China Marine
TsingTao Treasure

A marine returns to China in search of hidden treasure

BK08511251

BUZZ HARCUS

CHINA MARINE
TSINGTAO TREASURE

A Marine Returns to China
in Search of Hidden Treasure

Les (Buzz) Harcus

Wolfenden

Wofenden Publishers
P.O. Box 789
Miranda, California 95553
Voice/Fax: 707-923-2455
http://www.wolfendenpublishing.com
e-mail: wolfen@northcoast.com
        booking@inet.co.th

Cover and Interior Design:
Robert Stedman, Pte. Ltd., Singapore

Printed in Singapore

ISBN: 0-9642521-9-8

This novel is dedicated to those thousands of adventurous Marines who served in China over half a century ago prior to World War II, and afterwards during that hectic period from 1945 well into 1949, before the nation fell to Communism.

Today, many of these same Marines comprise the ranks of the China Marine Association, older, wiser, and with a sense of pride at having been a part of a unique life-changing experience in the annals of Marine Corps history.

CHINA MARINE
TSINGTAO TREASURE

A Marine Returns to China
in Search of Hidden Treasure

By

Les Harcus

CONTENTS

CONTENTS

Chapter 1

A VOICE FROM THE PAST

China! China! That's the second time thoughts of China had popped into Harry's mind that morning. "Thirty years," he grumbled to himself, "and I still can't put China behind me. And why does that damned phone keep ringing! Can't they tell I don't want to answer it?"

The incessant ringing cut through the hot stinging spray of the shower. Harry deliberately held his head under the nozzle trying to drown out the jangling, letting the steaming water course over his body washing away the grime of a ten-hour day.

His count reached twenty. Don't people know you hang up after ten rings? Still it continued. Disgustedly, he reached down and twisted the faucets sharply to off, yanked the shower door open, grabbed up a large towel and stepped out of the tub striding with deliberate steps toward the kitchen and the damned phone.

"Hello!" he snapped, jerking the phone to his lips. "Yes, this is Harry Martin –"

Harry stood in the kitchen doorway, the towel draped around his wet, shivering body, water puddling at his feet on the cold linoleum floor.

"You th' same Harry Martin that served in da Marine Corps back in China in 1948?" a raspy voice asked.

Harry paused for a moment, suddenly cautious, and then answered, "Yes. Who is this?" He was irritated at having to leave a steamy shower to answer the damned phone, and now some jerk wants to play question and answer games. "Who is this?" he demanded again.

"It's been a long time, Harry," the raspy voice answered, "an awful long time –"

"Speak up or I'll hang up!" Harry snapped, anger welling in his voice.

"It's me, Harry. Yer ol' buddy, Joe, Joe Gionetti," the voice cackled. Harry felt the blood drain from his face. He leaned against the doorframe for support. Joe Gionetti! Fear he hadn't felt for thirty years suddenly washed over him.

"How'd you find me?" he asked, a catch in his voice.

"Oh, hell, Harry," Joe replied, "Old Joe has know'd where ya' lived fer years, 'n fact, I know all about ya'."

Harry felt a slight wave of relief. If Joe had known his whereabouts all these years, he could have snuffed him out any time he wanted to. "Why are you calling me now, after all these years? What do you want?"

"Harry. I ain't mad at ya' no more. I let by-gones be by-gones," Joe said. "I figure what th' hell, we was jus' young punks back then –" He coughed, a long hacking cough as though he was trying to clear his throat. Several more times he coughed before continuing. "I jus' want ta' talk ta' ya' an let'cha know there ain't no hard feelings. You did what ya' had ta' do. I served my time an' it's over an' done with."

"It's not like you to forgive and forget, Joe," Harry replied, remembering the threats Joe had made. "Why call me now after all these years? What's the angle?" As he spoke, he began drying himself off, vigorously running the towel rapidly over his head, then down across his body, now a mass of goose bumps.

"I'm here at the VA hospital, Harry, over on Weiss," Joe rasped. He coughed again. "I got cancer. The docs think it's terminal –" He cut loose with another series of heart-wrenching coughs, then weakly continued. "This is th' only place I could get in, here in Saginaw." His voice sounded tight to Harry. He could hear his labored coughing again as he tried to clear his throat. "I got ta' see ya' Harry. It's important. I got ta' see ya' as soon as possible, right now! Can ya' come over ta' th' hospital an' see yer ol' buddy, Joe. Jus' fer a few minutes? It's important, fer ol' times sake."

Harry paused. Joe was as deadly as a rattlesnake. He only gave a moment's warning before he struck hard and deadly. There had never been any love lost between them. Joe repeated his plea. "I got ta' see ya' now, Harry. It's really important. If ya' could come over now, before 7:30, fer jus' a few minutes, that's all, I'd be much obliged."

Still drying off, Harry glanced at the clock on the stove. It was 6:45 pm. "Okay. Okay," he replied, but with a strong feeling of apprehension. "I'll be over in about half an hour."

"Thanks, Harry, I knew I could count on my ol' buddy. Be sure to get here by 7:30," Joe rasped. "7:30. See ya' soon."

"Yeah, soon."

Harry hung up the phone and finished drying off. What could be so damned important to Joe Gionetti that he'd want to see him after all these years? Shivering, he hurried back to the warmth of the bathroom. "Joe Gionetti –" he repeated the name several times while vigorously working up a thick lather on his shaving brush. Then, looking at his reflection in the mirror, he began lathering his face.

"Joe Gionetti, that sonofabitch!" His thoughts flew back to China, a tough, cruel China of long ago, back to when he was stationed there right out of boot camp in 1947, stationed with Joe Gionetti, and he automatically thought of Joe's rotten sidekick, Stan Drezewski.

It didn't take Harry long to find out Joe and Stan were deeply involved in black market activities. Scuttlebutt had it that they had salted hundreds of thousands of black market dollars away in special savings accounts back in the States before they got caught. Some of the old timers had claimed their take was in the millions – an unfathomable amount of money Harry recalled at the time, when as a lowly corporal, he was only making 75 bucks a month. It was harder, still, to believe the two skilled black marketeers got tripped up by a stupid, kid's mistake.

The sharp blade glided over his face as Harry reminisced about China. It seemed like yesterday, not thirty-two years ago, that he had been assigned to the U.S. Marine Corps base in Tsingtao. Tsingtao, an old historic seaport, bleak, desolate and foreboding that overcast spring morning when the U.S.S. *General J. C.*

Breckinridge docked. A Navy officer with the docking crew commented that this was a major port used by the U.S. Navy for the distribution of supplies to American troops stationed in north China that included not only Tsingtao, but Tientsin and Peiping as well.

Navy cargo ships unloading fresh stateside supplies were a common sight. Harry recalled the drudgery of unloading and transporting tons of supplies to the Old Japanese Compound, a series of tired red brick warehouses just inland from the dock area. The compound was surrounded by an equally tired red brick wall topped with coils of jagged barbed wire. Except for the main gate, the other three sides of the compound were ringed by a moat filled with dirty, slimy, stagnant water.

Each warehouse, called a "godown," contained stores of military supplies – canned foods, candy, cigarettes, C-rations, uniforms, boots, jackets, helmets, belts, winter clothing and every imaginable item to maintain the Marine garrison.

Guarding the compound was the responsibility of the First and Third Marine Battalions. They were a tough lot, dedicated, many battle-scarred veterans of World War II. At night the compound turned into a no-man's land with sporadic gunfire, as thieves tried to gain access to the supplies, and wiley Marines responded accordingly. In spite of the rigid security, a frightful amount of supplies ended up on the black market.

The duty of receiving and distributing supplies was the responsibility of the 12th Service Battalion. Harry was assigned to work with Joe and Stan, two old timers. A friendly relationship never materialized. With his rapid promotion to Corporal, by-passing Joe, who remained a Private First-Class, Harry felt the tension between them increase markedly. He soon found it necessary to pull rank on the two to get the work done. The tension never ceased.

Unlike Gionetti, who was always running off at the mouth, Stan Drezewski was more low key. He despised Harry, although he gave the impression he didn't give a damn about him. He did his work, kept his mouth shut, but he was always scheming. Harry had no use for either man. The two had arrived in Tsingtao in 1945 as part of the Marine Occupational Forces sent to secure the port and assist in the surrender of all remaining Japanese forces. In short order, they had established an efficient, well-entrenched black market operation. Pay-offs to authorities and the lack of sufficient evidence to arrest the two acknowledged black marketeers only prolonged their operation until the day they screwed up.

Chapter 2

FLASHBACK: OLD JAPANESE COMPOUND

Harry looked at himself in the mirror. Was this the same peach-fuzzed face he saw every morning on the dumb young corporal responsible for several godowns? He shook his head recalling the walk down the dusty road from the main gate every morning; large trucks passed by roiling up the dust even worse, and officer's jeeps added to the mess. The roadbed was raised and the ditches on either side usually contained dirty, scummy water. The road was the main artery between several rows of warehouses. The Command Post was a faded yellow house in the center of the Old Japanese Compound, FORMELLY the Japanese Command Post.

Dirty, ragged, smelly coolies were the chief means of labor, and cheap labor at that. Diseased, vermin-ridden and unwashed, the coolies nevertheless were good workers, but they were also artful thieves. They stole anything and everything that could be smuggled off the compound, in spite of stringent inspections.

Batu, Harry's Chinese foreman, was responsible for hiring the necessary daily contingent of coolies. Often, it seemed to Harry that he hired the same thieving scoundrels they had thrown out only days before. It kept Harry constantly on the alert.

Like happy children playing games, the coolies delighted in teaching simple Chinese phrases to those who wanted to learn. Harry was an eager student. He worked hard to master even the simplest Chinese phrases. It was more effective to give orders to the coolies in their native tongue. The coolies also responded more willingly to his requests.

Stan and Joe were a sharp contrast. They despised all coolies. They delighted in tripping or bumping into a coolie heavily laden with supplies, causing him to drop his load. Screaming obscenities, the two would beat the coolie unmercifully, then lift his fallen load on high and slam it down on his shoulders, reloading him. A swift kick in the behind sent the coolie on his way.

"Scum of the earth!" Joe always remarked, "Damned scum of the earth!"

The end of the workday was the time all Marines hated: coolie inspection. Searching through dirty, greasy, lice-infested hair, the half-dozen thin cotton jackets they all wore, making them drop their pants and bending over for an anal inspection, checking everywhere for stolen goods. Using a cut-off length of broom handle for the loathsome job, Harry recalled how he gingerly poked the stick up under each coolie's armpit, jacket by jacket, a favorite hiding place for stolen items. The stench of unwashed bodies often gagged him as did the sight of open runny sores, smallpox scabs and ugly deformities.

Harry crinkled up his nose as he recalled the day he searched La-Tor, the old man, the one who looked like the kindly Chinese peasant featured on travel brochures. He had ordered the old man to drop his britches, and then swatted him smartly across his buttocks to indicate he'd passed inspection. La-Tor crapped right on the spot. Gagging, Harry had dashed for the door and fresh air.

And, almost daily, a thief was caught. There was no pity shown by the Marines. The thief was whisked off to pay the price for stealing. The Marine's cardinal rule was no beating about the face or head; this left visible bruises. Bruises could mean a court martial. However, you could beat the hell out of the rest of their bodies and buttocks.

Joe savored catching a slant-eyed thief. He was a craftsman honing his special skills. Talking softly to the unsuspecting coolie, Joe would let him know it wasn't nice to steal from the American taxpayers, from Uncle Sam, from the Marine Corps. As he continued talking, a mounting rage grew in his voice, a contorted angry look across his face, and a sudden outburst of obscenities. Suddenly, he'd lash out, grab the coolie, throw him against the wall, punching and slapping him, screaming at the top of his lungs. If Stan were present, the unfortunate coolie got a double-dose of corrective medicine – shoved back and forth between the two. Faster and faster they'd push, punch and slap the helpless victim until he collapsed. There was never an outcry from the coolie. Each thief accepted the punishment, not for stealing, but for getting caught

The workday was finally ended when the Marines loaded on the trucks and rolled out of the main gate of the Japanese Compound. They had to ease through a sea of milling coolies bunched around the gate. The Marines couldn't help but admire the ingenious coolies who gleefully held up their stolen goods, laughing as they flaunted their catch. The Marines, with equal enthusiasm, responded with profanity and the universal finger salute. This, the Chinese returned, but many pointed their index fingers at the Marines as though they held a gun.

"Damn!" Harry yelped, feeling the razor cut. A thin sliver of blood appeared on his neck. "Pay attention to what you're doing or you'll slit your throat," he admonished his reflection. Quickly, he washed away the blood and pressed a piece of toilet paper tightly to the cut, staunching the bleeding. After a minute or so, he checked. Satisfied that the bleeding had stopped, he washed his face, and then liberally splashed after-shave lotion over his cheeks, neck, chest and body.

He took one long last look at himself in the mirror only to utter, "Joe Gionetti, what does that screw up have on his simple mind?"

Flicking off the light, he strode into his adjoining bedroom. The room was small but neat, the bed covered with a thick brown quilt. An early American chest of drawers stood against the outside wall between two tall windows. Several papers and magazines were stacked on the left side of the chest. On the right side were three pictures: one of a young smiling boy holding up a large bass; another of a slender young girl with a new bike; and a larger picture of himself, smiling, with his arm around a young, attractive dark-haired woman.

Beside the bed stood a small two-drawer end table. On it sat a huge piece of driftwood. Out of its center rose a large brass tube leading to a makeshift lamp. A brown burlap lampshade completed the rustic appearance. Jeff, his son, had made it at Boy Scout camp one summer twenty years ago. It was a birthday present. Harry still used it. The soft light from the lamp fell across the latest issues of "Penthouse" and "Playboy" that rested on the table.

Harry opened the top drawer of the chest of drawers, pulled out a T-shirt and shrugged into it, and then pulled on Jockey shorts. Stooping, he rummaged through the bottom drawer yanking out a black, ribbed turtleneck sweater and slipped into it. He crossed the room to the closet, stopping momentarily at the sight of his reflection in the full-length mirror mounted on the closet door. For just having turned fifty-three, he thought he still had a good build. He struck a karate pose. "Hah!" he challenged his reflection, and then laughed. He took pride in his physical appearance, exercising every day: thirty pushups, thirty sit-ups, deep squats, five miles of jogging when the weather permitted, especially now in the middle of January, and faithfully practicing karate. He had taken up the martial art many years ago to protect himself in case Joe or Stan came after him. He chuckled; now he was going to see Joe. Crazy.

He slid the closet door open and pulled a pair of black slacks off a hanger. He stepped into them, zipped up, and then slipped a black belt through the loops. Digging into the laundry basket, he came up with a matching pair of clean black socks and pulled them on. Lastly, for warmth, he pulled on his insulated, spit-shined black leather boots.

All the while he was dressing, his thoughts constantly slipped back to Joe Gionetti. He had to be one of the most rotten, conniving, dishonest guys he'd ever recalled meeting in or out of the Marine Corps. Stan Drezewski ran a close second, but Joe had to be the worst. Probably both were just as bad today.

He slipped a heavy medallion on a gold-link chain over his head, centered it on his chest, and checked himself in the mirror. Good. Sandy would like it; she'd bought it for him at Christmas. He looked forward to a romantic night with her. Carefully, he brushed a comb through his greying hair a couple more times. He smiled; his reflection looked good.

He went back to the dresser, reached into the second drawer, fumbled under his pajamas, which he no longer wore, and pulled out a .22 calibre Ruger automatic. He slapped a full clip into the butt, and then tucked the weapon inside his belt under his sweater. "Just in case," he mused. If he was being set up, at least he'd have a fighting chance with the gun, or with his skilled karate training.

He slipped into his leather jacket and glanced at himself one more time in the mirror. What a guy won't do to please a woman. But then, Sandy was something special.

"Christ!" he suddenly exclaimed glancing at his watch. It was 7:10 p.m. "I forgot all about Sandy being at the bar. She'll be there the same time I'm seeing Joe. Dammit!"

Chapter 3
THE YEARS IN BETWEEN

Quickly, Harry moved through the house making sure the lights were on in the kitchen and living room, all the timers set to turn on or off at staggered times. Then, he partially inserted the lamp plug for the hallway lamp but carefully trailed a thin black thread from the plug to the front doorknob. The plug was in deep enough to make contact, but loose enough so that any intruder opening the door would break the connection and the lamp would go off, a warning signal he'd devised years ago after he'd been robbed. Since the robbery, the place was lit up at night giving the appearance of someone in the house. House break-ins were quite common, especially with all the dopers who needed money to feed their habits.

The robbery had cost him his new color television set, the old 30-06 Winchester Western Model rifle his dad had given him the first year he started deer hunting, an AM-FM radio and his wide-angle binoculars, the ones he used at the beach to check out the sexy, bikini-clad girls with rich brown tans, big bouncy breasts and well-rounded asses — but that was before Sandy.

At the kitchen door adjoining the garage, he momentarily paused to survey the place before leaving. In spite of his being a bachelor, the place looked tidy. A smile broke across his face — neither his mother nor his ex-wife would have believed it possible he could keep a place looking at least half way decent.

He slammed the kitchen door behind him and got into his car knowing he'd have to hurry to finish his business with Joe to meet Sandy as soon as he could. The Pub was no place to leave a beautiful woman alone, especially a knockout like Sandy.

The engine growled as he turned the ignition key on, coughed, then caught hold. He let it idle for a minute or so to warm up. It was quite cold for January, yet warm enough this year that the shipping channels were still open, a phenomenon that surprised even the port of Saginaw, still able to ship outbound to the world.

Harry sat shivering in the beat-up '73 Pinto, all Laurie, his ex-wife, had left him after the divorce. He listened for the engine's special last clattering sound that would let him know the car was ready to go. "C'mon, Betsy," he chattered. "Let's go!" She was an old rust-bucket but she ran well, and she was paid for. Betsy just seemed the logical name. At 82,000 miles, she used some oil, but she was good transportation. Besides, Harry figured, someone might ram the damned thing some day, and he could collect from Ford when the gas tank ruptured and the car burned up – if he survived.

Ah it was purring now. He dropped the shift lever into reverse and backed out of the garage, stopped momentarily to close the garage door, and then got back behind the steering wheel, flicked on the lights and backed out.

Stopping across the street to shift gears, he looked back at the small bungalow. Not much to look at but it was home. He and the bank were proud of it. One day, he kept telling himself, he'd remodel the damned place: new living room, new kitchen, a bathroom with a sunken tub and built-in Jacuzzi, and a "macho" bedroom with a king-size waterbed and mirrors on the ceiling; a real stud palace.

He grinned. It was a far cry from the big rambling house he'd lost in the divorce settlement, but this place was special to him; it was his home, his castle, and he was enjoying life the way he wanted to.

The divorce hadn't been amicable – Laurie saw to that. He ended up with the Pinto and a couple thousand dollars. But, looking back, he guessed it was worth it.

Laurie had always bought things they didn't need to impress people he didn't care for, and he spent most of his time trying to figure out how to pay the damned bills. Luckily, the kids split after college in pursuit of their own careers. It was then, after the kids were on their own, they finally agreed they had nothing in common anymore: just two souls existing independently in a large overpriced house, pursuing different paths to reach their own separate goals.

He'd only seen her once since the divorce, about two years ago at Sissy's wedding. She was there with her new husband, a successful criminal lawyer. Big deal. It gave him satisfaction knowing he gave the bride away.

The look on his boss's face was one Harry would never forget. The divorce was final and it was time to make many drastic changes – beginning with his job. He was tired of the damned phonies he worked with every day as director of public relations, the things he had to do to keep his job, the glad-handers, picking up bar tabs for lushes, scrounging up hookers for out-of-town bigshots, and tired of promoting what he felt were worthless products. He'd told his boss to shove the job, as the saying goes, "where the sun don't shine!"

Free of the job and marriage, he'd stashed the Pinto at his son's place and returned to the sea working as a deckhand on a cargo ship sailing to distant ports. At sea was a good place to be, to think, to clear his mind, to review his life, to set new goals, to challenge his future. He was 49 then, and starting life anew was an awesome challenge, a chilling experience. He deliberately downplayed his education; a Master's Degree in Public Relations wasn't really helpful to an ordinary deckhand.

Initially, it was exciting traveling to distant Pacific ports-of-call, seeing the world from a different perspective. After several sexual experiences, he found himself backing off, not avidly pursuing every whore on the beach, not like the younger seamen. He no longer had to prove his manhood; he was virile. Besides, he dreaded the thought of getting the clap or some incurable venereal disease. At the bars the younger guys easily picked up the good-looking women. They laughed and kidded him, the old man, about his out-dated techniques. It hurt, but it was true.

After two years he quit the sea. He had proven his worth to himself. He had advanced to a position of helmsman but he found the sea no longer held the fascination it did when he was younger. With praises for a job well done, he hit the beach and headed back to Saginaw. He kept his papers current though, just in case the wanderlust to sail again came back.

Back in Saginaw, he pursued one of his other loves: carpentry

He got a job with a construction company building residential homes, office complexes and shopping malls. Working with his hands was a challenge to both his mind and body, proving to be mentally and physically rewarding. One day he'd hit it rich, but on his own terms, through hard work, honest effort and a hell of a lot of luck.

The blaring of a horn startled him as a car swerved around him, jarring his thoughts back to the present.

"Asshole!" he yelled after the departing car. Another case of "Saginaw Syndrome!" He'd never lived in a town where there were so many bad drivers. They ran stop signs as if they didn't exist; floored it on amber lights and ran red lights without a qualm of guilt – let the other guy worry. And they could throw away the speed limit signs: each driver drove between ten and twenty miles an hour over the speed limit, changed lanes without using indicators, disdainfully gave you the finger if you honked, and swore a blue streak at you. If nothing else, he had learned how to drive defensively.

Roaring off down the street, he shifted the car to second, and then third, now cruising along, his mind still on the past. The bachelor life had done wonders for him. He'd found the small bungalow, making a down payment with the meager savings he'd acquired at sea. He'd set a demanding regimen for himself exercising daily, losing about twenty pounds within the first couple of months. Today, he was proud of his physique; he was stronger, leaner and more muscular. His attitude was positive. He read mind challenging magazines and books, although he did enjoy an occasional adult magazine to stimulate an active mind. He chuckled to himself as he recalled signing up for a Wok Chinese cooking course at the local college. He had become somewhat of a gourmet cook.

Sandy popped into his mind. She was far different from the other women he had pursued. An attractive thirty-one year old divorcee, they had seemed to hit it off from the time they had first met a year ago. No talk about marriage – an understanding they had reached early on, and neither broached the subject. Sex was a real turn on for her; she was aggressive, yet coy, submissive at times, inventive, making the most of each moment together, savoring each experience. He grinned as he recalled letting her talk him into going to a porno film, the first one he'd ever gone to, to "break him out of his Victorian mold" she had said. He'd come alive after that. She was an excellent teacher; he an apt student.

Tonight would be special. He was anxious to see her. He had thirty days vacation accumulated and wanted to steal away with her to a warmer clime like the southern gulf coast, maybe South Padre Island, some secluded out-of-the-way place where they could relax and enjoy each other.

A couple of times the idea popped into his mind to ask her to marry him. Then he shrugged it off. Maybe one day, maybe on vacation they could see how compatible they were. It would be warm and cozy, just the two of them. Any place would be better than here and this damned cold weather.

Once again, he rehearsed the way he was going to pop the question: order Margaritas, talk about how nice it would be to vacation in a warmer clime, really lead her on, and then ask her to go with him. She was bound to say yes. She was bound to!

Now, all he had to do was get through his meeting with Joe – and he knew he'd make short work of the visit.

He drove north on Bay Road to Weiss, then right. Before he realized it, the VA hospital was suddenly on his left. He'd traveled the mile and a half in moments. Yet, all the while, his thoughts had been elsewhere

Pulling into the parking lot, he picked a parking space as close to the entrance as possible. Gusting wind-whipped clouds of snow billowed across the lot amidst the sparse number of cars. Harry shut off the engine and sat quietly. Events leading to the trial of Joe and Stan raced through his mind. Why, he wondered, after all these years, after all the deep bitterness, why did Joe want to see him now?

He stared out across the parking lot, his vision blurred by the blustering snow, yet not seeing the snow, thinking only of the events that lead to the trial.

Chapter 4
TSINGTAO: SPRING 1948

It was cold that Friday morning back in April 1948.

The dirty snow was melting; spring was in the air. Crocuses were breaking through the snow at the side of the administration building. Already his buddies in the 12th Service Battalion were talking about baseball, planning to knock hell out of the First and Third battalions. The sun broke through the morning haze It felt good to Harry, warming him through the thickness of his green field jacket. Northern China was bitter cold in the winter; chilling and damp in the spring and suffocatingly hot in the summer. Tsingtao was a hell of a place to be stationed, especially as it was located next to the sea.

Today was a good day, pay day, a day to enjoy life. But it would all change rather abruptly. Joe had seen to that.

Arriving at the Jap Compound, Harry overheard Ming Lee, a batu, complaining to Sergeant Rupp about a beating Joe and Stan had given to a young coolie boy they had caught stealing. The boy had cracked ribs and numerous bruises on his body, arms and legs. Sergeant Rupp told Ming Lee to come back after lunch and he would help him file a formal complaint, but at the moment, he was due at the command post.

On leaving the office, Ming Lee was confronted by Joe, who began screaming at him telling him he was a no-good, lying bastard, that all coolies he sent to work for them were lazy, dirty, no-good thieves.

Ming Lee snapped back, incensed at the remarks made about his crew, defending them, standing his ground, facing Joe squarely, trying to convince him he was wrong. For his effort, he was suddenly punched fully in the face by Joe. He fell backwards, landing in the aisle. Before he could recover, Joe had rushed him again, kicking him viciously in the stomach. Ming Lee gasped, clutching at his mid-section. Joe didn't let up. He seized the injured man, bodily picked him up, and then slammed him hard against the solid wooden doors of the warehouse.

Hearing the commotion, Harry rushed from the office, saw what was happening and raced down the aisle toward the two men. This time, Harry vowed, Joe had had it. It was time for a showdown.

Joe didn't see Harry coming. Still swearing threats at Ming Lee, Joe flung the warehouse doors wide open, grabbed the bloodied foreman by his shirt and flung him out the door into a ditch overflowing with mud and trash.

"You bastard!" Harry screamed at Joe, smashing a solid right cross to his jaw that sent him reeling backwards down the aisle. Joe fell to the deck "C'mon, you sonofabitch!" Harry screamed. "See if you can handle someone your own size!"

He stood over the fallen Marine, fists clenched tightly, moving in small circles, ready to knock him down again. His face was livid with anger. "C'mon, Joe! Try me! I'm ready!"

Joe lay back on the hard cement nursing his jaw, fearful of Harry's anger. Rising slowly, his eyes on Harry, he got to his feet, turned and started walking away. "Screw you," he clamored. "I ain't gonna have it out with you right here, not right now!"

Harry watched the departing figure, a bit surprised that Joe surrendered without a fight. Joe had been spoiling for such a confrontation for the past few months. Instead, he walked away. It wasn't like him. Like a rattlesnake, he'd strike again. Harry knew he could book on it.

Turning, he started out the door to help Ming Lee. With the aid of several coolies, he helped the mud-spattered man to his feet. With rags the other coolies gathered up, he began wiping the mud and crud from Ming Lee's body.

"Leave th' stinkin' gook alone!" a voice shouted. It was Joe who suddenly reappeared in the doorway.

"Make me!" Harry snapped glancing at the sallow-faced Joe. There was no response and Harry continued wiping off the mud, apologizing to Ming Lee as he did, saying all Marines weren't like

Joe. The batu nodded; he understood. Then, hurt and humiliated, he hobbled off toward the main gate taking his crew with him.

Joe spewed obscenities after them. Stan appeared in the doorway next to Joe. Harry now understood where Joe had gotten his sudden bravado; his sidekick was there to back him up. Gleefully, Joe described the incident to Stan. They stood laughing and gloating like a couple of snotnose kids.

Not wanting to tangle with both of them, Harry returned to the office. Later, he reported the incident to Sergeant Rupp. An old China hand, Rupp shrugged it off. "The batu will have his day," he added philosophically. "In the meantime, those jokers can do the coolies' work!" And thus, it was two grumbling, sweating Marines who broke their backs unloading stateside supplies the rest of the day.

Chapter 5

BREAK-IN AT THE JAP COMPOUND

Arriving at the warehouse early the following Monday morning, Harry found the padlock to the front door had been cut and cleverly forced back together giving the impression the warehouse was locked. Passing guards wouldn't have noticed unless they rattled each of the locks, which they obviously hadn't. Harry dispatched Private Novak to the command post on the double to report the cut lock to Lieutenant Donaldson.

Within minutes, the Lieutenant, accompanied by Sergeant Major Warden and Sergeant Rupp, arrived, their jeep splattering mud and gravel as it came to a grinding halt in front of the warehouse.

Harry showed them the lock, still in place as he had found it. With guns drawn, the three cautiously opened the door and entered. Harry followed, staying behind, picking up an ax handle as his weapon. The Marine work detail stayed outside watching as the foursome disappeared into the darkness.

It was an eerie feeling knowing someone had been inside, knowing something valuable might be missing, but what? Harry thought. And the search continued down the musky aisles.

Suddenly, Harry realized what was bothering him. It was so obvious and yet, it wasn't. It was like looking at the Eiffel Tower and suddenly realizing it was missing. All that was left was an empty space.

"The cigarettes!" he blurted. "The cigarettes are missing!"

All eyes riveted on the space where just last Thursday and Friday they had stacked more than three hundred brown corrugated cardboard cartons of fresh, stateside cigarettes nearly to the roof. Now they were all gone.

Lieutenant Donaldson immediately placed the area off limits and called for the Military Police. Next, he ordered the Marines to return to the main compound.

Even as the trucks loaded with Marines were heading for the main compound, the investigation was underway under the direction of Warrant Officer "Shorty" Donelson, a thirty-year man whose career dated back to World War One.

The Marines had a special respect for the man. No one screwed around with Shorty Donelson. He didn't take lip from anyone, no matter what their rank. He was blunt, fair, and let the chips fall where they may. From the top brass to the lowest buck private, Shorty was held in high regard.

Shorty had been wounded in Belleau Woods where he won a Silver Star for bravery under fire. He was captured early in World War II, surviving the Bataan Death March, only to spend the rest of the war in a Japanese prisoner of war camp. A wiry, feisty man, Shorty was a battle-toughened Marine committed to giving only name, rank and serial number to the enemy. No more. The Japanese tried repeatedly to beat this negativism out of him, but to no avail.

His tough demeanor set a tone for other prisoners. The merciless beatings he survived made headlines after the war when the trials of his Japanese captors was held. In spite of his debilitating experience, Shorty was one of the first of the prisoners to step forward and re-enlist, ending up in Tsingtao with the Military Police.

Even as the trucks unloaded the men outside the 12th Service Battalion barracks, inside, the building was already a scene of chaos. Word of the investigation had spread like wildfire. GI cans suddenly filled with fresh stateside supplies of candy bars, cookies, crackers, canned pineapple juice and other coveted items not yet available through the official base PX outlet. In addition, excess clothing, outlawed rifles, machine guns, pistols, bayonets, knives, swords and other Japanese souvenir weapons were hurriedly stashed on the fourth floor in the cramped quartermaster room, from whence the corporal in charge had conveniently absented himself for about an hour in order not to get involved.

Although slated to return to the states in a few months, Harry opted to hide his favorite weapon, a K-bar, the one he kept honed razor sharp, so he wouldn't lose it to a souvenir-hunting MP. He'd already lost his prized Japanese Nambu pistol during a sweep of the barracks in the summer of '47. It had really burned him up that no one at MP headquarters knew anything about his missing pistol, which, he finally figured, was probably some Captain's war souvenir now. This time, he took special pains to wrap the knife in an oiled cloth and hide it where no one would find it.

Chapter 6

THE MP INVESTIGATION

By mid-morning two truckloads of MP's had arrived and sealed off the barracks. No one in; no one out. Shorty Donelson set up his interrogation room in the guard shack located just inside the main entrance to the building. Word spread quickly that he had a long list of Marines to interrogate, although scuttlebutt indicated only a few were prime suspects. Within fifteen minutes, the first man was called down to the guard shack.

"Harry," Joe said in a sneering voice, after having walked past his bunk several times before stopping, "If they ask ya' anyting 'bout me, tell 'em I was down at th' ballpark all mornin' Saturday, 'n I was at th' slopshoot all afternoon. Ya' remember, don'cha?"

Harry looked up from the book he was reading. Joe seemed unusually nervous. "No. Can't say I did," Harry replied "I saw you and Stan gassing up a couple of trucks over at the motorpool Saturday morning –"

"Naw, ya' din't!" Joe snapped, cutting him short. "We wasn't anywhere near th' damned trucks."

"Well, I was just coming out of Tarver Gym. I could have sworn –" He stopped. Joe's dark, glowering face sent a warning of danger. "Well, yeah, maybe I was mistaken, looking into the morning sun."

"Take it from me, you was mistaken!" Joe's finger was jammed close to his face. "You jus' tell Shorty what I told ya' 'n everyting will be jus' fine"

He turned abruptly and stalked off to the far end of the room joining Stan, who had been keenly watching them. Harry watched the two for a moment. They were having a serious discussion. Stan suddenly glanced past Joe, glaring at Harry. With a shrug of his shoulders, Harry settled back on his bunk, his attention once again focused on the dirty book currently making the rounds of the barracks. Shit, he thought, no sense in making waves. Anyways, he knew he'd seen them at the motorpool, but, ah, to hell with it.

Harry hadn't realized how keyed up he was about the investigation until an MP stuck his head through the doorway and barked, "Martin, Corporal Harry Martin!" Harry literally leaped to his feet. He felt the eyes of Joe and Stan following him as he left the room.

He was ushered into the first floor guard shack where he stood at attention before the desk, his eyes riveted on a picture of President Truman hanging on the wall behind, Shorty's head. Shorty was intently reading a file and didn't bother to look up.

"Be seated, Corporal Martin," Shorty said after a moment, more a command than a request. Harry sat stiffly on the hard wooden chair. His stomach was churning. He was innocent, but he felt guilty as sin. He glanced around the small room. It was sparsely furnished: a scarred old wooden desk, two old wooden chairs, including the one he was sitting on, a filing cabinet and, in one corner, a cardboard box that served as a wastebasket.

The room had been repainted. About a month before he had arrived on base, according to one of the "old-timer's," a Corporal of the Guard had received a "Dear John" letter from his girlfriend, got really depressed, stuck the barrel of his duty .45 in his mouth and pulled the trigger. It took a couple of days to clean up the gore, and the room was repainted.

Shorty pulled out his familiar MacArthur corncob pipe, filled it, tamped the tobacco snuggly into the deep bowl, and then, with the help of three long kitchen matches lit it to his satisfaction. He took a deep puff and blew out a cloud of sweet-smelling smoke. It hung in a layer just above their heads.

Shorty's eyes riveted on Harry's. "You have a good service record, Corporal Martin. I see you made corporal's rank shortly after you arrived in China. That's good. You must be pretty sharp, pretty knowledgeable about a lot of things to get your stripes that quickly."

Harry nodded. Why that comment? Dammit. He earned his stripes and was even being considered for sergeant's examination.

"I understand you were the one who found the lock cut, noticed the missing stacks of cigarettes."

"Yes, sir."

"Even the guard patrols hadn't noticed the cut lock. Pretty dumb, don't you think?"

"Yes, sir." What was the point? Harry wondered.

"Who was driving the trucks last Saturday?" Shorty asked leaning across the desk, his eyes boring in, unwavering. "Stan and Joe?"

The question caught Harry off guard. He paled. He felt suddenly clammy. His stomach warned him he might vomit. His eye contact broke from Shorty's as his gaze fell to his hands. They were trembling.

"Who drove the trucks?" Shorty's voice was soft, but firm.

"I-I –" Harry stammered. If Shorty yelled at him right then he'd either puke or shit his pants.

"Now, son, we have witnesses who saw two trucks leave the motorpool early Saturday morning. We're sure it was Stan and Joe. We also know you were at Tarver Gym that morning and would have been passing the motorpool about the time the trucks were getting gassed ready to leave." He took another long drag on his pipe. "Are you a member of the gang?"

"No sir!" Harry retorted, sitting bolt upright in his chair. "I'm not a part of that gang, nor do I want to be identified as a part of that gang, sir."

Shorty grinned. "I didn't think you were, but you do know who the drivers were. It was Stan and Joe, wasn't it?"

"Yes, sir," Harry responded hoarsely, clearing his throat, suddenly relieved.

Shorty sat back in his chair. He made several penciled notations on a pad before he looked up again.

"What did they tell you to do, lie? Tell me."

"Uh, Joe, uh, he said to tell you he'd been down to the ballpark all morning and at the slopshoot that afternoon."

"The damned liar," Shorty snapped. "But you did see them driving the trucks?"

"Yessir. They were gassing them up and then drove them out the back entrance by the Third Marine barracks. I just thought they were on some kind of special assignment."

"Thank you, Corporal Martin. You're free to go."

Shorty stood up abruptly ending the questioning, extending his hand. Harry shook it; it was tough, leathery. Harry did an about face and left the room.

An MP intercepted him outside the guard shack and directed him to the lecture hall where other 12th Service Battalion personnel were seated. There was no talking. All eyes faced front. Harry was surprised to see Joe and Stan seated in the front row facing a low stage. The scene was reminiscent of the harsh regimentation he had endured during boot camp at Parris Island. A boot was nothing more than a piece of dirt to be stomped on by an overzealous drill instructor.

Chapter 7
BLACK MARKET THIEVES NAILED

Time dragged by slowly. Except for an occasional muffled cough, there was almost absolute silence. Harry glanced down at his watch. He'd been there almost an hour. The room was becoming unbearably hot. Sweat trickled down his face. It reminded him of the day he arrived at the 12th Service Battalion. The commanding officer had stood on this very stage and warned them that they were only guests in this country, and to respect the Chinese. He also warned them that this battalion had the highest venereal disease rate on the compound, and expected the new men to bring that ignominious recognition to a halt. Four more Marines were ushered in by the MP's. Time marched on.

Suddenly the door at the side of the room was thrown wide. An MP called out, "Ten Hut!" The men jumped to their feet, erect, shoulders squared, eyes front. Shorty Donelson strode into the room and up onto the stage. He turned, his eyes scanning the roomful of Marines. He puffed on his corncob pipe. After a minute or so had passed, he nodded to the MP, who called out, "At ease!"

"You men have been sweating today because some son-of-a-bitch decided to make a profit off Uncle Sam, and in the process, each of you suddenly became a suspect, many of you with excellent service records, cited for heroism under enemy fire during the war, giving your best to make the Marine Corps the best outfit in the world," Shorty began.

He took several more puffs, blowing clouds of aromatic smoke out across the audience. His face was hard, emotionless.

"You should all be pissed! You should all be really pissed off! One of your fellow Marines let you down. You, his buddies, the guy you work with, break bread with, drink with and bunk with. He let you down to make a fast buck off the black market."

He turned and tapped his pipe on the edge of an ashtray on the small desk behind him. The burned ashes fell out. All eyes followed his every move. His timing was superbly dramatic, Harry thought.

"Actually," Shorty Donelson continued, turning back to the attentive Marines, making a slight nodding motion with his head to several MP's, who started moving down the aisle toward the stage. "We have two sons-of-bitches!" His finger pointed directly toward Stan and Joe. "Joe Gionetti and Stan Drezewski!" A murmur raced across the room at the disclosure.

"Arrest those two men!" Shorty snapped. Quickly, the MP's moved in grabbing the two startled black marketeers and took them into custody.

"Take those scum out and handcuff them to my jeep," Shorty commanded. Then, he turned back to the audience, holding up his hand for silence. "For those of you who don't know what the hell happened, we found the shipment of cigarettes that were stolen over the weekend from the Old Japanese Compound. We got lucky. We caught the damned gooks with the loot as their ship tied up in Shanghai this morning. These two bastards made $30,000 dollars on the deal. We'll get that back, too."

As he spoke the MP's were dragging Joe and Stan toward the door. Joe turned, catching Harry's eye, and screamed at him, "You squealed on me! You squealed on me! I'll kill you for that! You ain't seen the last of me. I'll kill you one of these days!" Still screaming, he was yanked from the building.

The trial was short, the evidence overwhelming. Two key witnesses, Ming Lee and Harry, tied Joe and Stan indisputably to the crime. Harry's testimony placed Joe and Stan at the motor pool; furthermore, Harry had seen them drive the trucks off the base. During his testimony, Harry felt Joe's eyes boring into him, deep with hatred, his sunken face a constant scowl. Stan fidgeted, glancing at Harry occasionally, then glancing away. He seemed anxious to have the trial over with. As he left the witness stand, Joe pointed his finger at him and bent it as though pulling a trigger.

"One of these days, Harry, I'll get'cha," he said as Harry passed close by him.

Ming Lee took great interest in the trial. He willingly gave detailed testimony about the events of that Saturday, the two trucks entering the compound, the use of a Chinese coolie workforce he was unfamiliar with, noting the trucks left and returned to the compound twice. He explicitly identified Joe and Stan as the drivers of the trucks. No amount of haranguing or badgering by the defense attorney could shake his story. Harry had smiled at the time; Sergeant Rupp had called it right; the batu would have his day.

The two were convicted of masterminding a black market operation and found guilty of grand theft, the unauthorized use of military vehicles, breaking and entering a military facility, theft of supplies and the sale of those supplies to known black market agents. Additionally, they were charged with forging an officer's name on the military pass to gain access to the Japanese Compound.

On an overcast, drizzly Wednesday morning during the first week of May, the 12th Service Battalion stood at attention in front of the barracks listening as Sergeant Rupp read the trial details. The severity of the sentence sent a shock wave through the ranks. Twenty years for both with not less than fifteen being served at the federal penitentiary at Leavenworth.

The reading concluded, Sergeant Rupp gave the command "Right Face!" and the men marched up the hill to the messhall. Except for the rattling of metal trays and cups, and the slap of "shit on a shingle" hitting the cold trays, the messhall was deathly somber.

Within days rumor spread that the black market money had not been recovered, that it was hidden somewhere on the main compound. Feverishly, almost 2,000 Marines scoured every nook and cranny of the base, digging into the old Japanese gun emplacements on the back hills, around the perimeter of the ball diamond, everywhere, but nothing turned up. Like the others, Harry spent his remaining time in China looking for the money. He finally headed home empty-handed, got discharged from the Marine Corps at the Great Lakes Naval Station and, except for an occasional thought of the threat made by Joe, thoughts of China soon faded as life as a civilian saw a new set of demands placed upon him.

Suddenly Harry shivered in the darkness of the unheated car. Several minutes had elapsed as he recalled the trial. Joe's threats had always been there, tucked away in the back of his mind, but still there. During the first few years as a civilian, he had expected to be cut down brutally one day by an avenging, escaped Joe, or by one of his underworld accomplices. However, as time passed, the threat faded.

There had been college, marriage, raising a family, seeing them through twelve years of grade school and then college, and the divorce. Now, finally, he had found a semblance of happiness in his present job, and in the warmth of Sandy.

He smiled when he thought of the countless hours spent learning Karate, advancing to a black belt, capable of protecting himself in any event. His instructor said he had a killer's edge, that he should never be afraid; he was one of the best. Now, he was going of his own volition to see the man who had vowed to kill him thirty years ago. He shook his head. The whole damned thing seemed absurd.

Chapter 8
VISIT TO THE V.A. HOSPITAL

Harry jogged across the parking lot deftly following the footsteps of someone who had preceded him through the deep snow. He felt a chill running up his back. Was it the cold, cutting wind, or was it facing Joe Gionetti?

The Veteran's Administration Hospital was built in the typical bureaucratic architectural red brick style of the late '40's, replete with huge lampposts standing rigidly, much as soldiers at attention, on either side of the entrance, a large cement arch. Harry yanked the door open, packing new snow against the arch, and stepped inside. There was a hushed quietness in the reception area. The faint scent of disinfectant filled his nostrils. The reception area was dimly lit, more than likely to eliminate non-essential lighting and conserve energy, he thought, reflecting on the current energy shortage.

Harry moved quietly over to the reception desk, stopping to peer down at a white-haired volunteer who was obviously unaware of his presence, busily continuing to work on a visitor report sheet.

"Pardon me, ma'm," he said softly, clearing his throat.

"Oh!" she exclaimed, startled, glancing quickly up, clasping her hand to her chest. "Oh, Lordy! I didn't see you there. You gave me quite a start!" Slowly the color returned to her blanched face. "What can I do for you?" she asked, a slight tremor evident in her voice.

"Sorry," Harry offered in the way of an apology. "Didn't mean to scare you." He gave her a warm, friendly smile. "I'd like to see one of your patients"

"Who do you wish to see?" she asked generating a weak, flustered smile in return.

"Joseph Gionetti."

"Joseph Gionetti. Certainly –" she repeated. She began fumbling through an archaic filing system mumbling to herself, "Gionetti, Gionetti, Gionetti, oh, yes, Gionetti, Joseph. He's in room 302."

"Thank you," Harry said starting toward the elevators.

"Sir. Your name, please," she called after him. He turned back. She was holding up a pen and a visitor's log. "Mr. Gionetti is in intensive care so we must keep accurate records of all visitors." He signed the log and passed it back across the desk. Laboriously, she wrote his name on a visitor's pass before handing it to him. "There," she smiled, "now don't stay too long. He's a very sick man. Visiting hours end at 8:30."

Harry acknowledged with a nod, thanked her, and started for the elevators. He looked down at the card he held. ROOM 302 GIONETTI, JOSEPH. He stuffed the card in his pocket.

Reflections from lights at the end of the hall danced snake-like across the highly polished linoleum tile floor. The interior of the hospital was spotless considering the age of the building.

Harry pushed the up button. He could hear equipment clicking and the whirr of electric motors as the elevator approached. The doors opened and he stepped inside, moved to the back of the car and turned around facing forward. As the doors started to close, two men quickly stepped on board. One was a tall thin man, bearded, wearing a white doctor's coat. The other, an older, portly man, also obviously a doctor as he was wearing a stethoscope around his neck. He was puffing on a large cigar. Harry crinkled his nose at the noxious smell. He looked above the man's head. A sign stated SMOKING PROHIBITED BY LAW VIOLATORS SUBJECT TO $50 FINE OR 90 DAY IMPRISONMENT. Harry looked back over at the doctor; he winked, amused.

The doors opened at the second floor and the two doctors stepped off, but not before the fat one took a deep draw on his cigar and blew a huge cloud of acrid smoke inside the elevator as he stepped off.

"You son-of-bitch," Harry said in a quiet, even voice as the doors closed. He pressed three and the cables clattered, the motors whirred and in moments the doors opened onto the third floor. Harry stepped out and stood for a moment letting his eyes adjust to the low intensity lighting. Gotta conserve energy, he thought, especially now-a-days.

He made his way down the corridor, his rubber heels squeaking on the highly polished floor. An attractive nurse wheeled a pill cart past him. He took a moment to glance after her. Not bad, he grinned. The nursing station was quiet. One nurse sat with her back toward him monitoring an electronic board. He was about to interrupt her when he spotted the corridor sign: Rooms 300- 320. He headed down the corridor and located Room 302. It was the second room off the nursing station. The door was open.

Harry paused outside the door and listened. He asked himself for the umpteenth time what the hell he was doing here? Joe was a no-good scum. Why was he here? Even as these thoughts crossed through his mind, he was unzipping his jacket, easing his hand inside under the edge of his turtleneck shirt, closing over the cold steel of his .22 automatic, his index finger curling around the trigger.

A curtain was drawn about halfway across the room separating the room into two sections. The first bed was empty. The TV was blaring. Someone coughed. It was a long, drawn-out, guttural cough. The person was obviously trying to expel phlegm from deep in his throat. He coughed, coughed again, and then gave a long moaning sigh of relief. Harry eased forward, peeking around the edge of the curtain.

He stopped short, startled, for before him lay a tired-looking, emaciated old man propped up in bed, his head resting on several pillows. His cheeks were caved in; eyes dull, sunken deeply into his head. At the head of the bed on a patient dresser, Harry saw false teeth resting in a glass of water. Glancing back at the man, Harry saw tubes protruding from his right arm leading up to an IV bottle suspended above his head.

This tired, withered old man was Joe Gionetti?

Harry slipped his hand off the gun and drew his sweater over the weapon. "Joe, Joe Gionetti," he said stepping past the curtain to the end of the bed, still uncertain. The head rolled slowly around on the pillow, the dull eyes opening wider.

"Harry, is that you, Harry?"

"Yeah, it's me, Joe," Harry replied, detecting a slight smile breaking across Joe's face. He walked around to the side of the bed reaching for Joe's extended hand. It was gnarled, twisted with arthritis. There was no strength to his grip.

"Things ain't been going too good fer ol' Joe, Harry," Joe whispered in a hoarse voice. "Things jus' ain't been good at all."

"I'm sorry to hear that," Harry whispered back, wondering why he was whispering. Then he cleared his throat and continued. "What can I do for you? Your telephone call seemed quite urgent."

Harry watched as Joe painfully struggled to rise to a more comfortable position on the pillows. He looked pathetic; not the belligerent Joe Gionetti who had threatened to kill him, not the same bitter guy he'd dreaded meeting for over thirty years.

"Come close ta' th' bed, Harry," Joe said, and motioned to a chair next to the bed, "I want ya' ta' see this show on TV. It comes on now, all about our new relations with China." His voice cracked. Reaching up, he wiped his mouth with a balled-up wad of tissues, then coughed and wiped again. "I saw th' program earlier today. The announcer said they'd play it back agin t'night at 7:30, that's why I called ya', Harry, there's somethin' I want ya' ta' see." He glanced at the clock on the night stand. "It's 7:30 now." He picked up a hand-held TV remote control unit and pressed the button clicking the stations around until the public broadcasting station came on. "Now watch this," he repeated.

Harry squared the chair around, sat down, and adjusted his vision to the small television set mounted on the far wall. The station break had just ended and the next program was about to begin.

Chapter 9

VIEWING CHINA FILM DOCUMENTARY

"China Today: A Documentary on the New China," the announcer stated over the titles. The sing-song strains of Oriental music filled the background, still familiar after all these years. The announcer recounted a recent tour of the Orient he had taken, including some of the major cities in China, those enchanting, mysterious cities so often frequented in days past, in that decadent period before Communist China.

Harry smiled at the remark and scrunched down in his chair, crossing his legs, getting comfortable. He glanced over at Joe; his eyes were glued to the tube.

The first city was Shanghai, bustling, busy Shanghai, it's Huangpo River teeming with huge foreign ships, high-sterned junks, ferries and many smaller junks and barges. The colorful Bund along the waterfront looked the same as it did when he was last there, Harry thought, still teeming with people. He noticed several new attractions as the camera took them on a tour of the park. Glancing down at his wristwatch, Harry saw it was 7:37 p.m. Joe sure as hell didn't invite him up just to watch a documentary on China. What was the catch?

He glanced back at the screen. The action had shifted to a boat slowly wending its way up the river past the large ships and along the busy docks. Flags of many nations waved from the sterns of the ships, fluttering in an early morning breeze. The silhouette of the city stood stark against a clear blue sky.

Harry remembered Shanghai. It was his first taste of China, his first shoreleave. Alone, he'd taken a rickshaw through the busy streets ending up outside the Enlisted Men's Club in the heart of Shanghai.

A mob of Chinese had stopped the rickshaw about 200 feet short of the club entrance. He recalled his first frantic thoughts about the yelling, tattered mob – they all looked alike! The rickshaw boy demanded more money than they had agreed on. Harry objected, pulling only a dollar from his wallet. The boy shook his head, said something to the mob, and then demanded more. They argued as the crowd pressed tighter around them. For the first time, Harry felt fearful for his life.

"Leave that man alone!" called a tall, brawny Marine MP who came charging through the sea of yellow faces, recklessly swinging a large billy club and swearing profusely. The crowd fell back before him, dodging the flailing club. Fearfully, the rickshaw boy grabbed the dollar from Harry's hand and took off running, his rig bouncing behind him.

"You dumb jarhead!" the MP exclaimed gruffly, grabbing Harry by the arm and shoving him through the gates of the Enlisted Men's Club. "Don't ever flash your money before a mob like that again. They'll pick you clean as a bone in seconds."

Shaking, Harry turned to comment to the MP but, instead, snapped to attention, as he had learned in boot camp when in the presence of a sergeant, and the MP was a Master Sergeant.

"Hey, you okay?" the Sergeant asked, and then suddenly broke out into a big toothy grin. "Just out of boot camp?"

"Yes sir," came Harry's nervous reply. "Parris Island, Sir." He stiffened at attention.

The grin was still on the sergeant's pitted face. He shook his head, and then said, "Well, you're out of boot camp now. You're a Marine. And you don't call a sergeant, sir, and stand at ease for chrissakes!"

"Yes, si-I mean sergeant," Harry replied, suddenly relaxing.

"Now, private, I want you to always carry your wallet in your front pocket. It's harder for the gooks to get at. Too many of you 'boots' end up losing your wallets and getting cut up by these damned cutthroats. Be safe. When you leave here later, make damned sure you leave with several other Marines – and keep your belt buckle handy. A swinging buckle does a lot of damage. Now go inside and have a good time. Drink one for me."

"Right," Harry grinned stuffing his wallet in his front pocket, "and thanks."

"Don't mention it," the MP called over his shoulder as he moved off fighting his way through the crowd to rescue a couple of sailors. "You god-damned gooks!" he yelled, "Leave those men alone!" His flailing club bounced off backs and heads.

"Look! Look close now, Harry!" Joe rasped interrupting his thoughts. "See! See!"

Harry watched the screen intently. There was the port of Tsingtao. Christ, he thought, it, too, hadn't changed that much in the past thirty years. There was the ornate pavilion at the end of the pier at the entrance to the harbor; the travelogue announcer called it the Rebounding Wave Pavilion, then the Mayor's house perched high on a hillside, and the downtown area where most of the bars had been located, including the Enlisted Men's Club. Three places suddenly flashed across his mind: Gizmo's Night Club, Sammy's Place and the Tivoli Restaurant, three of his favorite hangouts. The camera moved to the dock area and the blackened, red brick fence surrounding the Old Japanese Compound. A chill ran through Harry; it was still being used.

"Watch close now!" Joe shrieked excitedly "This's what I wanted ya' ta' see. Watch close!"

Chapter 10

THE REASON FOR THE VISIT

The camera took them up a winding road around a hill and up to the main gates of Shantung University. Shantung University, hell! It was the old Marine Corps compound. Excitement swept through Harry. It was as if he'd never left the place. It seemed like only yesterday he had walked through those gates. The camera continued inside. Nothing seemed to have really changed. Yes, there were some cosmetic differences, new facades on buildings, more shrubbery and lots of beautiful flower gardens, but the basic layout was the same. The old baseball field adjacent to the main entrance, to his right, was still there, now the athletic field with students playing soccer. Even the old chain-link fence the Marines had put up to keep the gooks out. Harry grinned when he saw the dip in the gully where the fence didn't quite touch to the ground. Many times he'd crawled under the fence there next to a small drainage ditch, coming in late from liberty, bypassing the guardhouse at the main gate.

A new athletic building stood where the old Tarver Gymnasium had stood. It collapsed back in 1948 just days after the trial, he recalled. The old Third Marine barracks building was still there, but now converted into a dormitory with some classrooms. Students were sitting about on the lawn under the tall shade trees exchanging small talk, studying, enjoying a warm spring day. Many were walking to classes, all with happy, smiling faces.

Then he saw it – the old 12th Service Battalion building. Christ! he uttered to himself. It hadn't changed at all.

"See, Harry! See!" Joe grabbed at Harry's arm excitedly, holding tightly. "Watch this part. Watch this part!"

The barracks stood just the way the Marines had left it back in

1949. There was a growing lump in his throat. As the camera moved in closer, Harry could see the basic structure hadn't changed at all. Maybe a new coat of paint and a new name over the entrance to the building – but it was their old barracks. He knew he could walk inside today and go right to his old room on the second floor. It was incredible.

A view of the side of the building caused a start. Even the steps they'd built on the side of the building were still there, potted plants adorning each step. Harry smiled to himself. The Chinese probably didn't realize the skullduggery the Marines had gone to in order to build the steps. They led to the fourth floor, to the storage area where they used to sneak in Chinese whores for parties.

"How about that, Harry! Ain't that som'thin'?" Joe rasped.

"Yeah. Fantastic," Harry responded, a twang of nostalgia grabbing at his guts, a "wonder what it'd be like to be there today" feeling.

"That's what I wanted ya' ta' see," Joe rasped. "That's why I wanted ta' see ya', Harry." His bony fingers continued to dig into Harry's arm. "Yessir, that's why ol' Joe wanted ta' see ya'."

Harry glanced at Joe. Excitement radiated from his tired face, and his eyes were alive with a sparkle Harry once knew. Why was he so excited about seeing the old barracks? Hell, neither of them would ever set foot on Chinese soil again in their lifetime, much less see the inside of the old barracks.

Joe pressed the automatic tuner. The sound and picture faded abruptly just as Harry recognized the next city, Peiping, with its golden roofed Forbidden City. Joe lay back against the pillows gasping for breath, holding his hand to his chest and smiling.

"You all right, Joe?" Harry asked, a tone of concern in his voice.

"Yeah, jus' gotta let my excitement die down fer a few seconds, gotta bum ticker, too, ya' know," he replied. He continued sucking in air in short gasps, pursing his lips to exhale, not taking his hand from Harry's forearm.

Harry sneaked a glance at his wristwatch. They had only viewed twenty minutes of the travelogue. By now, they were showing different scenes of Peiping and he wanted to see more of that old fun town, especially the market, or the Hotel De Peking, and the fifth floor balcony where the whores roamed from room to room. Why'd he shut it off just as it was getting interesting?

"How'd ya' like ta' make a fast million bucks, Harry?" Joe asked in his low raspy voice.

"Come again?" said Harry thinking he had misunderstood. He twisted around in his chair facing Joe. Joe was lying there, smiling, a toothless smile, looking somewhat like the cat that swallowed the canary.

"How'd you like ta' make a fast million bucks?" he repeated.

"Fine," Harry quipped. "Who do I kill?"

It was a flippant retort that seemed to freeze on Harry's lips. Joe's face turned deadly serious, his dark eyes boring into Harry's – the cold, calculating eyes Harry recalled from the trial.

"What's it all about?" Harry said with a half-grin, a shrug of his broad shoulders. "Are you serious?"

"I want ta' make a pact with ya', Harry," Joe replied, his eyes still boring in ominously. "I know ya don't give a damn fer me 'n probably never did." He paused for a moment, seeming to search for the right words. "But, hell, I never cared a lick fer you either. But yer honest, 'n I know you can be trusted. I know I can count on ya'."

"What kind of pact?" Harry asked, somewhat surprised that Joe thought that much of him to call him honest. "Why old honest Harry Martin, who might just rip you off?"

Joe grinned. "Shit, Harry. I know all about you I've been here fer quite a spell –"

"And how the hell did you get into a VA hospital with a dishonorable discharge?" Harry countered, suddenly realizing Joe shouldn't be there.

Joe grinned again. "I got ways." He gave a wave of his hand. "Anyhow, I knowed you was from Saginaw. I knowed they had a vet's hospital here. At first I was going to knock you off, but then, what th' hell, I was falling apart anyways. I checked around. You got a good reputation and yer honest. I also know yer divorced, got two growed kids, yer independent as hell, but yer as poor as a church mouse right now. Yer gonna need a lot more dough ta' take care of that young skirt ya' been playin' house with, yeah a lot more dough, an' ol' Joe can help ya' get it."

Harry sat back thoughtfully amused, impressed at what Joe had just told him. The old bastard knew all about him. It suddenly dawned on him that Joe could have knocked him off any time he'd wanted. What was he leading up to?

"I need yer help, Harry," Joe continued. "I gotta share my secret with someone who can help me. I ain't got much time left 'n I need someone to share my pact with me. I think yer th' man." He coughed up some more phlegm, wiping it away with a fresh wad of tissues. "If I tell ya' my secret, ya' gotta swear ta' keep it a secret n' help me. Okay?" His eyes burned with a fire that made Harry shrink back, yet he couldn't break free. Joe's eyes never wavered, searching Harry's to the depth of his soul. "If ya' ain't gonna help me, get th' hell outa here right now!"

Harry held up his hands to stop Joe's sudden distrust. He was intrigued by the mysterious overtone, at the excitement he found in Joe's harangue. "Whoa! Hold on! Yeah, I'll keep your secret. What is it?"

Chapter 11
JOE'S HIDDEN CACHE

Joe seemed to be pondering his decision to share his secret with Harry. Then, he motioned toward the window ledge. "Bible. Get it," he insisted. Harry got the bible and handed it to Joe, who rested it on the bed tray. "Shake on it and hold yer hand on this here bible at th' same time."

This is a switch, Harry thought, Joe suddenly turning religious. He rested one hand on the bible and shook Joe's gnarled hand with the other. "I swear to keep your secret."

Joe leaned back on the pillows closing his eyes. Harry waited, watching. Had he passed the acid test? After several seconds, he wondered if Joe had died. He was so quiet. Would he ever know the mysterious secret? At that moment, Joe opened his eyes. With a crooked finger, he motioned him closer.

Harry leaned forward.

"Closer," Joe whispered.

Harry leaned over the bed until his face was only a couple of inches from Joe's. "Harry," came Joe's voice in a hoarse whisper, " I got over two million bucks stashed away in th' top of th' ol' 12th Service Battalion buildin', up where we used ta' keep our weapons, over two million bucks, Harry, 'n I'll share it with ya'."

"Get off it, Joe," Harry replied. "At the trial they said it was 30 grand, not two million."

"Harry, what'd you think, I'm a fool? 'Course I'm not gonna say two million. You forget, Harry, I'd been stashing a long time. I'm the best, Harry. Two million, I tell ya'."

Harry let out a low whistle and backed off looking at Joe. He suddenly realized that Joe, the old scoundrel, the stupid black marketeer was not as stupid as they all thought. He was serious; it showed on his face.

"I know it's still there; th' buildin's still standing just the way I remember it," Joe continued. "I stashed th' money away in a secret place that even th' stupid MP's 'n dumb chinks couldn't find, not even that double-crossing snake, Stan, jus' me." He cackled. "Jus' ol' Joe –"

Harry suddenly felt pity for Joe. The man was obviously deranged. What a fool, what a pathetic fool. He'd slipped over the edge. If there were money, it wouldn't be there now, not after all these years.

"We'll share th' money, ol' Joe n' you, Harry. You get it 'n we'll share it. Okay?"

"Two million dollars, all black market money that you stashed away? If so, that money belongs to the government, not you."

"No!" Joe snarled. "It's my money! I paid th' price fer it. I did my time. I paid th' price! Screw th' government! Screw th' Marines! Screw them damned commie chinks! It's my money! I know it's still there n' I want it!" His eyes were snapping with anger, his voice trembling. He seemed on the verge of hysteria.

"Calm down," Harry said, holding up his hands. "If you say the money's there, that's good enough for me. You know I don't give a rat's ass one way or the other, I just don't want you suddenly dropping dead with a heart attack. If you say it's there; it's there."

"It's there," Joe said, falling back on the pillows.

After a minute or so, Harry said, in a calm voice, "Joe, listen to what I'm going to tell you. It's been over thirty years since you stashed the money away. I don't think it's there anymore. Now think about it. It's probably rotted away by now, or the chinks found it when they remodeled the building, or the rats have chewed it up. You don't really think the money's going to be around anymore, not after thirty years?"

Joe grabbed Harry's arm pulling himself up to a sitting position. A fierce scowl masked his face, eyes flashing angrily "Goddammitt, Harry! It's there! I know it is. All big bills. I sealed them in heavy plastic 'n hid 'em in a big aluminum container. Big bills, $100, $500, $1,000, big bills, all there, all I gotta do is have someone go 'n get it 'n bring it back. That's all, jus' that simple!"

His voice suddenly faltered and he began coughing, the series of coughs racking his frail body. "Gimme some water," he gasped, wiping at his mouth with another wad of tissue. "Damn, jus' one good shot of whiskey'd do the trick." He dropped the wad of tissues in the wastebasket. "Even a shot of rotgut whiskey –"

Harry had jumped up at his request for water, reaching across the patient stand for the water pitcher and glass. In that moment, he felt a tug at his waist, and suddenly he was staring down the barrel of his own .22 held in Joe's gnarled left hand.

"Sit down, Harry," Joe commanded, motioning with the gun. Harry felt his face flush, a prickly sensation ran up his back and neck, and his hair felt like it was bristling. What a stupid move, reaching across the stand like that. Stupid! Never trust a rattlesnake, his dad had always cautioned him; they strike without warning.

"You always pack a rod, Harry?" Joe questioned.

"Uh, well, sometimes –"

"Only when ya' come ta' see ol' Joe, eh?" he cackled. He looked down at the gun, examining it momentarily, then turned it around and handed it back to Harry, butt first. "Like I said, I could'a knocked ya' off anytime I wanted to, but I figured what's been done is done. Put it away."

Still flushed, Harry slipped the pistol back inside his waistband.

"Put th' safety back on or you'll blow away th' family jewels," Joe admonished.

Harry gave an embarrassed grin as he took out the pistol, snapped the safety on, and then tucked it back in his waistband.

"Th' only time I'd come after ya' now is if ya' was ta' double-cross me," Joe said picking up the water pitcher and pouring a glass of water. Harry realized then, the wily old bastard had been wise to him, had figured he'd come packing a gun. Joe took a deep drink of water.

Chapter 12
DANGER: JOE'S EX-PARTNER, STAN

"That's all my loot over there, Harry," Joe said, and settled back resting on his pillows, seemingly more at ease now that he had Harry's undivided attention. "Th' only way anybody'd find it is if I told 'em – or they took th' place apart – 'n ya' jus' saw th' damned place is still standing, jus' th' way it was before"

"I don't know," Harry replied doubtfully. "I still say no money could last this long. It's been over thirty years since you hid it. Thirty years! Nineteen Forty-Eight versus Nineteen Seventy-Nine. That's a hell of a long time. Think about it."

Yet, all the time he was trying to convince Joe it was a hopeless cause, he found himself doubting his own reasoning. He recalled Joe as being exceptionally careful about his property. All the guys in the barracks knew he squirreled away his money, but they always figured he'd sent it back to the states. Hell, they had nearly torn up the whole damned Marine compound looking for the missing black market money. Now, here was Joe telling him it was hidden back in the barracks in Tsingtao, China.

"Listen ta' me, Harry. Listen ta' what I'm tellin' ya'. Th' money's there. Believe me, it's there! We'll split it right down the middle," Joe rasped, ignoring Harry's doubting comments. "A million fer you 'n a million fer me. How's 'at? Okay?"

Harry shook his head. It was far out. It'd be a miracle if the money still existed. Yet, it was a tempting offer – one million bucks. He and Sandy could really enjoy life then – the good life.

"Whatta' ya' say, Harry? Are ya' in?"

Harry mulled the deal over a couple more seconds. What the hell, he thought, why not. "Okay. It sounds plausible, and I could use a million bucks. Now, what's the catch?"

The look on Joe's face turned from that of a winning grin to a perplexed scowl. "There ain't no god-damned catch. You get th' money n' bring it back here ta' me. We split it fifty-fifty! No damned catch! I'd rather split it with you than have that bastard Stan get his hands on it."

Harry's eyebrows jumped. This was the second time Stan's name had been mentioned. "Does Stan know where the money is? Is he after it, too?"

"No. Hell, no!" Joe snapped, but there was a change in his voice that Harry caught. His eyes shifted away. "He's been after me fer years ta' tell him. I vowed I'd never tell him. I gave him th' slip back in New Jersey. He'll never find me." He gave a half-hearted laugh. "He'll never find me. Nossiree, 'n he'll never get his murderous hands on my money, never!"

Harry felt uncomfortable knowing Stan was aware of the money. If he was after it there could be trouble, especially if Stan knew just how much money. "What does Stan know about the money?" he asked.

"Nothin', really," Joe replied He suddenly seemed edgy.

"Don't lie to me," Harry fired back. "I don't like cat-and-mouse games. I don't want to get sucked into something where I'll end up fighting for my life, losing it over some damned cache of money that might not even exist anymore. It isn't worth it to me. Tell me about Stan or the deal's off. You understand? And no lies."

"Yeah," Joe nodded. "I understand. No lies. Stan knows there's money but he don't know where it is or how much. Honest. He got me drunk one time back in Passaic 'n I kinda let him know I had my dough stashed away back in Tsingtao. We got ta' laughin' about it, ya' know – my money there 'n th' commies not lettin' anyone in their damned country. It was funny at th' time. Ol' Stan had pissed all his money away, that what th' feds didn't get back. He's been flat-assed busted fer years. Pulls stick-ups, steals purses, strong-arm stuff. Anyways, later when Kissinger n' Nixon went ta' China 'n opened up new relations with th' commies, th' picture changed. Ol' Stan came back after me. He wanted to know all 'bout th' money. I wouldn't tell him a friggin' thing, not one damned thing. He busted me up somethin' awful. I was in a hospital fer three weeks. I snuck outta there one night, bad hurt as I was, cause I knew he'd be back. I got th' hell outta' Jersey 'n away from that bastard. Honest, Harry, I didn't tell him one damned thing. Nothing."

Harry sat staring at Joe, not knowing whether to believe him or not.

Chapter 13

NEW PARTNERS: JOE AND HARRY

"Time for your pills, Mr. Gionetti," came a soft female voice. Harry swiveled about catching sight of the attractive nurse he'd seen earlier pushing the pill cart. She had a warm smile for Harry as she moved past him to Joe, bending over to give him pills, making sure he took each one with a swallow of water.

Nice legs, Harry thought, admiring the view under the raised hemline. Nice ass. It's a good thing she's not a mind reader.

Joe gagged down the pills, muttering as he took each one. The nurse laughingly cajoled him, encouraging him.

"There. All done," she said, and turning to Harry, she continued, "It's almost the end of visiting hours, sir." She gave Harry that winning smile. "Mr. Gionetti needs his rest."

"I'll be leaving shortly," Harry acknowledged.

As she adjusted items on the cart, and then proceeded to leave the room, Harry sat thinking, contemplating what to do. There was a good possibility of getting into China now that the United States had recognized the country, now that relations between the two countries had improved to the point where travelers were visiting China in ever-increasing numbers. Maybe it was a long shot, but just maybe he could get to Tsingtao and get the money. Stan posed another problem, though. Somehow, he believed Joe, but the fact that Stan knew about the money bothered him. He was sure Joe hadn't told him; Joe was the kind who would never part with anything unless he had a hand in the deal. Stan was the deep thinker, the kind who'd kill for the information. Obviously, if Joe had escaped from him, then the secret would only be between Joe and him.

"Will ya' get th' money fer us, Harry?" Joe asked, a pleading tone in his raspy voice. "We'll split it, partners, fifty-fifty, just like I said. Ol' Joe jus' wants one more good fling before he cashes in, one more good fling."

"Well," Harry said hesitantly, not wanting to commit himself, yet finding the challenge of getting that much money too tempting to resist. "I got vacation time coming – seeing as how the bottom has dropped out of the building business because of inflation and high interest rates." There goes my vacation trip with Sandy, he suddenly thought, but then the thought of a longer vacation with her, even a prolonged honeymoon, perked him up. "Maybe I can swing it, partner." With a grin, he held out his hand and Joe grasped it holding it tightly as possible with his pain-twisted fingers.

"Yer th' only person I've ever asked, n' th' only one I'll tell where my stash is, 'zactly where ta' find it."

Harry noticed his eyes were wet. Joe quickly rubbed his sleeve across his eyes. "Ya won't be sorry ya' did this fer ol' Joe, Harry. Ya' won't be sorry, th' money's there, you'll see, I ain't lying, it's there."

Harry grinned at the sudden burst of enthusiasm. "Hell, Joe. If I can get to Tsingtao, and if I can get into the old compound, and if I can get into the old barracks, and if I can get the money, then I know I can get back okay," Harry quipped. "It's just all the 'if's' that bother me."

That brought a raspy laugh from Joe.

"Now, just where is the money?" Harry asked. "Just where do I find it?"

"Come close, closer," Joe whispered, motioning Harry close to his lips. "I don't want any damned nurses or doctors list'nin' in."

Harry listened intently as Joe described in detail exactly where the money was hidden and how someone could get it. Christ, Harry thought, it was so simple, yet so well hidden – the work of a genius. If I'd had my wits about me thirty years ago I could have figured it out, he chastised himself, then added, maybe.

"That's slick the way you hid the money," he said when Joe stopped. "Really ingenious."

Joe fell back on the pillows, coughing, hacking up more phlegm, wiping it away with a new wad of tissues.

"Now ya' know my secret," he rasped. "Yer th' only one I've ever told 'n I'm holding ya' responsible fer bringing' back my share."

"How the hell did you ever think of hiding it like that? You must have had a lot of help to get the contraption built to your specifications, and then getting it placed in the wall without any of our personnel being aware of it."

Joe glared at him. "Don't press me, Harry," he snapped. "I got it done n' I'm th' only one who knows jus' where th' loot is –'cept, now, fer you."

"Don't worry. I'll keep your secret. I was just curious. No offense. Just asking." Harry held his hands up to show he meant nothing by the inquiring remark. Hell, he thought, for two million bucks just for the taking, he could care less what happened thirty years ago. All he had to do now was get to China, get the money and get back and share it with Joe. Simple. Bullshit!

"Penny fer yer thoughts, Harry?" Joe cut in.

"Just thinking about China and how I'm going to pull this off."

"How ya' get there n' get back is yer problem. You jus' bring it back 'n we'll split it like I said, fifty-fifty. Jus' bring back some dough so I can have at least one good fling before I croak!" Joe laughed, but it was a raspy, guttural laugh. "I'd like ta' latch onta' a young chick like you got. She's a hot number, right?"

Harry nodded, a sudden thought of the passion he and Sandy shared so often crossing his mind.

"Yeah, I could show some chick that there's a still life in this ol' stud. Right, Harry?" He laughed.

"Right, stud –"

"Yeah. At least one more good fling before I croak. Dames, booze, at least I'd go out ballin' 'stead of layin' here dying with this damned cancer."

He coughed, coughed again, his face turning red. He grabbed up more tissues, continuing to shudder, coughing hard, his tired body racked with each spasm.

Harry watched helplessly, fearful that Joe might die at that moment. It was the worst siege of coughing yet. Suddenly, Joe moaned, simultaneously wiping a big gob of phlem with his wad of tissues, streaking it across his cheek, then fell back on the pillows with a deep sigh. Harry handed him a glass of water which Joe took, drinking deeply.

Finally, clearing his throat, Joe settled back on the bed exhausted, his head nestled deeply in the pillows, eyes closed.

Harry stood up, zipping up his jacket. "You need your rest, Joe. You lay back and sleep. I'll figure out a way to get to China'; don't worry about it. Right now, I gotta hurry, got a heavy date with Sandy and I don't want to keep her waiting."

Joe nodded weakly giving a slight wave of his hand.

"I'll check back in a couple days. I've gotta give a lot of thought to how I'm going to get to China. See ya' later, partner."

As he headed for the door, Joe called after him. "Se ya' later, partner."

Chapter 14

PROBLEM: HOW TO GET TO CHINA

Riding down on the elevator Harry smiled to himself; old Joe hadn't lost any of his street savvy. the old fox! He'd spotted the gun, probably expected it; he was still the deadly adversary. Harry knew he'd have to be on the defensive all through their partnership. There was no telling at this point whether he was being set up for a double cross. Be on guard, he warned himself.

The elevator door opened and he stepped out onto the main floor.

"Hold the elevator!" a man's booming voice called sharply.

Instinctively, Harry reached back to hold the doors open. Turning, he saw the portly cigar-smoking doctor hurrying for the elevator, still puffing on his cigar. As he got close, Harry removed his hand and the elevator doors snapped shut.

"Oops," Harry said wearing a sarcastic smile on his face as he strode past the wheezing doctor toward the lobby.

"Son-of-a-bitch!" the doctor muttered after Harry.

Retribution, Harry thought as he zipped up his jacket. Blow smoke in my face. Hah! God, I feel good! He pulled his collar tight around his neck, got his ignition key in hand, pulled on his gloves and headed out the door into the storm. It was blowing hard with snow gusting across the parking lot in billowing white clouds.

Walking with his head bent, shielding himself from the storm, Harry almost ran into a couple of men heading toward the hospital. Glancing up, he'd caught sight of them at the last moment, a bearded guy and an Oriental. Abruptly, he moved sharply to his right to avoid them. It was safer to stay away from strangers. Even in winter there was a high incidence of muggings in Saginaw, even in a hospital parking lot.

At his car, he unlocked the door, started the engine, and then let it idle for a few minutes before driving away. He glanced at his watch. It was 8:45 p.m. The duty nurse should have kicked him out of there at 8:30. His visit had lasted longer than he had intended. Sandy was probably furious by now, especially if she was stuck with Butch and Marlene. Knowing them, they'd be laying it on heavy suggesting he'd probably stepped out on her, was probably making out with some other female.

He drove south on Michigan Avenue. It was slippery. He slowed down for better control of the car. Another few blocks and he'd be there and straighten things out with Sandy. Maybe they could still catch a late dinner, take in a disco and wind up the night enjoying each other in her bed.

How the hell was he going to get to China? The thought was there constantly, and compelling to the point of irritation. Two million bucks! All for the taking – if it was still there!

The whole idea was so damned far-fetched. It was like the other get rich schemes he'd pursued. He'd already spent a small fortune on the Michigan lottery. Instant winner. Hah! They should have named it Instant Loser, a more accurate description of the game. Horse racing was equally costly. Now, he was faced with a two million dollar long shot.

"Shit," he muttered under his breath. "I'll probably have to spend the fifteen hundred I saved for my vacation with Sandy on this damned wild-goose chase. If I fly to Japan or China it'll wipe me out. If there's nothing there, I'll really be flat-assed busted. China, half way around the damned world from Saginaw. Jeez!"

His thoughts shifted again. His passport was current, his sailing papers up to date. Maybe he could fly out to "Frisco" and ship out on a freighter headed for China. But his thoughts kept shifting, fragmentary thoughts, how to get there, how to not spend every last cent, but always returning to point zero. How the hell was he going to pull it off?

He peered through the thick snow building up on the windshield. The glass was icing over. The worn wiper blades skimmed ineffectively over the icy buildup. His field of vision was getting smaller and smaller and the defrosters were laboring at full power.

He was on Hamilton Street now, only three blocks from the Pub.

A police car was driving away as he came to a stop across the street from the Pub. Several people were clustered about talking and gesturing after the departed police car. Harry searched the crowd looking for a familiar face. "She must be inside," he said to himself.

Reaching under his sweater, he slipped the pistol out and slid it under the passenger seat. It wouldn't be cool to carry a piece inside the bar. Suddenly, he slammed back hard against his seat. "How the hell do I get to China? How the hell do I pull it off?"

It was aggravating. He had to come up with an answer, and soon. Joe was in bad shape. He didn't have a lot of time, not with cancer. The more he thought of it, the whole damned idea of getting to China, and the whole idea never left his mind for one moment since Joe told him where the cache was hidden, the more maddening the challenge of getting there became.

"Tomorrow. I'll think about China tomorrow!" He shrugged, smiling to himself. "Tomorrow." Yet, thoughts of China persisted. "How do I get to Tsingtao? Is the money still there? Hell, the chinks must have scoured the building thoroughly after the Marines pulled out. They must have found it – but maybe they didn't!"

He saw Ginger and Ted getting out of Ted's new Porsche and heading for the Pub. Ted was a "leech" and no one knew it better than Harry. "Better get in there and protect Sandy from his hot hands," he told himself.

China. He tried to ignore it, to push the thoughts aside, out of his mind, but it was like trying to ignore an elephant standing on your foot.

He jerked the keys from the ignition, got out, locked the car and headed across the street. He glanced back momentarily, a paranoid habit he'd picked up somewhere along the way, always double-checking everything. The car was safe. He laughed. His friends kidded him constantly about his beat-up old "Betsy," but he had the last laugh. At least it was paid for, and it ran damned good. Maybe it used oil, but it was still good transportation. Maybe next year he'd be driving around in a new Mercedes convertible. Damn! Right back to China.

Chapter 15

TROUBLE AT THE PUB

On entering the Pub, Harry stopped momentarily to let his eyes adjust to the dimness. A pall of smoke hung across the room. It burned his lungs. He'd quit smoking ten years earlier realizing he'd become a slave to the weed – cigarettes and coffee, cigarettes and sandwich, cigarettes and beer. First thing in the morning and the last thing at night. Two on the way to work, a pack or two at work, day in and day out. He was always coughing to clear his throat. At times he thought he'd cough his damned head off. And the burns: new suit, the sofa, the new leather chair, on the dresser, on the car seat – just carelessness, and costly.

One day he quit cold turkey. It was hell for a few weeks but he did it and he was really proud of himself. Even his kids told him they saw a dramatic change in his personality. He was warmer, more caring. Laurie hadn't noticed, or if she had, she didn't encourage him. But he felt good. It was a personal achievement, one of many he faced alone over the next few years until he got his freedom. Now he accepted the choking smoke philosophically; it was the price he paid to be with friends.

As his eyes grew accustomed to the room, he recognized several familiar faces. He nodded and waved as he made his way toward the U-shaped bar where Gunther was on duty. The place was packed wall to wall with bodies, and some really nice bodies at that.

The Pub was one of the popular watering holes in Saginaw. Located in Old Town, the Pub catered to a younger set, twenties and thirties crowd. Harry felt like a misfit at his age, yet everyone seemed to accept him, more than likely because of Sandy.

The attractiveness of the Pub was its simplicity: bare brick walls with mortar oozing out between the old bricks, just as the walls had been built at the turn of the century. Large booths lined each main wall, the table tops thick wood slabs from the lumbering days. Like the walls, the rough-hewn plank flooring was also original, adding to the bar's unique atmosphere. Older wags said the bar had once been a stable.

In sharp contrast, tall multi-colored director's chairs circled the U-shaped bar. Harry waved to several more acquaintances as he eased onto one of the just-vacated chairs, acing out a young, bearded, longhaired kid.

"Hi, Harry. What'll it be?" Gunther said slapping a napkin down in front of him.

"Make it a light draft, Gunther," Harry replied. "What's all the excitement about? I just saw a police car pulling away."

As he spoke, he carefully scanned the room. More familiar faces, but Sandy's wasn't one of them. Maybe she was in the can.

"We had a doozy fight," Gunther replied, setting a frothy glass on the napkin. "Al's cleaning up the last of the mess now." He nodded over his shoulder toward the far corner. "Sent some poor sailor to the hospital, put Butch in the hoosegow and sent Marlene home drunk. The bitch!"

Harry craned his neck to see beyond Gunther's huge frame. In the far corner lay a demolished chair next to the broken popcorn machine, it's glass facing shattered on the floor. Al was busy sweeping up broken glass and popcorn.

"Butch in jail? How'd it happen?" Harry asked and pulled a roll of bills from his pocket, peeled off a single and tossed it across the bar top toward Gunther. As he spoke he continued searching for Sandy. "Fats" Johnson was in one of his usual heated arguments at the dartboard – but still no Sandy.

"Hi, Harry. How's tricks?"

Harry swiveled around as blonde, blue-eyed Janie, his favorite chesty waitress, slid in next to him.

"Two light drafts," she called out to Gunther stopping him before he could reply to Harry's question.

"Not bad, Janie. Not bad." Harry replied trying not to stare

65

down at her full breasts. One thing about Janie he'd learned: she was proud of what she had and loved to flaunt it. Tonight was no exception. Her breasts, which would make any average girl feel inferior, were accentuated by a tight-fitting sweater and, as Janie didn't believe in wearing a bra, her hard nipples pushed taut against the fabric. Skin-tight corduroy jeans and calf-high western boots completed her bold outfit.

"I'm free tonight if you're interested," she said, winking at Harry. He grinned and winked back. "Thanks I'll keep that in mind."

She smiled showing strong, straight white teeth. She ran her tongue casually around her upper lip. "You do that. It could be interesting." On an impulse, she grabbed a bar napkin and quickly jotted her address on it. "If you need me, I'll be home at this address after two." She folded the napkin and stuffed it in his jacket pocket. "If I can be of any help at all –" she whispered rubbing her firm breasts against his arm as she departed to deliver her two light beers. Harry watched after her. Nice ass, too, he thought.

"Yeah, some sailor off one of them foreign ships loading at Wickstrom elevators made a pass at Marlene," Gunther said leaning across the bar. "And, well, you know how hot-tempered Butch is. None of us expected it, least of all the sailor. All of a sudden Butch lowered the boom. Pow! He beat the hell out of the poor guy."

"Yeah, that Butch has a mean temper," Harry said taking a deep swallow of beer. "Course, a lot of the problem with Butch is Marlene; she still thinks she's the same hot little thing she used to be years ago when she was a teenie-bopper. I bet she came on strong with the poor sailor, that old 'come on' routine –"

"She did just that, Harry," Gunther nodded "I watched her when she came in tonight. You could tell there were bad vibes between her and her old man. She was cold as a witch's tit to him. Completely ignored him. The first thing she does is down a boilermaker, then she orders another and then starts down the bar socializing, playing up to guys, rubbing her boobs against them. When she came to the sailor he probably thought he'd found a good thing, probably didn't know she was Butch's woman, and made a pass at her. She really played up to him, his 'cute' foreign accent. He got turned on and, pow, Butch turned him off. The bitch. Personally, I think Butch would be a hell of a lot better off without her."

"Naw. I think they deserve each other. I've see them operate for two years now. Butch is the same way with women. He likes to hustle 'em, give the gals a lot of attention which, in turn, really pisses her off. Naw, they deserve each other. That, I'm sure," Harry said and took a quick swallow of beer, then started to laugh.

"What's so funny?" Gunther asked, puzzled.

"You don't suppose they're into kinky sex, ya' know, getting each other all worked up by doing these crazy things, then, horny as hell, they go home and knock off a good one?"

Gunther grinned. The more the outlandish thought sounded plausible, the bigger his grin grew until it turned into laughter. It hit him hard and he slapped his big hand hard on the bar. "That's a good thought, Harry. Goddamn, I never thought of that." He roared. Harry laughed harder, tears streaming down his cheeks as he watched Gunther, infected by his hearty laughter.

Still shaking his head, a chuckling Gunther moved off down the bar to serve another customer, still wiping tears from his eyes.

Harry wiped at his eyes, and then took another swallow of beer, emptying the glass. "Another one, Gunther," he called down the bar. He peeled off another single and slapped it on the bar next to his empty glass. He looked around the room; still no sign of Sandy. How long can a female stay in the john?

"Have you seen Sandy tonight?" he asked Gunther, just setting a fresh glass of beer in front of him.

"Yeah. She was here earlier. She got pissed off at having to wait for you and took off with some young stud." He tried to keep a straight face, but the twinkle in his eyes betrayed him.

"Okay, smartass. Where is she? Is she hiding somewhere?"

Gunther stood grinning down at him, the smile pasted on his broad face.

"C'mon," Harry pleaded. "We've got a date tonight. I'm already late —"

"Harry, when are you gonna make an honest woman out of that cute little doll? Ya' gotta pop the question soon. It's the only decent thing to do."

"I will. I will." Harry hunched forward motioning Gunther close. "I've been giving some serious thought to it. Honest. I think I can convince her. Got an idea that might do the trick. Now quit stalling. Where the hell is she?"

"Gone." The smile faded. "She took that dumb drunk Marlene home after the fight. She probably doesn't want to see anyone; Marlene barfed all over her. What a mess, and that cute little Sandy looking like she just stepped out of a Nieman-Marcus catalog. Marlene puked all over her. The damned drunk!"

"No shit? Damn!" Harry swore. "Did she say whether she was coming back or not?"

"I doubt it. She was a mess from head to toe. She said she'd get Marlene home – then she was going home. Sounded like she was calling it a night."

"Damn. No message for me?"

"Naw. She was pissed off about Marlene – said you'd understand."

Harry slammed his hand hard on the bar. "Damn! If I'd been on time she might have missed the whole incident." He shook his head, then a grin started breaking across his face as he looked up at Gunther. "You can bet your last dollar I'll hear about this later."

But, secretly, inside he felt relieved that she was home. There were too many young studs hanging around the Pub. Always, there was that gnawing feeling inside that she might dump him for a younger guy, yet she seemed satisfied. He couldn't figure out why, but it made him feel good.

There was a day, he recalled fondly, when they were lying naked, making love in front of an open patio door that looked out across a field of golden wheat ripening in the late summer sun. "Ya' know what I like about you, Harry," she said, gasping, at the same time knocking his stiff arms outwards so he fell tight against her, bringing forth a grunt of delight as his full weight pressed down, driving his manhood deeper into her. "We have a lot of fun together. We enjoy the same things, making love in the afternoon –" her hungry lips met his, tongues momentarily dueling – "hanging out together, holding hands, sharing, touching, you're not old, not as old as your age. You're young and you'll always be young. I don't want anyone else. I'm happy. You make me happy." She wrapped her legs around his waist squeezing him tightly to her. "Now make me happy again."

Harry grinned remembering the moment. The remark about his age had stuck with him. Yet, each time a young, good-looking stud appeared on the scene and started to hustle her, he got an uneasy feeling, wondering if this time he might be the "Mister Right." She had married Mister Right once before only to find out he was Mister Wrong. Now, a free spirit, she enjoyed life with no strings attached. "I just don't want to get involved any more than we are right now. Don't talk marriage. Not now. Let's just enjoy what we've got, okay?" She had said it quietly, but emphatically. He had accepted it although the twenty years difference in their ages still nagged at him.

Chapter 16
LOVE LOST FOR THE NIGHT

"Hi, Harry, how's it going?" Harry swiveled around in time to see Al moving behind the bar under the lift section, dumping a dustpan full of broken glass into a wastebasket. "Gunther tell you about your damned friends, Butch and Marlene?" he asked.

"Hold on," Harry exclaimed, raising his hands defensively. "Acquaintances, yes; close friends, no. Don't put me in the same category as those two."

"Goddamn them," Al said putting his broom and the dustpan away. "This is the last time for those two. Butch is gonna pay for all the broken glass, broken chairs, broken popcorn machine and my time to clean up the mess! I run a good clean place. I don't need that macho stud or his hot-ass wife on the premises. Piss on 'em! They can take their damned business elsewhere. They're nothing but grief!"

Harry nodded in agreement. "Maybe this'll teach them a lesson, an important and expensive lesson. Was the sailor hurt bad?"

"Hell yes he was hurt bad! Had to haul him away in an ambulance. Hell yes he was hurt!" He drew himself a beer. "The swabbie was getting happily loaded. He wasn't hurting anyone. Marlene deliberately teased him, leading him on. He probably figured he was in for a good time with her. The poor slob. He didn't know what hit him; it happened so fast. Butch punched him so hard you could feel his jawbone crack. Then Butch gave him several quick body punches and finally smashed the guy in the face again. He went sprawling backwards across the room, fell over a table and chairs, his hand smashed the glass on the popcorn machine, and when he hit the deck, the damned table landed right on his leg. You could hear the bone snap like the crack of a rifle shot."

"Yeah, and Al was over the bar and smacked Butch on the back of his skull with his billy club before Butch could land another punch," Gunther chimed in. "Butch went down in a heap and Marlene started screaming bloody murder. She was trying to get at Al, and she was screaming and carrying on something awful. Christ, what a mess. I called the police and they were here in a couple of minutes."

"Police ambulance took the poor swabbie over to St. Mary's Hospital emergency ward," Al added. "Medics said he had a broken leg and broken jaw."

"That poor guy will be out of commission for at least six to eight weeks," Harry said, shaking his head. "How'd Sandy get involved? Was she hurt?"

"Naw. Poor kid. She was trying to get Marlene calmed down. The dumb bitch just stood there screaming and yelling at me, at everybody, that I'd killed Butch. She dropped to the floor flopping over the guy, carrying on like he was dead. Sandy finally got her on her feet after Butch started stirring. Then what does Marlene do but puke her guts all over Sandy. Geez! Poor kid!"

"Sandy shoulda' punched her lights out right then and there," Gunther said. "Instead, what does she do but take the drunken bitch home."

"My invitation's still good, Harry," Janie said sliding in next to him, her bosom pressed firmly against his back. "Sandy's out and I'm available. Two drafts, Gunther," she said without taking her eyes off Harry. "I understand you're really good. I'd like to find out."

"Somebody's been telling tales out of school," Harry said, a coolness in his voice.

"Best offer you'll get tonight," Janie shrugged, picking up her two drafts. "I'm damned good, too!" She swiveled around and walked away.

"She – it!" Harry muttered. Still, he caught himself looking after her, the swing of her shapely hips as she walked away.

"And Butch is in the cooler for the night," Gunther said returning from the cash register. He caught the agitated look on Harry's face.

"Hey, don't pay any attention to Janie She's just her usual horny self. If it wears pants and there's a bulge in the front, she after it. She'll have some guy in tow before the night's over. That's just Janie. What else can you say?"

"Yeah. She's harmless, but a lot of fun" Al grinned as he reached up for a glass. He was tall, muscular, with thick blonde hair that contrasted with his reddish-blonde mustache. He was of Swedish extraction with deep blue eyes peering out from his sharp angular face. A devil-may-care smile crossed his face.

As Al drew a beer, Harry saw the familiar scorpion tattoo on his right wrist, a souvenir of "Nam." He never mentioned the war but you knew he still lived it. He was one of five survivors of the Scorpion platoon. His buddies said he was the devil in hand-to-hand combat; quick, fast and deadly.

Gunther was older, about age 48. A generation earlier, he'd fought his way across Korea from the Inchon invasion, and on up to the Chosin Reservoir where all hell broke loose. Half-frozen, in constant fear, they had fought for their lives back across Korea's cold, rugged mountains before an unrelenting foe until they were evacuated. The blaring of Chinese trumpets still pierced his nightmares, chilling him.

Al shook his head. "Yeah, that poor swabbie never knew what hit him. Out for the count. Probably still in emergency. Hey! Gunther! Make sure we check our insurance coverage. I don't want any damned lawsuits. Better yet, call our damned lawyer, that's what we pay him for."

"Another one?" Al asked grabbing up Harry's almost empty glass and refilling it before he could answer. He slid it back down the bar. Harry fumbled in his pocket for a loose bill. "On the house, Harry, I treat my good customers on a rare occasion." He grinned, lifting his glass. Harry hoisted his glass in silent salute, and then took a long swallow.

"Hi Harry. What're you doing here?" Fats Johnson said stopping beside Harry, his pudgy fist clutching several darts. "I thought I saw you going into the vet's hospital about two hours ago. What's the matter? You're stomach acting up again?" He threw a beefy arm around Harry's shoulder. "Christ, we can't have you hospitalized. Who would we beat at darts?" He laughed heartily. It brought a sheepish grin to Harry's face.

It was true. Ever since he teamed up with Sandy, he'd lost his skill with the darts, buying many a round of drinks for the opposition. But, he had to admit to himself, his love life had greatly improved since he met her.

"Yeah, that cute little Sandy's got your old ass tacked up on the dart board," Fats chortled. "And you know we just love sticking it to you!" Fats continued, chuckling at his remark, much to Harry's growing embarrassment. "You must have hidden talent, Harry, 'cause it sure don't show in darts." His comment brought a round of laughter causing Harry to squirm even more.

"You got ulcers from worrying over buying us drinks all the time?" Fats chided.

"Is somethin' wrong with you?" Al asked, suddenly concerned.

"No. I don't have ulcers and I'm okay. The only thing wrong with me is my suffering pride and thinning wallet from buying for you turkeys all the time," Harry replied jokingly. "Actually, I stopped by the hospital to see a guy I used to know way back when, hell, before any of you were even a gleam in your old man's eyes." He laughed. "Naw, this guy's got terminal cancer. The docs don't expect him to live more than a year at the outside, maybe six months. He saw I lived in town and wanted to see me, shoot the breeze, the good old days, do him a couple of favors."

"Cancer. Geez! That's too bad," Al said. "He didn't get mixed up with Agent Orange or any of them chemicals, did he?"

"Hell no. He's World War Two vintage, too early for that defoliant crap." His gaze took in the heavy pall of smoke hanging across the room. "He probably got cancer from smoking too damned many cigarettes."

"Funny, Harry, funny –" Al deliberately reached to the back bar and picked up a partly smoked stogie. He re-lit it and blew a cloud of sweetish smoke into Harry's face. "That's why I quit cigarettes. They can kill you. Cigars, well, they stink, but you sure as hell don't inhale them like cigarettes." He took another puff and blew a smoke ring at Harry. "Cigars give you class without killing you." He laughed. Harry waved the smoke ring to one side.

"It's your turn, Fats!" came a shrill female voice from across the room. "Let's go!"

"Keep your pants on!" Fats retorted. He slapped Harry on the back. "Sorry about your friend, Harry. Just glad it's not you, though. Join us for a round. We need a sucker-er, an angel to buy for us." Laughing, he headed back across the room yelling at the girl to keep her pants on.

Harry turned back to Al who had just started washing an accumulation of about twenty dirty glasses. His movements were quick, sloshing each glass in an agitated manner; wash, rinse and sterilizer, then setting the glasses on the far sink to dry before hanging them up in the overhead slots ready to use again.

"Yeah, I feel sorry for Sandy," Al called over his shoulder. "She looked like a million bucks."

"Excuse me, please. I am looking for some information, please –" a voice interrupted.

Harry turned glancing over his shoulder at the sound of a foreign accent. He found himself looking at a tall distinguished man with a neatly trimmed beard and mustache who was just moving in next to the bar. Harry noted the officer's cap with the scrambled eggs sat squarely on his head; his coat a traditional officer's black. Dark blue eyes peered from under bushy eyebrows.

"A sailor was injured in a fight here tonight?"

Chapter 17

A SLOW BOAT TO CHINA

The barroom rang with the sound of happy revelers, the sound of rock and roll, even Fats course language at losing a game, but the question posed by the officer seemed to cut through all conversation like the cutting edge of a Bowie knife.

Stealthily, Al reached under the bar to where his billy club lay in wait, grasping the hard walnut stock tightly in his hand. "Yeah, there was a sailor hurt in a fight here tonight. Why?"

"Der sailor, Alex, is my close friend. I vant to know vere he vas taken so dat I might go to him."

Al relaxed his grip on the billy club. "You ain't here to mix it up, are you?"

"Mix up?" The man had a quizzical look on his face.

"Fight," Harry interjected. "Mix up."

"No. No fight. All I vant is to find Alex. He is a member of my vatch, my vork detail, und I vant to find him so I can help him."

Al released the club back to its resting place. "He's over at St. Mary's Hospital in the emergency ward. Sorry about the fight. I was just telling Harry, here –" he nodded toward Harry who tipped his finger to his brow – "that I don't like fighting in my bar. I like to have happy drunks and big spenders, not fights."

"Yeah," Harry added. "Fights happen even though Al and Gunther do their best not to let them get started. I'm sorry about your friend, Alex."

"Tank you," the man replied. "I go now to see him. Vere is dis St. Mary's Hospital? Do you tink dey vill release him so dat I might take him back to der ship?"

"No way, pal," Al responded shaking his head. "Your friend's got a busted leg, busted jaw and several good cuts. He'll probably be out of commission for a couple of months."

"No!" the sailor gasped. "Oh, Lord! Ve sail in two days!" He clasped his hands to his head. "Oh, no –" he groaned dejectedly settling onto one of the bar stools. "Poor Alex. Ve vill haf to sail vis out him. Ve need him. I don't vant to leaf him behind. He is my right hand, I need him, I count on him –"

"Hey pal, don't worry about Alex. They'll take good care of him at the hospital," Harry interjected, trying to reassure the man. "It's a good hospital and they take real good care of sailors, don't they, Al?" He glanced over at Al looking for support.

"Uh, yeah, sure. He's in real good hands, honest –" Al added quickly.

The sailor rubbed his hand across his brow. "Two months, dat is terrible, dat is a long time to be in der hospital –"

"Hey, pal –" Harry said trying to comfort the man. "Don't worry. They'll take good care of him. Honest!" He felt sorry for the man wishing there was something he could say, could do, to cheer him up. "Where you from, pal?" he said for starters.

"Stockholm. Ve are members of der crew of der grain carrier *Otto J. Nurad,*" the officer replied almost inaudibly. "Ve are loading grain right now for der first International Trade Commission shipment to China."

Harry, who had just taken a big swallow of beer, almost choked when he heard the word "China." Setting his glass gingerly down on the bar, he turned to the officer and, in a slightly strained voice, asked, "You said you were sailing to China?"

"Yah. China," the man replied. "Ve vill be sailing to Shanghai und on up der coast to der port of Tsingtao. Ve sail on Saturday morning as soon as der ice breaker can clear a channel for us."

A euphoric feeling suddenly flooded throughout Harry's body like the warming taste of good brandy. His heart was pounding so loudly he thought everyone in the bar could hear it. My god! China! Shanghai! Tsingtao! He could hardly believe what he'd just heard. He felt giddy, light-headed. He had to hear it again If it was so; it had to be a good omen.

Trying to control his growing excitement, he leaned closer, practically pushing his face into the officer's face. "You did say Tsingtao, didn't you?"

"Yah. Tsingtao. It is a small seaport located on der Shantung peninsula across from der southern tip of Korea. Vy? Do you know of it?"

"Do I?" Harry exclaimed, a broad grin breaking across his face. "Hell yes I know it, like the back of my hand. It was a second home to me, stationed there with the Marine Corps." He continued grinning; it was a silly grin, a happy grin. It probably didn't mean a thing to the sailor, Harry thought; he probably thinks I'm stupid grinning like this.

"What's your name, pal?" Harry asked breaking free of the stupid grin, suddenly more attentive to the man. In the same breath, he called to Al, "Two beers, Al. One for me and one for my friend –"

"Peter, Peter Selham," the man said.

"For my friend, Peter Selham," Harry continued. He dug deep into his pocket and pulled out a wad of bills, peeling off a couple of singles, and slid them across the bar to Al as he set two frothy glasses of beer before them.

"No. Please. Tank you, but I should go to my friend, Alex," Peter said, but his eyes were already fixed on the glass of beer.

"C'mon," Harry encouraged. "Just one to let you know we're your friends." He slid the beer closer to Peter. "Okay?"

"Vell, just vun –" His hand closed around the wet glass.

"My name's Harry, Harry Martin," Harry said pointing to himself, "and it just might be that fate brought us together tonight." He raised his glass to Peter. They clinked glasses and drank deeply.

"Two more, Al!" Harry called out, pulling out more money.

Play it cool, Harry told himself. Listen closely, work all the angles, use the old think tank. China might be closer than you imagined just ten minutes ago. He looked down the bar where Al was drawing two beers. Hurry up, man, he thought; gotta keep Peter here, gotta talk to him, gotta figure out how to get on board his ship. Maybe I could replace his friend, Alex. Yeah, maybe, just maybe –

"No more, please. I must go to Alex, but tank you anyvays, Mr.

Martin." Peter stood up, adjusting his cap, as Al arrived setting the glasses down in front of them, grabbed up Harry's money and headed down the bar to wait on another customer.

"Just this one. It's paid for," Harry encouraged heartily. "Go ahead." He watched as Peter, hesitating for a moment, reached for the glass. "Ya know, Peter," Harry said, breathing a sigh of relief, "I was thinking about your friend, Alex, and that he's going to be hospitalized for several weeks, almost two months, probably longer. Maybe he could meet your ship in New York or one of your other stops before you head out for China."

"No. Dat is not possible. Ve can't vait for him nor can he meet us elsevhere," Peter replied. "Ven ve sail it vill be straight to Shanghai vis no stops. Alex vill haf to fly back to Stockholm. I am sorry for him. He is my assistant und I depend heavily upon him. I vill miss him. He vill haf to be replaced. Dat vill be hard as ve are sailing vis a minimum crew."

Harry's heart skipped a beat. Play it cool, he reminded himself. Make the man want to hire you. Fill him with bullshit – but get on board that ship! "What kind of work did Alex do?" Harry asked attentively, but with a forced nonchalance.

"Alex vas my assistant. He vorked on my vatch primarily as my helmsman, but he vas helpful in many odder vays. He vas my right hand."

"That's too bad. I know how important a man like Alex is to the team, especially being a helmsman in the operation of the ship. I used to be a helmsman when I was in the merchant marines." He said it casually, but notably, letting the information sink in: here was a helmsman – and available for hire. "By the way, what do you do on board ship?"

"I am der first officer."

A biggie! Harry grinned; this was the second in command of the ship. This was the guy who could best influence the captain. He took a swallow of beer. "Yeah, Peter, working on ships is exciting. I used to work on a cargo ship a few years back. Really enjoyed it. I know how important someone like Alex is to the team. His being laid up is a real loss. You'll need a good helmsman to replace him."

Again, he emphasized helmsman. "It takes a lot of training to achieve that position. I know!" He took another swallow, tipping the glass, draining it. "Two more, Al," he called down the bar

Peter held up his hand in protest.

"Just these two and then I'll personally deliver you to St. Mary's Hospital. I promise. Just consider me your friend. Okay?"

"Vell, jus' dese two, den, Harry, friend –" Peter eased onto the barstool grinning broadly, strong white teeth showing through the bearded foliage.

Harry met his grin with his own but it masked a feeling of relief. "Yeah," he continued with his assault, "I did a lot of work similar to what Alex did on board ship, was promoted to helmsman my second trip out. I've always enjoyed the sea, the smell of salt air, the rolling swells, the pitch of the deck under my feet, new ports, new foods, new adventures. Yessir, I really enjoyed that kind of challenge."

He reached across the bar and took the fresh brews, sliding one glass over to Peter. He glanced at Peter. He was staring at the fresh beer, still cupping the last glass which was still almost full. With a wink, Peter lifted the glass and drained it, then reached for the fresh one.

"I should not drink so much," Peter said. "I cannot be of much help to Alex if I am drunk." His voice had a slight slur to it. "I am not used to your American beer." He grinned as he pulled the fresh glass before him.

"Yeah. Sometimes I wish I'd never left the sea," Harry continued. "I wish I could set sail again and visit some of those strange exotic places again, especially China. I really enjoyed Shanghai and Tsingtao. Yeah, I really envy you, Peter. How long do you figure you'll be gone before you return to Stockholm?"

"A year or more, but first ve must return here to Saginaw for der second shipment of grain and take dat back to China. Two trips from here, Saginaw, to China before ve can sail for Stockholm."

"You mean you're shipping out to China, dropping off the grain and then coming back to Saginaw for a second shipment – and then back to China again?"

"Yah. Six months to China und back just for der first shipment, den anudder several tousand tons of grain, und anudder six months going back to China, und den on home to Stockholm, und to my vife und family." He gazed intently at his glass of beer. "It is a long time to be avay from my family und friends, a long time –"

Harry let out a long low whistle. "Yeah, that is a long time." But already his mind was alive with thoughts: If he could just get hired on board Peter's ship he could get overseas, get the money, and be back in less than six months. Old Joe could have his share of the loot for his big blast and he could start planning his future with Sandy. Six months away from her was a long time, but then, six months from now he could be enjoying the good life.

"Ya know, Pete, you don't mind if I call you Pete, do you?" He continued, not waiting for a reply. "I was stationed in Tsingtao for two years with the United States Marine Corps. I got to know that seaport like the back of my hand. I could probably even show you a few places that'd curl your hair, that is, if the town hasn't changed that much." He laughed. "It's too bad I'm not sailing with you. I could serve as your helmsman and right hand. I'm a damned good worker, a hard worker and a damned good sailor. I know my way around ships. I learn quick. Yessiree, I could really be of great help to you,"

Peter listened uncommittedly, nodding between sips of beer as Harry droned on selling himself, not objecting when Harry ordered more beers, continuing to drink, nod and listen.

"Yeah, all my papers are in order so in case I get the yen to go back to sea I'm all set." He took a deep swallow of beer, emptied the glass, and then banged the empty down on the bar. "China! God, I'd love to go back there again. I'd quit my job right now if there was a chance to sail to China, Shanghai, Tsingtao." He looked at Peter, a warm, winning smile breaking broadly across his face. "By god, Peter! If you want me to, I'd be real proud to serve with you on this trip to China, take Alex's place just for the one trip to help out. Yessiree, it'd be a pleasure to work with a real gentleman like you on board ship. Do you think you could use me? I'm ready!"

Peter looked at Harry through heavy eyelids. "Vell, Harry, I don't know, ve vill see –" It was non-committal. "I like you. You sound like der right man for der job." Rising, he drained his glass then let it drop to the bar where it broke, cracking into two large pieces. Al was there in a flash but Harry interceded saying they were just leaving, tossing a fiver on the bar.

"I vill haf to talk to der captain about you," Peter said, and then hiccupped. He stood unsteadily on his feet, weaving slightly. "You are a good man, Harry, my friend. You call me tomorrow at der Vickstrom Company grain terminal. Dey haf a direct line to der ship. I vill talk to der captain – but I don promise anyting. I see about you. Captain Andress vill listen." He slapped Harry heartily on his back. "Yes, you are my friend, but now I must go to Alex –" He started toward the door weaving unsteadily, stopping to grasp a chair to steady himself. He turned grinning, a stupid grin "I-I feel my drinks –"

Harry grabbed him, putting his arm around him for support. "I told you I'd drive you to the hospital," Harry said. "What are friends for if you can't use them? C'mon." Unsteadily, they headed for the door. "See ya, Al, Gunther –"

"Yeah. Hey, button up. It's cold out there," Al called after them.

"It must be zero out," Harry said through chattering teeth as they got into his car. It was cold inside and they sat stiffly listening as the engine growled several times before begrudgingly turning over and catching hold. Harry let it warm up for a few minutes waiting for that final purring sound. "No sense in stalling out every five feet," he said, shivering, glancing over at Peter, who hiccupped.

"S'cuse me," Peter slurred, and then hiccupped again.

Harry nodded rubbing his hands together. Damn but it was cold. Then he heard the purring sound and they were off.

"Vy do you vant to go to China?" Peter asked haltingly, his eyelids drooping even further.

"Cause I got a wanderlust. Cause I want to go someplace. Cause I want to see China once more before I die," Harry replied smilingly. He shivered. Reaching forward, he shoved the heat controls to high and felt the first faint traces of heat. "I don't have any ties here. No wife. Kids on their own. I can take off any time I want to. I'm in the construction trade right now but because the country's in a recession

I'm barely making ends meet. My boss would probably be glad to let me go for a few months. Hell, I can always get my job back later when construction picks up. Sides, I got a lot of vacation time coming to me. I can take it any time I want to –" He snapped his fingers for emphasis. "Right now, as a matter of fact!"

"Yah. I can understand vanting to go back to sea. Yah, it is der good life, especially for dose of us who love it. Yah, I sink I can vork out somesing for you. You call tomorrow."

Harry dropped Peter off at the hospital's emergency room entrance. As he let Peter out, he said, "Just tell them you're here to visit the injured sailor. They'll take good care of you. I'll call in the morning."

"Yah, in der morning. Tank you, Harry, friend," Peter called slamming the door shut and then shuffling off toward the emergency room entrance.

Harry watched after him until he disappeared inside, then spun the Pinto around and headed for the VA hospital.

"Yahoo!" he yelled at the top of his lungs. "China here I come!" He could almost feel the money in his grasp. He had to tell Joe the good news – right now!

Chapter 18

STAN'S IN TOWN, JOE'S DEAD

A glance at the dashboard clock showed 11:30 p.m as Harry wheeled the Pinto into the VA Hospital parking lot. It was almost empty. Only a few cars remained, most probably belong to staff members, he thought. He wheeled in next to one of the cars as close to the hospital entrance as possible, shut off the engine, locked the car and headed for the entrance jumping and kicking his way through the snowdrifts like a kid frolicking in the first snowfall of the season. He felt good. "China, here I come," he chuckled to himself. "Ol' Joe will cackle his fool head off at this stroke of luck. Harry, you smooth-talking son-of-a-bitch," he chided himself, "you're on your way to China!"

He grabbed hold of the huge door handle and yanked. The massive door swung open and he stepped inside. "Humpf!" he snorted, surprised at the door being unlocked. "Don't they know the place should be locked up this late at night? Hell. Anybody could come in the joint and rip them off."

Standing inside, he waited for a moment for his eyes to adjust to the dim lighting. He moved down the hall and across the lobby toward the reception area. No one was on duty at the desk. He looked around; the lobby was deathly quiet, the odor of antiseptic lingered faintly in the air. He heard the whirring of the elevator. "At least they're working," he said starting for the elevator.

A nurse rounded the far corner of the hallway, her shoes squeaking on the highly polished floor. She stopped abruptly at seeing Harry. "Ohh!" she gasped, then, quickly, in an authoritative voice, demanded, "What are you doing here? Visiting hours were over at 8:30." As she spoke, her bold facade began to crumble and she slowly edged her way backwards hoping to reach the safety of the corner and a chance to dash for her life.

"It's okay, nurse," Harry said raising his hand in a friendly gesture, speaking in a reassuring tone of voice. "I'm Harry Martin. I was here earlier this evening to visit one of your patients, a friend of mine." He moved slowly toward her stopping under one of the center hall lights so the nurse could get a better look at him. "I just got some good news I want to share with him. It can't wait. It'll only take a minute, just a minute, that's all. Honest"

"What's your friend's name?" she asked, closely scrutinizing Harry just in case she might have to identify him in a lineup later for rape or god knows what.

"Joe. Joe Gionetti. He's in Room 302."

"Oh. Oh yes, Mister Gionetti," she acknowledged. A sigh of relief escaped her lips, but at the same time, a look of sorrow crossed her face. "Mister Martin, I - I'm sorry, you're friend died unexpectedly this evening."

"What?" Harry stood stunned, staring at her, not wanting to believe what he had just heard. She stepped forward touching his arm. "It was a shock to all of us."

"Not Joe, " he whispered. "He was in good spirits when I left him earlier. You must be mistaken. Joe. Joe Gionetti. Room 302."

"I'm sorry." Her hand held tightly to his wrist. She looked up into his face with searching eyes. "It was a shattering blow to all of us. He seemed to be making such good progress, was responding well to chemotherapy. I'm so sorry."

Harry felt sick to his stomach. "Not Joe, " His voice grew husky. "He said the doctors had given him six months, maybe more, maybe a year. Hell. He had a lot of living to do yet!" He slumped back against the wall. "Joe had a lot of living to do yet, a lot of living. You must have him confused with someone else. Joe was okay when I left him. He was okay."

"I'm sorry. It was Mister Gionetti. Apparently he choked to death. We really won't be sure until they autopsy." She pointed toward one of the lobby chairs saying, "Won't you sit down. You look ill."

He shook his head. "I'll be okay, just a minute, it's just such a shock."

"It was to us, too," she said. "I was on duty when one of his two friends came running down to the nursing station for help. By the time I got there with a couple of others he was dead. It was tragic We tried to revive him but couldn't get a pulse or heartbeat. Both of his friends said they did all they could for him before we got there. They felt badly."

"Friends?" Harry said the word softly. "Friends?" The word cut through his muddled thinking like a knife. He stared hard at the nurse, looking at her as though in a daze. Joe was dead. Friends? What friends? Joe had said nobody visited him. Nobody knew he was in the hospital. Joe had called him, one of his archenemies, for help. Who were his friends?

"I thought I was the last visitor tonight. I left his room shortly after 8:30, well beyond the end of your visiting hours. In fact, a nurse reminded me that visiting hours were ending just as Joe and I finished talking. Who were his friends and how'd they get in to see Joe after hours?"

"They came just after visiting hours and, well, because they had come from such a long distance, Chicago, the doctor allowed them to visit Mr. Gionetti for a few minutes."

"But who were they?" Harry pressed.

The nurse hesitated for a moment. "One was an Oriental man who's name I can't recall. But the other man, his cousin, was a Stan," and again she shook her head.

"Stan!" Harry exclaimed. A chill rocketed through his body, his mind in a sudden panic. There was only one Stan, Stan Drezewski! And he was from New Jersey, not Chicago! "Was it Stan Drezewski?" he asked.

"Yes, I think that's his name."

"Mr. Martin, Mr. Martin —" she was shaking his arm — "You don't look well at all. Are you sure you wouldn't like to sit down for a few minutes? I could get you a sedative."

"No." Harry shook his head. "I'm all right, really, just shocked." Yet his stomach was churning, his mind in a knot.

Why was all this happening all at once? Why had Joe called him tonight of all nights? He had known for years where he lived, his family, his kids, Sandy. Why call him tonight? He must have known Stan was dogging him.

Somehow, Stan had found out where Joe was hospitalized and had come to find out where Joe had hidden the money. He must have found out, then killed Joe. It had to have happened that way. It was murder.

"Can I get you a sedative, water –" the nurse asked shaking him, getting his attention.

"Huh? What? Oh. No. I'm-I'm okay, shocked, but okay," he assured her forcing a smile onto his face. She smiled back. "I just wanted to make sure –"

Harry looked down at her. She was fairly attractive, probably in her mid-thirties, slightly overweight, large-breasted, which the harsh overhead light tended to enhance because of the starched, white uniform.

"What did his cousin, Stan, look like?" he asked, turning his eyes from her breasts to her face.

"An older man, maybe in his fifties, bushy eyebrows, dark, deep-set eyes and a bushy salt and pepper beard and mustache. He was about your height. I think he was wearing an old Mackinac hunting jacket. Ummm, that's all, although his voice was harsh, demanding," she shrugged.

It was Stan. He had found out where Joe was, came here to find out where the money was hidden, then killed him. It had to have happened that way. Damn, Harry thought. Damn!

"Did Joe try to get in touch with you when they arrived?" Harry asked. "Did he try to ring you, press the call button or something? Was he alive when the two guys arrived?"

"Yes. I had stopped in to see him right after visiting hours just after a man had left –"

"That was me," Harry interrupted.

She acknowledged with a nod of her head, and then continued. "He seemed in unusually good spirits, even gave me a thumb's up sign and wink when he saw me. He did look tired, though. He was watching the last of some educational program on television, something about China." She paused for a moment. "When I left his room I noticed two men standing by the nursing station. I told them visiting hours were over but they showed me a pass from the duty physician. I cautioned them that Mr. Gionetti was quite ill and not to tire him. The next time I saw Mr. Gionetti was when one of the men came running for assistance. You know, it might have been the excitement of seeing so many visitors in one night. He was frail and –"

"But he didn't make any attempt to use the emergency call button? It seems to me that a man on the verge of death would have made an effort to use the button."

"Well, " she responded, then snapped her fingers. "I do recall they said they had been talking to him when he suddenly had a choking spell. They tried to help him but he collapsed. That's when they came running for help."

Harry recalled the wrenching, gagging coughs that racked poor Joe, yet it was too co-incidental that Stan should suddenly appear on the scene and Joe, just as suddenly, ends up dead. They had to have found out where the money was hidden, killed him and fled. What gnawed at him at the moment was whether they knew about him?

"Mister Drezewski said he was Mister Gionetti's only living relative," the nurse said. "He apologized that they didn't have enough money for a decent burial. I told him the hospital would make the necessary arrangements. He asked that a Catholic priest give the last blessing."

Harry nodded. "Joe should have a proper burial."

"We do this routinely," she replied.

Harry felt a loss and yet, he couldn't shed any tears. It was just the sudden loss of a human being, and knowing deep inside he'd been murdered. Damn Stan. And who the hell was the Chink?

"Uh, was anything said about me visiting Joe earlier before those two arrived?" Harry asked.

"No. Not unless Mr. Gionetti mentioned you to them."

Let's hope not, Harry thought, not those two. "Well, thank you for the information about Joe. I'm sorry about his untimely death," he said, starting to back toward the entrance.

"If I can be of any further help, please come back. I'm Margaret

Lendowski. I'm usually on duty at this time every night."

"Thank you, Mrs. Lendowski."

"Miz Lendowski," she quickly corrected.

"Miz Lendowski," Harry repeated, "You've been very kind. I may take you up on your offer if I need any additional help or information."

"Maggie. Call me Maggie." She smiled warmly, inhaling deeply at the same moment, accentuating the fullness of her bosom.

"Maggie –" He turned, heading back out the entrance of the hospital. Poor Joe. He'll never have a chance to spend his money. Then it struck him; neither would he! "Shit!" he muttered under his breath as the sharpness of the winter night engulfed him. He pulled his collar tight around his neck. The best thing to do is forget about the money, China, the whole damned thing. Pretend it never happened. If Stan and the Chink know where the loot is, let 'em have it. They're probably well on their way already. No sense in asking for trouble from those two. He gave a philosophical shrug. Oh well, it was fun dreaming about going to China and picking up a cool two million dollars.

The wind blew sharply whipping through his jacket, chilling him. He bent forward, head tilted downwards against the wind. "That's it!" he suddenly exclaimed. "The two guys I almost bumped into in the parking lot earlier – Stan and the Chink!" The thought panicked him. If they had recognized him, he might be dead, too.

Chapter 19

THE STALKING BEGINS

The darkness of the night, the howling wind and blowing snow and the ever changing shadows added to the panicky feeling clutching at Harry. He quickly unlocked his door, checked inside for any unwanted visitors, then jumped inside, locked the door and jammed his key in the ignition. The engine sprang to life which gave him a feeling of relief. He had to get out of here, go home, rest and forget the whole damned incident.

"Damn!" he exclaimed as he turned on Weiss Street. "Sandy! I forgot all about Sandy!" He glanced at his watch. It was 11:45, too late to stop by her place. He'd call her in the morning and apologize, even set up a date for tomorrow night.

As he headed for home, his mind became keenly alert sifting through the events of the evening and the strange twist of events to this moment. Joe's death bothered him the most because he knew Stan had caused it. He'd skip calling Peter. No need to go to China now; no need for a job on board ship. It had been one hell of a bazaar night.

The windshield wipers swung ineffectively back and forth across the frosted windshield as a thin coating of ice built on the glass. The defrosters didn't work worth a damn. He had vowed all fall that he was going to get the defroster fixed before winter set in, and here he was with the same damned defective defrosters. Harry hunched forward squinting through the small oval opening in the icy windshield. "A few more minutes and I'll be able to crawl into bed and sleep off this damned bad evening," he muttered.

As he slowed to turn into his driveway he caught a glimpse of a car parked across the street from his house. His headlamps caught the silhouette of two people seated inside. Almost simultaneously, he noticed his living room light was off. Someone had been inside, had tripped the string and unplugged the light, something the intruder wouldn't have noticed, but it alerted Harry that something was wrong.

"Damn —" he swore for he had already turned on his directional indicator to turn. Quickly, he applied pressure to the accelerator pedal and continued past his driveway, not speeding up perceptibly, but enough to keep his momentum going. He shielded his face, pretending to scratch his cheek as he moved past the parked car. Slowing, he wheeled into his neighbor's driveway on the corner. It was a circle drive that came out on the side street. Harry applied his brakes, the red taillights turning the fresh snow blood red, and slowed down almost to a halt. Shutting off his lights, he eased the car slowly on down the driveway onto the side street out of view of the parked car. After a half block, he flicked on his lights and headed the Pinto for State Street and freedom to breathe, and think.

Wheeling into a Wendy's all-night diner, he stopped at the drive-in speaker, ordered a large black coffee, and then drove around to pick it up. As he waited for change from his fiver, he thought of the parked car. He was sure the two persons were Stan and the Chink. They must have found out about him from Joe. Just how much had Joe told them?

He accepted his change, and then drove to the far end of the lot easing his car in amongst several others, blending in so as not to be seen from the street. Shutting off his lights, he sat in the darkness and sipped at the steaming brew.

If they had gotten the location of the money from Joe, why were they still in town? Why were they at his place? He took another sip. On the other hand, if they didn't get the information, but knew he had visited Joe, then they probably figured he knew where the money was hidden and they'd have to get the location from him. One murder had already been committed. The stakes were high and it was obvious that these guys wanted the money at all costs.

If that's the case, he thought, then he had a better chance of getting the money before them. One thing was certain: Joe had definitely been on the level about the hidden money. He was dead because of it.

"Okay, Harry, what're you going to do?" he asked himself aloud. "You either shit or get off the pot. If you want the money, you go for it. If not, you might end up like Joe."

Mentally, he clicked off his options. He was sure he could get on board the ship through Peter. His passport and sailing papers were in order. With the construction business in a slump, and with vacation time available, he was sure his boss would let him off for two or three months with no problems.

He continued sipping at the coffee, his eyes constantly scanning State Street and the parking lot around him, watching for any vehicle like the one he'd seen parked in front of his place.

If the money was still there, and if he could get his hands on it, it'd buy a lot of happiness for him and Sandy, and pay off a lot of bills, but not if he was dead.

Gulping down the last of the coffee, he dropped the empty cup over on the floormat, flicked the headlamps back on and slowly eased onto State Street. Traffic was light. The snow had stopped. He drove back toward his place cutting diagonally across his street about a block behind where the parked car would be. It was still there.

He headed back to the VA Hospital. There were several questions he had to ask, and he needed answers.

The parking lot was barren except for the several staff cars still clustered together in a dark mass. Harry scanned the area carefully. He parked close to the cluster, shut off the engine and lights, and then scanned the area again. "Christ. I'm getting paranoid," he muttered as he hurried across the lot to the hospital entrance. He was surprised at finding the door still unlocked. Letting himself inside, he stopped momentarily to let his eyes adjust to the dimness, and then started briskly down the hallway hoping to bump into the same nurse as before.

"Can I help you?" a deep male voice asked from the shadows behind him. Harry stopped in his tracks, turning slowly toward the voice. A security guard stepped out from the shadows adjacent to the entrance, his hand resting on the butt of his large service revolver.

"Uh, yeah," Harry replied. "I was in here just a little while ago, came back to visit a friend of mine, but the night duty nurse said he'd died. I was so shocked that I left without getting all the details. Is it possible for me to talk to her for a minute?"

"Sure. I guess so." The guard advanced closer, hand still resting on his revolver. "Can you give me the nurse's name or describe her?"

"Ummm, it was Miz," – she emphasized the Miz part – "but, jeez, I can't recall her name. She was about five foot seven, dark hair, dark eyes, probably in her mid-thirties. Good figure and well endowed," he said, making a gesture with both hands as though holding up a couple of melons. "The overhead light really bounced off her, uh –"

The guard chuckled. "When you said well endowed, I knew you meant Miz Lendowski."

"Yeah. She's the one!" Harry replied with a grin.

The guard laughed again. "Yeah, she makes working on this night shift worth all the effort." He eased his hand off his pistol. "You wait here. I'll fetch her." He headed down the hallway, heels clicking on the hard polished surface.

Harry waited, running several questions through his mind, and then glanced up at a hall clock. It was 12:30. At that moment he heard the squeaking of rubber soles accompanied by the clicking of hard leather heels. Turning, he saw the smiling, well-endowed Miz Lendowski.

"Hi," Harry waved cordially as the two approached. "Sorry to bother you again, Miz Lendowski."

"Maggie," she replied, beaming. "I knew you were quite upset when you left earlier. I hope you're feeling better."

"Much better, thank you."

She had stopped only inches from him. He couldn't help but glance down at her breasts, amply highlighted by the overhead light.

"I, uh, wanted to check a couple of things over with you," he said forcing his eyes from her breasts, glancing quickly down the hall, and then over to the guard who was grinning, watching him. Harry turned back to the nurse, who also wore the faintest sign of a grin. Damn. He felt like a schoolboy caught gazing at forbidden fruit. Even his comment had come out stupid – check a couple of things! Christ! "What I mean," he said clearing his throat, "is that I need some answers. You mentioned Stan Drezewski and the Oriental. Did he have a name?"

"I checked at the visitor registration for their names after you left. Neither had registered. They shouldn't even have gotten past the receptionist. She was probably flustered when the doctor allowed their late visit." She suddenly gasped. "Oh. The man, Stan, called him by name. Uh, Ming, I think. Yes, it was Ming."

"Ming?" Harry mulled the name over in his mind. There was no Ming that he could recall in his past. Ma, yes; Ming, no "Had you ever seen him before? How old was he? Any idea?"

She shook her head. "Like they say about those Orientals, they all look alike. But I never saw him before. Age? Probably in his late twenties, maybe thirty."

Harry chuckled at her remark. "I know what you mean when you said they all look alike. I was stationed in China many years ago. It's true."

She laughed.

"What about Joe's personal effects?" Harry asked. "His bible, address book, savings book, check book, letters, anything like that?"

"Mr. Drezewski took everything. He was insistent that he take it now, inferring we'd steal from the deceased. I did have him sign for everything he took."

"What things?"

"Mr. Gionetti was an indigent patient. He literally had nothing of value. The bible was ours, one per bed. All he had was his wallet, a few dollars, an out-of-date driver's license, social security card and a folded scrap of paper with a telephone number on it. I think it was a local number. His address book was apparently blank because the bearded one, Stan, commented snidely that even his name wasn't in it. That's it. Nothing of value. Mr. Gionetti was a pauper."

"You didn't happen to see the telephone number?"

"Just a glance. It was a local exchange. 793, something. I can't recall the last digits." Then she laughed. "I have a hard time even remembering my own telephone number."

Harry smiled at her remark. But the first three digits were the beginning of his exchange. It might be his number. Joe had called. All they had to do was check the phone book or contact information. It was that simple

"And you said they'd hold an autopsy on the body?"

"Yes. Although someone like Mr. Gionetti was dying of cancer, there might be extenuating complications that actually caused his death. We routinely autopsy each deceased person to determine the exact cause of death. It's doubtful that we'll find anything unusual, but we must autopsy."

Harry nodded. He was sure they'd find Joe had been murdered. Most likely smothered or choked. He had no further questions to ask. "Thank you, again, Miss – Maggie," he said.

"If I can be of further help to you, please come back," she replied reaching out and taking his hand. "Anything at all." And her hand slid lightly from his, her soft fingers trailing down his fingers.

Harry smiled. He'd caught the meaning, the invitation from the touch of her fingertips. He stole one last glance at her bosom. Dolly Parton eat your heart out, he thought. He glanced over at the guard who was still watching him, the smirk still on his face. "And thank you, too, Mr., ah –"

"Swanson, Mel Swanson," the guard replied touching his fingers to the brim of his visor. "Sorry about your friend."

"Mel, Maggie," Harry repeated the names, acknowledged with a smile and then he was walking back toward the entrance of the hospital.

Chapter 20
LUCKY SANDY TONIGHT

Outside the wind had subsided and the sky was a blue-black, punctuated by millions of bright, white stars. Earlier in the day the weatherman had forecast an additional six inches of snow that night. He had added that the next day would be bad with drifting snow and many school closings. Hah! It was clearing. Never trust a weatherman.

Harry observed his parked car for several seconds. From his vantage point everything seemed to be okay. He moved quickly to the car. No strange footprints around it. He unlocked his door and glanced inside. No hidden visitors. Watch out for paranoia, he warned himself.

The engine was still warm and started immediately. He sat back letting the car idle while he tried to sort things out in his befuddled mind. If Joe had told them where the money was, they should have been long gone. But they were still here. Either they were sticking around to silence him so he wouldn't go after the hidden cache, and the thought scared him, or, and it struck him all of a sudden like a bolt of out the blue; they didn't know where the money was; Joe hadn't told them!

Once again, he drove past his street looking down the block toward his house. The car was still there. He couldn't go home. "Lucky Sandy," he chuckled driving on, then heading north on Center Road. He drove over to her apartment complex pulling into the parking lot where he found an empty space next to her gray Mustang. Shutting off the engine, he looked around the lot, now almost a conditioned reflex. "Christ!" he muttered, "I'm really getting paranoid. They'll be jumping out from the shadows next to get me."

He retrieved his pistol from under the seat, and slipped it inside his belt before getting out of the car.

He glanced toward the apartment complex. Sandy lived on the second level at the back corner. He could see her bathroom light on. She always kept a light on. Just a habit left over from her childhood she had responded when he asked her about it.

Her apartment faced out on a two hundred acre field. On warm summer days they enjoyed strolling about the apartment in the nude, touching, rubbing, caressing each other, arousing subtle erotic feelings, then making love in front of the open patio door, their passionate rhythm in tempo with the gentle undulating movement of the golden, wind-swept wheat.

Harry jiggled through his keys until he found the key to the security door, and then let himself inside the building. Next, he got out the special key she had made just for him – passionate purple with a circle of lovemaking positions stamped into the metal. He gave a light chuckle. She had said, "No nookie without a new key."

Quietly, he made his way up the stairs to the second level, and then down to her apartment. Slipping the key in the lock, he turned it and quietly eased the door open. "Damn," he muttered under his breath, "she didn't throw the deadbolt again." How many times had he talked to her about it? Throwing the deadbolt was for her own protection, especially in this crazy drug-centered town. It only took a second, and it could save her life. He closed the door behind him and slid the bolt shut.

The light from the bathroom shown softly through the apartment. He stood still for several seconds until his eyes became accustomed to the dimness, and then he moved across the living room to the bathroom. Her freshly washed dress, bra, panties, slip and stockings were draped over the shower curtain bar drying, drops of water still spattering on the tile floor.

Peering into her bedroom, Harry could see Sandy lying half under the covers. A heavy quilt was thrown back toward the foot of the bed. She kept the room at 72 degrees – to hell with the government. If she wanted heat, she'd have it! Crap on dialing down to save a couple of bucks, especially considering the way the government wasted billions.

She was wearing a thin, lacy nightie, the sexy brown one with the spaghetti straps he'd bought her for Christmas. The right strap had slipped down over her shoulder exposing one full, firm breast peeking out from under the thin nylon covering, it's pouty nipple standing mischievously erect.

Harry felt a sudden overpowering urge to take her. Quietly, he crossed to the bed easing gently down on the edge of the bed without disturbing her. He licked his lips, then leaned forward and softly swirled his tongue around the turgid nipple. Sandy emitted a soft, low moan responding to his touch, which brought a smile to his face. Suddenly, without warning, she sat bolt upright, in the same movement cracking Harry sharply across the side of his face with her hand, knocking him off the bed where he landed unceremoniously on the floor. Before he could regain his balance, he was looking down the business end of a snub-nosed .38 pistol that Sandy had grabbed from under her pillow, and now held firmly, aimed at his head.

"One damned move and I'll blow your head off!" she hissed. Harry froze, still in a crouching position. He knew she meant business. With her free hand, Sandy reached over and yanked the cord on the bed lamp. Light flooded the room. "Harry!" she exclaimed. "What the hell are you doing here?"

With a sheepish grin, Harry rose shakily to his feet looking down at her. "I, uh, missed you tonight, and, uh, well, I got horny,"

"Horny!" snapped Sandy, glancing at the clock on her nightstand. "Horny! Harry, it's one o'clock in the goddamned morning – the middle of the night!" Her dark brown eyes flashed with anger. "You must be nuts!" She still held the pistol on him only now her hand was trembling. She shook her head. There was a slight catch to her voice when she spoke again. "I could have shot you, might have killed you."

"Could you lower the gun please," Harry said.

"Oh!" she said and then dropped the gun in her lap.

Harry looked at her, at the tousled chestnut-brown hair falling in cascades around her shoulders contrasting sharply with the milky whiteness of her exposed breast.

Suddenly realizing she was exposed, Sandy plopped her breast back inside the nightie and yanked up the thin strap. "I'm a working girl, Harry," she said. "I've got to get some sleep. This is Saturday already. A bank loan officer has to look perky on the job. You missed your chance last night, so go away. Get the hell out of here! Go home! I don't give a damn what you do with it, but you aren't getting anything tonight. Understood? This working girl needs her sleep! Good night!"

She shoved the pistol under her pillow, yanked up the covers, snapped off the light and rolled over on her side with her back toward him.

"Good night, Harry," she said coldly.

Harry looked at the dimly lit form. He knew he'd blown it for the night. But, damn, he couldn't go home either; not with a welcoming committee camped outside his door.

"Good night, Harry," she repeated icily, jerking the covers up over her head.

"Ahhhmmm, can I use your phone?" he inquired in a syrupy voice.

"Sure. Just leave a quarter." Her muffled voice was still cold.

Boy, she's really pissed, he thought as he left the room heading for the kitchen. He snapped on the light by the sink. Sandy kept a listing of emergency numbers pasted over the wall phone. He skimmed the list with his index finger looking for the number of the city police. It was 911, the universal number. Picking up the phone, he dialed.

"Central dispatch. Officer Johnson. May I help you?" a voice responded.

"Yes. I'm the security guard over at the VA hospital. One of our patients died mysteriously this evening and the two men who had visited him last, a middle-aged guy with a salt and pepper beard, and an Oriental guy, were seen leaving the room in a big hurry. Well, there wasn't much I could do as they left, but, anyways, I never gave too much thought to the incident until now. I just got home from work and I saw them two characters parked in a car about a block down the street from me. My wife says they've been parked there for over two hours. She's scared. Her neighbor friend in the house where the car is parked out front, has called my wife several times. She's scared to death. I'd appreciate your checking them two out. It'd sure give my wife peace of mind. 'Course, there's probably nothing to it, but I'd appreciate you fellas checking out that car. Okay?"

"No problem, sir. We can dispatch a patrol car over there in a few minutes. Now, what's your name and address, and the location of the car?"

Harry hesitated. What the hell was the name of the security officer? "Swanson. Mel Swanson," he said barely recalling the name in time. Then he gave an address in the next block up the street from his, then his neighbor's address across the street from his house, the location of the car.

"Thank you, Mister Swanson. We'll check it out for you," the officer said.

Harry smiled as he hung up the phone. They might catch Stan and the Chink and hold them for investigation in the death of Joe. At least by taking them into custody, it'd allow him time to get home, get a suitcase packed, close out the house and get out of town. Surprisingly, he had made up his mind to go for the money after seeing the car still parked there. He seriously doubted they knew the location of the money or they'd have been long gone. There was no doubt in his mind he was the only one who knew the exact location, and now the money would be all his.

As an after thought, he sifted through his change, extracted a quarter, and left it next to the phone. She'd get a chuckle when she saw it.

Flicking off the light, he started past her bedroom taking a moment to glance at her huddled form. He smiled. Vividly he recalled the way she sat up in bed, the way that supple, tantalizing white breast with its pouty nipple had protruded invitingly from her nightie. She loved to have her breasts caressed, nipples teased roughly to tautness. He'd begin slowly, his tongue swirling around and over the tender buds, nipping gently, biting ever so lightly. Soon her breathing would change, gasping, softly moaning, responding to his demanding tongue, to his now exploring hands. And his mouth would move over the warmth of her perfumed, satiny skin, exploring all the erogenous curves and valleys of her inviting, responding body. Legs would splay wide to his exploring touch. And, shortly, she would reciprocate with equal, lusting intensity.

Harry rubbed his hand across his groin; he was hard as a rock. What the hell, he shrugged. Softly, he crossed back to the bed and slipped out of his clothes. Naked, he reached forward pulling the covers down and lightly kissed her exposed shoulder trailing kisses up her neck. The fragrance of her perfume added to his excitement. Gently, he tugged at her shoulder easing her over on her back, a sigh of exasperation escaping her lips. Harry ignored it, continuing soft, wet kisses along her neck as his hand slipped the thin straps down over her shoulders exposing her beautiful coral-tipped breasts. Tenderly, he trailed kisses down across her breasts seeking one, then the other, rolling turgid nipples between his lips, nipping gently.

"Ohhh, Harry," she moaned softly, aroused, her breath warm in his ear. Rising up, he kissed the fullness of her lips, felt them part and their tongues began a gentle duel. His hand moved under the covers, up under the hem of her nightie. Her body responded willingly, her breath coming in short, rasping gasps, legs parting to his touch.

"Are you going to rape me?" she gasped reaching out for him.

"Uh, huh," he replied as his kisses intensified, his tongue searching, demanding.

"Ummmmm, then get under the covers," she murmured between heated kisses. "I like getting raped under the covers in the winter."

Harry grinned as he crawled under the covers, easing over on top of her. "Is this what you had in mind?" he whispered.

"Yes, you horny old fart —" came her muffled reply as he entered her, driving deeply, and then she wrapped her legs around him.

Chapter 21

PACKING FOR CHINA

Harry awoke with a start. The dream was all too real! Stan and the Chink had caught up with him but he escaped by running up an endless staircase. He recalled vividly it had no railing. He ran upwards, ever upwards, his chest heaving, his body strained to the max, trembling, his legs feeling like lead weights. Still they pursued him, gaining. He knew when they got too close he'd have to jump or they'd kill him.

Gasping, perspiring profusely, he sat up abruptly in bed. He shook his head. He knew if he jumped, he'd die. Someone said they had read in a dreams interpreted book that if you jumped in a dream you'd never hit bottom, but would die of fright. The comment had always stuck with him. Glancing around in the darkness of the room, he realized where he was: Sandy's place. Then it all came flooding back to him, the death of Joe, the car parked at his place, and Sandy, the warmth of her perfumed body. He glanced at the luminous dial of her clock on the nightstand. It was 3 a.m. He ran his hand across his brow; it was wet with sweat. He let out a long sigh of relief. He was alive. He saw Sandy slept on, undisturbed at his sudden awakening.

He hated to get out of her warm bed but he had to get home for a few minutes to get clothes and papers. He had to go to China. It would be for them. Quietly, he eased out of bed and got dressed. He slid the .22 Ruger into his jacket pocket, slipped into his boots and let himself out of the apartment. He'd be back before she realized he was gone.

The hallway was clear. Stopping in the entrance foyer for a moment, he zipped up his jacket, pulled up his collar and pulled on his gloves Outside, the parking lot was dark, the sparsely spaced street lamps providing a minimal of lighting across the lot. A sharp wind cut through his clothes. It was probably bringing in more storm clouds. He hurried to his car, unlocked the door and got in. It was frigid. The engine was sluggish, turning over begrudgingly several times before catching hold.

As Betsy warmed up, he turned on the radio and adjusted it to a local station playing "oldie moldies." "Well, nightowls," the announcer exuded in a staccato delivery. "It's really cold out tonight. How cold? Glad ya' asked. As the key bird says, 'Key, key, key-rist, it's cold out!" He laughed at the joke. "Right now the temperature stands at a frigid minus ten, that's ten below zero, and people, that is really cold. On top of that we have winds gusting up to thirty-five miles an hour bringing the windchill factor to, I guess, around minus forty degrees. Now, that's really cold!" He laughed again.

Harry reached for the knob to change stations but hesitated as the strains of an old familiar tune came to his ears. "Well, we'll try to warm you up with some good old music right now," the announcer continued. "Here's an all time old favorite. 'I'd like to get you on a slow boat to China,' and that's the place to be today, I guess, what with our government opening up trade."

The music flooded the car. Harry laughed. How appropriate. He turned up the volume. Turning on his lights, he headed his car toward home singing along, pleased that he could remember most of the words of the song. Approaching his street, he again crossed it first looking down toward his house. The car was gone. Good. He circled the block and came back up his street. Nothing out of the ordinary. Police probably routed them out of the city or have them in jail. I hope they're in jail for Joe's murder, he thought.

The warning light was still off in the living room but other lights were still on throughout the house. He pulled into his driveway, stopped, opened the garage door, and then drove inside. The garage door was quickly closed behind him.

Easing the .22 out, holding it at the ready, he moved silently to the side door leading into the kitchen. He could tell by the splintered wood that the door had been jimmied. He cursed under his breath;

he should have locked the garage door when he left. Pushing open the door, he listened. There was no sound except for his nervous breathing and the pounding in his chest from his rapidly beating heart. Slowly, methodically, he searched each room. Christ, he thought, is this the way Kojac would do it?

Satisfied that no one else was inside the house, he flicked on the kitchen light. Surprisingly, whoever had been inside hadn't disturbed the place, at least not that he could immediately determine. He examined the door lock. Although the door had been forced, the lock was still in working order. With a screwdriver and several toothpicks, he repaired the screw holes, and then forced the screws back into the lock holes. He tried the door. It closed perfectly, the lock holding. Good. Now, he had to pack and git. No sense hanging around running the risk of getting caught by Stan or the Chink.

From under his bed he hauled out his old weather-beaten suitcase, threw it open on the bed, then quickly started grabbing clothing from the dresser and stuffing it into the limited space. Socks, shorts, T-shirts, work shirts, a couple of dress shirts and even three ties, work pants and a couple of dress slacks, warm turtleneck sweaters and a pair of dress shoes suddenly filled the suitcase.

"Damn!" he muttered aloud. He stood scratching at the back of his head. What else could he carry clothes in? "Ahah!" he exclaimed with a snap of his fingers. Rummaging around in the back of his closet, he came up with his old Marine Corps seabag. It had served him well over the years for camping and for hauling dirty clothes to the laundromat. Just the ticket for his extra gear, he thought as he opened the bag and hastily began stuffing more clothes inside. Blue jeans, work shoes, his sewing kit, a blanket, sheets, pillow and pillowcases, two heavy wool sweaters, even his new bulky, alpaca-lined jacket, the warm one he should have worn tonight to ward off the cold. From the bathroom he grabbed his shaving kit, shaving gear, toothbrush and toothpaste and several other sundry items. Then, the seabag was full.

From his rolltop desk in the corner of the living room he picked up his checkbook and savings book. At least whoever was in the place wasn't after money, he thought. Reaching up under the top of the rolltop where it recessed, he extracted an envelope, his "mad money," and peeled off $500, enough to tide him over until he started receiving wages on board ship – and, somehow, he knew he would sail with Peter Selham when his ship headed outbound for China. Lastly, he picked up his sailing papers and passport. With a growing sense of urgency, he moved through the house, turning down the heat to 50 degrees, checking the lights, re-stringing the black string to the living room light and making sure all windows were closed and locked. In the basement, he shut off the water. Now, he could leave.

In the kitchen, he paused, and then shook his head. One more thing to do. Picking up the phone, he dialed. The phone rang for about a minute before a sleepy voice answered. "Jeff. This is dad," Harry said.

"Oh, hi, dad," the sleepy voice replied, then yawned, then reacted. "Dad! Do you know what time it is?"

"Yes, but it's important that I talk to you right now. Listen, and listen good."

"But it's three-thirty in the morning –" Jeff protested.

"Listen." It was a command. "I'm leaving town for a combination business and vacation trip. The deal just solidified last night. I'm packed, ready to leave right now. I want you to check my house daily. I left the timers on, shut off the water. Pay any bills that come due and I'll reimburse you when I get back, just as I have before. I'll probably be gone three or four months; just an ocean trip. I'll be in touch with you by mail."

"What the hell is this all about?" Jeff demanded coming fully awake. "It's not like you to take off on some kind of ocean trip, especially this sudden, and in the middle of the night. Where are you going? Where can I get in touch with you?"

"Don't worry about me, Jeff. I'll be all right. I'll write you with all the details. Just keep an eye on my place, pay any bills, and I'll settle with you when I get back. I got a deal of a lifetime and I can't turn it down. I love you, Jean, Tommy and Tammy – and Sissy and Bill. Take care. Must run. G'bye."

He hung up the phone, a big lump forming in his throat. He was committed now, all the way.

Jeff was a good son. Harry knew he'd watch the place as he had done on several previous occasions when he'd gone on vacation. He made good money at the bank, in line for a vice-presidency in the trust department. He could pay his bills just like before. Besides, this time he'd be paid back with interest.

No sense in calling Sissy. It was her first pregnancy and a call in the middle of the night would only upset her. Jeff would give her a call in the morning. They were close for brother and sister. They knew their dad wasn't one to go off half-cocked. Besides, he'd write them a letter in the next few days and explain what he was doing – well, almost everything.

Then, the thought suddenly struck him. The damned ship wasn't supposed to sail until Sunday! That meant he had to hole up somewhere for another twenty-four hours. Damn! He couldn't stay here. Stan and the Chink might come back. Damn! Sandy would be asking all kinds of questions if he stayed at her place. No. He had to find a way to board the ship early. He'd call Peter right after Sandy went to work. Peter would understand his eagerness to get on board ship, to get settled. It was his best hope.

His eyes fell on his stereo unit. Should he take it? No. They must have something comparable on board ship. Still, and suddenly he was kneeling by his record collection pulling out several albums, his favorites: Harry Reser, Johnny Ford, The Flint Banjo Club and a couple of other banjo favorites. He sandwiched the albums in the middle of the suitcase where they wouldn't get warped or broken. Gathering several pictures off the dresser, and his latest magazines off the nightstand, he stuffed them all into the suitcase, then closed and locked it. Lastly, he snugged it down with a thick leather strap. In his top drawer, he found his old combination lock. He snapped his seabag shut and locked it. Grabbing up the two pieces, he headed for the garage where he dumped them in the back of the Pinto.

Perspiring freely, urged on by a growing sense of danger, he moved quickly back inside the kitchen to the counter where he had left his

.22 automatic, picked it up and stuffed it inside his belt. Then, he left, locking the door securely behind him.

The street appeared empty as he peered cautiously out the garage door window. He threw the door upwards, backed the car out, quickly slammed the garage door shut and locked it. This time he didn't look back.

Chapter 22
STAN'S PARTNER: THE CHINK

Sandy, lucky Sandy. He'd spend the rest of the night there and after she left for work in the morning, he'd call Peter, get permission to come on board, and he'd be on his way. He'd leave her a note explaining, letting her know it was for the two of them, that he loved her. She'd understand.

The parking lot of Sandy's apartment complex was just as he'd left it only a short time before. She probably hasn't missed me, he thought as he glanced up toward her apartment, and then grinned. The bathroom light was off. Nope. She'd noticed he was gone. More than likely, she got pissed off, flicked the light off and most likely threw the deadbolt.

She's reasonable, he told himself as he parked back by her car and then took an extra moment to throw a blanket over his gear to hide it from the prying eyes of strangers. He took the steps two at a time to the second floor. Charm her, he told himself, let her blow off steam, and then explain. She had to understand.

He stopped short of her door; it was ajar. He felt a prickly sensation coursing through his body. Something was wrong. He grabbed his pistol from inside his belt, slipped off the safety and curled his finger around the trigger. He focused his mind on the interior layout of the room. If someone was in there he had to move fast to catch them off guard.

Taking a deep breath, body tensed, he suddenly threw himself forward bursting through the door knocking it wide open, dashing inside, diving and rolling across the room to the far corner. Two shots rang out thudding into the wall just above his head. "Sandy! Stop! It's me!" he yelled. "Sandy!"

A bullet shattered the top of the chair he was hiding behind. It was clear in that second that the shooter wasn't Sandy. Harry returned fire jerking off three quick shots. There was a startled scream, then the curse of a male voice in the darkness. A slug shattered the arm of the chair Harry had just scooted behind trying to get a better bead on his assailant. Harry fired two more shots in the direction of the last shot. A shadowy figure broke for the door Harry fired, the bullet splintering the doorframe as the person ran from the room down the hallway.

The room was suddenly deathly quiet. Harry listened, ears keenly tuned, alert to any sound beyond the pounding of his heart, and his gasping breath. Nothing.

After what seemed a lifetime, but was only seconds, he reached up and flicked on a lamp on the end table. The room filled with light. Cautiously, he rose up looking carefully around the room, gun ready. He began a methodical search of the apartment. The kitchen was empty as was the bathroom. He hadn't heard a sound from Sandy. The door to her bedroom was closed. He knocked on the door. "Sandy!" he called, but there was no answer. Was she being held by others in her bedroom? Gun at the ready, he viciously kicked open the door, flicked on the light, then nearly vomited.

Sandy lay naked across the bed, the brown nightie tightly knotted around her neck, open eyes staring vacantly at the ceiling. Harry grabbed at the nightie, untied it, and then checked her carotid pulse. Nothing. She was dead.

Screaming, "Murderer! Murderer!" he rushed from the apartment taking the steps two at a time as he ran out into the parking lot. Whoever it was; he had to be here. He couldn't have escaped that fast. He had to find him, kill him!

The lights of a car suddenly blinded him as, with squealing tires, it hurtled toward him. Harry stood his ground, raised his gun and fired point blank into the car's windshield. At the last possible moment he dove to safety as the car roared past him, but not before he'd seen the passengers, the bearded man and the Oriental. Stan and the Chink. Tires squealing on the black macadam, the car swerved across the lot heading for the main street. Harry scrambled to his feet racing across the lot to intercept them, stopping to fire time and time again until his weapon clicked empty. The car disappeared into the night leaving him standing numbly in the darkness.

The wail of sirens filled the air; but it was too late to help Sandy. Harry stood sick at heart, cursing Joe, Stan and the damned Chink. A patrol car screeched to a halt by him, the red and blue lights painting an eerie scene across the apartment's brick walls and parked cars. An officer jumped out, gun in hand aimed at Harry. "Freeze!" he commanded. "Drop your weapon."

Harry turned toward the voice. Dazed, he looked from the officer down to his hand, at the gun still clutched tightly in his fist.

"Drop it now," the officer repeated, his voice stern.

Harry relaxed his hand and the gun slid away clattering to the icy pavement. The officer slipped the end of his pencil through the trigger guard picking up the weapon as another officer came around the police car holding a shotgun leveled at Harry.

"What's coming off?" the policeman asked. The shotgun never wavered. "We were informed shots were fired."

"Upstairs, she's dead," Harry choked. "They killed her." His body began shaking spasmodically as the full agony of what had happened hit him. He began sobbing, tears streaming down his cheeks. "The bastards killed her."

Lights had come on all over the apartment complex. People gawked out their windows. Several braver, more curious ones, even ventured out into the cold night in only pajamas and robes to see what the shooting was all about.

The first officer dropped the pistol into a plastic bag and placed it in the squad car. "Keep an eye on him. I'll check inside," he said heading for the apartment building entrance. The gawkers quickly made way for him as he moved past them into the building.

"You the only one involved in the shooting?" the second officer asked.

"No!" Harry replied. He raised his hand to wipe at the tears that refused to stop.

"No sudden moves!" the officer warned raising the shotgun higher toward Harry's head.

"You guys just passed the killer's car when you came down the street," Harry said. "I pumped it full of holes, shot out the windshield. You must have seen it. Get on the radio now! Tell 'em the car's a black '78 Ford sedan. It was headed toward town."

"If others are involved, we'll get 'em," the officer replied.

"Listen to me! They're getting away!" Harry snapped. "Call now!" He started toward the officer. "Call now!"

"Freeze! One more stupid move like that and I'll blow you away. That I know."

"There's a dead woman up there," the first officer said joining them, holstering his pistol. "Strangled to death. Bullet holes all over the place. I'll call homicide." He continued on to the patrol car.

"Tell 'em to look for a black '78 Ford sedan with two guys in it!" Harry called after him. "I pumped several rounds into the car. I know I shot one of the bastards up in the apartment. Call it in, a '78 Ford sedan with two guys in it."

Within minutes, two more police cars came screeching onto the lot. One was an unmarked car, the other a command car. The first officer directed detectives into the building. The Command Sergeant ambled over to where the second officer stood, shotgun still leveled at Harry, now handcuffed.

"What have we got here, Becker?" he asked the officer, and then stopped, a surprised look on his face. "Well, hello, Harry," he said moving toward the prisoner.

"Hi, Frank," Harry responded, relieved that it was Sergeant Frank Cavitch, someone he knew and trusted.

Frank turned toward Officer Becker and they talked in whispered tones for several seconds. Then, Frank turned back to Harry. "Ya' want to tell me what happened here, Harry? Officer Becker says you were found out here in the parking lot with an empty pistol in your hand, and that there's a dead woman upstairs."

"It's Sandy," Harry replied in a choked voice.

"The hell you say!" Frank gasped. "What the hell happened?"

"I don't know. I'd been over earlier tonight. Everything seemed all right. I told her I was going on vacation for a couple of weeks.

She'd already said she couldn't get away so I told her I'd go home and pack and be right back." Harry said, stretching the truth.

"When I got back here, I saw her bathroom light was off – you know how she always kept the light on, how we always kidded her about it –" Frank nodded, recalling Sandy's peculiar eccentricity.

"When I saw the light was off, I had a feeling she was pissed off at me because I was going on vacation and this was her way of letting me know I wasn't welcome. Anyways, when I got to the second floor and found her door open, I knew something was wrong. I got my gun out and charged in, and rolled to the far side of the room. Someone shot at me. I shot back. I know I hit him – it was a guy – 'cause he screamed, and then shot back at me. I know I got him good, but he escaped."

"How'd you happen to have your gun handy?" Frank questioned.

"Was out plinking rats at the county dump earlier today. Had it tucked under the seat of my car," Harry lied, immediately continuing his story. "Didn't want to leave it in the car. Someone might have broken in and stole it."

Frank nodded accepting the explanation.

"Anyways, when I was sure there was no one else in the apartment, I started checking. I found Sandy on the bed with her nightie twisted around her neck. I freaked out, came running down here to the parking lot looking for the bastard. They tried to run me down – two of them, a bearded white guy and an Oriental. I emptied my gun at them but they got away. That's when your men arrived. I tried to get them to put out a dragnet. Shit! It was like talking to a brick wall."

"Sorry, Harry. They have a procedure to follow."

"Yeah, but they could have caught the bastards!" Harry retorted. "Now they got away. You'll have a hell of a time catching them."

"We'll catch 'em, Harry," Frank assured him. "We'll get 'em."

"Sergeant Cavitch, the lab boys and medical examiner are here," the second officer interrupted. "They'd like you and, uh, the suspect upstairs."

"Sure," Cavitch said turning back to Harry "It's cold out here, Harry. Do you think you could go back to Sandy's apartment?"

Harry was suddenly aware that he was shivering violently.

Yet, return to Sandy's apartment? See her again, dead? He hesitated looking at the building, and then at the still staring face of Frank Cavitch.

"Yeah, I guess so," he mumbled, yet seemed unable to move.

Frank grasped Harry's arm and firmly, but gently, steered him toward the apartment building entrance. "Ya' know, Harry, I can't figure out why Sandy didn't use that snub-nosed .38 she always keeps handy?"

"I can't either," Harry replied "Like I said, I stopped by earlier tonight to surprise her. She surprised me. When I let myself in, I found myself looking down the barrel of her gun. I can't figure out why she didn't use it. She keeps it under her pillow, ready."

"What time did you leave here?"

"About three. I had to get home and throw my stuff in my car. I wanted to get an early start. I told her I'd be back. I knew she was upset about my going alone. I told her I'd bring her back a souvenir. Know what she said?"

"What?"

"Yeah, probably syphilis."

Frank chuckled. "She was always the one with a quick comeback. Damn. We'll miss her. Damned fine woman."

They followed a trail of blood into the building and up the steps to Sandy's apartment. "At least I got the son-of-a-bitch!" Harry said through gritted teeth. Inside the apartment a team of officers were examining bullet holes in the walls, furniture and the shattered doorframe. The bedroom door was closed.

"Lieutenant O'Toole, this is Harry Martin," Sergeant Cavitch said to one of the plainclothes detectives. "He arrived on the scene at the time an intruder was in Sandy's – the lady's apartment and exchanged shots with the person."

Lieutenant O'Toole nodded in recognition of Harry's presence. "You're acquainted with the deceased?"

"We, uh, dated regularly. Yes. I knew her well," he replied quietly.

"Tell me what happened from the time you arrived on the scene and how you found the deceased," O'Toole said scanning the room.

"And take the cuffs off him," he added.

"Her name is Sandy," Harry replied sharply as Frank unlocked the cuffs. She had been someone, a human being, not just a corpse She had been full of life, love, outgoing, caring, not simply "the deceased," as the Lieutenant had so coldly put it.

Harry repeated the story he'd told Frank earlier The Lieutenant's interest perked up when Harry described the bearded white man and the Oriental.

"Lieutenant!" came a voice from the bedroom "We found her gun."

Lieutenant O'Toole excused himself and hurried into the bedroom. Harry waited, glancing about at the activity in the room. Frank stood unmoved, also watching. O'Toole came out carrying a gun. "Is this her gun?" he asked holding the weapon up before Harry.

Harry nodded, recognizing the pearl-handled gun.

"It hasn't been fired. It was under her body."

Lieutenant O'Toole took Frank to one side speaking earnestly to him. Harry watched them but his attention was drawn to voices speaking in the bedroom. "Whoever did this was a sadist," one voice exclaimed "He broke every finger on both hands, then her arms."

"It's like something from a Chinese torture chamber," a second voice added. "She had to be in such pain that he probably strangled her to put her out of her misery."

Harry gritted his teeth. It had to be the Chink.

"Lieutenant," a plainclothes detective said, rising from where he had been digging into the far wall. "These are .45 caliber slugs we found in the wall. The guy was packing a heavy piece. You're man, there, is lucky he wasn't blown away."

Harry shuddered at the thought of being hit by a .45 slug, knowing the explosive power of a slug when it hit and when it exited, ripping out meat and bone with it.

"You're damned lucky," Frank said re-joining him. "Damned lucky."

Harry nodded. His eyes suddenly filled with tears as he saw a body bag being carried out on a stretcher from the bedroom. His body shook with pain, wracked with guilt that he'd ever got her involved in his crazy night. Tears streamed down his cheeks and he couldn't stop them. Frank put his arm around his shoulders consoling him. "I'm really sorry, Harry," he whispered. "You two made a great couple." But even his words couldn't stem the flow of tears or suppress the excruciating pain.

The medical examiner came out of the bedroom stopping momentarily to talk to Lieutenant O'Toole. "We'll do a complete autopsy on her. At first glance, it had to be strangulation, but we'll have to establish whether she was sexually assaulted as well."

O'Toole turned back to Harry and Cavitch. "We'll need a statement from Mister Martin. Sergeant Cavitch will take you down to the station. We'll also keep your weapon for evidence. You'll get it back after the trial of whoever committed the murder, and don't worry, we'll get the responsible party."

"Are you going to hold me or can I drive my car to the station?" Harry asked.

"No. You're not a suspect. Sergeant Cavitch can arrange for an officer to accompany you to headquarters."

As Harry and Frank stepped out of the apartment, Harry stopped and motioned Frank closer.

"What's up?" asked Frank.

"The autopsy. If they examine her body thoroughly, they'll find penetration, uh, well, we, we made love sometime after midnight and, uh –"

"Don't worry, Harry," Frank nodded "I'll explain it to the medical examiner."

Chapter 23
FINDING A PLACE FOR THE NIGHT

Harry dictated a statement to the trimly uniformed black female officer, and then watched as she finished typing. "If this is a true statement, then sign it," she said ripping off a copy and handing it to him along with a pen. Harry read the statement and then signed it. She took the statement to another office.

Harry leaned back, exhaustion sweeping over him. The night had turned into a nightmare. Sandy was dead. Joe was dead. He had to get out of town because he knew he was next.

Slumping back in his chair, he closed his burning eyes, wondering if the money was worth it. Blackmarket money, dirty money, and it had caused two deaths already. Tears welled in his eyes. He pulled his handkerchief from his pocket dabbing at his eyes, but the tears wouldn't stop. Sandy. So young, so vital, now she was dead. He couldn't bring her back. All his plans for them destroyed.

His attention was drawn to two police officers a short distance down the hallway having a lively discussion. "I mean it," one said. "I'll bet they'll find the slugs from the dame's apartment match those taken out of Johnson and Tillman's squad car. They're both damned lucky to be alive. Those .45's blew the hell out of their car."

"Tillman's still critical," the other replied. "One slug still buried in his chest. But as far as the slugs, no way they were from the same gun. The shootings took place miles apart. There's more than one .45 caliber automatic in Saginaw."

"Five bucks says I'm right. Put up or shut up," the first officer demanded.

"Five bucks? Hell, you're on, like taking candy from a baby."

"Good," grinned the first officer shaking hands on the bet. "Oh,

I forgot to tell ya', a bearded white guy and an Oriental were involved in both shootings."

"Damn you!"

The first officer scurried off past Harry with the second officer in hot pursuit, swearing a blue streak after him as they raced down the corridor.

Stan and the Chink. Harry knew it had to be them.

"Mister Martin. You're free to leave now," the young black officer said offering a consoling smile. "We'll get in touch with you if we need to. The investigation will be continuing. Thank you for your cooperation."

Harry nodded as he wearily rose to his feet. "Oh, what about my vacation?" he asked, as the China trip suddenly popped into his mind. "I was getting ready to go on vacation. I planned to be gone for a month or so."

"You're not a suspect, so I see no problem. Just leave word where we can get in touch with you."

"You can get in touch with my son, Jeff," Harry said writing his name, address and phone number on a slip of paper.

"Okay, Mister Martin. Have a nice vacation." She stopped, covered her mouth. "I'm sorry, that sounded tacky, after what you've been through. Uhmm, rest assured, we'll catch the murderer."

Harry nodded, turned and walked away. Have a nice vacation? That was tacky.

Outside the police station, Harry stood in the crisp cold of the waning night trying to clear his mind, trying to figure out what to do next, where to go. His mind was muddled, cluttered with thoughts to the point of exhaustion, the same exhaustion that tugged at his tired body.

He had to stay out of sight. He couldn't go home. Not back to Sandy's place. He had to remember her as before, the good times. Yet, he had to stay hidden from Stan and the Chink, and he knew they'd be looking for him and his beat-up Pinto.

He jammed his fists into his jacket pocket. Damn! He'd have to rent a motel room for the next twenty-four hours. Even then, it would be risky. The two were probably driving around scouring the area for his car, checking motels. Jeff? Sissy? No. No sense in endangering their lives. He felt a piece of paper in his pocket. Pulling it out, he saw it was a bar napkin. He opened it. Janie's address. He studied the napkin, and then shrugged his shoulders. Only a couple blocks away. What the hell, it was a place to flop, a place to catch a few winks.

Harry knocked on Janie's apartment door several times. There was no answer. He listened at the door. No stirring inside. She's probably not home anyways, he thought, probably shacking up with some young stud somewhere. He yawned. If he could just find a place to flop for a few hours. He felt physically exhausted, mentally drained, ready to drop. A couch, even a thick carpet would do just fine.

As he turned to leave, he heard the doorknob rattle. The door opened just a crack and an eye peered out at him from behind a security chain "Harry! What're you doing here?" Janie whispered, startled at seeing him.

Harry forced a smile. "I decided to take you up on your invitation," he lied, holding up the napkin.

"But it's so late," she said. She gave an exasperated sigh. "You're timing's lousy."

"I'm sorry. Like you said, my timing's lousy." He caught himself starting to yawn, clapped a hand to his mouth. "I got to partying, ran across your address, and decided to stop by –"

She gave him a sleepy smile. "That was eight hours ago."

"Yeah. Right. You probably got company, so, I'll leave." He yawned, stretching, his eyelids getting heavier.

"No. No company, just –" She looked at the poor guy and shook her head. "You look beat, Harry, just a second." There was a rattle of the chain being unhooked, slapping against the wooden doorframe, and then the door swung wide for him. He stepped inside. Janie closed the door behind him. She stretched, her full breasts straining against the terrycloth robe pulling the material taut. "You're welcome to stay," she whispered. "It's just that I'm too beat right now, too pooped to participate, if ya' know what I mean. Maybe later, huh? D'ya' mind?"

"Naw. I understand." He felt sudden relief. If she had wanted sex he'd have been a loser. After all that had happened, he couldn't have risen to the challenge. "I'm tired, too," he said." Too much beer." He looked around the small living room spotting her sofa. "Maybe I could just flake out on your sofa for a while." He crossed the room and sat on the edge of the sofa, kicking off his boots as he unzipped his jacket. Balling the jacket, he stuffed it under his head like a pillow, and then laid back on the small sofa. "Just a couple of hours," he said with a weary smile.

At seeing his large frame stretched out on the small sofa, his feet dangling beyond the arm rest, Janie gave an exhausted sigh, shook her head and said, "C'mon, Harry, come sleep with me."

She pulled him to his feet, and then gently nudged him along a hallway toward her bedroom. In spite of the shades being pulled, the room was fairly well illuminated from an outside streetlight. Harry sat down heavily on the edge of the bed and raised a tired face toward her. "Go ahead and get in," she whispered. "I gotta take a pee."

Harry stripped to his shorts and crawled into the still warm bed pulling the covers over him. He vaguely heard the flushing of the toilet as sleep overcame him. Janie closed the bedroom door, stripped off her robe and, naked, crawled in next to him, cuddling her smooth, warm body tightly to his backside.

Chapter 24
CONFIRMING PASSAGE

Harry gasped for breath. He'd emptied his pistol at the speeding car and stood clutching the smoking weapon in his hand, watching as the bullet-riddled car disappeared in the darkness. He blinked his eyes open. It was a dream, part of the continuing nightmare. But where was he? He felt the pressure of a body against him. Sandy? No. She's dead. He'd seen her naked on her bed, the nightie tightly knotted around her neck.

Slowly he rolled over in order not to disturb whoever it was. A face came into view. Janie! Then it came back to him. Yeah. Janie. The napkin. Now he remembered. He was in Janie's bed in her apartment. Slowly the jumbled events of last night fell into place. He'd needed a place to stay, found the napkin in his pocket and came to her place.

She rolled over onto her back, still soundly asleep. Her flaxen blonde hair swept out across the pillow, an aura of innocence enveloping the soft features of her face. Glancing past her, Harry saw the clock on her nightstand. Almost 10 a.m. He had to call the ship.

Quietly, he slid from the bed and stood up. Stretching, he let his hands fall to his side, then glanced down and smiled. His shorts were still on. She must have been tired. Maybe all the stories he'd heard about her voracious sexual appetite were overly exaggerated. Anyways, she hadn't touched him.

He crossed into the living room where he spotted a phone next to the sofa. It was resting on top of the phone directory, a stroke of luck. In seconds, he found the number for Wickstrom grain elevators and dialed.

"Wickstrom Terminal. May I help you?" came a pleasant female voice.

"Yes. I wish to speak to the First Officer on board the ship loading grain for China, the —"

"*Otto J. Nurad,*" she said sweetly, picking up on his momentary hesitation. "One moment, please. I'll connect you to the ship." There was a long pause, and then a deep voice with a foreign accent answered.

"Bridge. Vat is it?"

"First Officer, Peter Selham, please." Harry said.

"Von moment." There was a long pause, and then a familiar voice came on the line. "Yah. Peter Selham. May I help you?"

"Peter, it's me, Harry Martin," Harry said somewhat excitedly into the phone. "You remember me from last night down at the Pub?" Quickly he recounted their meeting and how they had discussed the possibility of his working on the ship as a replacement for the injured seaman. What the hell, the thought flashed through his mind, don't tell me the guy's forgotten me already. Christ! I spent enough on booze for him last night.

"Yah! Yah! Harry Martin! I remember!" Peter called into the phone interrupting Harry's rapid discourse of the previous evening. He laughed heartily. "Yah, my friend, Harry. I know you. Yah!" Harry breathed a sigh of relief. "Yah, ve haf a spot for you on board," Peter continued. "I haf spoken to Captain Andress about you. He vas impressed dat you are older und dat you haf served in der Orient before. He looks forward to meeting you."

"Great! Thank you, Peter," Harry said, an expansive grin spreading across his face. "I really appreciate all your help."

Suddenly he was excited at the thought of traveling, getting away, leaving last night behind, escaping. Work at sea, good hard work, would get his mind off the last night. Time might heal, but it'd never erase what he and Sandy had shared together.

"Harry. I'm sorry to say dat you must get down to der ship as qvickly as possible," Peter interrupted. "Ve leave Saginaw today, instead of tomorrow, as I had informed you last evening. Der icebreaker, Mackinaw, vill be clearing a path up der river for us und ve depart no later dan two o'clock. Can you make it?"

"Yes. Yes I can make it," Harry blurted. "I'm on my way now. I'll be there shortly!"

"Good. Ve vill be expecting you." The phone went dead. Harry jumped into the air and clicked his heels. "Yahoo! China here I come!" he called out in a hoarse whisper intended only for his ears. "Money be there!"

Restraining his enthusiasm, he picked up the phone again and dialed. After three rings the phone was answered. "Tom. Harry here," he said to his boss. "I, uh, I got some bad news this morning. My mom is real ill out in Phoenix. She needs my help. Uhm, would you mind my taking off for a while to help?"

"No problem, Harry," Tom replied. "I know how those things happen. My mom just had a mild stroke. She's better now, but I was really worried for a while. I know how you feel. Go ahead. Get back to me later, and say 'Hi' to your mom for me."

"Thanks. Will do. You know how you've been cutting back on crews because of the lack of work during this damned recession. If you don't mind, I'd like to take off a couple of months to help out, take some of the pressure off your budget, too."

"The only thing that'll help my budget is stronger people in the new administration in Washington getting the economy rolling, and getting the national budget under control!" Tom snorted. "Harry, you take off as long as you need to in order to care for your mother. Don't worry about your job. I'll always have a spot for you. Good help is hard to find."

Harry uncrossed his fingers as he hung up. All loose ends were taken care of. Now he could go to China. Even if he found the hidden cache of money, it would be a hollow victory: Joe and Sandy were dead. If only Sandy was alive the whole trip would be worth it.

It was time to get going, to get down to the ship. He started back toward the bedroom, and then stopped when he caught sight of an open package of jelly rolls on the kitchen counter. Padding into the kitchen, he grabbed up a jellyroll wolfing it down in a couple of bites, then ate a second, then a third. In the refrigerator he found a half gallon of milk and took a couple of deep swallows.

Feeling better, he headed back to the bedroom.

Janie slept on undisturbed, having rolled onto her side. As he watched her for several seconds, he was impressed by the serene, relaxed look on her face. There was no denying it; she was a very beautiful girl. As quietly as possible, he slipped into his clothes, and then headed for the door. He stopped, his hand on the doorknob, and glanced back at Janie. A devious smile crossed his face; he had to know. She was always bragging about what she had to offer, what the hell, why not check it out? Returning to the edge of the bed, he knelt down and gently raised the covers gazing at her nakedness.

"Whew," he breathed with a disbelieving shake of his head at the beautiful form before him. He lowered the covers. She's got it all – beautiful face, terrific body and brains, but just not my type.

Sitting on the sofa, he pulled on his boots, then shook out his jacket and slipped it on. He froze when he heard a moan coming from the room adjacent to Janie's. He listened. Was someone sick? Whoever it was might wake Janie. The moaning increased in tempo. That's all he'd need having someone wake her up and then what? He had no interest in her.

Crossing to the room, he eased the door open. His eyeballs popped wide. Petite, blonde, blue-eyed Tina, one of the other waitresses, was thrashing about under a muscular black guy, a stud he'd seen giving Tina the eye down at the bar. They were oblivious to his presence, pummeling at each other, her white breasts bouncing in tempo to his thrusting, her pale white legs wrapped around his black buttocks, gasping, moaning. The smell of marijuana permeated the air.

I'm turning into a damned voyeur, Harry thought watching a moment longer. Then, quietly, he closed the door. As he turned, he accidentally tripped over a sewing basket spilling the contents. He recalled Janie said she loved to knit in her spare time. A half-finished sweater had tumbled out. Quickly he scooped the sweater and ball of yarn, needles and other material back into the basket. A roll of Velcro landed on top of the heap. On an impulse, He stuffed the Velcro into his pocket, pulled out his wallet and left three singles in the basket.

Then, silently, he let himself out of the apartment.

Chapter 25
TYING UP LOOSE ENDS

Driving east on Shattuck Road, Harry turned on the radio. The newscaster was reporting late breaking news. "Closer to home, two Saginaw police officers are recovering in St. Mary's Hospital after they were gunned down when they responded to a neighborhood complaint call. Two heavily armed men seated in a car opened fire on the police as they approached. Both officers were seriously wounded but were able to return fire. A police spokesman said they emptied their weapons at the fleeing car. Road blocks are being continued in and around the city of Saginaw as police continue looking for the bullet-riddled car."

Harry shook his head. They were still on the loose. Damn!

"Saginaw also recorded its tenth murder last night," the announcer droned on. "A young divorcee who's name is being withheld pending the notification of next of kin, was brutally murdered in her west side apartment about three o'clock this morning. Police would say only that she had been strangled, although a shootout occurred in her apartment when a male companion momentarily trapped the suspected killer in her apartment. Police report the suspect was wounded in the exchange of gunfire, leaving a trail of blood into the parking lot where an accomplice picked him up and they both escaped in a bullet-riddled car. Police investigating the incident believe the two men are the same two men involved in the earlier shooting with police officers. Police described the two suspects as armed and dangerous. One is a white male, middle-aged, with a salt and pepper beard. The other is a younger Oriental male. Anyone seeing these two persons or a car with numerous bullet holes in it should contact the Saginaw police."

Harry reached down to shut off the radio but decided, instead, to see if there was any brighter news that might cheer him up on an already depressing day.

"In farm news," the announcer continued, "the first shipment of grain under the new 'preferred nation status' is destined for Communist China. The Swedish grain carrier, *Otto J. Nurad*, out of Stockholm, will leave the port of Saginaw later today, one day ahead of schedule, with a full load of grain for the starving folks in China. The ship will be escorted by the icebreaker, *Mackinaw*, into Lake Huron for the trip that will take it down the Detroit River and across Lake Erie into Lake Ontario, where it will enter the St. Lawrence Seaway. From there, the ship will pass through the Panama Canal and on to China.

"Authorities say the extended shipping season on the Great Lakes was caused by a mild fall, unusually higher temperatures, and rain through January up until about a week ago. They say *Nurad* will most likely be the last ship out of Saginaw, and one of the last through the Welland Canal, and the seaway, before the shipping season ends."

Harry snapped off the radio.

Wheeling into a florist shop, he ordered a large spray of flowers and penned a note, "All my love, always, Harry." He told the florist to contact the police department and ask for Sergeant Frank Cavitch. He would know what funeral home Sandy's body would be sent to. "Make sure the flowers are placed by the head of the casket," he added, as he jotted Sandy's name on the envelope. He wrote a check for the spray, then left.

Within minutes he was northbound on Seaway Drive headed for the Wickstrom grain terminal. As he rounded a curve he could see the large, massive grain elevators standing tall against the lead-gray sky. Beyond the elevators sat the ship.

Otto J. Nurad was a gigantic grain carrier. Its long black hull was topped by a white and tan painted superstructure with red trim. The closer Harry drove, the more massive the ship appeared. It was the largest ship he'd ever seen. White steam billowed into the sky from its single stack.

Pulling onto the Wickstrom elevator property, Harry drove along a road angling back toward the elevators located close by the river. He stopped when he found the office, a small building hidden in the shadow of one huge elevator.

Stepping inside, he was met by a vivacious, bosomy redhead who stepped to the counter with a friendly smile lighting up her face.

"Hi," she said in a warm voice. "What can I do for you this morning?" She leaned forward rising up slightly allowing her ample breasts to rest on the glass-topped counter.

Lucky counter, Harry thought at that moment. He also decided not to give her one of his normal, nasty comebacks on what she could do for him this morning "I'm signed on board the grain carrier, there," – he pointed in the direction of the ship – "and I just got word we're supposed to sail today –

"Sorry. I don't know anything about the ship's sailing schedule," she interjected apologetically.

"No." Harry cut in. "I'm interested in where I can leave my car for a couple of days. My son will be down to pick it up."

"Oh, that's no problem," she replied. "Park it around in back over by the far end of the terminal. A lot of guys leave their cars there if they're going to be gone for just a few days or a week. No problem, no charge –"

"Thanks. Much obliged," Harry grinned. "Uh, say, could I use your phone to make a local call? Call my son to let him know where to pick up my car."

"Oh, sure," she replied reaching over and sliding a phone toward him. Harry picked up the phone and dialed Jeff's number. The phone rang several times. He noticed the clerk still watched him, standing to one side offering an excellent profile of her trim young body. He winked. Flustered, she turned and walked back to her desk. Harry caught the swing of her trim buttocks. Nice. Still no answer so he let it continue ringing. She was looking again. He smiled. She smiled. He winked again. She looked away and started typing on an invoice. Damn but she's a cute trick, he thought.

After a couple of minutes, he hung up. "No answer," he said looking in her direction, and loud enough for her to hear. "He must have left his office for a few minutes."

She stopped typing. "Leave the number and I'll give him a call for you." She smiled, crossed to the counter, and again rose up allowing her bosom to rest on the glass top. She pushed a piece of paper and pen toward Harry. "Jot down his name and number," she said in a throaty voice "I'll call him for you, no charge."

Harry grinned as he took the pen and quickly jotted Jeff's name and number on the paper along with the make of his car. He glanced up at her. She was watching him intently. He was half tempted to jot down one of his smart comments but decided against it; she was too much like Sandy. He shoved the note back across the counter to her.

She read the note and nodded. "No problem. I'll call him. Is he as good-looking as you?"

"Spitting image," Harry quipped back. "Only twenty-five years younger –"

"Oh?" Her eyebrows rose at the remark. "I'll make sure I tend to this personally."

"And married," Harry added.

"Damn." She thrust out her lower lip in a pouty gesture. "Just my luck."

"Thanks, anyway, uh, Miss –"

"Jean," she replied, "and still single."

Harry laughed. "I'm sorry, Jean. Only one son, but I do appreciate your help. Just tell Jeff where the car is parked. He's got a spare key."

"No trouble," she replied, smiling. "I'll keep an eye on it for you. You have a good trip."

"Okay." Sandy was sassy like that he thought. Tears blurred his vision. Turning abruptly, he hurried from the office. In the car, he took a deep breath, and then drove around in back parking it next to a huge snow bank.

He unloaded his seabag and suitcase, locked the door, and pocketed the keys. This done, he lifted the seabag up on his shoulder, picked up his suitcase and headed for the ship.

Chapter 26
THE *OTTO J. NURAD*

Otto J. Nurad was overpowering, longer than a football field and almost as wide, Harry estimated. The closer he got to the ship, the more impressive was its massiveness. It seemed to be an unending wall of steel plate, larger by far than any ship he'd ever sailed on before. He stopped at the bottom of the gangway realizing that when he walked up the steps there was no turning back; he was committed to go forward, regardless of the outcome.

Before going aboard, he looked back across the Saginaw skyline. There was a tug at his heartstrings. He knew he should stay for Sandy's funeral, for the kids, and for his friends. But more than anything, he knew he had to get away. He had to occupy his mind with work, anything to keep his mind from dwelling on Sandy's death. He had to go. It would be a short time, three or four months, six months at the most. There was more – the adventure of returning to China, the thought of finding hidden millions.

Turning, he headed up the gangway. Stepping on deck, he looked forward, and then aft. There was no one in sight. He noticed the decks were relatively clear of snow and ice. He also saw that the ships hatches were already in place and sealed for the voyage. The ship was obviously ready to sail. Setting his seabag and his suitcase down, he glanced about again. There had to be someone on deck somewhere.

At that instant, a sailor stepped on deck from one of the hatchways. "May I help you?" he asked with a thick Swedish accent.

"I hope so," Harry replied cheerily. "I'm here to see your First Officer, Peter Selham."

"Yah, I vill get him," the sailor replied. "Please vait here." He disappeared back through the hatchway leaving Harry standing on deck. He could feel the chill of the cold steel deck through the bottoms of his boots. After several drawn minutes, he began shivering. This is a hell of a way to greet your new helmsman, he thought.

"Hello, Harry Martin. Velcome aboard." Turning, Harry saw a grinning Peter Selham stepping through the hatchway. He grabbed Harry's hand shaking it vigorously. "Tank you for coming so soon. It is short notice but ve are getting set to sail. Come, Captain Andress vill see us now." Turning to the sailor who had accompanied him on deck, he ordered, "Take his gear to my cabin."

The husky sailor effortlessly grabbed up the seabag and suitcase and disappeared through the hatchway. Peter led Harry along the deck. "Vatch out. Der decks are slippery in spots," he cautioned, skirting a patch of ice, as he led Harry forward, then up a ladder towards the bridge.

Inside, the cabin was warm and comfortable. An array of dials, lights and other sophisticated electronic gadgetry filled the center control panel. Although he recognized most, Harry admitted to himself there had been some significant changes in the few years since he'd last been to sea.

Forward of the control panel in front of the huge windows facing the bow stood a tall, powerfully built man sharply attired in a black uniform with gold braid. He sported a neatly trimmed mustache and beard. At the moment, he was involved in a heated exchange with a smaller, scowling man in grease-stained clothing.

Harry gathered from the animated exchange that the Captain was winning the battle of words. He and Peter stood to one side. Peter appeared somewhat embarrassed at the topic of discussion and, as Harry listened, he realized it involved him.

"I don't care, Ernst! You could haf sailed on dis ship since it rolled down der vays in 1957. You could be der most senior man on board, but you are a machinist's mate und I vill not promote you to der position of helmsman simply because you vant it. I make der decisions on dis ship as to who vill vork on der bridge. Dat is final! I vill discuss it no ferder! Now go below, ve sail shortly."

"Aye, sir!" Ernst growled, snapping off a brisk salute, the scowl etched on his face. He turned seeing Peter and Harry, and glared at both as he stalked out of the wheelhouse.

"Peter," the Captain said turning his attention to them, a broad smile quickly replacing the frown. "Und who is vis you?"

"Sir. I haf der new man, Harry Martin," Peter said gesturing toward Harry.

"Ah, yes, der American –" The Captain approached, extending a large, beefy hand that enclosed Harry's within it. "I'm Karl Andress, Captain of der *Otto J. Nurad*." Harry felt the man's strength through his firm, but gentle, grasp.

Beneath shaggy eyebrows, Captain Andress' steel-blue eyes searched Harry's face. Andress knew himself to be a good judge of character. Character showed in a man's eyes, in his handshake and in his appearance. What he saw and felt pleased him. The American seemed all right.

"I'm pleased to meet you, sir," Harry replied knowing he was being sized up at the moment. The handshake was firm. He hated limp, wimpy handshakes. He recalled his dad always telling him a solid handshake was more sincere, more telling of a man. Harry was impressed by the Captain's size, towering at least six foot six, and probably topping two hundred and fifty pounds. He seemed sincere; one who left no doubt as to who was in command, regardless of the situation. Harry liked him immediately.

"Peter told me how helpful you ver in getting him to our shipmate, Alex," Captain Andress said. "Dat vas too bad about Alex. But den, dese kinds of tings happen. You haf no control over such situations. Ve truly appreciate your help. It is not often today dat vun meets a helpful stranger in a strange land. Tank you so very much."

"It was the least I could do," Harry replied. He knew the captain was making a decision on whether to hire him. "I'm sure you would have done the same for me if I had been in your country, and in a similar situation"

"Yah. You might say it vas fate dat brought you und Peter together," Captain Andress added with a breaking smile. "Peter informs me dat you haf sailed on merchant ships before as a helmsman. Your papers are in order? Is dat correct?"

"Yah, yes, yessir. I do have all my papers in order and up to date." He fumbled inside his jacket pocket, somewhat surprised at his sudden nervousness, and then extracted a packet of papers which he passed quickly to the Captain.

Captain Andress sifted through the papers. "Passport, union papers, quarantine requirements, good, good, all seems in order. Excellent." He handed the papers to Peter. "Check dem more thoroughly," he said turning back to Harry, who wondered why he felt so nervous all of a sudden. Just as suddenly, he shrugged it off. He was always nervous for job interviews.

"Peter tells me you served in China before. Ven?"

"Back about thirty years ago. I served with the United States Marine Corps in Tsingtao for a couple, three years. We had to evacuate in 1949 when the Communists overran the Nationalist forces and took over the Shantung peninsula and, of course, all of China."

"Yah," Captain Andress acknowledged with a knowing grin "I vas in Shanghai at der time China fell. I barely got my ship out of der harbor. Dey vas shooting at us as ve sailed out der river into der China Sea." He laughed heartily. "I vas really scared. It vas my first command. Dat vould haf been terrible to lose a ship on der first voyage." He stopped, a distant look in his eyes as he remembered that moment in history, then gave a deep sigh. "But enough, ve vill haf time to talk und spin tales about der good old days later. Right now, Peter vill check out your papers. If all is vell, you vill sail vis us. Okay?"

"Okay," Harry replied.

Peter, who had been sifting through the papers while the two talked, shuffled them back into a semblance of order, saying, "All papers are in order, sir," he said; "I'll sign him on."

"Good." Captain Andress beamed. "Velcome aboard Harry Martin. It vill be nice vorking vis you."

"Thank you, sir. It's good to be on board ship again." They shook hands all around. Harry breathed a sigh of relief. He was underway.

"Peter. I vant Harry to vork vis you taking on Alex's duties. He vill bunk vis you. Ven you haf time, show him der ship und introduce him to der crew." With that, Captain Andress turned away from them, back to the task of getting the ship ready to depart. He seemed intent on what was happening on dockside as a long contingent of cars arrived stopping at the gangway.

"Oh, Mr. Martin," the captain asked, not turning his attention from the delegation of people alighting from the cars. "How old are you?"

"Just turned fifty-three, sir," Harry replied with a questioning look in Peter's direction. Peter shrugged with an "I don't know why the question" look.

"Good. Are you married?"

"No sir," Harry replied.

"A vidower?"

"No sir. Divorced." Why the sudden inquisition, he wondered.

"Oh, sorry. How long haf you been divorced?"

"Several years." The old goat is blunt and to the point, Harry thought. The captain's back was still toward them. Harry glanced over at Peter again. Peter shrugged, not understanding the line of questioning either.

"We raised two kids, but found out we weren't compatible anymore, so we got divorced."

"Sorry. I did not mean to pry," Captain Andress said turning back to face Harry.

The hell you didn't, Harry mused.

"But you are not attached at dis time?" he continued the line of questioning.

"No sir. I'm older, free, virile and full of piss and vinegar!"

Captain Andress chuckled at the remark. Peter, too, wore a big grin. "Ahhh, you haf a good sense of humor, too, Harry. Good. I like dat." He turned to Peter. "Get Harry settled on board now, please. Ve haf much to do."

"Come," Peter said ushering Harry from the bridge leading him below deck to the ship's galley where they took a moment to enjoy a steaming cup of coffee.

Harry looked around the galley. It was neat and clean. The

bulkheads were white with yellow trim. The aroma of food being prepared wafted throughout the galley. It smelled good and he was hungry. If the food was as good as the coffee, there'd be no complaints from him.

"Vell, Harry,' said Peter, "as Captain Andress said, velcome aboard." He reached across the narrow table and shook Harry's hand again. "Let me tell you a bit about our ship. Der *Otto J Nurad* is a grain carrier of Swedish registry, out of Stockholm, Sveden. Der ship is 730 feet long mit a beam of 75 feet. Ve are propelled by Kockmust-DeLaval steam turbine engines und twin screws. Ve are carrying vun million, five hundred tousand cubic feet of grain to China. Ve haf a crew of tventy-nine including you, und vun cook. It is a vell-disciplined crew. If dere are any disputes or misunderstandings, you see me first. If I can't handle it; I see der captain. Usually, however, most misunderstandings are settled qvickly between myself und der disagreeing parties. Ve are a good crew, a hard vorking crew, und ve do haf disagreements on occasion, but rarely. Ve also haf a good sense of humor, as you vill soon learn."

After a long sip of coffee, Peter continued. "Dis is der galley. Coffee is alvays available und ve haf vun of der best cooks in der vorld on board. Yes, I tink you vill like being vis us. I know I vill enjoy vorking vis you."

"Thank you," Harry replied, watching as Peter downed the last of his coffee. "I know I'll enjoy working with you and the others –" he was cut short as Peter suddenly rose.

"Ve must go," Peter said glancing at his watch. "It is getting later." He set his half empty cup on the counter and started away. Harry quickly gulped down the last of his coffee and followed suite.

"Dis is my quarters. Alex shared it vis me. You vill share it now," Peter said on entering his cabin. Harry stepped inside. It was a fairly Spartan cabin with bunk beds, a desk, dresser for both bunks and individual lockers adjacent to the door. "Dat is your locker und you get der top bunk. Ve share der desk und, as you can see, der is plenty of reading material."

Harry leafed through the stack of magazines, and then laughed. I don't read Swedish," he commented wryly.

"Ve do haf some English magazines somevere," Peter grinned. "I get dem for you." Then he winked. "Maybe by der end of der voyage ve haf you speaking Svedish."

"Or I'll have you all speaking and reading English," Harry retorted.

While Peter used the bathroom, Harry opened his assigned dresser drawers and began unpacking, hastily placing wrinkled clothing in the drawers as neatly as possible

"I had dem clean out der drawers first ting dis morning," Peter said coming back into the room, zipping up. "After your call dis morning, I knew ve vould haf a new man on board today." He stood to one side watching as Harry continued to unpack his belongings. "Take your time. Ve are not in dat big a rush."

Harry nodded, continuing to unpack at the pace he'd set for himself. Working from the bottom up, he soon had two of the drawers crammed with work clothing. The last drawer, which was the top one, he used for his underwear and socks.

"Vat is dis?" Peter laughed, reaching across and yanking out a pair of pink satin bikini panties trimmed in white lace, from a stack of Harry's shorts. Harry turned beat red. Sandy's panties. They must have got mixed in with his underwear when they did their laundry last week.

Peter held up the panties, and then sniffed them. "Ummm, a light delicate perfume. Your lady friend has good taste."

"Gucci," Harry said reaching for the panties. "It was her favorite. I bought it for her last Christmas. She was a friend, a very close friend." He stuffed the panties back in the drawer under his shorts.

Peter sensed a change in the tone of Harry's voice, in his mood. If something was bothering him, it was none of his business. Perhaps later, he might wish to discuss it.

"Vell, I vill leave you to continue unpacking und getting settled in," Peter said starting for the door. "Ve vill need all hands on deck shortly ven ve set sail. Hurry, please, und bundle up. It is cold out dere."

Harry nodded yes, as he dumped the contents from his seabag on the deck. As the door closed, he reached under the shorts and took out the panties, just holding them in one hand, then clutched them in his fist. The bastard didn't have to kill her. After a moment, he stuffed them under his pillow.

In the locker, he hung up his work trousers, slacks, work shirts and dress shirts, ties and the quilted jacket. Dress shoes and works shoes ended up in the bottom of the locker. The albums, the latest adult magazines, books and his shaving gear ended up on the only shelf. His sewing kit and the roll of Velcro ended up in the top drawer. In minutes, the place was tidy again, everything tucked away or hung up. He took a moment to relieve himself in the bathroom, the head as it is known on board ship. It was small with a stool, lavatory, a shower and a locker for towels and toiletries.

With a sense of urgency, he hurriedly changed into work clothes, donned the heavy quilted jacket, pulled on a knit cap, pulled on heavy gloves and headed topside.

Chapter 27
HEADING OUTBOUND

A brisk wind blew downriver, swirling gusts of snow before it. North, toward Bay City, dark, ominous clouds blocked the horizon. Peter moved along the deck giving orders to crewmen, relaying messages from the bridge via his hand held walkie-talkie. He introduced Harry to the other members of the work crew. There was a quick doffing of gloves, fast handshakes, and hurriedly pulling the warm gloves back on.

Under Peter's direction, the crew moved toward the bow pressing to free up hawsers from heavy snow and ice build-up, chopping briskly, chips flying everywhere.

Harry rested for a moment, gasping from the feverish pace. Looking up, he saw the huge icebreaker *Mackinac* coming upriver toward them, relentlessly crunching through the massive field of pack ice. *Mackinac* drove forward rising high on the ice, crushing down, breaking the massive floes into smaller chunks, moving ever closer to *Nurad*, and then passed along the starboard side. Harry looked over the railing at the huge chunks of ice, some a foot thick, churning, tumbling, sliding along under the cold, hard steel hull as the icebreaker moved on by.

"She vill be turning around in der next tirty minutes und ve must be ready to follow her out of der channel," Peter called out extolling his men to work harder. "Ve must vork hard und fast now!"

Harry grabbed up his axe and turned to joining the others at the task of freeing the hawsers and winching mechanism. They worked furiously, perspiring beneath their jackets in the zero temperature, lungs aching with every gasp of frigid air.

The ship's whistle blew spewing a large plume of steam upwards through the crisp air. Harry jumped at the sudden intrusion. The others laughed.

The wind picked up in intensity. Harry shivered as the sharpness of the cold air cut through his heavy jacket. Glancing about, he saw he wasn't alone. Others were gasping, shivering in the cold.

"Done!" yelled a crewman, and the men stepped back to rest.

Harry stepped to the railing and looked astern. *Mackinac* had made its turn and was now heading back. The whistle blew again. The crew stood by ready to haul in lines, watching for a signal from Peter.

On the dock a group of dignitaries were completing last minute formalities and waving farewell to Captain Andress as he strode up the gangplank. A TV remote crew with a mini-cam unit recorded the whole incident, the departure of the first shipment of grain to China from the port of Saginaw. Harry recognized TV commentator, Larry Duke, standing before the mini-cam talking to one of the dignitaries, obviously from the Wickstrom terminal.

"Hi, Mom!" Harry called, waving at the camera, not resisting the ham in him, waving as they all do before a television camera, and then stopped abruptly. "Shit!" he exclaimed ducking below the level of the railing. If Stan or the Chink, or even his boss, saw his face on TV that night on the news, they could put two and two together. "Dammit! Stupid move, Martin!" he admonished himself as he scurried to the starboard side of the ship.

Mackinac was just passing by. It was a long, low-decked ship. The superstructure was forward. It had one stack, tan with black accents. The vessel churned steadily forward through the ice floes driving the ice aside, rolling chunks along between the two ships.

"Cast off the bowlines!" came the command from the bridge. The dock crew freed the large hawsers as the winch behind Harry suddenly groaned to life reeling the huge hawser up on deck. The dock crew guided the hawser, while the deck crew reeled it on board and secured it.

"Cast off the stern lines!" came the second command, and Harry knew the aft crew was humping their backs to get the hawsers secured on deck.

"All work crews now secure!" came the command. "Stand by to sail."

Released from duty, most men immediately headed below deck for hot coffee and rolls. A few stayed behind waving at the people still braving the chill day as they stood on the dock watching, waving after the departing ship.

Harry could feel the ka-thump, ka-thump, ka-thump of the huge shafts moving the massive twin screws. It was an exhilarating feeling, one he felt each time he shipped out; a feeling of excitement, of adventure, and a feeling of loneliness at sailing into the unknown.

He walked toward the bow, stopping to look over the edge of the railing, fascinated as the ship picked up momentum, knifing through the chunks of ice, rolling them into the murky waters of the Saginaw River.

At that moment a shaft of sunlight broke through the clouds, splashing the ship in radiant brilliance. Harry squinted, shading his eyes. Looking astern, he had a panoramic view of the Saginaw skyline and the grain terminal. Well-wishers, slowly diminishing in size, were scurrying to their cars and warmer locations.

January is a lousy time of the year, Harry thought. At least by the time he got back it would be warm and green. The thought flashed through his mind – and Sandy would be buried almost six months, but never forgotten.

He shivered. In spite of the cold he wanted to stay and watch. He looked forward at the stern of the icebreaker, watching as the two ships wended their way carefully down the winding river toward Saginaw Bay and Lake Huron. On the starboard shore the old mosquito control headquarters stood bleakly surrounded by snowdrifts. What the hell do they do in the winter months, he wondered.

Ahead, the ominous clouds all but obliterated Bay City. The town was in the midst of a heavy snowstorm. With chattering teeth, Harry finally relented; it was time to go below and get a hot cup of coffee and join the rest of the crew.

"Over here, Harry!" called Peter at seeing Harry enter the galley, motioning for him to join with the others. Harry acknowledged, holding up an empty cup, that he'd get his coffee first, and then join them. The coffee was black and steaming hot, just the way he liked it. The rolls were warm, freshly glazed.

"Harry, dese are some of der crew members you should know. You vill be vorking vis most of dem on dis voyage," Peter said waving his hand in a broad arc at the assembled array of sailors.

"I know you von't remember all der names at first, but I introduce dem jus der same. Dis is Hans, Helmut, Jorge, Deiter und Sven." Harry walked around the table shaking each man's hand, trying to remember each name. He was acutely aware that they were all young men, much younger than he, probably in their mid-twenties or early thirties. He suddenly felt like the old man of the crew. Yet, in minutes, he was earnestly engaged in conversation and feeling more comfortable by the minute. He grinned at the mixture of language: Swedish, fractured English and slang.

The men seemed to show more of an interest in Harry after Peter explained that Harry had been to China before. None of them had ever been to the Far East. They plied him with questions about the Orient, the food, the girls, the places to have fun. Harry laughed. He explained that it had been quite a number of years since he'd been to China, but that he was sure the girls were just as attractive and just as available as before.

The crew listened intently as he described Shanghai, Tsingtao and Peiping, or Beijing, as he understood they called it now. He embellished his stories with colorful descriptions of the ways of the Orient, along with several vivid sexual encounters. There was an eagerness in their eyes to taste the Orient. "I hope the Orient hasn't changed too much in the last thirty years," he said. "I know you'll enjoy it."

"Vell, I must take Harry up to der bridge und get him acclimated to vat his job duties vill be," Peter said apologetically, putting a stop to the flow of questions. "You vill be able to talk to him later. I vant to tank all of you for your hard effort. Ve are undervay. Soon ve vill be basking in varmer climates."

Chapter 28

CONFRONTING THE CHINK

The snowstorm had engulfed the ship while they were having coffee in the galley. Visibility was greatly reduced. *Nurad* followed closely astern the *Mackinac* as it approached Bay City. Peter and Harry stood at the back of the cabin watching quietly as Captain Andress and the pilot moved the ship cautiously downriver toward Saginaw Bay.

Harry could barely make out Brennan's Marina. Sailboats and cruisers were nestled snuggly in their cradles under a thick blanket of snow awaiting the first warm breath of spring.

Bay City was a blur of lights. The Lafayette Street Bridge was raised, backing traffic up for several blocks in either direction. Horns blared and people stood outside their cars shivering in the cold watching the two ships moving under the yawning spans of the open bridge. Many people waved. A few gave the universal salute for the inconvenience. No one on board waved back. Captain Andress blew the ship's whistle. People jumped. He laughed.

A couple more bridges and, soon, Bay City lay behind, lost in the swirling snowstorm. Even the old Defoe shipyard stood silent, a ghost of the past, and then was swallowed from sight.

Over his shoulder Harry could hear the clipped commands of the pilot and the firm suggestions of Captain Andress. He was impressed at the ease with which the helmsman responded to orders, making necessary course adjustments on command.

It was hard to believe *Nurad*, the first of the new super carrier class, as Peter had pointed out, could actually carry a million and a half bushels of grain, and that all was destined for just two ports: Shanghai and Tsingtao. Harry smiled recalling that when he was a kid dawdling over his food, his father would reprimand him in a monotonous tone of voice: "Eat all the food on your plate. Just think of all the poor starving kids in China."

The smile broadened as he recalled using the same line on his kids when they were growing up and dawdling over their food, only then, he used the phrase, "poor starving kids in Southeast Asia."

"Vy don't you two go eat," Captain Andress suggested rather brusquely, probably anxious at having too many people on the bridge. Peter nodded and they hastily left.

"I vill show you your job later ven it is more calm," Peter said as they made their way to the galley. "Der Captain hates to have odders running his ship. It gets tense."

They joined several other crewmembers going through the cafeteria-style line. Harry's eyes roamed over the mouth-watering array of food. He sniffed at the tantalizing odors wafting from the steaming trays: polish sausage and sauerkraut, hashbrowns, buttered beans, hot fresh baked bread and cabbage salad. He followed Peter's lead picking up a tray and utensils and proceeded through the line. A young boy dished out the food. Harry cut off a big chunk of crock butter and dropped it on the hot steaming bread, watching it melt. His saliva glands were working; he was hungry. He hadn't had a decent meal since yesterday, just the rolls and milk at Janie's apartment earlier that morning. His tray was soon filled with hot food. At the end of the line he also managed to pick up an orange and apple.

"Geez," Harry commented setting his tray down next to Peter's. "If I eat this much for each meal I'll be four hundred pounds by the time I get back to Saginaw."

Peter laughed. "You can go back for seconds, too," he added.

Harry shook his head no as he delved into the food. Yet, surprisingly, he did go back for dessert, something he rarely did as he was trying to control his weight, trying to maintain a slim hundred and sixty-five pounds.

It was dusk by the time they left the galley. Peter excused himself to check on several items with the captain. Bundling up, Harry stepped out on deck. It was cold. He stuffed his hands into his warm gloves and moved to the railing. The storm had passed as quickly as it had come. *Nurad* had cleared the Saginaw River and was well out in Saginaw Bay. In the distance, the sun sat low on the horizon, large red-tinged clouds contrasting with the blue-white snow. Red sky at night, sailor's delight; red sky in the morning, sailor take warning. Harry spoke the saying aloud recalling the many times his dad had said it when he had taken him fishing early in the morning off Harbor Beach. The saying had always stuck in his mind.

On shore, lights were blinking on as people burrowed in for another cold winter night. He wondered how many actually dropped their thermostat setting to 65 degrees at night, and put on another sweater. Another bureaucratic decision from Washington: save fuel, dial down. How many bureaucrats dialed down?

The wind was biting cold sending a shiver through him. The brilliant redness was fading into a dullish gray as the skies surrendered to the onset of nightfall. Along the edge of the ice pack a few foolhardy snowmobilers raced their machines across the ice. Dumb, Harry thought. Anyone hitting an open patch of water at night would disappear along with their machine – sometimes forever.

And then he was thinking of Sandy. His eyes glistened with tears. He wiped at his eyes but the tears continued to trickle down his cheeks. He looked around; he was alone. Bowing his head, he said a silent prayer for her. He was going to miss her. Whoever did it should burn in hell.

Glancing at his watch, he saw it was 7:30 p.m. No, he corrected himself. He had to convert his thinking to shipboard time. It was now 1930 hours. When in Rome, he mused. He glanced once more at the shoreline and the many twinkling lights. Overhead, the sky started to clear giving way to a brilliant array of stars. It was time to go inside, to get warm, to get ready for his first stint at the midnight watch. He knew he should rest for a while in order to be awake and alert when he joined Peter on the bridge.

In his cabin he peeled off the thick jacket and started to throw it on his bunk, but stopped. He held it up, examining it. An idea was forming in his mind. Of course! He turned the jacket inside out.

The quilted stitching carried through the jacket. Each quilted section was about six inches by four inches, just what he needed. He could tailor the jacket to hold the packets of money. Any excess money could be stashed in the bottom of his seabag, which he had already decided to modify with a false bottom, even false sides if needed, in order to carry all the money.

"Hot damn!" he exclaimed jubilantly. "Hot –" The word stuck in his throat. Standing in the bathroom doorway was a man holding a .45 automatic. It was aimed right at his head. Harry looked at the man's face, an Oriental. The Chink!

"Harry Martin?" the Oriental asked knowingly.

Harry nodded, watching the man closely. The Chink threw a folded copy of the Saginaw newspaper at him. Harry caught it and opened it.

"Bottom of the page!" the Chink snapped in flawless English.

Harry glanced down. Bold headlines leaped out at him.

CHINA TO RECEIVE MICHIGAN GRAIN.

He scanned the article quickly. It described the *Otto J. Nurad's* mission to carry grain to Shanghai and Tsingtao, departing on Sunday. But then, they had moved the sailing date to today, Saturday. He glanced at the date, Thursday's newspaper. His bowling night. He hadn't read it yet. But then, he hadn't read any newspaper in the last couple days. Hell, yesterday at this time the ship's sailing hadn't meant one damned thing to him. And then that damned phone call from Joe. Events had changed his life drastically in the past 24 hours.

"So?" Harry responded, dropping the paper on the desk, looking back over at the Chink. How in hell did he sneak aboard, Harry wondered.

"So this, wise guy," the Chink replied. "It was easy to put two and two together and figure out how you aimed to get to China. All I had to do was get on board and find you, and here we are."

"Cozy, ain't it?" Harry snapped. "How'd you get aboard?"

"None of your business! Your being here tells me you know where Joe's money is hidden. I want the information, now."

Harry stood silently. If he told him, he was a dead man. He observed the Chink deciding to play a waiting game. Maybe Peter might return. Maybe they could overcome him. He noticed the Chink stood slightly stooped, his coat caked with what appeared to be mud. His left arm seemed to dangle freely. Harry suddenly realized it was dried blood staining the sleeve, not mud.

"You look like you might have stopped a slug or two. You're bleeding." Harry motioned at his arm. "Either the cops got you or I did in Sandy's apartment —"

"You got lucky," the Chink retorted. "But don't plan on pressing your luck. One false move and you'll be dead, too."

"Where's Stan?"

"I wish I knew!" the Chink hissed. "The bastard dumped me after I got hit. I don't know where he is, but I'll beat him to the money. He'll pay for this. I'll live, live long enough to get the money and kill that bastard!"

Waving the gun menacingly, he moved across the room to within a couple of feet of Harry. "Now, where's the money?"

"I don't know —"

The gun smashed down across Harry's shoulder knocking him backwards to the bulkhead where he dropped to his knees. Harry grabbed at his shoulder, stifling a cry of pain. The Chink moved quickly, driving the point of his shoe into Harry's stomach. Harry gasped, then balled up on the deck, sure he was going to vomit. "You son-of-a-bitch," he hissed, barely able to breath. The Chink hit him a glancing blow across the back of his head with the automatic. Harry saw stars momentarily, then blackness.

The feel of cold water on his face brought him around. Groggily, he looked about. His dresser drawers had been dumped and his clothing strewn about the cabin. Turning, he again faced the gun and the stoic-faced Chink.

"Where's the money hidden?" the Chink asked in an even tone of voice.

"Go to hell. If I tell you, I'm dead." Harry rasped.

"You're just as good as dead, smart guy. You'll be as dead as Joe and that stupid broad; just as dead." He thrust the gun up under Harry's chin, forcing his head awkwardly backwards. "Now, for the last time," he hissed, "where is the money hidden? Where's Joe's black book with the information in it?"

"I don't know," Harry gasped. "Joe was gonna tell me when I came back to let him know I was going to China. There's no book, either. You guys took all his possessions – everything he had."

"You're lying!" the Chink hissed forcing the gun deeper into the soft flesh of his throat. "The only reason you're on this damned ship is because you know where the money is!" He jerked the gun away and brought it down sharply across Harry's face. Harry jerked, grabbing at his face, feeling warm blood trickling through his fingers.

"Your last chance, tough man. Where's the money?"

"Go to hell, you god-damned gook!" Harry spat. He pulled his bloodied hands from his face glaring at the Chink. "You can go straight to hell!"

The Chink's foot suddenly snapped upwards catching Harry in the groin. Harry screamed, doubling over in pain. "You had it, tough man," the Chink said looking down at the writhing figure clutching at his groin. "Get on your feet. We're going for a walk."

Harry rolled over onto his knees. Raising his head, he looked into the Chink's smirking face. The gun was still leveled at his head, right in the middle of his face.

"On your feet, tough man. We're going for a walk."

Harry rose unsteadily to his feet clutching at his groin. The sharp pain was now a throbbing ache. He caught a momentary glimpse of himself in the mirror on the back of the locker door. His face was streaked with blood.

"We're gonna take a walk to the back of the ship, tough man, only you aren't coming back."

"Why'd you kill the girl?" Harry gasped.

"I didn't like the way she parted her hair! What are you? Dumb? She wouldn't talk. I tried to get her to talk but she wouldn't talk. So, I got rid of her,"

"She didn't know anything about this."

"She still doesn't."

"Her gun," Harry said. "She had a gun. How'd you get the drop on her?"

"She woke up with my .45 in her mouth, so no argument. We

had a nice chat."

"Chat! You bastard! You broke her fingers and arms —"

"Part of my gentle art of persuasion. Wrong answer; snap!"

"You didn't have to kill her!"

"Nightie was up around her neck already. All I had to do was twist it. No more crying out. Incidentally, good body."

"Bastard!" Harry screamed, angrily lunging for him, ignoring the gun. The Chink deftly stepped aside, slamming his weapon hard against his skull. A karate kick followed just as quickly sending Harry bouncing off the bulkhead onto the deck.

"Now, get up and no more heroics," the Chink said motioning with the gun for him to rise and head for the door. "Open it slowly," he commanded. Harry opened the door; the corridor was empty. "Move out slowly and head for the back of the ship."

Harry stepped into the corridor prodded along by the automatic pressing tight against his ribs. He had to make a move and fast, but how? The guy was obviously a skilled killer. One nervous twitch and he'd be dead. He kept walking.

They stepped on deck. The temperature had dropped considerably. It was bitter cold with a sharp, biting wind. Harry shivered in the frigid night air. The Chink prodded him along, continuing toward the stern. Harry held onto the railing. The deck was still slippery in places.

"Damn!" Harry cursed as he slipped, falling hard on his knees. Hurriedly, he regained his footing, glancing backwards just as the Chink lost his footing. As he rose, Harry spun about and gave a sharp left heel kick to the Chink's stomach. The Chink gasped and, as he started to crumple, Harry followed through in a fluid movement, with a thrusting upward kick to the Chink's head, snapping his head backwards. The Chink's body followed the momentum of the kick with an upward movement that carried him up and over the ship's railing. His screams were lost in the shrill wail of the wind and pounding of the engines.

Harry steadied himself against the railing. There was no sign of the Chink, nothing but dark swirling water. "For Sandy," he whispered.

Shivering uncontrollably, he made his way back toward his cabin. Luck was with him; there was no one in the corridor. Quickly, he returned to his cabin. Inside, he washed his face and checked the cut. It was superficial, just a lot of blood for the moment, but his face was swollen and tender to the touch. He dabbed at the cut with peroxide, and then covered it with an adhesive bandage. His stomach and shoulder ached, but nothing seemed broken. A couple of days would take care of the aches.

In a matter of minutes he restored the cabin to a semblance of order as it had been before the altercation. It was clean, no sign of a struggle, no sign the Chink had been there, nothing. No sense in reporting a stowaway on board if there wasn't one, so no sense of reporting a man overboard either.

He sat down at the desk running through the events of the last twenty-four hours. Now he was certain that Stan didn't know the location of the money, only himself. From this moment on, he knew he had to be on guard against Stan, or any of his hired thugs.

Chapter 29
ALMOST LOST OVERBOARD

"Vot happened to you?" asked Peter staring at Harry's swollen face as he joined him on the bridge for the midnight watch.

"I slipped on a patch of ice on deck and fell against the railing," Harry lied. "I'll be okay. Just a little sore now."

"Vell be careful. Der deck will be getting slipp'rery even more now dat ve are moving. Vun hand for der ship, vun hand for yourself. You could slide right overboard und not be noticed."

"Right," Harry grinned. "Don't worry. From now on I'll be super careful."

"Good. Now I show you your duties," Peter said. He began a methodical, painstaking review of the complex responsibilities of the watch. Harry listened carefully, asked questions and generally familiarized himself with the job. When he took command of the wheel it gave him a momentary start; everything he had learned before as a helmsman flooded back and he felt a sense of ease, felt the ship respond to his touch as he followed the commands of the First Officer, Peter Selham, who checked his every move.

"Ve pick up anodder pilot ven ve get to Port Huron," Peter said, when Harry asked what had happened to the other one. "Der odder vun got off ven ve cleared der river. You ver below decks at der time."

Nurad continued in the channel created by the icebreaker *Mackinac*. Harry's eyes took in the various gauges and illuminated dials, as well as keeping an eye on *Mackinac*. He listened to the crackling communications between the two ships, kept an eye on the compass and followed orders. Soon, the monotony of the job came back to him. It was demanding, yet there was a certain monotony about it. It was the same as it had been on other ships.

All jobs had a certain amount of monotony inherent in them. You just can't get the perfect job, he rationalized, or even if you did you'd soon find fault with it. Sameness and monotony were often interchangeable.

Hot coffee was available and, over the next few hours, Harry drank several cups. As the night droned on he could feel stiffness overtaking his body from the beating the Chink had given him. He'd have to exercise when he got off duty, work out the kinks. Still, as he stood at the wheel, the events of the last twenty-four hours continually see-sawed back and forth through his mind. It seemed incredible that a simple phone call could screw up his life so badly, and in so doing, cause the death of three people.

There was no doubt that Joe's hidden cache of money really existed from the way it was being pursued. Yet, thirty years was a long time ago; a lot of things could have happened to it. The way the Chink talked, apparently not even Stan knew the exact location.

The Chink. Harry's jawline tightened at the thought of the man. He had no reason to kill Sandy, just killed her for the hell of it. The bastard! Vividly he recalled the Chink going over the railing. They might fish his worthless body out of the bay in the spring but there was nothing to tie him to the ship. Nothing. Besides, he might never be found.

Off to his right along the Michigan shoreline he could discern small towns and villages, their clustered lights appearing like a swarm of fireflies in the darkness.

Early on, Peter had struck up a conversation talking about a myriad of things relative to the operation of the ship but, as the night wore on, Harry sensed a change in the line of casual questions, that Peter was pumping him for personal information.

He was persistent; questions, then more casual conversation, then more personal questions. Harry responded with some of the highlights of his business career, sailing experience and such. Nothing about his love life, which he sensed was kind of what Peter was interested in. Having seen Sandy's panties, he was sure Peter wanted to know more about the girl who owned the panties. Yet, he couldn't come right out and bluntly ask, or could he?

"I am not trying to pry into your personal life, Harry," Peter said, sensing a hesitancy on Harry's part. "I just vish to know more about you so dat ve can vork better togedder. It vill be helpful to me. You do understand, yah?"

"Sure thing. No problem," Harry replied making light of it. "Happy to oblige." A smile crossed his face. I suppose I'd want to know more about a new shipmate, he reasoned, especially a guy I picked up in a foreign port. But then, I don't suppose I'd want to tell him every minute detail about myself or my love life.

At 0400 hours they were relieved by the next watch. Peter turned in immediately wanting to catch as much sleep as possible as they'd be needed on deck before too long if the storm continued to build. Harry agreed, and in short order, in spite of lingering pain, he was snoring in harmony with his cabin mate.

Dawn broke ominously. Heavy-laden clouds blocked out the horizon. Rolling white caps crested across the cold, black waters of Lake Huron as far as the eye could see. Wind-whipped spray splattered the length of the ship freezing almost instantly. Railings, lifeboats and rigging were encrusted with ice. Across the deck ice grew thicker and thicker as the ship continued on course. The heavily laden ship labored, heaving and tossing, groaning under the incessantly pounding waves.

Harry awoke finding Peter dressed in cold-weather gear, just leaving the compartment. In spite of his exhaustion, he knew he might be needed. Dropping lightly to the deck he hastily dressed in cold-weather gear and headed topside.

Harry found himself humming a refrain from the song, "The Wreck of the Edmund Fitzgerald," as he stood in the back of the wheelhouse, as directed by Peter. The weather was as rotten as it was that cold November day when the Fitzgerald sank in Lake Superior with all hands lost. The story of the tragedy had soon turned into a popular folk ballad. Writers and sailors spent countless hours pursuing theories as to what caused the sinking. Of course, he told himself, there's a hell of a lot of ships that never made it across Lake Huron either. Hauntingly, the tune stuck with him.

Nurad seemed to hug even closer to *Mackinac* as it made a compass turn heading in a more southerly course. Before too long the Blue Water Bridge at Port Huron came into view. It was a welcome sight. Shortly after, with another pilot on board, they were wending their way down the St. Clair River. The storm hit with gusting winds and a heavy snowfall. Within a short time a thick covering of snow engulfed the ship from stem to stern.

At noon Peter took command of the watch, with Harry at the helm. Captain Andress joined them on the bridge. If he was concerned, it didn't show in his face or eyes. The challenge of sailing through the storm, beating the odds, was apparent as the captain looked forward through the huge windows, and then took in the ship from stem to stern. He motioned Peter to his side for a brief exchange, and then turned his attention to the pilot assuring him they would take the storm in stride. Both listened intently to the Coast Guard weather reports. The storm would be blowing over before too long followed by possible sunshine through breaks in the clouds. Captain Andress smiled. Turning, he switched on the radio.

The sound of a familiar voice caught Harry's attention. Glancing about, he concentrated on the voice: Art Nathan, his favorite newscaster in the Saginaw market. Harry was surprised that the radio station's signal was so clear. Glancing at his watch he saw it was 1230. Art usually gave an update on all the news happening in the Saginaw valley at this time. Casually, Harry reached over and turned up the volume.

"Police are continuing their search for the two men who wounded two Saginaw police officers Friday night. Evidence now links the two with the murder of a young Saginaw divorcee. A police spokesman said the two police officers were recovering. He added that one of the suspects is believed to be badly wounded from an exchange of gunfire in the slain woman's apartment. A bloodstained, bullet-riddled car pulled from the Saginaw river this morning is believed to be the fugitive's getaway car. However, the two suspects are still at large –" Harry gave a deep sigh of disgust, snapping off the radio as he did. Stan was still at large.

Harry failed to notice the inquisitive glances from Peter and the Captain at the way he had abruptly snapped off the radio.

South of Algonac, at the mouth of Lake St. Clair, *Mackinac* radioed it was turning about, heading northbound. It made a wide sweeping turn, bidding them fair weather and good sailing. The ships exchanged ear-piercing blasts from their whistles. Captain Andress thanked *Mackinac* for its assistance, slapped the pilot on his broad shoulders for a job well done, and said they were really under way now. Astern, Harry could see *Mackinac* punching it's way northward, fading into the swirling snow.

Soon they were down bound in the Detroit River. The downbound and up-bound lanes were fairly clear of ice. Harry could see the curling smoke of at least three ships ahead of them. Detroit and Windsor lay under threatening storm clouds. Snow flurries continued. Peering through the huge wheelhouse windows, Harry could make out the Renaissance Center, the Blue Cross Building and Cobo Hall. Then they were sailing under the Ambassador Bridge. Ahead lay Lake Erie and the St. Lawrence Seaway. Captain Andress took command of the ship suggesting they leave the bridge, grab a bite to eat and prepare to clear ice from encrusted points on deck.

Peter wolfed down his food, almost cleaning his plate before Harry got seated. "Sorry to rush you, Harry," he apologized, as he picked up his tray of dirty dishes. "Ve must get up on deck und vork vis der odder men to get rid of dat ice buildup. See you on deck." He took one last gulp of coffee before dropping his tray at the counter, and then left.

"Slave driver!" Harry called after him, jokingly, as he turned to his food. Eating voraciously, washing almost each gulp down with coffee, he finished in short order, although it felt like the entire meal clogged up in his throat. Done, he dropped his dirty dishes into the tray and headed topside.

Joining the other crewmembers he turned to with an axe, chipping ice from the boat davits. Suddenly, while rounding the superstructure on the boat deck, Harry slipped on a patch of ice as the ship pitched, landed on his back and found himself sliding toward the railing. He dropped his axe, which went sailing over the edge, and, in a desperate movement, lunged, throwing his body to the left where he grabbed a railing stanchion. Quickly he wrapped his arms around it holding on for dear life, only the stanchion was so thickly coated with ice that it made his situation more precarious. Reaching around as far as he could, Harry grabbed onto his jacket sleeve clutching tightly to the material, his body dangling over the edge of the ship. He yelled at the top of his lungs for help. His clothing soon became soaked from the freezing spray chilling him to the bone. It was only a matter of time before he'd lose his grip on the wet material and he'd be lost overboard. He continued to yell with added fervor.

Looking frantically along the deck, he saw a man had stopped and was just staring at him: the man with the scowl who'd been arguing with Captain Andress when Peter first brought him to the bridge. Harry yelled for help but the man only smiled, then suddenly turned and walked away.

"Hey! Hey!" Harry screamed after him. "Help!"

Knowing he couldn't hold on much longer, Harry desperately swung one leg up, repeating the movement several times until his heel caught on the lip of the deck. Slowly, carefully, he pulled himself up until most of his body was on deck, although he was still far from safety. A line suddenly fell in front of his face. Looking up, he saw two crewmen standing back by the boat davit holding onto the other end of the line. "Grab der line. Ve pull you!" they shouted.

At the point of total exhaustion, Harry laboriously wrapped the line around his arm several times, and then was dragged across the deck to safety.

Shaking with exhaustion, his lungs heaving from the labor, Harry managed a weak, gasping, "Thanks. I don't think I could have held on much longer. I'm sure glad that guy sent you."

"No vun sent us," one replied. "Ve heard your call for help. Der line was der best vay to save you."

Harry looked from one to the other. "Interesting," he gasped. Rising slowly to his feet, walking stiffly in his wet, leathery hard frozen clothing, he let them lead him to safety within the ship. He thanked them again for their help, then headed below to his cabin. The thought passed through his mind; why did the man with the scowl leave him?

Chapter 30
DOWNBOUND, MEETING THE SHIP'S COOK

The midnight watch went without incident. Captain Andress came onto the bridge exchanging comments with the pilot as *Nurad* followed a line of down-bound vessels heading across Lake Erie. At one point he stepped behind Harry and chided him for not wearing a safety line when he was working on the boat deck. "Fastest vay for a man to be lost overboard."

Harry took good-natured ribbing in stride. He decided not to mention the man with the scowling face. He'd talk to him later.

After their watch was relieved, Harry made a beeline for his bunk. Still exhausted from his near meeting with fate, he closed his eyes but jumbled thoughts tumbled back and forth in his mind, thoughts that had no answers, only asked more questions. Peter had fallen into his bunk and was snoring. How could a guy fall asleep so easily, Harry wondered. He punched his pillow several times, rolled over again for the umpteenth time to find a comfortable position, and even resorted to counting sheep but all failed. Yet it did happen; sleep came as a veil of quiet relief.

The noon watch found them still crossing ice-laden Lake Erie. There were two ships ahead of them in the down-bound lane and they were all heading for the Welland Canal. *Nurad* arrived at the canal late in the day and moved easily through the number one lock. After several more miles, it prepared to drop the 46 feet in ten minutes in each of the next three locks until it finally moved out into Lake Ontario. Ahead, in the St. Lawrence Seaway, lay the locks at Iroquois, Eisenhower/ Snell, Beauharnois, Ste. Catherine, Cote and St.Lambert.

On rising late in the day, Harry dressed for duty, headed topside to the galley and ate heartily, joshing with several crew members, feeling a bit more at ease as a member of the crew now. He checked the galley. No sign of the man with the scowling face. One day soon they'd meet, he was sure of that. How big was this ship anyway? With time to kill, he stepped out on deck, making sure he held onto the railing. He gazed off across the Canadian landscape. It was dusk, light snow falling. The town of Cornwall appeared ahead of them. *Nurad* moved silently past the town as it continued up the St. Lawrence Seaway.

Arriving on the bridge before midnight, Harry met the new pilot, a craggy-faced, white-haired man by the name of Harold Cobb. Both Harry and Peter soon learned that Harold had a running gift of gab. Harry found himself enjoying the folksy manner, akin to Mark Twain, as the seasoned pilot spun yarn after yarn about the seaway, puffing on his ever-lit pipe. Even Peter cracked a smile now and then about the man's outlandish yarns. And so the watch went, moving along through the seaway, periodically stopping to lock through, and then continuing the voyage.

Waking around 1000, Harry glanced out the cabin porthole. It was a dull day with snow still falling. Below him, Peter's snoring seemed louder than usual. I'd love to put a pillow over his face, Harry thought as he rolled over, closed his eyes and tried to go back to sleep. But it was a fruitless effort; he was wide awake and the snoring was too loud.

It was time to rise. The thought came to him, why not take a tour of the ship as long as he was awake this early. He always felt better when he knew the inner workings of the ship he was on, kind of like knowing the lay of the land. Besides, it would keep his mind off Stan and Sandy.

Showered, dressed, and having grabbed a light breakfast in the galley, Harry stepped through the first hatchway as he started his self-directed tour of the ship. He moved along the corridor at a fairly brisk pace. Perhaps, he thought, he might find an indoor jogging area as the top deck was too precarious for such activity at this northern latitude. Physically, he felt much better, his mind clearer than it had been for a couple of days. He knew he had to keep his mind from straying back to past events and, rather, to concentrate on what lay ahead. Already, he had started working on modifying his jacket. Once ashore in Tsingtao, he had to get up to the old Marine Compound, get into the old 12th Service Battalion Building, get into the old storage room and find the money. Then, but there was always Sandy. She was there on his mind.

"Ooooops!" he gasped, coming around the corner of a dark corridor. Shocked, he had collided full on into a woman. A woman! Instinctively he grabbed her so she wouldn't fall.

"Oh!" she yelped at the same moment, his strong arms still around her, holding her.

"We've got to stop meeting like this," Harry quipped. "The rest of the crew is getting suspicious."

"Vot?" she asked, somewhat puzzled, pushing free of his hold. "Vot did you say?"

"Sorry, just a little American humor," he replied, stepping away, an embarrassed smile crossing his face. "Oh, uh, I'm Harry Martin. I just joined the ship a couple of days ago in Saginaw."

"Oh. Der American," she acknowledged with a nod of her head. "Yah. I haf heard of you." She started fussing, straightening her blouse "Yah. I know you."

"All good, I hope," Harry retorted. "Are you okay? That was a pretty hard jolt. I hadn't intended to bump into you, into a girl – uh, it was an accident." A nice accident at that, he thought, looking her over. Not bad. A natural blonde, warm blue eyes, strong white teeth, full, sensuous lips and a nice slim figure. Forty-ish, he figured, but still a beautiful woman. "You are okay, aren't you " he repeated, expecting a name.

"Yah, yah. I am okay," she said, fussing with her hair.

"And your name is?"

"Osa. Osa Peterson." Their eyes met. "I'm der cook," she added.

"You are?" An incredulous look came to his face. This gorgeous woman was the cook! Teasing, he said, "I thought you might be a fashion model on vacation. The cook! Wow!" She seemed amused at his comment, a hesitant smile breaking across her face. He continued. "The food is terrific, excellent, superb." His tongue seemed to stumble over his eyeteeth in trying to say the right thing. "You sure know how to cook, I mean, uh, I never imagined having such excellent fare aboard ship, especially this ship, that is, from such a beautiful woman, er, such a beautiful cook."

Osa laughed at his rambling flattery. As seldom as she got any compliments, she enjoyed the moment, but more so, she enjoyed his boyish squirming. It was refreshing.

"Tank you –"

"Harry, call me Harry," he was quick to reply.

"Harry, dat is nice of you to say dat. Tank you." Her smile was warm, infectious, and she had a twinkle in her eyes. "I must go now und prepare der lunch. I vill see you again, yah?"

"Yah, er, yes. Yes, ma'm, you certainly will," he smiled back at her. "You certainly will."

He watched the undulation of her buttocks within the trimly tailored slacks as she walked down the corridor. Nice, he thought, real nice. Sailing on ships had certainly changed radically since the last time he was at sea. Now they let women on board. Terrific. He let out a sigh as she disappeared around a corner. Then, with a shrug of his shoulders, he continued his exploration of the ship. "Osa, Osa Peterson," he said aloud. Nice name, nice lady.

The ship proved more complex than he had anticipated and, after a while, he stopped. He'd explore it a section at a time, and he certainly had plenty of time. Captain Andress estimated it would take the best part of two months to get to China. Yes, he had plenty of time.

Early lunch was a disappointment. The food was excellent but where he had anticipated seeing Osa, she was not to be seen. He shrugged it off; he'd see her again. He joined several other crew members, getting involved in small talk, trying to improve communications, to become more accepted, better acquainted and to learn names. Periodically, he glanced in the direction of the serving counter. At one point he caught a glimpse of Osa through swinging doors behind the counter. Their eyes met for a fleeting moment, then she was gone.

Probably married to one of the officers, or a member of the crew, he thought. Still, he was aware that except for Peter and the Captain, and perhaps a couple of others, the rest of the crew was younger, much younger than her. And he shared a cabin with Peter, so it couldn't be him. But who? The Captain? Naw, he was way too old for her. Chief engineer? He looked about the same age. Maybe. Maybe he could find out from Peter on the noon watch.

"Osa?" Peter repeated the name Harry had just mentioned, and then grinned. "She is our cook." With that comment, Peter closed any further discussion on the subject. The pilot interrupted ordering Harry to bring the ship starboard two points of the compass. The explanation of why a female cook was on board was not made and so the watch continued its boring, monotonous manner as *Nurad* wended its way northeast up the seaway.

Coming off watch at 1600 hours, Harry decided to continue his exploration of the ship. He started in the corridor where he had bumped into Osa earlier. He hoped to get as far as the engine room. Engines, especially huge ones used to drive ships, were always fascinating. He admired the genius of those who engineered the design of huge engines, those who built them, and those who installed them in ships – to witness them work to perfection.

A door suddenly opened ahead of him and Osa stepped out. She appeared startled at seeing him. "Vot are you doing here?" she demanded, at the same moment taking a hurried look up and down the corridor.

"Exploring the ship. Why?"

"Dis whole area is off limits to der crew. It is der Captain's orders. You should not be here. He vill deal vis you severely."

"I didn't know," Harry said. "I'll get on back –"

"Shh," she cautioned holding her finger to her lips. "Qvick. Come inside. Somevun is coming."

She grabbed his arm pulling him into her cabin, quickly closing the door behind them. She held her fingers to her lips again warning him not to move or make a sound. Harry could hear nothing but he couldn't stop admiring her. She was attractive in her white blouse and navy blue skirt, her hair pulled back tied with a ribbon. After several seconds, the thought crossed his mind that it was a sneaky way for her to get a man in her cabin.

A sharp knock on her door startled him, driving the thought from his mind.

"Yes," she sang out. "Who is it?"

"Uncle Karl."

Osa's eyes widened in fear. "My uncle, Captain Andress," she whispered to Harry in a trembling voice. "You must hide. Qvickly!"

Harry glanced about the room. It was small, about the size he shared with Peter. A large bed occupied one corner. It was covered with a bright print quilt and adorned with several small throw pillows. Leaning back against the pillows was an old, tattered Teddy Bear. The bed, he could hide under the bed. No, not enough room.

"Just a minute, Uncle! I vas jus' getting ready to take a bath," she called out stepping to the closet and grabbing a robe off a hook. "Qvickly!" she snapped, as she slipped the robe on over her blouse and skirt covering herself. She glanced furtively at Harry as she kicked her shoes off. "Jus' vun minute, please."

Harry made a dive for the bed; solid base. The closet was far too small for his large frame. "Hurry," she implored in an agonized whisper. Harry stepped into the bathroom. There was a tub with a shower curtain around the inside. It would have to do. He stepped inside, closed the curtain and pressed himself back as tightly into the corner as he could, ducking his head slightly because of the shower nozzle. Damn. It dripped.

Osa closed the bathroom door, slipped the ribbon from her hair letting the long golden tresses fan out, then rushed to let her uncle in, somewhat flushed at the sudden turn of events. Harry could hear Captain Andress enter, and they began speaking in Swedish. The dripping faucet was becoming a wet source of irritation. Reaching down, he grabbed the handle and gently twisted it. Inadvertently, he turned it the wrong way and a steady stream of water gushed out. Harry stood under the faucet fearful to move, the water continuing to run, soaking him.

"Vell, I cannot stay," Captain Andress said. "I hear your vater running and I must get back to running der ship." As he started through the door, he suddenly poked his head back inside. "Dis man Martin I told you about. He is very nice. I haf good reports about him from Peter. I vill take it upon myself to formally introduce you to him. You two haf much in common. He, too, is a college graduate mit a master's degree. I am impressed by dis man. I vill tell you more about him later. Go and take your bath, I vill see you at dinner."

"Yes, uncle. Now I must hurry and get ready for dinner." Osa breathed a sigh of relief as she closed the door behind him. Turning, she rushed into the bathroom and flung back the shower curtain. "Qvickly! You must get out of here –" but she stopped, suddenly breaking into hysterical laughter at seeing Harry standing before her soaking wet.

"Oh, I am so sorry –" she managed to say between bursts of laughter. "Der ship's plumber vas supposed to fix der faucet vhile ve were in port." Tears streamed down her cheeks as she shook her head, laughing.

Harry found himself laughing, too. In spite of his soaked, miserable feeling, he had to admit it was funny. He stepped from the tub, water dripping on the thick carpet, accepting a large bath towel from Osa, who could not contain herself, continuing to laugh, giggle, and wipe away tears streaming down her cheeks.

"I think I'd better leave now," Harry said dabbing at himself ineffectually with the towel. "I enjoyed your pool party but I think I'd feel better in dry clothes."

Osa doubled over laughing harder. "Oh, Harry, I am truly sorry." She followed him as he crossed the room leaving a trail of water where he stepped. She glanced out into the corridor. "Now," she said and he hurried past her into the corridor. "I'm sorry," she called after him in a husky whisper.

He swore he could hear her laughter even after the door closed. He continued squishing his way down the corridor hoping he wouldn't run into anyone and have to explain his condition.

Captain Andress peered around the corner of the corridor behind Harry. A fatherly grin broke lightly across his lips. He tamped fresh tobacco into his pipe, lit up, and continued toward the bridge.

Chapter 31

SPRUCING UP FOR THE LADY

Two showers and shaving twice in one day? Harry mumbled looking at himself in the mirror. "C'mon, Harry, get hold of yourself," he chastised his reflection. "Sandy's not even warm in her grave and Osa, well, she's a very nice lady, so don't get any funny ideas about her. She's a lady and you damned well better remember that!" Then why am I slapping on the expensive aftershave lotion? he asked himself. Dressed in freshly pressed work clothes, taking pains to look neater than usual, he glanced again at his reflection. Hell, he thought, she doesn't know I exist anymore than any other member of the crew.

Osa had enjoyed her bath, luxuriating in the bubbling lotion that left her skin soft and smooth. She had dried leisurely, powdered, applied makeup and generously perfumed with Chanel, something she never did just to work in the galley. Harry Martin. He was cute, she thought. Older, but cute, a nice personality. For his age, the American was rather good looking, in a rugged sort of way, yet well-mannered, suave, yet youthful, and, according to Uncle Karl, well educated. She laughed lightly as she recalled him standing in her tub soaking wet, like a huge wet sheep dog.

Slipping on her robe, she lay back across her bed examining her fingernails, her robe falling open exposing long, slender legs and well rounded hips. She definitely needed a good manicure, she thought, hastily yanking the robe closed over her legs. It would be one of the first things she got when she arrived in port.

Sitting up, she looked into her dresser mirror at herself "I tink he is cute!" she blurted. She gave an exasperated sigh "Osa!" she said, glaring at herself. "Vy do you say dat? Vy are you taking all dese pains? You are chust der cook! Besides, he probably hasn't given you a tought. You are chust an old dried up vidow. He probably has all kinds of young girlfriends at home in Saginaw."

She glanced at the clock on her dresser. "Oh!" she gasped. It was time to go and serve dinner.

Harry found himself outside the galley early. He glanced at his watch. It was stupid being here so early. Dumb. He started to walk away but bumped into Peter.

"You are hungry, too?" Peter chided, rubbing his stomach. "I am famished. I had to come down und get in line early. I don't know vy but tonight I am really hungry."

"You took the words right out of my mouth," Harry replied. "For some odd reason I really worked up an appetite"

"Dere's someting about you –" Peter said staring at him. "Yes. You are all dressed up." His eyes took in the length of his friend. "Are ve dining formal tonight?"

Harry gave an embarrassed grin. "Naw. I just got dressed up now so I won't have to change for watch later." He hoped his little white lie was acceptable, and then they pushed through the galley doors.

Surprisingly, there were quite a number of the crew in the galley already enjoying hot coffee and a chance to get out of the cold weather. Just then, the mess boy stepped behind the counter and announced the food line was open. There was a sudden rush as men dashed to the starting line grabbing up trays and utensils. As a ranking officer, Peter stepped to the head of the line, pulling Harry with him. Salty protests erupted about cutting into line but were met with equal fervor by Peter. "Don't complain," he admonished. "Vhile you sleep tonight, ve will be guiding der ship. If ve don't eat now der ship may accidentally sink." His comment was met with more good-natured, salty remarks.

Osa came out of the kitchen concerned about the sudden noise. At seeing Peter and Harry first in line, she stepped to the counter and started serving.

"Vell, Osa, dis is a surprise, being served by you," Peter commented as she dished out food. "Und don't ve look lovely dis evening? Is dis some special occasion? You look absolutely beautiful, so radiant," He glanced back at Harry. "Und Harry, too, he is all dressed up tonight. I feel out of place. Maybe I should go und get on my dress uniform, yah?"

Osa's face had turned crimson. Harry's face, too, had turned a shade of pink. Neither looked at the other.

"You should get dressed up vunce in a vhile, Peter," she snapped back. "It makes you feel human." She turned to Harry. "Don't pay any attention to him. He is jealous because some people get dressed up. I tink you look nice."

"Thank you," Harry replied. In spite of a full white apron, she did look radiant, as Peter had said. There was a certain sparkle to her blue eyes as she smiled at him, full lips slightly parted. "And you look terrific, too," he added. "Just terrific."

"My, my," Peter interjected. "Mutual admiration. I'm sorry dat I mentioned der two of you ver all dressed up at all. Please excuse me." He feigned an injured look.

"Oh, Peter!" Osa exclaimed apologetically "I didn't mean to hurt you. After all, I am a voman und I do like to get dressed up vunce in a vhile to remind me dat I am a voman. All you tink of me is a cook, just a cook!"

"Und a darned good vun at dat!" Peter retorted.

"Oh! You men!" Osa snapped with a tone of exasperation. "Here," She slapped food on Peter's tray. "Go und eat. Get fat. Go! Go!" Peter roared with laughter as he walked away.

"Und you, too," she said turning her attention to Harry, slapping food on his tray. "You men are all alike! Go! Go get fat like Peter!" She turned moving to the next man, slapping food on his tray with the same admonishment.

"Ahhh, dat voman," Peter commented as Harry joined him. "She is a vunderful person. I hope she don't take me serious. I like to tease her. She needs her spirits bolstered."

"She's a fine lady," Harry added. "I met her while I was getting oriented to the ship. I guess I didn't realize women were allowed aboard ship –"

"Just dis vun." Peter interrupted. "In her case, it is different, special."

"Yeah. I kinda gathered that," Harry replied. "She's more than a cook; she's the Captain's niece."

"Dat is right. He brought her along on dis trip because he vanted her to see der vorld. Und vat better vay dan on his ship?" he said and gave a slight chuckle.

"She's more than just an ordinary cook, though," Harry said. "I noticed she's wearing a wedding ring. Is she married to an officer or one of the crew? Except for you and the Captain, the rest of the crew seem a little young for her. No offense intended, ya' understand."

Peter laughed. "No. She is not married to any of der crew. She is a vidow. She lost her husband last year in a terrible auto accident."

"I'm sorry to hear that," Harry replied, his attention perking up. "Was she badly injured?"

Peter hesitated, holding his forkful of mashed potatoes before him, and then motioned Harry closer. "I vill tell you dis," he said in whispered confidence. "Der tragic part of her husband's death vas dat he vas killed vis a beautiful young girl – how you say it – vis a hooker? Both ver killed instantly."

"With a hooker?" Harry frowned in disbelief. "Why chase young stuff when you have a woman like Osa at home?"

"I don't know. It vas tragic. Der deaths und der publicity about her husband, who vas a prominent attorney in Stockholm, just about killed poor Osa. She had to get avay, und Captain Andress asked her to sail vis us. Our cook had retired dis past year und it vas good timing. Der trip und der job of cooking for dis crew vould keep her occupied und her mind off her troubles."

"Good thinking," Harry responded thinking of his situation. "Hard work gets your mind off your problems. I know."

"Yah. Und to top it off, ve got us a darned good cook." Peter laughed patting his stomach.

"I agree," Harry replied with a grin. "I'm going to have to exercise twice as hard to work off all these calories."

"Und remember," Peter cautioned, shaking his fork in Harry's face, "all dis information is strictly confidential. Don't say anyting to Osa. I don't vant her to know I told you"

"Not a word. Scout's honor," Harry said crossing his heart with his index finger. "I have a better appreciation of the lady now. Not a word."

"Dat's der ticket! Dat's der vay Captain Andress vants her treated, a lady. He is very fond of her, and voe to der man who hurts her. He is extremely protective of her. I should varn you dat der section of der ship ver her cabin is located is off limits to all crewmembers. No man dares enter dere visout der Captain's permission. No sir, he is very protective of her. He vants to help her overcome her grief from der tragedy. It must hurt to lose somevun you ver so close to, somevun who shared your life und den to lose dem under such tragic circumstances. Tch, tch," he added with a forlorn shake of his head.

Harry laid his fork down. A lump the size of a baseball had suddenly formed in his throat. It still hurt; it hurt like hell. Every time he thought of Sandy he choked up. What a senseless waste of life. The Chink should burn in hell.

Peter was staring at him.

"Uh, I'll see you later on watch," Harry said. "I guess I'm not as hungry as I thought." He picked up his tray and left.

Peter looked after him momentarily, shrugged, and then continued eating. Osa glanced up from where she was serving, surprised at seeing Harry leave so abruptly. She hurried over to Peter wiping her hands in her apron. "Is Harry sick? He didn't finish his food, und I have prepared cherry pie for dessert."

"I don't know. He seemed suddenly upset. I don't know if it vas someting he ate or someting I said. It certainly couldn't be der food. It is excellent, as usual."

Osa smiled at the compliment. But it bothered her that Harry left so abruptly, and without even a nod or word to her.

Chapter 32
HEAVY SEAS AND SEASICKNESS

Nightfall found *Nurad* steaming up the St. Lawrence Seaway making good time in spite of the continuing foul weather. Harry stepped on deck for a couple of minutes for a breathtaking view of Quebec, its lights shining brightly through new falling snow, neon signs gaudy, the streets bustling with activity. Sandy would have liked this city with all its hustle and bustle. It was the kind of place she would have chosen for a romantic, getaway weekend: laughing, smooching over a delicious meal, teasing, feeling the sexual tension building and knowing they'd end up in the sack wrapped up in each other's arms, grunting and groaning in ecstasy. He shook his head; it was all gone now. Grimly, he turned and stepped inside the first hatchway; it was time for duty on the midnight watch.

A new pilot had come on board. Unlike the previous pilot, this one was all business. He worked closely with the command officer guiding the ship along the last leg of its journey up the St. Lawrence river. At the helm, Harry responded attentively to commands, keeping the ship on an even northeasterly course toward the Gulf of the St. Lawrence and the Atlantic Ocean.

Harry's thoughts turned to Osa. Her husband must have been some kind of jerk. She was one sweet, classy lady. Classy. She had an outgoing personality and good looks. Why cheat on someone like that? She deserved better.

"Keep your eyes open, now, Harry. Ve vill see more traffic as ve get closer to der Gulf of der St. Lawrence," Peter said easing close to him.

Within a couple of hours *Nurad* was moving to a new rhythm. Harry sensed it at the helm, a different feel to the ship as it plowed through large rolling swells, much different than the waters of the river or the Great Lakes. The rising, falling swells of the North Atlantic Ocean moved the behemoth to a new tempo.

Rounding Cape Breton Island, *Nurad* started its southward journey toward the Panama Canal.

Second Officer Helmstrund, their relief, mentioned that Osa was in the galley early this morning and had prepared an excellent breakfast. Surprised, Peter and Harry headed for the galley on the double.

Peter stopped momentarily on deck to gaze out across the dark, somber ocean. "Can you feel it?" he asked Harry, who had stopped by his side. "Der is a different feeling underfoot ven you sail on der ocean."

"Yeah," Harry replied. He was already aware of the change as the ship rose, dropped, pitched sideways and then rose again. Even at this moment he sensed a squeamish feeling grabbing at his stomach. He knew he had to get to the galley and get food into him quickly or he'd be seasick. Why, he never knew, but he always got seasick the first day on the ocean. Once having regained his sea legs he was all right.

"C'mon, Peter," he urged. "Let's go eat."

Hurriedly he moved through the serving line. Osa had prepared a sumptuous breakfast of eggs, bacon, fried potatoes, sausage and buttered toast. Harry failed to savor all the culinary delights but quickly filled his tray, giving Osa but a scant nod of recognition as he hurried off to a table where he began wolfing down his food.

"I didn't realize you ver so hungry," Peter said joining him. "Of course, I admit I am starved but you, you dashed right trough der line, und you hardly said a vord to Osa."

"Sorry," he said.

"Since ve get into der ocean und der rolling of der ship, I find I eat more. Is dat how you feel?"

Harry looked over at his friend and nodded, not missing a forkful of food. He knew he had to get food in his stomach. There was nothing worse than the dry heaves. A twinge passed through him; it was coming, that sick, nauseous feeling, the sudden perspiration, the gulping, trying to keep everything down. Glancing up, he was aware that Peter was staring at him. Then, he saw others were also staring at him, even Osa, who had stopped serving, a puzzled look on her face.

"Vat is der matter?" Peter asked. "You don't look too good."

Harry shook his head no. Already his stomach was doing flip flops. He grabbed up the sausage and toast, rolled them in a napkin and stuffed them in his jacket pocket. Then, amidst knowing smiles he bolted for the passageway and the main deck.

Peter found Harry leaning out as far as possible over the railing heaving his guts out. Harry knew from past experience that you puke cross wind or you got it back all over you. He retched until he thought his stomach was going to turn inside out and he could taste his asshole.

"Are you better now?" Peter asked, patting Harry gently on his shoulders. "Do you vant some dramamine? It helps –"

"Uh-uh," Harry moaned gazing down at the windswept waters. "It makes me sick." Unable to retch anymore, his stomach feeling like a boiling cauldron, he let Peter help him to their cabin. Weakly, he kicked off his shoes, shrugged out of his jacket and, with an effort, climbed up into his bunk totally exhausted.

"If you vant, you may use my bunk. It is closer to der head," Peter offered. "Just don't puke on it, okay?"

"Nooo," Harry groaned. "I'll be okay, honest" With a pasty look, he added, "I'll be all right in just a little while. Just let me rest."

Peter stood by the bunk grinning. He knew seasickness was no laughing matter. Anyone who had ever been to sea had experienced it. Anyone who said he hadn't been was a damned liar. "Remember, I'm in der bunk below you so, please, don't trow up wisout warning." With that, Peter stripped to his shorts, crawled into his bunk, pulled the covers up over his head, eased closer to the bulkhead and, shortly, was snoring.

Harry slept fitfully, changing positions often. Whenever his stomach started churning he rolled on one side or the other. There was nothing left to upchuck.

Damn Peter. Damn his snoring. How could he sleep so soundly

when I'm dying. He twisted about on the bunk then spotted his jacket. "Make sure you have plenty of food in your stomach," a former shipmate had once said to him. "Its the best thing for fighting off seasickness."

Reaching out, Harry grabbed his jacket and dragged it up onto his stomach. Fumbling through the pockets, he found the napkin with the toast and sausage. Lying back, he began nibbling at the food, feeling it moving slowly down into his rebellious stomach. He paused time and again, and before long realized he'd eaten all the food. Then he lay still waiting for that infernal, internal signal that would trigger his mad dash to the head. Surprisingly, nothing happened. Soon, sleep overcame him allowing his exhausted body to relax.

On wakening, he found Peter standing beside his bunk watching him. "You ver moaning und groaning so badly I could not sleep. How do you feel now?"

"Lousy. I don't know if I'm gonna die or live. I always get seasick the first time out, but I can't recall it lasting this long before." He gulped, feeling a churning in his stomach. Peter jumped back out of the way. "I'm really sick this time," Harry said. "Really sick!" Perspiration stood out across his face. He gritted his teeth. He couldn't throw up anymore; he couldn't!

"If you cannot make it, ve can send you back to der mainland vis der pilot boat," Peter said in a matter-of-fact manner, almost as though this was a common practice. "Dey vill be departing shortly."

Harry grimaced at the remark. At the same moment, his stomach churned with renewed fire. No! No! He couldn't leave the ship now. Not now! He was committed to his mission. To stop now was to face a life he didn't want to face, not Saginaw, not alone without Sandy. He forced a smile onto his face, a somewhat pasty smile, but a smile. "You can count on me, I want to sail with you, count on me."

"Dat is der ticket," Peter grinned. "I haf plans for you. You are a good man, Harry Martin. You rest now. I vill see dat food is brought down to you. I must report to der bridge now but I be back soon."

Harry heard the door close but his mind was contemplating the statement Peter had made – plans for him? He closed his eyes. He'd probably die of seasickness and never find out, and then he fell asleep.

Chapter 33

THE COOK TO THE RESCUE

The gray cement walls of his cell were overpowering. Harry lay in his bunk not believing the travesty of justice that had happened to him, to be accused and found guilty of the murders of Joe, Sandy and the Chink. The damned lawyers. They twisted his words, had turned the trial into a sham. Stan had sat there with a smirk on his face, star witness for the prosecution. Outside his cell he could hear the steady tapping of hammers as they constructed the gallows. "No!" he heard himself screaming. He was innocent; it was Stan. They had the wrong man! The pounding grew louder and louder. He closed his hands over his ears but the pounding continued. It was a bad dream; that was it, it had to be a bad dream. He had to wake up. The pounding continued, growing in intensity.

Suddenly he sat bolt upright staring through glazed eyes at the wall, only it was a gray steel bulkhead, not a gray cement wall. Sweat beaded across his forehead; his whole body clammy wet. Gingerly, he reached out and touched the wall. Steel. Not a prison cell. He saw light. It was the porthole. A nervous laugh escaped his lips. Through the porthole he could see the rolling ocean and wind-whipped waves. It had been a dream, a horrible dream, but the pounding continued.

He glanced at the door. Someone was knocking. "Yes," he called out.

"Harry. It is Osa. I haf brought food for you," came her muffled reply.

"Come in, please," he called with a sigh of relief. So much for the gallows; so much for a very bad dream. Quickly he ran his fingers through his hair hoping to smooth down his tousled look, trying to look a tad more presentable. Osa peeked inside, eyes bright, smiling. "Hi. I haf food for you. Are you hungry?"

The thought of food caused a momentary churning in his stomach. "I guess I could make a stab at it," he said, rolling over and resting on his right elbow, looking down at Osa as she stepped to the desk and set down a white towel-covered tray. She looked attractive in a white sweatshirt, the sleeves pushed up, and blue slacks. Her hair was pulled back into a long blonde pigtail. As she peeled back a corner of the towel the aroma wafted upwards. Harry inhaled deeply. "Smells good."

"You eat. I vill be back later, okay?" There was a sympathetic tone to her voice, a sympathetic look in her eyes as they met his.

He offered a weak smile. "Okay," he said, almost in a whisper.

She smiled, happy to see a more lively look on his stubble-covered face. "See you soon," she said and left.

The door closed and Harry shucked off his covers and rolled over the edge of the bunk slowly lowering himself to the deck. He held on tightly to the bunk frame for support sensing the pitch and roll of the ship. Although giddy, he felt a smidgeon stronger.

Unsteadily, he crossed to the desk, pulled out the chair and plopped down on it. Lifting the towel, his eyes feasted on hot, homemade vegetable soup, oyster crackers, a grilled cheese sandwich and a pot of steaming coffee.

He slowly pecked away at the food, alert to any sudden twinge that would send him dashing for the head. Nothing happened. He continued eating. The food stayed down. Before he realized it, he had devoured the sandwich, slurped down the soup and was downing the last of the coffee, all without the faintest inkling of nausea. With a sigh of relief, he let out a healthy burp, climbed back into his bunk, yanked the covers over himself and within a matter of minutes had dozed off.

Sleep was short lived, however, for he awoke to find Peter and several crew members standing beside his bunk. "Vell, how is der landlubber?" Peter grinned. "Yah," said Hans. "Ve vill haf to get a helicopter out here to ship you home. Vunce a landlubber, alvays a landlubber!"

"Yah, he has rubber legs, not sea legs," another chimed in. "Maybe ve keep him for shark bait."

The good-natured ribbing continued at Harry's expense. He took it in stride. He deserved it for he had been through it before, every time he had sailed. Even he was guilty of mocking seasick shipmates when they had spewed their guts out.

A knock on the door interrupted their fun. "Come in," Peter called. Osa's smiling face peeked inside. "I came to get der dishes –" The smile disappeared at seeing all the men around Harry. Of a sudden, she realized they were harassing him.

"Shame on you!" she exclaimed angrily. "He is sick. You are picking on him. Out! Get out! All of you!" Like a protective mother hen she moved quickly into the cabin. "Out! Out!" she cried as she shushed them out the door, amidst their laughter and half-hearted protests. Slamming the door shut after them, she turned only to see Peter still standing by the bunk, grinning like a Cheshire cat. "You, too," she glared. "Out!"

"But Osa," he protested. "Dis is my cabin. I live here!"

"Oh! Dat's right!" She snapped acknowledging the fact. "Vell, den, don't pick on Harry." She waggled her finger under his nose. "You should know better dan dat."

Peter backed off, still grinning. "Okay, okay, I behave myself, honest. I von't pick on poor Harry."

Harry watched, amused at her sudden defense. Her anger dissipated when she saw the empty tray. "Good!" she beamed. "You haf eaten all der food. How do you feel now?"

"Good. The food was good. I even kept it down."

"Good! Good!" she exclaimed. She went to the bathroom, grabbed up a washcloth, wet it, wrung it out, then returned and gently wiped the perspiration from his face. The moistness felt cool and refreshing to him. Her hand was soft, gentle, as it moved over his unshaven face. He closed his eyes enjoying the attention. "You stay in bed. I vill bring dinner down to you later. You must build up your strength." She tucked the covers around his neck as she spoke.

Gathering up the tray of dirty dishes, she started for the door.

Peter stepped to the door opening it for her. As she passed him, she said, "Und if I hear of any more shenanigans, you and dem vill get bread and vater for a veek!"

Peter laughed heartily closing the door after her. "Dat Osa. She is vun fine voman. Vun moment she is cool und aloof; der next a clucking mudder hen. I tink she likes you, Harry –" But his words fell on deaf ears, Harry had fallen back asleep.

Harry woke to the fanning of pages. Glancing over the edge of his bunk, he saw Peter sitting at the desk glancing through a Swedish girlie magazine.

"Don't wear out the pages," Harry admonished.

"Oh, Harry, you're avake. Good." Peter dropped the magazine back in the desk drawer and stepped over to the bunk "You look trough dose pages at all dat young stuff. Whew! I don't know vat I vould do if I ever had such an opportunity vis vun of dos girls."

Harry laughed. "Sex sells. Women are getting bolder, want to show off their charms, what better way than in a magazine that caters to men."

"Yah, but I guess I am getting older. I like der old fashioned morals. I like it der vay it vas vis my wife, dating, kissing, long walks, an occasional touch. Save it for der vedding night."

"World's changing, Peter. Some colleges are even encouraging guys and girls to live in the same dormitory. I don't like it, but what the hell. I'm just one voice. But, then –" He stopped, for the thought of Sandy suddenly came to mind. She had been in college during that period, had spoken about the crazy times in her co-ed dorm. The sexual revolution had happened. She was emancipated; she was a part of the revolution. In fact, she had changed him. She had an aggressive appetite for sex. Would he ever find another jewel like her?

"Do you tink you'll be up to vorking on the midnight vatch?"

Harry's eyes widened. "I missed the noon watch?"

"You ver sick. I took care of it. No problem."

"Shit!" Harry swore. "Yes, I will make it tonight. You can count on me." He tossed off the covers, stretched and dangled his legs over the edge of the bunk. Easing himself onto the deck, he stood quietly holding onto the bunk frame for support. After a moment, he began walking around the cabin. "I'm almost there," he grinned at Peter as he continued, picking up the pace. "I'm really feeling better." The nausea was gone. He twirled around and stopped, slapping Peter soundly on his shoulder. "No kidding. I'm gonna live after all." Peter chuckled at the remark.

There was a knock at the door. Harry grabbed the doorknob and flung the door wide open. Osa stood before him with a tray of food.

"Harry, vot are you doing out of bed?" she said, startled at seeing him standing before her. Then, as her eyes took in his total being, she gasped for he was dressed only in his undershorts. Just as quickly, her head turned, eyes suddenly transfixed on the doorframe.

"Oops! Sorry," he said at her embarrassment, and turning, he grabbed for his pants, pulled them on and zipped up.

"I'm going to live, I'm gonna live," he said, laughing, grabbing her around the waist, dancing her around the cabin.

"Stop!" she screamed balancing the tray precariously, fearful of spilling its hot contents across the deck. "Harry, stop it! I vill spill der food!"

"Hey, I feel a hundred percent better."

"You are crazy," she laughed, breaking free, quickly setting the tray on the desk. "Crazy!"

"Aw, Osa, I feel good, thanks to you," he replied, peering over her shoulder as she uncovered the tray. "Uhmmm." His eyes swept over the mouth-watering array: boiled fish, mashed potatoes, green beans, fresh-baked bread with melted butter on top and a pot of coffee. "Beautiful! And I am hungry!"

"Sit und eat," she beamed, pleased at the compliment, further pleased at his speedy recover.

Harry needed no urging. He sat down and began eating, complimenting her several times about the delicious taste, which made her glow. "Oh, and Osa, thank you for your personal service. It's greatly appreciated."

"You are velcome," she replied with a slight curtsy. "Dis is der first time I haf served a crewmember in his cabin, but den, dis is der first time I haf ever seen such a really seasick sailor."

The teasing remark elicited a sour look from Harry. "Funny," he said. "Funny."

"I suppose I vill haf to go to der galley if I vant to eat," Peter said wearing a pained expression.

Osa caught the remark. "You get sick und I bring you food, too. But don't tink I give maid service. Just food. I don't go to men's cabins. It is wrong. You get sick. I feed you, und no more!"

"I didn't imply anyting" You were an angel come to my rescue, Harry hastily interjected. "I thank you for arriving in the nick of time." He raised her hand and softly brushed it with his lips.

"Ohhh, Harry," she cooed. "You embarrass me." Flustered, she jerked her hand back. "I-I must go now und set out der food for der odders. Uh, you must get dressed for vork, yah?"

She scooped up the tray of dirty dishes and hurried to the door. As she opened it to leave, she gasped. The clenched fist of Captain Andress had just started down to knock on the door.

"Uncle Karl!" Osa exclaimed shrinking back, almost dropping her tray.

"Osa!" he said, astounded at seeing her. "Vot are you doing here?" He glanced beyond her at Harry, then saw Peter and was relieved that the two weren't alone in the cabin. "Are you tending to der ill now?"

"He vas too sick to go to der galley," Peter added hastily.

"Ahhh, so it vas easier to feed him in der cabin."

"Yes, uncle. It vas." Osa felt intimidated by her uncle's stern look. He wouldn't dare think that she, that she and Harry-heavens no!

"Und how are you feeling now, Harry?" the Captain asked turning his attention to him, stepping into the cabin as he spoke.

"Better, sir. Much better. This morning I didn't think I was going to make it, but through the grace of God and Osa's fine cooking, plus the spirited support of the crew –" he gave a sideways glance in Peter's direction – "why, it looks like I'll survive. I'll be ready for duty tonight."

Captain Andress beamed at the remark. "Dat is good, Harry. Dat is good."

"Und did you do der honors of formally introducing Harry to my beautiful niece, Osa?" he said looking at Peter.

"Uh, dey had already met, sir," Peter replied. "In der galley earlier."

"Good." Captain Andress glanced at Harry, then Osa. "Osa is a vunderful, girl, Harry. I am very proud of her, except at der moment. I am disappointed in her —"

"Vy?" demanded Osa, surprised at the remark, looking askance at her uncle. "Vot haf I done?"

"Vell, you know dis part of der ship is off limits to females. You should not be here." Although his voice was stern, there was a twinkle in his eye as he winked at Peter. "You know how I feel about people being in off-limit areas."

"But Harry's sick," she protested. "He needed nourishment."

"True. All I said vas dis area is off limits, much like your part of der ship is off limits to men. Dat's all." He scratched at his beard for a moment, and then added, "Of course, I'm sure dere are circumstances dat occur ven rules might be broken, such as now, to assist a sick person."

Peter scratched his head. What was the man driving at?

Captain Andress turned his attention to Harry, taking in his unkempt appearance, mussed hair and swarthy whisker growth. "I suggest you get cleaned up before reporting for duty," he said as he headed for the door, "und dis time don't take a shower mit your clothes on." The door clicked shut behind him.

Osa almost dropped the tray of dishes. Her eyes darted to Harry, her uncle knew.

"Ven did you take a shower vis your clothes on?" Peter asked somewhat perplexed at the captain's comment.

"Uhhh, I stepped into the shower to check out a dripping handle. I accidentally turned it the wrong way and got soaked. The captain thought it was funny."

"Oh." Peter smiled, accepting the explanation. He glanced at his watch. "I vill see you later. I got tings to take care of."

As the door closed behind him, Osa looked at Harry. "I am so embarrassed," she said. "Uncle Karl knows you ver in my cabin. He vill tink I am not a nice girl."

"I doubt that. I think he understands it was an innocent mistake on my part." He laughed. "It was dumb and I'm sure I must have looked dumb walking down the corridor soaking wet.

"You did," she said, laughing. "You really did."

Their eyes met, locked on each other for a moment, and then her eyes shifted to the tray of dirty dishes. "Uh, I must go to der galley to serve dinner. I see you later?"

"Yeah, later. I gotta get cleaned up and ready for duty."

Once again their eyes met. Harry felt prickly warmth as he gazed into hers. Again, she shifted, breaking eye contact. What was it about her that bothered him? Here was a mature, fully blossomed woman, yet she wore the aura of innocence of a young maiden.

Osa, too, had felt a tingling warmth radiating through her and immediately broke eye contact. She didn't want to be accused of flirting. "Goodbye," she said of a sudden and quickly let herself out.

Chapter 34

TRAVERSING THE PANAMA CANAL

Foreboding snow clouds changed to fleecy white as *Nurad* moved ever southward leaving the cold, surging, wind-whipped swells of the North Atlantic for warmer, calmer waters and the soft caress of the tradewinds.

Huge masses of ice clinging tenaciously to the ship's superstructure broke free with sharp, cracking sounds, crashing into the ocean or shattering across the steel deck and spilling over the side. Many hours were spent by the crew chopping ice free and heaving chunks overboard.

Within a couple of days the weather changed dramatically climbing into the 70's, and Harry found himself digging into his locker to get out light-weight work clothes.

As they moved further south beyond Florida and into the Caribbean Sea on a steady course toward Panama Canal, Harry began seeing a greater variety of ships in the shipping lanes.

Duty watch became more demanding. He was constantly scanning the horizon, and then the radar scope, then back to the horizon for visual location of ships. Through his binoculars he distinguished ships of varying sizes and makes: tankers, freighters, containerized cargo ships, super tankers, passenger ships, small coastal freighters and countless colorful yachts of all descriptions happily sailing the placid waters of the Caribbean.

The *Otto J. Nurad* arrived off Panama Canal early one morning just after daybreak and waited its turn to enter the Port of Cristobal. On deck, having gone off watch and yet too excited at being at the Panama Canal to hit the sack, Harry stood watching the passing scene. He felt a big lump in his throat at seeing two large American aircraft carriers and four destroyer escorts move past them, old glory waving boldly in the slanting rays of the morning sun. Almost automatically, he snapped to attention as the ships passed. The red, white and blue never looked better.

Then it was *Nurad's* turn to enter the Panama Canal and began its 51-mile, fourteen-hour journey to the Pacific Ocean.

Harry walked along the upper deck stopping periodically at the railing to observe the intricate task of moving the behemoth upward eighty-five feet through the Gatun Lock's three levels. He listened to the crisp commands of the pilots to the harried, nimble lock workers, themselves a sharp contrast to the slow-paced civilians ambling along the shoreline. *Nurad's* 730-foot length and 75 foot beam was easily accommodated in the 1,000-foot length and 110 foot width of the locks.

The morning had turned hot and muggy. Harry perspired freely. Even the faintest of breezes was welcome although it had no effect on the humidity that hung heavily in the air. On glancing down at the main deck he was surprised to see the man with the angry scowl staring up at him. It was the man who had watched him as he frantically struggled to haul himself back aboard ship when he'd slipped on the ice and almost slid overboard. The scowl remained unchanged, the eyes dark, contemptuous.

What the hell is bugging you? Harry wondered, deciding the best thing to do was confront the man and settle any differences. Harry hurried down the steps to the main deck but the man had disappeared. He was nowhere in sight. Puzzled, Harry finally gave a shrug of his shoulders. So much for effort. One day they'd meet and then they'd settle any misunderstanding.

As the ship raised upwards in the lock, Harry watched fascinated, marveling at the powerful structure. This was truly one of the engineering marvels of the century and one of the great man-made wonders of the world.

Once free of the locks, *Nurad* started its slow journey across the twenty-five mile length of Gatun Lake. A sudden shower swept across the lake and Harry made a quick dash for cover under the back superstructure, almost bumping into Osa who was just stepping on deck.

"Oops!" he cracked. "We've got to stop meeting like this."

"But I just came on deck," she said, perplexed at his remark.

Harry chuckled. "Just an old American saying. Forget it."

They stood back under the overhanging deck out of the rain. Just as quickly as it began, the rain stopped. Already, the deck was steamy as the evaporating water rolled in a snaking fog across the hot steel plates.

"It is beautiful here," Osa said taking a deep breath, gazing out across the lake.

"Yeah, it is," Harry replied, studying her out of the corner of his eye, the golden blonde hair, and looking cool and comfortable in a white, lightweight, sleeveless cotton dress.

Harry wiped the perspiration from his brow. "It's too hot, too muggy," he added after several moments. "I prefer the northern climate. I like the changing seasons: spring, summer, fall and winter – and skiing."

"You ski?" There was excitement in her voice, in her eyes, as she looked at him.

"Yeah. Downhill and cross-country. Why?"

"I ski, too," she beamed.

"Really?" Harry's interest perked up. "Where do you ski?"

"My family lives in der middle part of Sveden at der base of a large mountain, a little town you vouldn't know. Dey operate a ski resort. It has become a very popular ski resort for downhill skiers. Ven I am home in der vinter, I am alvays skiing. I luf it!"

"You must be a good skier."

"Vell, I like to tink so. I am a member of der ski patrol."

"I'd say you're a good skier then. Me, I'm more the intermediate class skier, too advanced for the 'bunny hill' but not quite up to the mogols. Of course, the hills in northern Michigan can't compare with the mountains of Sweden. But, we do have a lot of fun."

"Yah. Ve can ski five, sometimes eight kilometers down der slopes of der mountain. You should come to Sveden. I vould be happy to show you how ve ski."

"Thanks for the invitation," Harry grinned. "Maybe I'll take you up on it one day."

"I am serious. Der invitation stands."

"Accepted." His grin broadened. "And cross-country?"

"Oh, yes. Ve haf many kilometers of trails trouout der countryside. It is very healthy." She took a deep breath, and then laughed. "I sound like you. I, too, enjoy der changing seasons."

Harry laughed, wiping his forehead again. "Here we are both sweltering from the humidity in this 90 degree weather, in the shade, yet, and we stand here talking about skiing in the winter, the foul weather we just sailed out of. I think we're both crazy."

She laughed. It was a deep, throaty laugh. "Ve are silly. If anyvun overheard us dey vould tink ve vas a little, how you say it, mit a loose screw?" She pointed her finger at her head making a small circular motion.

"Right. Screwy. Lost our marbles," Harry added. She laughed harder. He liked the sound of her laughter; it was wholesome, honest, not forced.

The sun sparkled off the water. Along the shoreline thick foliage grew right down to the water's edge. A light, warm breeze rippled the surface of the lake.

"I understand the trip through the canal takes about fourteen hours," Harry said after a bit. "I've never been this way before."

"Nor haf I." Her reply was quick. "I tink it is very interesting I - I also enjoy talking vis you."

"Oh?" he said, pleased.

She gave a nervous smile. "Vat I mean is dat you are nice, comfortable to talk to, uh, you make me feel at ease, dat is, good. Oh! It is hard to explain –"

"No, don't explain. I know what you mean," he grinned. "I enjoy talking to you, too. You make me feel good." And she did, he admitted to himself.

Of a sudden, he wished he could unload, tell her of his problem, but he couldn't; he couldn't share his problem with anyone. Besides, she had her own problems. It was best they stick to small talk. At least he had someone to talk to and that was helpful.

"Uummm," she inhaled deeply. "Can you smell der fragrance?"

Harry sniffed. "Yeah. It's that sexy perfume you've got on. Love it."

"No," she giggled. "It is not my perfume. It is der vild flowers in der jungle. Dey smell like dat."

He took a deep breath. "Are you sure? I'd swear that's the scent I caught in your cabin the other day."

"Harry!" she exclaimed, suddenly glancing about to make sure his comment wasn't heard by others. Except for her uncle and his fussing concern for her well being, no man had entered her cabin. It was her personal domain, a place where she could escape from the pressures of her daily routine or fall exhausted across her bed to sleep, escaping the haunting, tormenting memories of Rudy – Rudy in the arms of that young slut. A memory which constantly reminded her of her own feelings of sexual inadequacy.

"Whew! Look at the size of that ship coming along now," Harry said, interrupting her thoughts. "C'mon. Let's get over to the other side and watch it pass."

He grabbed her hand and pulled her along after him to the other side of the ship where they stood at the railing watching. It was a huge Japanese freighter, one of the newer containerized ships carrying thousands of cars to the east coast. Help the defeated bastards and put Americans out of jobs. Harry knew full well the loss of jobs in the auto industry in Saginaw, Flint and Detroit, but it seemed our government doesn't give a damn, he thought.

He was suddenly aware that he was still holding her hand. Reluctantly, he released it. Osa caught the movement, disappointed as her hand fell free coming to rest on the railing. Unnoticed, she moved it closer to his.

The Japanese waved and they waved back, laughing.

"Vell, are you two enjoying dis beautiful weather?" Captain Andress said, approaching them, a wide, paternal smile on his face. "Osa, you look absolutely lovely. I haven't see you look so radiant, such nice color in your cheeks. Dat is good. Dat is good."

Osa blushed at the remark. Why was it, even at her age, he treated her as he did when she was a little girl. She was an adult now and, yet, just the way he spoke to her, especially now in front of Harry, why did she blush like a little girl? She looked away, angry with herself. After a moment, and composed, she turned to her uncle. "Uncle Karl, you embarrass me –"

"Come, come, child. It is true. It must be der salt air und sunshine," he teased, winking at Harry. "You look so youthful. Here you are getting younger and younger und I, I am getting older by der minute. Tch. Tch. It is not fair, now is it, Harry?"

"No, sir," Harry replied. "She is getting prettier." He was grinning at her embarrassment, but more so, grinning because he felt like a kid caught making time with the boss's daughter, and it was imperative to say something witty.

"Oh, you men are all alike!" Osa said with a feigned sigh of disgust. Yet, she was pleased at Harry's comment, especially in front of her uncle.

"It's a scorcher today," Harry said, changing the subject.

"Yah. But ve vill be picking up der cool breezes of der Pacific Ocean in a few hours und den ve vill make good time as ve head directly for Shanghai," replied Captain Andress.

Harry nodded. He liked the man. For being in his sixties, he was pretty sharp, alert. Today, dressed smartly in whites: white shirt with Captain's epaulettes, white shorts and even white calf-high socks and white shoes, the man seemed to tower over him. He was the epitome of the command officer.

"Do you like our cook?" he asked almost casually of Harry as he reached out and pulled Osa close to him, hugging her to his side. "She is a good cook, yah?"

"Excellent. I've never tasted better cooking." Harry felt somewhat embarrassed for Osa who looked quite uncomfortable trapped by her uncle's huge arm, unable to escape.

"Uncle Karl, please," she said, struggling to break free.

He laughed, releasing her from his grip. "Okay, okay, I am just teasing. I luf to tease her, der vay she turns beet red. Ven she vas a little girl she alvays took off her clothes und ran around naked. I vould tease her und she vould turn beet red all over her body –"

"Uncle!" exclaimed Osa, glaring at him. "Don't tell dat!"

Captain Andress threw his head back roaring with laughter. "Okay I am sorry." He wiped at his eyes, still chuckling, much to

183

her discomfort. "I shut up," he said, his body still shaking with laughter. "Besides, she vas only tree or four years old." He patted her hand. "I don't tell dat story any more." Osa breathed a sigh of relief but dared not look at Harry. Why? She didn't know.

"Dis voman is really remarkable, Harry. Did you know dat?"

"How so?"

"She is not only a good cook, but she has a brain. She vas a schoolteacher, a professor at der University of Stockholm. Yah. She has an advanced degree in home economics. Dat is vat she taught at der university."

"Very admirable," Harry said looking at Osa. "That's a demanding area of study."

The anger she had felt at the embarrassment caused by her uncle softened when she looked up and caught Harry looking at her. Again, sudden warmth coursed through her body.

"But she vas restless, vanted to get avay," the captain continued. "So, I talked her into taking a sea voyage. Besides, our cook had qvit und ve needed a good cook. My men ver starving on der food der previous cook fed dem. Lots of complaints. Now, ve eat good. Und der trip has done vunders for her complexion. Don't you tink so?"

"Yes, I do," Harry said without taking his eyes from her. "She's getting prettier all the time."

"Ahhh, you men," Osa said stepping away from them. "I haf better tings to do dan stand here und haf you discuss me. I must prepare der food for lunch."

"Vait!" Captain Andress said grabbing her wrist, pulling her around. "You are not der only smart vun here. Dis man, Harry Martin, he is a scholarly person, too. I haf reviewed his papers thoroughly. He holds a master's degree, an advanced degree like yours, only in public relations –"

"Now you embarrass me," Harry quipped with a sheepish grin. But in his mind he was quickly recalling the papers he had provided. There was nothing in them to indicate he had a master's degree. Interesting. Someone did some research on him, more than likely before they even entered the St. Lawrence Seaway, and they must have approved, or he'd have gone ashore on the pilot boat.

"Yah. A master's degree, und single," the captain added. "Dat is interesting, yah?"

"Oh?" Osa hoped her utterance wasn't that noticeable, but saw they were looking at her. "Lunch, I just remembered. I must go. Lunch," she said and walked quickly away.

"Save me a cup of coffee and a hot roll," Harry called after her. "I forgot all about breakfast."

Captain Andress looked from Harry to the departing figure of his niece. "She is a vunderful girl, a smart vun, too. But she is still just a little girl to me."

"A beautiful woman the way I see it," Harry countered. "She has a good personality. I enjoy talking to her." He leaned back against the railing turning his attention to the Captain. "I don't recall a copy of my resume amongst my sailing papers."

Captain Andress winked. "Isn't it amazing vat a simple phone call can accomplish in providing information."

"I see." Harry scratched his chin. "And –"

"I know all about you, Harry Martin. Oh, you haf my deep condolences on der death of your young companion. Dat vas tragic." He paused for several seconds watching as a large tanker moved by. "Italian," he said motioning toward the ship. "Dey don't run a clean ship. Dirty. Everyvhere is dirt und rust. Look along the length of the ship. Rust everywhere. Bad. I sailed on vun of dere ships just vunce. No more."

Harry watched after the departing ship waiting for the other shoe to drop. Was there something, some point the Captain wanted to get across?

"Yah, der police officer who responded to my inquiry knows you real well. He is a sergeant," Harry nodded. It was Frank. "Und he spoke very highly of you, even made it a point to tell me of all your good qualities. He also pointed out dat you are not a suspect in der girl's murder. He said dey are still vorking on the case."

Harry nodded again. "That's good to hear. Good to see the investigation is continuing." One day, when his journey was completed, he'd have to sit down with Frank and tell him about the Chink, that the murderer was dead. Yet, the journey was far from ended; Stan was still on the loose and there were thousands of miles yet to cover.

"I vas impressed by your education and qualifications. I found myself vundering vy such an educated person vould vant to sail on a lowly grain carrier?"

"To get away," Harry replied. "I had met Peter in the bar that night when the young sailor was injured and before Sandy was murdered. I got to talking with him about shipping out again, kind of toyed with the idea of sailing on your ship seeing as you were one hand shy. I'm a carpenter and right now the building trades business is at rock bottom. I figured I could ship out with you for six months. I'd be earning money and then when I got back, maybe the construction business might have picked up and I'd go back to my regular job."

"Yah, I see," Captain Andress nodded. "And der girl?"

"When she was murdered I freaked out. I knew if I stayed in Saginaw it meant seeing all our old friends and acquaintances, going to the same haunts, same bars, places where we had been before and had so much fun, and now –" He paused, gulping, trying to force down a huge lump in his throat. "I'd be wondering all the time why I hadn't got to her quick enough to save her life. It's terrible seeing the one you love like that."

"I understand," Captain Andress said, patting Harry paternally on his shoulder. "I understand."

"All these thoughts preyed on my mind. I had to get away, keep myself busy as hell in order not to think back –" He stopped, turned away blinking back tears. They watched in silence as another ship passed.

"How long did you say you haf been divorced?" the Captain broached after several minutes.

"About five years. Why?" Harry felt a sudden irritation at the question, an intrusion into his privacy. His divorce was none of the Captain's business. One more question and he'd tell him his personal life was none of his damned business.

"Just curious." He brushed an imaginary speck of dirt off one epaulette. Leaning on the railing he looked forward past Harry.

186

"Yah," he sighed, "I tink dis trip vill be good for you, und Osa, too. I tink so."

Harry let the remark slide by, turning to look forward as another ship hove into view.

"Vell, I must get back to der job of running dis ship," the Captain said, straightening up. "Second Officer Helmstrund is good but he needs a bit of supervision yet. Vun of dese days he vill be a darn good officer, probably a captain of vun of our vessels." As he started away, he paused, and then looked askance at Harry. "Der section of der ship Osa is in is still off limits. She is a nice girl. I vant to keep her dat vay. Understood?"

Harry felt a flush of anger. He knew he'd been in her cabin. There was no sense in trying to explain at this late date.

"Understood," he replied stoically.

"You haf permission to explore all der rest of der ship, but not dere." Then he was gone.

Harry slapped his hands hard on the railing. If that old coot thinks I've got any romantic notions about his niece, he's got another think coming. I don't need that kind of involvement!

Chapter 35

A FRIENDLY PASS; A SHARP REBUKE

Nurad continued its journey around the Gamboa Reach, through the Gaillard Cut, and on along the Empire Reach. Like many of the other crew not on duty, Harry spent the entire morning since coming off duty on deck enjoying the never-ending panorama unfolding before him. Reluctantly, he had forced himself into the galley for an early lunch before reporting for duty on the noon watch.

It was business as usual. Captain Andress was on the bridge observing his first officer and pilot as they brought the ship smoothly along the passageway. Harry stood alert, quickly responding to commands. At times he had an uncomfortable feeling that Captain Andress was staring at him. *No, I'm not gonna seduce your little niece, for chrissakes,* he mused. *I've got enough problems without getting involved with her.* And then his watch was over.

Before long they were approaching the Pedro Miguel Locks, only a short distance from the Pacific Ocean. While the ship prepared to lock through, Harry unconsciously looked about him. It occurred to him that he hadn't seen Osa since early lunch, and then only for a cheerful wave and silent "Hi!" *Poor girl, the Captain had embarrassed both of them.* She probably had better things to do than stand on deck and watch the passing scene. He shrugged. *Nice lady, just not my type.*

Osa stepped on deck as the ship began its final descent through the Miraflores Locks, the final 85 feet to the level of the Pacific Ocean. She moved to the railing, breathtaking in a flowery sundress that clung to her lithe body, enhancing her womanly charms.

Harry glanced at his watch. Just under fourteen hours for the passage. Out of the corner of his eye he caught sight of her. He was tempted to call out but hesitated. Perhaps, after the teasing she had received from her uncle that morning, she preferred to be alone. Pretending he hadn't seen her come on deck, he moved to a spot away from her on the other side of a lifeboat davit.

Osa saw him walk away. She stood disappointed. Maybe he preferred not to talk to her because her uncle had subjected them to his boorish teasing. She gave an exasperated sigh. Should she return to her cabin? No. She had purposely bathed, perfumed and put on this dress especially for him. It was a new summery cocktail dress she had bought in Stockholm to celebrate her last birthday, only it got lost in the explosion of nasty events surrounding Rudy's death. It had hung in her closet for months. She had wondered at the time she was packing for the voyage why she brought it; now she knew.

Taking a deep breath, she strode down the deck and around the boat davit coming to a halt at the railing next to him, her hand resting a scant few inches away from his.

"Hi," she said, her voice soft and friendly.

"Hi," he replied, turning, taking in her beauty, the way the dress accentuated her charms. There was an intriguing sensuousness in the warmth of her smile, the look in her eyes. A slight breeze fanned her blonde hair curling it around her soft bare shoulders. He caught a whiff of perfume as the breeze wafted the heady fragrance to his nostrils. It was a light, delicate fragrance, very expensive. Sandy loved to indulge in a sensual application of perfume, even on the most intimate parts of her body. Did Osa apply perfume just as indulgently?

"You look beautiful this evening," he said.

"Dis?" She seemed flattered he noticed. "Just an old dress I brought along. Vun seldom has a chance to get dressed up on board a ship"

"True, but very nice."

She smiled. Inwardly, she was pleased he noticed. Why was it she felt so comfortable around him? And single. Why would a man his age be single? She'd have to talk to Uncle Karl for he seemed to know quite a bit about Harry Martin, and she wanted to know more about this man, too.

Nurad had finished locking through and their attention was, now, drawn to a bright red and black pilot boat pulling along side. Just as quickly their nimble-footed pilot descended a ladder and dropped lightly onto the deck. The boat pulled away chugging back for shore as *Nurad* faced into a brilliant orange sun settling slowly into the darkness of the Pacific Ocean.

"It vas a beautiful trip," Osa said breaking the prolonged silence "I enjoyed it."

"Same here," Harry replied. "Sharing it with you made it even more pleasant."

A wistful smile came to her face. "Tank you. I enjoyed having der opportunity of talking to you, up to der point my uncle interrupted."

He laughed. "I know."

"Speaking of interruptions," he said, looking beyond her. She turned; the galley boy stood sheepishly, his hat in his hand. "Der galley is filling up."

"Oh, my goodness!" she exclaimed with a quick glance at her watch. "I didn't realize vat time it vas. I am late. I must go." She squeezed Harry's hand. "I see you later?"

"Just like Cinderella," he grinned, "life controlled by the clock." She gave an exasperated look, laughed, then hurried off. Harry watched after her, at the shapely movement of her buttocks under the clinging cocktail dress. The boy cut off his view moving in behind her following quickly in her footsteps.

I can't figure out what it was with her husband chasing some young stuff when he had a hot looking woman like her at home, Harry thought. He must have had rocks in his head.

Dinner was over before he realized it. In spite of the food-spotted apron she wore, Osa seemed to glow as she served food to the crew. As he had moved through the line Harry tried not to make eye contact for certain thoughts had begun creeping into his mind, lustful thoughts that would grow and demand fulfillment.

Back in the solitude of his cabin, he forced himself to concentrate totally on his China mission. Now that they had entered the Pacific Ocean, time was of the essence. There was much to be done. Yet, his mind kept wandering back to Osa, her warm smile, lilting throaty laugh, enticing perfume, full breasts and –

No! He cajoled himself. There is no place for her in your thoughts. Retrieving the money is the most important, singular thing that should be on my mind. Any thoughts of her, any thoughts about sex shall be stricken from my mind!

Opening his sea chest at the foot of his bunk, Harry pulled out his winter jacket, held it high and examined it. In the short space of time he had available to him he had already been able to accomplish certain changes in its outwards appearance. He had slit the inner nylon material and carefully pulled the alpaca lining out of each pocket. Each pocket was just a shade larger than the size of a dollar bill. When completed each pocket would be able to hold a packet of bills about two inches thick, hopefully all large denomination bills. Once the pockets were filled, they'd be sealed with the Velcro tabs, and then the jacket would take on its original bulky appearance. Now he was involved in the tedious task of sewing Velcro strips to the opening of each of the pockets.

Sewing had become a time-consuming part of his task. He found himself constantly on edge, fearful of Peter popping in on him, asking questions that he preferred not to answer. Yet, of late, he noticed Peter was extremely busy off running about the ship. He sensed the man was under a lot of tension and he did his best to stay out of his way.

He had only been sewing a short time when his thoughts strayed to Osa. Dammit! She looked so gorgeous standing on deck by the rail, the bare shoulders, rise and fall of her breasts under the clinging material of that sexy dress, and that look in her eyes. There was a message there, an invitation.

A sound outside the cabin interrupted his thoughts. Peter! Quickly he gathered up the Velcro, sewing kit and jacket and was stuffing everything into the bottom of his sea chest just as the door opened.

"Hello," Peter said stopping just inside the cabin, doffing his cap and sailing it across the room where it landed on his bunk. "Haf you lost someting?" he asked seeing Harry kneeling at the foot of the bunk

"No. Nothing. I was just checking for something in my sea chest." His fingers passed over the covers of his banjo albums. "I thought I'd give the crew a treat tonight," he said pulling out the albums. "Just a few good banjo recordings."

"Banjo music?" Peter asked quizzically.

"Banjo! You mean to tell me you've never heard banjo music before?" Harry held the albums up for him to see. "Why it's the native musical instrument of America, mom, apple pie, fun and happiness, sing-along and hand clapping music." He closed the lid on his sea chest and stood handing the albums to Peter. "These are my favorite albums. Think the crew would like a little American culture?"

Peter laughed as he glanced at each of the albums. "Yah. Good idea. I know of der banjo. Come. Ve go to der galley und play dem." He tucked the albums under his arm and together they headed for the galley.

The room was somewhat subdued, a sharp contrast from the hubbub at mealtimes. Crewmembers were relaxing, playing cards, reading, writing letters and involved in any number of lively discussions. Harry was surprised at finding Osa socializing with them. It was the first time he'd seen her in the galley in the evening. She had changed to gray slacks and a soft, pale blue pullover sweater Her face lit up at seeing Harry enter.

"Your attention, please," Peter called out. "Ve haf a special treat tonight. Harry has brought along some of his American banjo records vich he vill play for us. I tink you vill enjoy dem." He turned, thrusting the albums into Harry's hands. "Tell dem."

Harry stood awkwardly for a moment trying to think of what he could say about the music. "Well, there's not too much to say about the banjo. It's a different kind of instrument, a different kind of music. I think the best thing I could do would be to play the albums and let you decide for yourselves if you like it or not."

Turning to Peter, he asked, "Where's your record player?"

"Come," Osa said jumping to her feet. "I vill show you ver der record player is." She led Harry back to a small room on the far side of the kitchen. "Dis is my office und dis is our record player," Osa beamed. The smile on his face faded as he looked toward a corner shelf unit on which stood a record player that had obviously seen much better times. There was a stack of worn albums, most sans jackets, next to the unit. A cursory check shocked him; it looked like they had been through the war, their covers battered and scratched. Harry cringed; the albums he held were some of his prize albums.

"Ve haf der music piped into der galley to a couple of speakers. Dey vill hear it ven you put on your records."

Harry looked the archaic record player over carefully, then took one of the records that sat behind it, an album by ABBA, slipped off the jacket and placed the disc on the turntable. "I'll just check it first," he said to a watchful Osa. He turned on the power; the turntable began revolving. That was a good sign. Placing the needle down in the first grove, he adjusted the volume and tone, and then listened to the sounds of ABBA. The needle was good, good enough to use on his prized albums. "Good," he grinned at Osa, "good."

He stripped off the old record and replaced it with his Harry Reser recording. He set the needle down and banjo music suddenly flooded the room. He glanced up toward Osa only to find she had left. Disappointed, he turned back to his task, stacking the albums on the holder, and then headed for the galley.

Those in the galley were listening and smiling. Peter winked giving him a thumb's up. Several others nodded and gave the thumb's up sign of approval. Osa, too, was smiling. Harry acknowledged their approval, grabbed a cup of hot coffee and sat down next to Peter, across from Osa. "Dis is fine of you to share your music vis us," she said. Harry flushed. Was it the music or the way she looked at him with those warm, inviting eyes.

"Are you a musician?" she asked.

"No. I'm not," he replied somewhat apologetically. "I love the banjo, in fact had tried to learn the instrument one time but gave up, all thumbs." He laughed. "So, I buy banjo albums and play them. These are some of my favorites. I really dig banjo music."

"I like it too," she said, her smile broadening.

With hot cups of coffee, they settled back with the others listening to the music. When the album, "The Happy Sounds of the Flint Banjo Club," dropped onto the turntable and the first stirring sounds of "Alabama Jubilee" filled the room, the mood of the listeners became even more festive. Everyone was smiling now, clapping hands, tapping toes. Those who knew the words sang along.

"I really like dat music," Peter grinned. "It is happy music. I really like it."

"That group is just down the road from Saginaw in Flint, Michigan," Harry said. "I used to go and watch them perform quite often. A really great group, probably fifty banjoists."

"Are you a musician?" Peter asked. Osa laughed. He hadn't heard her ask the same question only minutes before.

"No. I play the radio, television and record player," Harry replied with a grin. "I was just telling Osa that I tried to play one once but I couldn't read music, didn't know what a chord was and couldn't fit my fingers to the strings. I think the instructor was relieved when I quit. Anyways, I always buy banjo albums. I play the music as background for parties and other fun times."

Soon another album dropped onto the turntable. Harry's eyes lit up, one of his favorites: Johnny Ford. As the distinctive artistry of Johnny Ford filled the air, the room became silent. Harry smiled. It always happened when Johnny played. The proverbial pin could drop and be heard in the silence of the room.

"He's a young fellow with a black patch over one eye," Harry whispered across to Osa. "I met him. He's the greatest. Best banjo player I've ever heard."

Osa sat back listening to Johnny Ford, a far away, pensive look on her face. Harry studied her features. Beautiful, he thought, absolutely beautiful. A flustered, embarrassed smile broke across her face when she glanced up catching him staring at her.

"Dis is nice," she whispered as the last strains of Johnny's record faded. She reached across patting Harry's hand.

Warmth spread through him as her hand gently came to rest on his rubbing lightly. A message? Naw, he thought; don't go getting any funny ideas about her. She's nice, but not your type. You want the dark-haired, dark-eyed, buxom, lusty brunettes with the ready smile and body to match. Still, her hand felt good as it had come to rest on his.

The evening flew by with those present asking him to play the records over several times. Harry obediently obliged, pleased they liked the music.

Peter looked at his watch, and then turned to Harry. He pointed to his watch. Harry got the message, time for the night watch. He turned to Osa. "I have to go on duty. If you don't mind, I'll leave you in charge of my albums. Okay?"

"Yah. No problem," she beamed.

"You'll guard them with your life, right?" he said grinning at her. "They're collectors items, very difficult to replace."

"Yah. You can count on me," she grinned. "Vis my life."

Harry laughed. "Good."

"Vere are der jackets?" she asked.

"Back by the record player," he replied.

"Show me, please," she said, a warm, come-hither look glowed in her eyes.

"Sure," he responded. "Come and I'll show you."

He ushered her from the galley back to where the record player was located. As he stood behind her, bending forward to show her the record jackets, his hand came to rest lightly on her waist. There was no protest. The faint, sensuous aroma of her perfume filled his nostrils. On a sudden impulse, he bent forward kissing her lightly on the nape of her neck. Osa flinched, glancing around at him, a surprised look on her face at his boldness. But before she could say anything, he pulled her close and kissed her, crushing her warm, full lips to his, and his arms encircled her pulling her tightly to him. In that moment, as he sensed her melting in his arms welcoming his touch, his tongue probed lightly against moist lips, and then, like a searing firebrand, slid deeply inside.

Although startled, she had seemed to accept the invasion, even moaning as their kiss grew in intensity, and then his hands slid down encompassing her solid buttocks, pulling her hard against his burgeoning erection.

It was then he realized she was struggling against him. "No!" she moaned. "No!" Jerking free, gasping, she pushed away from him. Her face registered neither anger nor passion, but abject fear. Wide-eyed, wiping the wetness from her lips, she stared at him with eyes which suddenly brimmed with tears.

"Dis is not right," she said in a trembling voice. "You should not haf done dat. I'm not dat kind of voman."

Harry thought she looked like a frightened schoolgirl who had just reacted to her first feel.

"Osa, wait –"

"I must go." She blurted, pushing past him.

"Well, I'll be damned," Harry muttered looking after her, then at the swinging doors. "I read her message loud and clear!" He jammed his hand in his pocket to adjust his slowly deflating erection. "The widow sent a message then changed her mind. I'll be damned!"

The galley seemed chillingly still when he returned. All eyes seemed riveted on him as though knowing of his dastardly deed. Already he was beginning to feel like a cheap hustler. If she had only stayed a moment longer, he could have apologized, could have told her he mis-read her "invitation." He was sure of one thing; he'd screwed up their friendship royally. Dammit! She was too nice for a cheap pass like that. What the hell had come over him to do such a stupid thing like that?

He stopped at a table where one of his friends, Sven, was reading, and asked if he would keep an eye on his albums as it was time for him to go on duty. Sven agreed. Harry quickly left the galley and headed topside. Dammit, Martin, he chastised himself. She's got enough troubles without a middle-aged stud trying to make a pass at her. It was uncalled for. He had to apologize – and soon!

In her cabin, Osa slammed the door shut, kicked off her shoes and threw herself across her bed. What gall! "I'm not dat kind of girl," she spat. "I did nossing to lead him to tink I vas dat kind of – dat kind dat Rudy vould chase after."

Tears trickled down her cheeks. All she wanted was to be friends; was that asking too much? Yet, when their lips had first touched, the warm sensation it had triggered, the fulfillment of yearning to be kissed again after so long. True, she had felt herself melting in his arms at that moment. A tingling sensation still coursed through her body as she recalled the way he had held her, the feel of his hands roaming over her body creating a feeling deep in her loins that ached for release.

She had felt dead inside for so long, so very long. Rudy had ignored her while he chased after young whores. She knew what he was doing. She wasn't stupid; she heard the gossip. She had turned away from him in bed.

When Harry forced his tongue between her lips, it was as though he were treating her like the tramps Rudy chased after. She shook her head. She was not that kind of girl! Not a whore! Harry had to be taught a lesson much like she had taught Rudy. What he did, it couldn't happen again. Never!

Chapter 36
FINDING TROUBLE, EXPLORING THE *NURAD*

Two full days, forty-eight hours, had passed and there had been no sign of Osa. Each watch began to weigh heavily on Harry, especially the midnight watch. Except for an occasional malfunction of the radar, which raised the captain's ire, nothing noteworthy happened, and he was left with his thoughts of the other night and his feelings of guilt. He had tried in vain to contact Osa to apologize. It was as though she had become invisible, at least to him. Others saw her, whether in the galley, along the corridor or on deck, but for him, she had seemingly disappeared.

Time and again his thoughts strayed to her, the guilt he felt about his actions further compounded when Peter returned his albums. Sven had given them to Osa, who turned them over to Peter saying she did not want to be responsible for them. There was no reprimanding intonation in Peter's voice indicating anything was amiss between the two of them; she had merely asked that the albums be returned.

Had Peter noticed anything different about Osa of late, Harry asked one night during their watch. Peter had thought for a moment, and then said she seemed pre-occupied in her work more than normal, probably some woman kind of thing. He shrugged it off. Woman are that way; unpredictable. Harry said he, too, had noticed it, that she seemed more aloof of late.

Dammit! It was a stupid thing to do, he told himself for the thousandth time. You don't build lasting friendships that way. Had he mis-read her body language, the smile, the touch of her hand? She hadn't really resisted when he first kissed her. How the hell could he apologize when he couldn't find her?

The thought occurred to him that maybe she was being serviced by one of the younger studs and she didn't want any complications in her life, but who? Hell, who knows! Even she had to get rid of her sexual urges, sexual frustrations, somehow. He did. All men did. Women must, too. Ahhhh, to hell with her!

He peered ahead into the empty darkness, another boring night was ahead. Yet, time and again his thoughts strayed to her, the warmth of her kiss, the firmness of her buttocks. Damn, but she had a good body for her age and she was damned attractive to boot. Then he snickered; the longer he was at sea, the more attractive she'd probably become.

At 0400 hours Second Officer Sigmund Helmstrund, a tall, blonde, steely blue-eyed Swede with sharp, chiseled features, joined them. He had a good physique, Harry noted, most likely from all the exercising he did. Every morning after his watch, Sigmund could be seen jogging around the deck. Harry decided the man was a bonafide health fanatic, always exercising, lifting weights and jogging.

The thing that bothered Harry the most about the Second Officer was his youthful arrogance and aloofness. If he could be taken down a peg or two, he'd probably turn out to be a pretty decent person. Harry recalled his dad saying first impressions weren't always the most reliable, but more often than not, pretty certain of a person's character. Then, too, Harry recalled that dad had said to keep an open mind, that someone we might dislike or distrust at first might end up being one of our strongest supporters. Maybe by the end of the voyage things might be different. One could only hope. The thought suddenly occurred to him; was Helmstrund Osa's lover?

There seemed to be a subtle rivalry between Peter and Sigmund that Harry noted early on. A chance comment overheard in the galley by one of the crewmen further substantiated his belief about the rivalry. There was a strong possibility this would be the captain's last voyage, that he was slated for the front office with a major promotion and that a new master would be assigned to *Nurad*.

The draw for command was between First Officer, Peter Selham, an older, seasoned veteran, and Second Officer, Sigmund

Helmstrund, a younger, more aggressive officer, and who just happened to be the son of one of the largest stockholders in the shipping line.

"I see you up and at 'em every morning after watch getting your laps in around the deck," Harry commented to Sigmund, glancing over at the man.

"Yah," Sigmund replied, "six kilometers."

"That's a lot of jogging. You must be in pretty good shape. Getting ready for the Olympics?"

Sigmund laughed. "No. Just staying in shape. Und speaking of staying in shape, I see you vorking out almost every evening. You are in good shape for an old man. I haf noticed."

"Old man! Old is a state of mind," Harry retorted looking askance at the young officer.

Peter kept his eyes buried in his binoculars scanning the horizon, but a smile had broken across his lips at Sigmund's comment.

"Oh,' he blurted, "I did not mean dat you –"

"You know the old adage: healthy mind, healthy body," Harry interrupted, and then laughed at the embarrassed look on Sigmund's face. "Healthy mind 'cept in certain matters," he added.

Peter could not contain himself. Lowering his glasses, he said, "Sigmund, vot he means is dat he is a healthy, dirty old man."

"Oh." And then Sigmund laughed. "I see."

"Harry is not like odder men his age," Peter continued. "He don't know how to slow down. You listen to his adventures some time. Dis man is someting else. His exploits vis vomen is mind-boggling."

"Oh?" Sigmund sighed with a different tone of voice, possibly a new respect for the old man.

"Yah. Use it or lose it," Peter chuckled. "Dat is der philosophy of Harry Martin."

Harry grinned looking over at the First Officer. Was there something in his comment that caught his attention? Did Peter know more about what had happened between Osa and him than he'd led him to believe? Maybe Osa had spoken to him about the incident. Damn!

"Vell, you two are relieved," Sigmund said throwing off a salute "I take charge for der next vatch."

Peter eased the binoculars over his head handing them to Sigmund as Harry released the helm to his replacement, Sven. He'd made up his mind that the sooner he found Osa and apologized, the better he'd feel. Better to have Peter think he was a dirty old man than to find out first hand from Osa.

He made a beeline for the galley. Yessir, he'd apologize as soon as he found her, if she'd let him.

Much to his chagrin, Osa was not there. In fact, she continued to be an elusive, invisible person. Harry soon got the distinct impression she was deliberately avoiding him. How the hell could he apologize when he couldn't even find her? Time and again he found himself analyzing his action. They weren't that bad. Hadn't she ever been hustled before?

Finally, after many attempts over several days, he gave up. The feeling he had sensed about her early on became naggingly clear: she was a prude. She had to be. No female had ever stayed pissed off at him that long after a pass, and all he'd done was steal a kiss and cobb a feel. She had to be a prude. To hell with her!

He turned his thoughts and energies back to other activities: strenuous exercise, letter writing to the kids, and modifying his jacket and seabag to accommodate his potential treasure.

Back in Saginaw spring was close at hand. Soon the snow would be melting, trees budding, grass turning a thick, rich green. Time to get out the old lawnmower. Had they found the Chink yet? And where was Stan? And why the hell do they allow such a beautiful woman aboard ship! It should be outlawed!

That night he confided to Peter that the routine was getting through to him. Did he have any suggestions on how to overcome his feelings of boredom? Peter pondered the question for quite sometime before answering. Had Harry ever completed his tour of the ship? It was important to know every aspect of the ship from stem to stern. It might prove useful one day to have such knowledge of the ship. Harry brightened. Yes, a good idea. He'd start that very day.

As an afterthought, Peter warned him not to stray off limits where Osa's cabin was located. It was definitely off limits. Harry nodded. Understood! Somehow, Peter must have found out, or at least sensed the coolness between himself and Osa. It was just as well. Exploring the ship would be more rewarding than pursuing an old broad.

Promptly, his exploration of the ship began that morning after a few hours of sleep and a hearty breakfast. Descending into the bowels of the ship proved interesting as he moved along the dim-lit corridors of gray painted steel.

His first stop was in the engine room where a cigar-chomping man with an officer's cap cocked back on his head hailed him over wanting to know what he was doing in the engine room. Harry introduced himself and found he was talking to Chief Engineer Gueder Svenson. Yelling above the constant ka-thunk of the engine and the high-pitched noise of the other machinery, the chief proudly showed Harry around his domain, taking pains, as he did, to explain the operation down to the finest details.

"How old is the ship?" Harry called out over the constant roaring sound.

"About twenty-four years old. It is a newer ship, a good ship."

"No danger of sinking?" Harry asked good naturedly.

"No!" Gueder snapped, and then caught the twinkle in Harry's eyes. "Dis is a good ship. Vell constructed. I haf been vis it since it vas christened. It von't sink. It is a good ship. You don't vorry."

"Good. I'm not much of a swimmer and I hate sharks," Harry replied, smiling.

"Ahhh, you tease me," Gueder laughed. He slapped Harry solidly on his shoulders. "You Americans, you luf to tease. Yah."

Harry asked if it was okay just to wander about. Gueder shrugged, it was okay but stay clear of any machinery where the greatest danger was present. He added that the coffee pot was on and suggested he stop back for coffee before going topside.

"Will do," Harry replied, giving a wave of his hand as he headed forward through an open hatchway. He walked along a dimly-lit walkway, almost feeling his way through the darkness between the sparsely placed lights. An inner feeling clutched at him, a feeling of the unknown that was ever pervasive in his mind as he moved along. More than once he stopped abruptly at seeing the shadowy figure of a rat scurrying off into the darkness. He hated rats. For a moment he considered the folly of his exploration, not being so damned adventuresome and turning back. Still, he pushed forward.

Going off on a right angle between two huge grain holds, he dead-ended against the steel plate of the ship's outer skin. It was damp and cold to the touch He pulled out a small penlight and flashed it along the steel wall toward the bilge. As he shivered in the cold dankness ready to retrace his steps, his light beam passed over a gob of what appeared to be putty. He shined the light on the gob. It was jammed tightly against a welded seam next to the outer skin.

"That's odd," he said aloud. Why have a gob of putty here? If the ship were leaking they should have put it in drydock for repairs. Putty sure as hell won't stand up to the pressure of thousands of tons of seawater. As he reached up to touch the wad, a rat suddenly leaped off the top of the putty.

"Christ!" Harry gasped, jerking his hand away, his body repelling backwards in the same movement. His head collided with something solid and he pitched forward onto the deck unconscious.

"Dat vill teach you not to snoop, you American bastard!" a guttural voice snarled. A wrench was still tightly clutched in his hand.

Harry awoke with a painfully throbbing head and shivering uncontrollably. Touching the back of his head gingerly, he felt a good-sized bump. What the hell happened, and then he recalled the rat. Yeah, it had jumped off the gob of putty. He had jerked back, must have smacked his head on a steel beam. He shook his head but a scream of pain stopped him. He knew his eyes were open but it was pitch black, and cold. Where the hell was he? Where were the lights? There had been dim lights before, now nothing. Reaching out, he felt wet, cold steel plating: the outer skin of the ship. Painfully, he rose to his feet, stopping when his head bumped against steel plate.

Standing hunched over, he wondered where the hell he was. His penlight was gone so that meant he had to feel his way around in the darkness. After bumping into steel walls several more times he concluded he was in an enclosure about five feet by five feet. "I must be in a storage compartment," he muttered. His fingers touched what felt like a handle. Grasping it firmly, he jerked the handle several times feeling it slowly giving each time he jerked until, finally, the door gave way and opened.

Stepping through the small doorway, he saw a series of lights along a passageway. He looked back into the small compartment. "Well, I didn't get there by myself," he muttered, as he briskly began rubbing himself trying to restore some warmth.

"Whoever put me in there had to have a lot of strength to carry me, and to dog down the handle that tight. Apparently someone on board this ship doesn't like me."

Except for the constant throbbing of the engines the area was silent. A smile broke across his face. "I can't believe Osa was that angry." The thought of her felling him caused him to laugh, bolstering his spirits. Not her, he mused, but someone did it. Slowly he made his way back toward the engine room.

"Where's the Chief?" he asked one of the oilers in the engine room.

"Eating. It is our lunch time," he called back, pointing at a clock.

Harry glanced at the clock. It was just after eleven hundred hours. No wonder he was so damned cold; he'd been unconscious for the best part of an hour.

Thanking the man, he headed topside on the double. Stopping in his cabin for a moment to clean up, he studied himself in the mirror. He didn't look any the worse for wear but there was a definite, painful lump on his noggin. "Well, maybe I'll find out who tapped me when I get to the galley."

The galley was full of noisy, hungry crewmembers. Harry moved through the line selecting his food, glancing about as he did to see if anyone had a look of surprise on their face. It didn't bother him that Osa was not to be seen. There has to be something more than me that's bugging the broad, he thought. Maybe it's her own guilt about her husband getting killed with some young bimbo.

"Helllooo, my American friend," called the Chief Engineer jovially waving Harry to join him. "Come. Come and join us." He patted an empty space next to him. Harry nodded and settled in beside him.

"Und how vas your trip? I tought you ver coming back for coffee?"

Harry looked at the man; there was no sign of surprise. His remark seemed sincere. "I got in deeper than I had anticipated," Harry lied. "Sorry about the coffee."

"You should not go below decks visout permission," a man sitting across from the chief admonished. Harry glanced across at the man; it was the one with the ever-present scowl and deep-set eyes, still cold with contempt. "You could get hurt badly if you don't know your vay around."

"Yes. Yes, you're right," Harry replied. "A person could get hurt if he doesn't watch his step." He deliberately rubbed his hand gently over the back of his head as he studied the man's face. There was no change in his expression. What was it about the guy that made him feel uncomfortable? Why was he so bitter? Harry had to know.

In a controlled demeanor, he extended his hand across the table. "I don't believe we've met, although I've seen you a couple of times. My name's Harry —"

"I know who you are!" the man snapped back, angrily slapping Harry's hand aside. "You are der vun who stole Alex's job from me. Dat's all I need to know about you. You damned American! You should haf been vashed overboard in der storm!"

"Ernst! Stop it!" Chief Svenson jumped to his feet glaring at the man. "He did not take der job from you. Captain Andress hired him for der position. Dat is final!"

"No!" Ernst screamed rising to his feet. "It should haf been my job. I earned it. I haf been vis dis company for tirty years. I deserve it more dan some damned foreigner!"

"Hey, look! I'm sorry about the job," Harry said trying to placate the man. "I didn't know you were in line for the job, but I needed a job too."

"Not on dis ship! Ve haf no place for you on dis ship!"

"Ernst. Stop it dis instant! Dat's an order!" the Chief bellowed.

Glaring at his chief, eyes flashing hatred, Ernst cried, "He is bad!" Turning back to Harry, he said, "You haf brought a curse to dis ship. Mark my vords, somesing bad vill happen to dis ship because of you!"

"Now hold on, pal," Harry snapped, bristling, having taken all the crap he'd take from the man. "I came on board to work. When we reach port back in Saginaw the job's yours. But don't go feeding a line of bullshit to these poor guys about a curse. Even I don't buy it. As far as I'm concerned, if you don't want to be friends, we won't be."

"Ve never be friends! Never! You vill pay, all of you vill pay for dis man being on board. Mark my vords. You vill all die!" He screamed hysterically pounding the table with his fist. "You vill all die because of him!"

All eyes in the room had focused on Ernst. The chief rushed around the table toward the man but Ernst had already grabbed up his tray and was stalking away. "You damned American pig!" he exclaimed over his shoulder. "You vill pay!" He threw his tray down on the dirty dish stand and slammed out of the galley.

Harry looked over at the chief, who stood with a bewildered look on his face. "Whew," Harry said wiping at his brow. "Is he always that pleasant?"

"Don't pay no attention to him," the chief said sitting down next to him. "Ernst is a sick man. Somesing is bothering him. I haf never seen him like dis before. He is a hard vorker but now he don't get along vis anybody no more. He vill never get anyvere on dis shipping line vis dat attitude."

"I don't want any hard feelings," Harry said. "I didn't realize the job meant so much to him."

"I tell der truth. He vas not eligible for der job. Ve told him dat a long time ago. He is better off in der engine room vere he is an oiler. I haf told him dat; Peter has told him dat. He vill not accept it. You can bet I vill talk to him ven I get back to der engine room. He vill be nice tomorrow. You vill see." By the tone of his voice and the look in his eyes, Harry knew Ernst would definitely be more agreeable the next day. Maybe then he could talk to the man.

"Come, now," the chief said thrusting his face into Harry's. "You must tell me about dose records of yours, der banjo music. I really enjoyed dem der odder night. Very good. Vat vas der name of dat vun man? Johnny Ford?"

"Yeah. Johnny Ford. The greatest banjoist I've ever heard since Eddie Peabody. A real artist."

That noon, while on watch, Harry reflected on the events of the past morning. Although his lunching with Chief Engineer Svenson was enjoyable, it hadn't proved profitable in finding out who cold-cocked him and locked him in the storage compartment. The most logical candidate had to be Ernst. Chief Svenson had turned out to be a real solid, down to earth guy, even extending an invitation to return for coffee anytime. Harry definitely planned on returning below decks because something was not right down there.

That evening he focused his energies into modifying his jacket. It was beginning to materialize as he had envisioned. There was still sufficient time to get the jacket and seabag done before they docked in Tsingtao. The danger of interruption had passed since they entered the Pacific Ocean for it seemed Peter was spending more and more of his off duty time on other tasks, and less time on the supervision of one, Harry Martin, for which Harry was most grateful.

Yet, as he worked, he had a feeling someone had been in his sea chest rifling through his belongings. Although nothing was missing, there was a feeling that someone was prying into his personal life. Why? He'd never go through another person's personal belongings. It wasn't right.

Chapter 37

SOMETHING AMISS ABOARD SHIP

Coming off duty the next morning, Harry decided to go below decks in order to settle his own curiosity about the putty, maybe even find a clue as to who had cold-cocked him. Breakfast could wait. Anyway, Osa would most likely continue to be invisible. Hell, any other woman would have shrugged it off, told him off, or settled for an apology, which, if she ever appeared, he would be glad to give.

Too, was it his imagination working overtime, for Captain Andress seemed to be avoiding him of late. Had the bitch gone crying to her uncle? His attitude toward her was hardening. The thought that she might be an A-Number One prude bothered him. Shades of his ex-wife.

Taking a moment to grab a larger flashlight from his cabin, he gingerly made his way down several levels by-passing the engine room, and headed directly toward the spot where he had his "accident."

Moving through a series of hatchways and sharp angled bends, he soon found himself on the same walkway where he had discovered the putty the day before. Turning on his flashlight, he shined the beam of light along the wet hull skin, then along the walkway. He had stopped almost at the spot where he'd first noticed the thick wad of putty wedged against the ship's outer skin. His penlight lay on the walkway. Retrieving it, he flicked it on, surprised that it still worked. Sticking it in his shirt pocket, he aimed the beam of his flashlight up along the welded seam stopping when the light shone on the gob of putty. He thought his eyes were playing tricks on him for something was sticking out of the putty, a thin rod that appeared to be a fuse. Could the putty actually be a plastique explosive?

The sudden clatter of metal on metal followed by a curse in Swedish startled Harry. Someone was making their way along the walkway toward him. Not knowing if he was up against a man with a gun, considering the sound of metal striking metal only moments earlier, Harry glanced about for a place to hide; there was nothing. Below the walkway was the bilge. His light reflected off the water, thinly layered with oil. Quickly he doused the light as the footsteps came closer, plodding along the metal walkway, ever closer.

Quietly, Harry eased over the edge of the walkway and lowered himself into the bilge. Dammit! It was rank, icy cold water. Clinging to the side of the walkway, he ducked back out of sight as a beam of light came swinging down the way.

As the person approached, Harry pressed even tighter out of view. The person stopped directly above him. Glancing up, Harry saw it was Ernst. He was reaching for whatever it was that was stuck to the putty. He examined it, grunted, and then stuffed it in his pocket. "Good," he muttered, then moved back along the walkway from where he had come.

Harry waited for several minutes until he was sure Ernst was out of earshot before pulling himself up onto the walkway. He was thoroughly soaked to the waist, shivering, and he stank of bilge waste. "Shit!" he muttered aloud. He pulled the flashlight from his back pocket. It didn't work. "Shit!" he cursed again. "What the hell is this all about?"

As luck would have it, his penlight worked, and he shone the faint beam onto the wad of putty. Reaching up, he pinched off a small gob of the material and stuffed it in his shirt pocket. There was no doubt in his mind that it was not putty. It had to be plastique explosive. Something was very rotten aboard ship and Peter had to be told.

At the moment, however, he was more concerned in returning to his cabin unseen and getting into some dry clothes. Luck was with him and he arrived back in his cabin unnoticed. Quickly he stripped off the wet clothes, emptied the contents of his pockets on the desk, and then threw his clothes into the shower stall. While taking a hot, steamy shower, he sudsed off his clothes. Now all he had to do was wring them out and throw them in the dryer.

Dressed in a clean outfit, Harry sifted through the waterlogged contents of his pockets lying on the desk. Money, credit cards and other notes were stripped from his wallet and spread out to dry. Keys, change and a small pocketknife went back into his dry pants pockets. Picking up the small wad of putty, or whatever it was, he examined it closely, rolled it between his fingers and sniffed of it. At the time the Japanese surrendered Tsingtao to the Sixth Marine Division at the close of World War Two, he recalled how the Marines had used plastique explosives to clean out some old Japanese gun emplacements entrenched in the hillside behind the Marine base. It sure looked like the same stuff they had used back then.

Why would Ernst be stashing plastique explosive along the ribbing of the ship? Was he planning to blow up the ship? Naw, that was too far-fetched. There had to be a simple explanation. He rolled the material between his fingers again. Damn, but it sure felt like the old explosives they had used so many years before. No. The thought of Ernst blowing up the ship was too far-fetched; it had to be putty. Hell, he'd ask Peter. He dropped the wad of putty on the desk, gathered up his wet clothes and headed for the laundry room.

Back in his cabin an hour later he dumped his clean clothes on his bunk, separated them and stored them neatly in his dresser. Turning to the desk, he found his money and papers had dried so he replaced them in his wallet. It was then he noticed the small wad of putty was gone. Thinking it might have rolled off the desk onto the deck, he dropped to his hands and knees looking for it. It was gone.

"Lose someting?" Peter asked coming into the room just then.

"Uh, nothing, just popped off a button," Harry lied. "I'll get another one and sew it on later." Now why the hell did I say that, he asked himself. And where the hell was the putty? How could he explain the stuff to Peter if he had nothing to show him, and he certainly didn't want to drag him below decks on a wild goose chase. He'd let it go for now. Later, he'd tear the cabin apart; the putty had to be there. In his haste to find it, he'd just overlooked it.

"You missed a good breakfast," Peter said. "Osa vas at her best today. She vas her old self again, happy, cheerful; I even got seconds. I can't figure out vat vas der matter vis her der last several days. It must haf been her period."

"Probably," Harry agreed. Wouldn't you know it, the day he skipped breakfast she shows up. Great! "Well, I'm skipping a few meals, getting too fat," he said. "Look." He grabbed a handful of flab around his beltline. "Love handles, that's what I'm growing. Love handles."

"Yah, you could skip a few meals to lose pounds but you should never skip breakfast. It is der most important meal of der day. Didn't dey teach you dat back in school?" Peter laughed "I must tell you of my teacher, Mrs. Zager, ven I vas a child. Almost religiously each day she vould say to all the pupils, 'you must not skip breakfast!'" He laughed again. "It is very funny how dat suddenly popped into my mind, dear, sveet Mrs. Zager, a real nice lady."

"I used to get the same message, but I'm still planning on skipping a few meals."

"Suit yourself, Harry," Peter replied as he plopped down on his bunk. "I hit der sack now. I am sleepy. I see you later."

"Yeah, see ya' later," Harry replied, as Peter rolled over on his side. "I'm not sleepy now. I'm gonna go up on deck and soak up a few hot rays."

Harry stepped on deck and crossed to the railing. The seas were running before them; *Nurad* was making excellent headway. Hawaii was to the northeast and the Philippine Islands lay ahead, but southward. China, their destination, lay dead ahead.

Although the tradewinds continuously swept across the ship, it was necessary to wear shoes on deck as the steel plating was hot from the strong rays of the tropical sun.

The day was like several of the previous days: an early morning rain squall, and then clear, mostly cloudless skies. A line of billowy, white clouds lay gently along the horizon.

Harry glanced back along the deck at the series of hatch covers on which many of the crew were already sunning themselves. A colorful assortment of deck chairs, mattresses stripped off bunks, and myriad colored blankets greeted his view. A few men were playing cards. Harry waved off playing cards. It was too hot.

He climbed up on the forward hatch, the men's area – no women allowed they had jokingly commented – and stripped down to his shorts, piling his clothing on Dieter's blanket. Dieter grunted approval and muttered hello. They shared the same blanket almost daily. Dieter was already covered with oil and lay unmoving. "Hot today," Harry said sitting down. Dieter grunted again.

Harry looked toward the stern at the last hatch cover. The men joked about it, off limits. Only for women, namely Osa. However, lately she seldom used it, nor was she there now.

Applying lotion liberally over his body, arms and legs, Harry stretched out on the blanket. He lay on his stomach gazing out across the rolling seas, watching the rise and fall of the railing against the horizon line. His vision was interrupted when Karl, the engine room oiler he had spoken to the first day below decks, stepped up on the hatch cover.

"You make a good door, Karl," Harry growled.

Karl laughed. "Sorry, Harry."

Harry glanced at his watch. Twenty minutes already. Time to turn over. He checked his watch constantly to make sure he turned over ever twenty minutes. It was like basting a turkey, but he knew the tropic sun was deceiving and you could get an extremely bad burn in only a short span of time.

Karl looked up at the blue sky. "Beautiful," he said, then threw his blanket out before him, spreading it wide. Quickly he stripped away clothing until he was left only in his undershorts. Then he liberally covered his hairy body with sunscreen. Settling down next to Harry, he picked up his binoculars and began slowly scanning the seas.

"Anything interesting?" Harry asked.

"Nossing." He paused a moment. "Yah. Der is a ship right on der crest of der horizon. I can't make out vat kind. Ahhh, it is moving away from us."

Harry rolled over on his back. "How's things down in the engine room?"

"Good. Busy."

"Say, you work with that guy, Ernst, don't you?"

"Yah. Vy?"

"Oh, nothing, nothing in particular. I met him the other day and it's apparent he doesn't want anything to do with the 'American'."

"Don't pay no attention to him. Ernst is a funny fellow. He is hardheaded. Even ve find him hard to get along vis, a funny fellow. You're better off visout him."

"Has he always sailed with you on *Nurad*?"

"No. He vas re-assigned to dis ship in Stockholm jus' before ve sailed. Der man he replaced, Otto, vas vun hell of a fine man. You vould haf liked him, fine sense of humor. He vas killed in an auto accident; der brakes failed on his new Volvo, very mysterious." He sighed. "Bless his soul."

Harry lay still letting the hot sun soak in, thinking of Ernst. Funny that even his own men don't care that much for him.

"He's not new to working on ships, though," Harry commented after a couple of minutes. "I can tell when a man's been around ships, and Ernst obviously knows the insides and outsides of ships, especially this ship, like the back of his hand."

"Oh, yah, yah. Ernst has been a sailor for many years. He vas on dis ship before ven it vas first christened. Den he vas transferred to our ill-fated sister-ship, N*uergren*. It sank in der Indian Ocean two years ago. Ernst vas very lucky. He had a bad injury at sea und had been transferred to vun of der mainland hospitals only hours before der ship sank vis der loss of all hands." Karl let loose with another long sigh. "It sank dat very night."

"Really?" Harry responded, glancing over at Karl. "I'd say providence is looking out for Ernst. He's a very fortunate fellow"

"Yah. Der ship sank in der deepest part of der Indian Ocean. No vay to recover it or to find out vat caused it to sink. Dere vas no distress call, nossing. Der ship jus' suddenly disappeared, sank vis all hands."

"Hmmm, interesting," Harry commented. Was it just coincidence that the Bonin Trench, one of the deepest parts of the Pacific Ocean, was coming up soon? Perhaps, he wondered, it might be more than mere coincidence.

"Mind if I look through your glasses?" Harry asked rolling around and up into a sitting position.

"No, please do," Karl replied, stripping the glasses' strap from around his neck and passing them to Harry.

Harry raised the glasses to his eyes and started a slow sweep of the horizon. As he came slowly along the length of the ship he was mildly surprised to see Osa climbing up on the last hatch cover. She looked captivating in a red-checkered halter top and cut-off blue jeans. He watched her intently as she spread her blanket out on the hatch cover, then stepped deftly out of her outfit revealing a seductive white bikini suit that fully enhanced her lithe figure. Osa knelt down on the blanket, uncapped a bottle of suntan lotion, and began rubbing lotion in an almost sensuous manner all over herself.

Was she putting on a show for the boys? Or, Harry felt, somehow, it was as if she knew he was watching her. Damn, he breathed, feeling a sudden twinge in his groin. Sandy always enjoyed the special way he rubbed suntan oil all over her creamy skin. Damn! He'd like to rub that lotion all over Osa's beautiful body, every inch of it.

Osa leaned forward onto her stomach, reached behind and unsnapped her bikini top, raising slightly to drop her straps, enough that Harry could see the fullness of her breasts stark white against her deepening tan. "Whew," he whispered. And then she was resting her head on her arm gazing out across the sea oblivious to him and the others.

"See someting?" Karl asked at the exclamation.

"Uh, no, nothing. Thanks for the loan," Harry replied, returning the glasses. He stretched. "Whew but it's hot." He glanced at his watch. "I guess I've had enough for awhile. I can feel that old sun burning through me. I'm heading for the shade. Good talking to ya'. See ya' later."

"Yah. Good seeing you, too, Harry."

Harry pulled on his pants, grabbed up his shirt, and headed down the deck with a jaunty step, trying to act nonchalant, but anxious to talk to her.

"Hi, Osa," he exclaimed, swinging easily up onto the hatch cover and looking down at her stretched out before him, her long tanned legs spread slightly apart, bare back inviting. There was no response; she certainly knew his voice, and knew who it was. "You better watch out so you don't get a bad burn," he continued. "This tropical sun is tricky. You can get burned and not even know it." He shielded his eyes. "Yeah, that sun is fierce today, and with your tender skin you'll burn fast." He knelt down beside her reaching for the bottle of suntan lotion. "Maybe I ought to rub some on your back, uh, just to be safe, okay?"

"No tank you. I just rubbed some on me a few minutes ago," Osa replied coolly, not bothering to look up. "I am perfectly capable of putting lotion on as necessary."

"Well, just thought I'd offer," Harry said backing off. "Just thought I'd offer."

He squatted on the hatch cover a short distance away still admiring her, finally forcing his gaze elsewhere, out across the rolling seas. After a prolonged silence, he turned his gaze back at her. She had not moved, not even to turn her head in his direction. "I missed you at the meals lately," he said. "Have you been ill?"

Osa's head twisted about and her eyes bore into his. "I haf been dere. I am der cook und I make sure der food is ready. It is my job, my duty." She turned away with a look of disgust.

"Oh," Harry mustered in answer. After another prolonged silence, the proverbial pregnant pause, he decided now might be the best time to apologize. "Are you still angry at me for stealing a kiss?" There, now if she had anything to say she could bring it out in the open for discussion. It wasn't that bad, at least he didn't think so.

"Yes. I am still angry," she replied, a chill to her voice. "I dont' like being treated like dat. I am a lady!" Their eyes met as she turned to him, anger clearly showing in hers. "Vat you did vas uncalled for. It vas cheap und vulgar."

"Hey! Hold on!" Harry responded sharply. "I didn't rape you. I just kissed you and copped a feel, what any red-blooded man would have done if he were close to such a beautiful woman."

"It vasn't okay vis me! You should not haf done it!"

"Okay. I apologize. It won't happen again."

"It better never happen again. I should be treated vis respect. I am not vun of your gutter whores. I am a lady!"

"Okay. Okay. I got the message. I apologize again. Now can we be friends?"

"Ve see." There was still a chill in her voice. She turned away seeming almost irritated at his continuing presence.

The thought flashed through his mind that this was the kind of cold-assed bitch you brought along to a party to sit on the beer to keep it chilled. That look and comment could have chilled a carload of beer. "Well, I'll be seeing you around," Harry said, standing, stretching. "Good talking to you." He jumped lightly onto the main deck and headed for his cabin. Time for a cold shower, he muttered under his breath.

Back on the after hatch cover, Osa wore a smug look. Good. He did apologize. Now he knows she is a lady and should be treated like one. Time would tell. Then she smiled; he had said she was a beautiful woman.

On the bridge Captain Andress had been observing the two. Harry was wrong to even be on that hatch cover. He was prepared to talk to Harry about being out of bounds again, and yet, his instincts told him to back off, to watch. As they talked, it became apparent to him that they might have had a small tiff, and now, with Osa smiling, it was over.

He had reviewed Harry's papers a dozen times. He was a good man, older, the kind that would make a good match for Osa. Now, if only she'd break down and get rid of her damned self-imposed, better-than-thou attitude, she might start enjoying life.

Chapter 38

THE FIRST MATE SOUNDS OFF

Reporting for duty that night, Harry was surprised to find Captain Andress on the bridge, his booming voice angrily directed at the First Officer. "As long as I am in command of dis ship you vill obey my orders. Is dat understood, Mr. Selham?"

"Aye, Captain!" came Peter's sharp response, crisply snapping to attention, his face a livid white under the brim of his officer's cap.

"Good. Carry on den. Traditions are important in our maritime vorld und ve vill follow dem." With that, he wheeled about and stormed out of the wheelhouse brushing past Harry with nothing more than a nod.

What the hell was that all about, Harry wondered, stepping to the helm and relieving his counterpart from the previous watch. Quickly he checked all the dials and gauges – the radar, the Loran, the compass. Peter stepped forward giving several orders for this watch. His voice was tight, sentences short, clipped. Then he grabbed up his binoculars and moved a distance away toward the front of the wheelhouse.

Boy, we're touchy tonight, Harry thought. He must have got his ass chewed out for something big. He shrugged, another exciting duty night.

The skies were overcast. Occasionally the moon shone through a break in the clouds washing the ragged edges of the clouds a silvery hue. Stars could be seen then, sparkling brightly in the blackness of outer space. On deck, many of the men had brought their mattresses up laying them on the hatch covers, enjoying sleeping under stars, caressed by warm trade winds.

Even though it was a balmy night Harry sensed a change in the seas, a little more turbulence. He felt the ship fighting back as they moved into heavier seas. There was a more pronounced rolling and pitching. A low-grade storm was fast approaching.

"Hold her steady on course," Peter snapped.

"Aye, Sir," Harry replied.

Soon we'll be changing course, heading northward into the East China Sea, Harry thought, and then they'd be sailing back into the coldness of the waning days of winter in China.

Peter roamed the wheelhouse like a caged lion, stopping to scan the dials, walking to the far end of the cabin, looking out across the barren darkness through his binoculars, continuing his prowling. His face was grim as though pre-occupied with thoughts.

"Something I can help with?" Harry offered as Peter stopped to scan dials and gauges. Perhaps by getting Peter talking he could relieve the growing tension.

"No," retorted Peter sharply.

"Just offering," Harry countered. "It might help if you talk, get whatever's bothering you off your chest. It always works for me."

Peter looked at him for several seconds, and then spoke. "Captain Andress is an old voman. He still tinks he is aboard an old tramp steamer like he commanded back in 1949. Dat vas over tirty years ago. He is out of date, out of step vis der times. He should be removed from command und put behind some desk vhere he don't do no harm. Der front office may feel he is good for dem but I vould fire him. He is just dat, an old voman. He-he vants to hold on to old, out-dated traditions, traditions dat haf no place in our modern vorld. Traditions! Bah! Can you imagine, he vants to celebrate der crossing of der International Dateline ven ve get to der 180th meridian. Dat is stupid. Dat tradition is so far out of date. It is a vaste of time und energy. He should be retired. It is getting more und more difficult to serve under der man!"

Harry was surprised at the invectives spewing from Peter. The man and the captain had served together for years. In fact, from what he had learned from the crew, the two officers made an excellent team. This tirade seemed out of character for Peter. Up till this moment he'd never said one unkind word about Captain Andress.

Was there something more than just a simple tradition bugging Peter?

"If you don't mind my saying so," Harry offered. "I think certain traditions are nice, important, like Christmas and Christmas trees, New Year's eve parties, birthday parties, Thanksgiving when we celebrated the landing of the Pilgrims in America, Halloween, the Fourth of July, kind of the foundation blocks you build on, knowing certain things are going to happen, if you know what I mean,"

Peter had listened somewhat impassively, and then gave a slight shrug of his shoulders in condescending agreement. "Yah I know vat you mean. But dis is a vorking merchantman. I don't tink it is necessary to haf dis particular ceremony. Dere are only a handful on board who haf not crossed der International Dateline. Personally, I could not justify it. Der captain enjoys it because he plays ruler of der Domain of Der Golden Dragon und has a chance to poke fun at der men. I actually tink he vants der ceremony in order to please Osa." He threw his hands up. "Shit! Maybe dis vun last time!"

Rain suddenly spattered across the bridge windows. The storm had arrived. On deck sailors scurried about quickly gathering up their mattresses and hurrying below deck as sheets of rain swept across the ship. *Nurad* rolled easily with the increased wave action.

Harry had watched after Peter, puzzled at his statement – vun last time. What the hell did that mean? Yet, just as suddenly, the tension in the wheelhouse lifted. Peter returned to the front of the wheelhouse, whistling softly to himself, staring out through the rain slick windows.

Harry's thoughts turned to the gob of putty. Although he had nothing to show, he felt he had to talk to Peter about his concern. After all, Peter had said early on if there were any problems they should be brought to his attention first.

"Peter, you know that guy down in the engine room, the one called Ernst –"

"Yes. Vy?" Peter turned abruptly at the mention of the man's name. "Vot about him?"

Harry was momentarily startled at the response. "Uh, I'm curious about him. He's not very friendly. I tried to introduce myself to him the other day but he wouldn't have a thing to do with me. I got the distinct impression he hated my guts. Called me a lousy American pig and that I had taken his job away from him."

"Ahhh, Ernst, vat can I say? He has a bad temper. I vouldn't pay too much attention to him." Peter waved it off with a simple gesture of his hand. "He vould like to be up here but Captain Andress und I felt you ver der best man for der job. In fact, I vanted you in dis job."

"Well, thanks for the vote of confidence," Harry replied, flattered at his remark. "But seriously, is Ernst the kind of man who holds a grudge to the point where he might do something dangerous?"

"How do you mean?" A serious look came into Peter's eyes. "Vot do you mean by dangerous?"

"Endangering the ship and crew?"

"No. Not Ernst. Vy do you say dat?"

"Well, after our talk the other day, I decided to tour the ship to become more familiar with it. While I was below deck, down in the area of the bilge where there's some small walkways, I found something wedged up against the skin of the ship. Well, it looked like putty at first, but before I had a chance to examine the stuff, I got hit on the back of my head and wound up stuffed inside a small storage bin –"

"Hit on der head?" Peter exclaimed. "Who hit you?"

"I don't know. A rat had jumped out and I had ducked back. Apparently my head hit something solid and, well, when I came to, I was in a small storage locker. Now you don't bump your head, knock yourself out, then wake up fifty feet away from the point of impact in a storage locker without someone's help.

"Anyways, I went back to that spot yesterday morning after I got off duty and found the gob of putty. Only this time, there was something sticking out of it, something that looked like a fuse. Before I could examine it, Ernst came walking along so I hid. Why? I don't know. I guess I don't trust the guy and this was not the time nor place for any confrontation. I hid and watched as he took the fuse out of the putty and walked away. After he left, I pinched off a piece of the putty and examined it. The more I handled it, the more convinced I became that it was a plastique explosive. I brought the piece back to the cabin to show you but, somehow, I lost it. Frankly, if that is a gob of plastique explosive up against the outer hull, that size charge could punch a hole in the side of the ship and all hands would end up on the bottom of the Pacific Ocean."

"Dat is a serious charge, Harry," Peter said, having listened intently to every word. "Ernst is not a madman." He scratched at his chin, turning, peering out the front windows. "Haf you spoken to anyvun else about dis?" he asked.

"No."

"You tink it vas an explosive?"

"Yes. I didn't know who to talk to about it. I felt it best that I talk to you. You could bring it to the attention of Captain Andress."

"Not yet," Peter replied. "I vill check all dis out first. Don't talk to anyvun, especially Captain Andress. I don't tink he should be unduly alarmed. I am sure dere is a logical explanation. Ernst is not like dat. I vill talk to him und den let you know."

"Fair enough." Harry felt relieved, glad that Peter would pursue it. "Probably my active imagination working overtime," he grinned, "but you never know."

"Yah." There was a wry smile on Peter's face. "Too long at sea can make a person's mind play tricks on dem."

Yet, the thought that someone might have placed an explosive charge on board ship must have rankled Peter for several times he came back to talk to Harry about it. "Vell, you can be sure of vun ting. I vill get to der bottom of dis. Please leave der whole ting in my hands. Ernst vill explain or I vill slap him in irons."

The bridge grew quiet once more. Harry sensed tension building by the way Peter paced, the way he fidgeted, the sudden scanning of the horizon, the dropping of the binoculars, the constant pacing.

"How much longer before we reach the Chinese mainland?" Harry asked hoping by changing the subject he could lesson the tension.

"Vat?" Peter snapped about. "Vat did you say?"

"China. The Chinese mainland. How much longer before we reach it?"

"Oh, China. Ve should arrive in Shanghai in five days if all goes vell. Der veather reports indicate relatively good veather, maybe some showers, and a possible squall. A small typhoon has passed vest of der Philippines heading northvard toward Korea und Japan. But it is vay ahead of us. Yah, Shanghai in five days; Tsingtao in seven, possibly eight days."

"Good deal," Harry beamed. "Hope we can get ashore in Tsingtao. I'd sure like to see the old place again. Might even recognize some of my old girlfriends." He laughed. "Hell, I could even fix you up, Peter."

Peter laughed, giving a negative shake of his head. "Tanks, but no tanks, Harry. Remember, you haf aged und dey haf aged. Und who vants to fool around vis some fifty-year old voman?" He cocked his eyebrow. "Yah, am I not right?"

"Yeah. Right. But then, I never turn down any free stuff."

Peter laughed heartily. "Harry, you are incurable! You never cease to amaze me for a man your age. You remind me of an eager young man out for his first taste of life und adventure, his first conquest of forbidden luf." He raised his binoculars scanning the horizon again. "I vill never understand vy you vould vant to come back to dis part of der vorld. It is probably just as bad und dirty as ven you left it. Vy come back?"

Was he making casual conversation, Harry wondered, or, perhaps, he had snooped through his personal belongings and was trying to figure out why he was modifying the jacket.

Yet, the thought of sharing his real reason for making the trip to China had crossed Harry's mind several times. Peter had been his logical choice. They were cabin mates. They had fostered a healthy respect for one another both off and on duty. Perhaps if he told Peter and enlisted his aid, it might prove useful to him in getting ashore in Tsingtao and, later, getting his booty ashore back in Saginaw.

But a gnawing feeling deep inside said no. It was something he couldn't explain, much more than just a gut feeling. He would wait. He knew the man, but how well? His vitriolic attack on Captain Andress earlier bothered him. It was so unlike Peter, the always quiet, mild-mannered and even-tempered one he had come to know and respect. No. He'd let it ride for now.

He glanced over at Peter, surprised to find him staring back at him as though awaiting an answer to his question.

"Ohhh, coming back. Well, when this crazy set of circumstances came about, finding out that I had a chance to return to China; I guess I just wanted to see it once more, see the changes – so here I am." Peter gave an understanding nod. Yet, Harry sensed he was obviously waiting for more. He continued. "You know how it is, Peter. As the saying goes: you only go around once in this old lifetime, so I'll take all the gusto I can get now. I don't expect to get rich in my lifetime, especially at my age, but I'm willing to take tradeoffs and get what I can get out of life. I hate to admit it, but I'm not getting any younger, so I take a chance now and then. China: this is the time."

"Yah. I know vat you mean," Peter said with a heavy sigh. "It vould be nice not to be a pawn to profit makers, but it costs so much just to exist today, to raise a family, to try to get into a position ver der real money is. It sickens me to prostitute myself to make odder men richer, but der only vay to get to der top of der heap is by playing der game using dere tactics. In a vay, I envy you. I vish I could vash my hands of all dis responsibility und do vat I vant to do, not vat I am committed to do."

His response came as a surprise to Harry. Hell, he thought, second in command of a ship rates good money, bonuses, perks. "What d'ya mean?" he asked, puzzled.

"Nossing."

"I guess if I were second in command of a vessel, I'd be happy," Harry said.

"Captain of a vessel is better," Peter replied.

"Are you slated for command?"

A wane smile crossed Peter's face. "Yah. I haf been promised a command ven dis mission is completed."

"Well, that's really great!" Harry replied enthusiastically. He grabbed Peter's hand shaking it vigorously. "Let me be the first to congratulate you."

"Tank you, but your congratulations are premature," Peter said retrieving his hand. "Too early, and please don't tell anyvun about dis," he cautioned. "It is still top secret."

"Mums the word. I won't tell a soul, but damn, that's really great!"

"Yah. I tink so." Then, in a somber tone of voice, he added, "I hope my vife vill finally be happy."

"Why wouldn't she? Wife of a captain! She should be very happy."

Peter shrugged. "She nags. Alvays nagging about the need for more money. She vants nossing but der best. Even my kids dress bedder dan der fadder. Nossing but der best."

He moved away, lifting the binoculars to his eyes, scanning the distant horizon. The storm had passed, the moon breaking through, stars twinkling above. Except for an occasional command from Peter, and the pervasive throbbing of the huge twin screws, the wheelhouse grew silent.

Harry thought of his former wife and the demands she had placed on their marriage. How similar, nothing but the best. He knew full well the pressures of a nagging wife, the need for more money, the need for a bigger house, two expensive cars, membership in the country club, entertaining, all important to their lifestyle. Yet, how often he had wished they could chuck it all, could have gone back and lived that simpler life they once knew, a time when they were struggling to make ends meet, and they always seemed to do it, and been able to spend more time with the kids, to let them know how special they were. But you can't go back. The distance between the two grew and grew until the divorce. At least he wasn't shackled to a bitching wife anymore or a job that was really the pits.

Working as a carpenter for the past few years had been the best. You worked with people you enjoyed. No phonies; just real honest, down-to-earth people. They were the kind who cared, who listened, who gave a damn about you. Sure, maybe they drank a little too much, swore a little too much, farted when they had to relieve themselves, but they lived life with a passion and made love the same way, and wasn't that what life was supposed to be all about.

Sandy had been a part of this group. Divorced from a drunken husband who was still chasing the bottle, she had determined to change her life around. At thirty-three years of age, she had determined she could be somebody if she wanted to, if she tried hard enough, and she knew she could also enjoy the pleasures of life at the same time.

They had met one night at the Pub. She was with a group of people Harry knew casually. Somehow, they had got paired off at darts. Harry hadn't objected; hell, she was a good-looking woman. She was good at darts. Good eye, good trajectory. He had stood back watching her. Good form, too, he had noticed almost immediately. Tight fitting designer jeans, shimmering black nylon blouse and, obviously, no bra, a real turn on seeing hard nipples pressed against the flimsy material. Damn but she was cute. And she had a warm, outgoing personality to match.

"Sandy, just call me Sandy," she had said when the match first started. He was good at darts but as the night progressed his concentration began to fade for he couldn't take his eyes off her. Soon he was losing consistently, much to the teasing of his friends and teammates. He ended up buying at least five rounds, and apologizing for his form, which was way off, while his competitor's was great. She had laughed at this, a soft, throaty laughter that made him tingle.

Al had called for the last round; soon the night would be over. Would he see her again? Did she have a steady boyfriend? Forget it, Martin, he had chastized himself; she wasn't even remotely interested in an old man.

His heart had skipped a beat when she tugged at his arm saying, "C'mon, Harry, the gang's coming over to my apartment for early breakfast." He didn't need a second invitation.

Scrambled eggs, sausage, hashbrowns, beer and coffee. He remembered it well. By four a.m. most of the revelers had gone. As much as he hated to, he had no excuse for staying. Stepping into the kitchen, he thanked Sandy for the breakfast, and for such a good time. She had squeezed his hand tightly. Then, to his surprise, had kissed him on his cheek, whispering, "Come back in about fifteen minutes."

Hell. He thought he had heard wrong. She couldn't mean him,

not a fifty-year old fart. He had pointed at himself. She nodded yes as she whisked away saying goodbye to more departing guests.

He had left with the last of the group. She smiled, winking at him as he eased out the door. Nonchalantly, he waved goodbye to the others in the parking lot, got in his car and drove off. He checked his watch a dozen times in the next fifteen minutes as he drove around. At one point he laughed aloud; she was pulling his leg. That had to be it. A young gal like her and an old fart. Naw, she didn't really mean for him to come back. He must have misunderstood, but she did whisper it to him.

He drove back to her apartment complex and parked. His heels had clicked sharply on the hard tarmac surface. Stopping at the apartment building door he had yanked on the handle. Locked! Damn! He knew it was too good to be true. She was just teasing him. He started to leave when he spotted the resident listing. Hell, he couldn't even remember her last name. Sandy, Sandy, what?

Running his finger along the listing, he came across S. Simpson. He noted it, then continued running his finger down the entire listing. It was the only name with an "S" for the first name. It had to be her. Sandy Simpson. He rang the button for her apartment. Almost instantly a buzzer hummed and the door unlocked. He entered and quickly moved across the small lobby and up the steps. At the top he looked down the hallway. She was standing in her open doorway, a warm, inviting smile on her face, a diaphanous black peignoir covering her lithe body.

"Bring her ten degrees to starboard," Peter commanded, interrupting Harry's reverie. "There's a small ship cutting across our bow about two miles ahead. Didn't you see it?"

"Sorry," Harry replied. "I was looking away at the moment." Glancing down at the radar screen, he saw the blip. The small ship was probably an inter-island steamer. Dammit, Harry muttered under his breath, once again looking into the darkness of night, so much for pleasant thoughts. He glanced back down at the radar screen. The blip was gone.

Nurad responded as he turned the wheel changing course. In a matter of minutes the small ship had slipped along well past the port side and Peter ordered Harry to resume the previous course.

Harry glanced down at the radar. The blip was there again. Maybe his eyes were playing tricks on him, or maybe the radar was malfunctioning again.

"Good morning, chaps," Captain Andress said stepping into the wheelhouse. A broad smile filled his face, a cup of steaming coffee in his right hand. Peter threw a quick salute. "How goes the night, Mr. Selham?" he nodded in courtesy to the salute. Even Harry felt himself stiffen to attention.

"Everyting is going vell, sir," Peter replied crisply. "Ve made a ten degree course change just minutes ago to avoid an island steamer crossing our bow, den corrected back to our regular course. Oddervise, der night has been uneventful."

"Good. How is dis man, Harry Martin, vorking out? It appears he is turning into qvite a helmsman. Does he do his job vell?"

"Yes, sir. Good," Peter replied with a faint grin. "He is earning his keep."

"Good. Good. Keep him busy und out of mischief."

Captain Andress winked at Harry as he passed by. "I couldn't sleep so I decided to come up to der bridge. You two seem to haf everyting under control." He scratched at his beard then took a sip of coffee. "By der vay, is der radar vorking okay now since der engineer fixed it?"

"I tink so," Peter answered. He glanced at Harry. "Is vorking okay?"

"I was about to mention to you, Mr. Selham, that when I checked the small ship on the screen a little while ago, it's blip didn't appear on the screen. It seems to appear, then disappear for several sweeps, then reappears. Now you can't see it."

Captain Andress studied the scope, the smile fading into a scowl. "Dis is der second time dat damned piece of equipment has malfunctioned. You vould tink a modern ship like dis vould haf better equipment on board. You call up der engineer right now und tell him I vant dat damned piece of junk fixed now!"

"Aye, aye, sir!" Peter snapped back sharply. He turned, picked up the bridge phone and called the chief electrician conveying the captain's request in very curt terms.

"He vill be up shortly," Peter said, hanging up the phone as he turned back to Captain Andress.

"Good. Make sure he fixes it right dis time!" With a broad sweeping glance about the bridge area, he gave a perfunctory salute and started away. "Carry on. I go down for Osa's breakfast." He patted Harry's shoulder as he passed by. "She's vun fine voman."

Harry offered an anemic smile in return. "She's very nice, sir," he replied, deciding it was better to offer a nice comment than none at all. A fine woman? Cold as a cucumber!

The sun would soon be rising, its thin rays reflecting off the distant clouds and a new day would be at hand. Harry was particularly pleased. At the change of watches, he would be duty free for the next twenty-four hours. The last twelve days had been unduly demanding. The time off would be a welcome relief.

Chapter 39

KING NEPTUNE PAYS A VISIT

"I vill check on der information you gave me last night about der putty und let you know," Peter said joining Harry for breakfast. "It does seem strange."

"I'd appreciate it if for no other reason than peace of mind," Harry answered as he dug into his grapefruit sending small jets of juice spurting in several directions.

They ate in relative silence, interrupted occasionally by crewmembers inquiring of Peter about the ship's current position. When he was through eating, Peter gathered up his tray and left. Harry settled back savoring one last cup of coffee. He sipped at it slowly enjoying the aroma, the warmth. Exhaustion tugged at him and he fought it. Maybe he'd hit the sack a little later. The next twenty-four hours were all his; no work, his own personal time, time to relax, to write those dozen or so letters he'd delayed writing, do some laundry, clean up the cabin, work on his jacket and seabag, or whatever struck his fancy. He yawned. Would one full day be enough time? His eyelids drooped. He yawned again, blinking his eyes several times. No, he didn't want to sleep just yet.

Osa came into the galley from the kitchen. Their eyes met. Harry winked. She started to smile, then froze, wheeled about and headed back into the kitchen. He grinned. *I didn't realize I'd been that bad,* he thought, as the grin widened. *Apparently my apology hasn't warmed her up one bit. It'll take a lot to melt that cold, cold heart, and I sure as hell don't have the time.*

He finished his coffee, piled the empty dishes on his tray and dumped the tray at the dirty dish window. Out of the corner of his eye he caught her looking at him. He waved. She turned quickly away. "Screw you," he said softly.

Stopping by the railing he gazed out across the sea. Martin, he scolded himself, get the bitch off your mind. You're going to have to concentrate every bit of your free time to your mission in China to retrieve that damned money.

Astern, the first faint light of a new day stretched across the horizon. Harry pulled his collar tighter around his neck as a chill wind swept across the deck. He could sense an inner tiredness tugging at his body. No sense in fighting it any longer; it was time to call it a night.

Harry blinked his eyes open. Peter was standing at his side of the bunk grinning ear to ear, shaking him awake. "Harry, I haf good news for you," he beamed. "I haf good news."

"What, what are you talking about?" Harry replied shaking his head, trying to come fully awake. "What good news?"

"Der putty. I confronted Ernst right after breakfast. I told him it appeared dere might be some unusual materials below deck dat could be dangerous. He vas puzzled. I told him dat you had seen a substance dat looked like plastique explosive along der ribbing of der ship next to der hull. He vas still puzzled. Den I told him about your exploration below decks und seeing him vis der putty, or vat ever it vas. All of a sudden his eyes lit up and he started laughing. He said vat you saw vas ship's putty. It is special putty used as a sealer. He took me over und showed me a can of der putty. Den I recalled hafing seen dis putty before. It is not explosives. No. Only putty." He laughed. "Dat is funny."

Harry gave Peter a questioning look. "He actually showed you the stuff?"

"Yah. Of Course. It is vat he said it vas, just putty. Ernst asked me to bring you down und he vill show you."

"This I gotta see," Harry said throwing off his covers and bounding out of bed. Quickly he dressed and the two headed below deck to the engine room.

"Vell, Mr. Martin," Ernst beamed as they came into view. He extended his hand, shaking Harry's vigorously. "I am sorry for der misunderstanding. Mr. Selham made me avare of your concerns und I vant to allay any suspicions you might haf. Come, please. I vill show you"

Harry and Peter followed Ernst as he led them back to a storage locker in a far corner of the engine room. Yanking open the door, Ernst pulled out a five-gallon can clearly marked as putty. "As you can see, dis is der kind of putty ve use in der ship for sound proofing, to seal joints, small pipe leaks und for odder minor repairs." As he spoke, he popped the lid on the can exposing the pale yellowish textured material for Harry to see. His voice was loud above the roaring sound of engines. "See, up here," he said pointing up along the edge of two adjoining steel bulkheads. Harry saw a thick seam of putty that looked much like the gob he had seen down in the bilge area.

"Is this the same stuff I saw along the outer skin of the hull the other day?" Harry asked, watching for his reaction to his question. Why did he feel so uncomfortable in his presence? Why was he so damned nice all of a sudden? A real Dr. Jeckyl and Mr. Hyde. It wasn't him, the angry, bitter Ernst. He was fawning, maudlin, definitely out of character.

"Same ting. Come, I vill show." He started away heading for the hatchway leading lower into the ship's bowels. Peter was right behind him. As Harry followed after them, he reached down and pinched off a small piece of putty from the can, rolled it up in a ball, then wrapped it in his handkerchief.

Ernst led them deep into the ship, then along the walkway to the spot where Harry had first seen the gob of putty. Strange, Harry thought; he'd led us to the exact spot. Stranger, too, was the fact that there were now several gobs of putty forming a seam along the ribbing next to the hull.

"See," Ernst said, pointing with his flashlight, then reaching up and pinching off a piece of the putty. He handed it to Harry. "It is der very same ting."

Harry felt the material. He smelled it. It smelled the same as putty back in the engine room, probably the same as the ball in his pocket.

"Well, I guess I was wrong," Harry said, handing the sample

back. "My apologies. When I'm wrong, I admit it. Sorry for the misunderstanding."

"No. Is not necessary to apologize," Ernst was quick to reply in an ingratiating tone of voice. "I jus' vant to make sure you know vat dis stuff is. No. Ve don't carry any kind explosives on board dis ship, especially a grain carrier. Vun bad spark und BOOM!" He threw his hands in the air to exaggerate his point.

"I get the picture," Harry replied.

"No. No explosives on dis ship, too dangerous," Ernst repeated.

"Dere," Peter said to Harry. "I tought you might be mistaken. Dat is vy I vanted to see for myself before reporting dis to der captain." He smiled. "Much ado about nosing, right? Ve don't mention dis to der captain. Okay?"

"Okay," Harry agreed. "You've satisfied my curiosity. No sense in making a mountain out of a molehill; no sense in mentioning it to Captain Andress." He shook hands with Ernst. The man's hand's were cold, sweaty. As their eyes met, he still sensed anger in spite of a forced smile.

Back in his cabin, Harry reviewed what had just transpired. Ernst was out of character, his answer too pat, and why all of a sudden were gobs of putty all over the place, especially down in the bilge. Somehow, Harry knew he'd been conned. Ernst was too condescending, making too much of an effort to allay any possible suspicions he might have. There had to be skulduggery going on down below.

Reaching inside his pants pocket, he pulled out his handkerchief and unwrapped the small ball of putty. He examined it closely, rolled it around in his hand and smelled it. It was putty; there was no doubt about it. In fact, it was drying much like putty does leaving a white-ish residue in his hand. Plastique explosives didn't crumble, and the sample he had from before was a different texture, definitely not putty. Somebody had made some fast "repairs" below deck between the time Peter came and got him and they returned to the engine room. Why hadn't Peter picked up on it? Was he that gullible?

Then he shrugged; maybe he was reading too much into the whole damned thing. Climbing back into his bunk, he pulled his blanket up tight around his neck. Thoughts of putty and plastiques faded as he dropped back to sleep.

The noise of a claxon blaring startled him abruptly awake. What the hell is this all about? Was it a fire drill? Had something dreadful happened? Ernst! Had he blown up the ship? Jumping off his bunk he grabbed his pants, pulling them on as he headed for the main deck. Stepping on deck, he was immediately confronted by two garishly dressed characters aiming what looked like vintage World War I Springfield rifles at him. "You are a prisoner of Neptune, keeper of der oceans," one said trying to keep from laughing, looking out with twinkling eyes from under an old GI helmet liner and stringy seaweed hair. They prodded Harry with the rifles motioning him toward the bow of the ship. "Go und learn your fate." Humoring them, Harry marched forward playing the role of prisoner to the hilt, knowing full well what was coming.

On top of the center hatch cover, resplendid in a flowing cape, a gold-painted cardboard crown set jauntily atop his mophead wig, sat King Neptune, alias a grinning Captain Andress. He was holding a large golden trident, wet seaweed trailing from the pointed tines. Flanking him stood his, also grinning, costumed court. Standing in trepidation before him were several hapless members of the crew, including Osa. Harry was shoved forward unceremoniously to join them.

Rising to his full height, now glaring down at the misbelievers, King Neptune spoke out in a booming voice. He berated these mere mortals for daring to cross the International Dateline, the Domain of the Golden Dragon, without paying tribute to King Neptune and the Golden Dragon. "All sailors who haf ever sailed der seven seas und der mighty oceans of der vorld, all pay tribute to me, King Neptune. You flotsam shall be no exception!" As he spoke, he looked askance at each, his eyebrows furled in mock anger.

Turning to his court, he bellowed, "Prepare dese lowly mortals for indoctrination into der Domain of Der Golden Dragon. I, in my dual role as Golden Dragon, Ruler of der vun hundred und eightieth meridian, vill oversee der ceremony."

Each prisoner was forced to crawl across the tarpaulin cover and kneel before King Neptune. Members of the court forced them to partake of a concoction that repulsively resembled dinner leftovers of stew, spaghetti, meatballs, bread, soup and other edibles all swirled together and topped off with a splash of green food coloring. To wash down the stew, they were forced to drink an ample helping of Dragon's brew from an oversized ladle. Harry gagged at the taste. It had to be stale beer, cooking wine and a strong dash of tobasco sauce. Still, like the others, he forced it down and was released to stand with the others by the railing. He noted Osa, too, almost gagged at the concoction but managed to drink enough to satisfy the watchful eye of King Neptune.

As the clustered prisoners huddled close together at the railing they were suddenly set upon by a group of screaming, gyrating, outlandishly dressed characters carrying buckets and large paint brushes. All were generously splashed from head to toe with water-based paint from the over-sized paint brushes, thoroughly drenched with blue and yellow colors that streamed down their bodies, mixing, turning to a muddy brown as the streams puddled at their feet and ran across the deck and overboard. Although sopping wet, no one laughed lest they get the whole treatment again.

And then the next assault struck, characters who sprayed them with shaving cream, working it in their hair and lathering it across their faces and bodies. Before they could catch their collective breaths, and most unexpectedly, the ship's hoses were trained on them. The powerful streams of water doused them thoroughly from head to toe. Harry twisted and turned trying to escape the full power of the hoses. The paint washed off quickly while the drowned rats stood watching as the last of the color washed overboard.

Several feet away from him, Harry caught a glimpse of Osa trying to compose herself. She was a mess; hair hanging limp and stringy, devoid of makeup, wet clothing clinging tightly to her lithe body, water still running in small rivulets down her deeply tanned legs. Yet, in spite of her disheveled appearance, he couldn't help but admire her natural beauty. Not bad for an old broad, not bad at all.

Towels were quickly dispensed followed by cold beer, sandwiches, the singing of salty sea chanties, laughter and general socializing. A carnival atmosphere enveloped the group with everyone singing, slurping down cold beer and having a fine time. Harry was surprised that Osa joined in. She even had a few pleasant words for him. How do you figure her out, he wondered. Terrific personality when she was warm; cold as an iceberg when she was pissed; and there was no doubt that she held grudges.

When he could no longer feel the tip of his nose, Harry excused himself. He'd had enough. It was time to go. Trying to maintain his equilibrium, he meandered back to his cabin, shrugged out of his damp clothing, toweled off, and then climbed back to the beckoning warmth of his bunk. Damn, he thought, as he drifted off, it had been one hell of a good party. He chuckled, then hiccupped and then laughed. It was a hell of a lot more fun than the simple dateline crossing ceremony held on board the troopship *Breckenridge* bound for China in the late 1940's. Aw, hell, it was fun. It was worth it just to see Osa sopping wet, and a damned good body for an old broad.

Chapter 40
THE LADY'S AN ICEBERG

Waking was an agonizing experience. Besides a throbbing head, Harry's mouth felt like it was stuffed with used cotton balls. Groggily, he glanced over the edge of the bunk. Peter was gone; no one to commiserate with. It was just as well, actually, for he didn't feel much like being sociable at the moment. Lurching forward, he rolled over the end of the bunk landing unsteadily on the deck. "A cold shower," he mumbled, stumbling toward the head.

Twenty minutes later, showered, clean shaven and dressed, a new, alert Harry Martin addressed himself in the mirror. "You look a hell of a lot better," he said to his reflection. His stomach growled. Glancing at his watch; he saw it was 1930 hours. Dammit, the kitchen would be closed. At best he might scrounge up a cup of coffee and sandwich from the dinner leftovers.

The galley was deserted. The newly indoctrinated members of the Domain of the Golden Dragon were probably sleeping it off, save for those on watch. He picked through the scraps of food finding enough to make a sandwich. It would hold him until breakfast, he thought, munching away.

The sun was low on the horizon when Harry stepped on deck picking at his teeth with a toothpick. He took in several deep breaths of air, and then strolled leisurely along the main deck toward the bow, stopping now and then to lean on the rail gazing out across the ocean. Clouds stretched out across the distant horizon in flaming reds and golds, contrasting sharply against the dark blue ocean. The air was still, warm but soon cool evening breezes would sweep across the ship.

Reaching the bow, he paused at the port rail. Leaning far out over the railing he watched the bow slicing through the swells like a huge knife. Dolphins darted alongside the ship leaping high in the air, disappearing beneath the surface and then breaking free, leaping high once again in a continuing rhythmic pattern.

Moving around the bow Harry was somewhat surprised at seeing Osa standing at the starboard railing looking pensively toward a magnificent sunset.

"Hello," he said, approaching her. "I thought I was the only one on board ship who appreciated beautiful Pacific sunsets."

Osa turned, startled at hearing his voice. "Oh, it's you."

She seemed somewhat disappointed at his presence. She offered a half-hearted "let's be friends" smile. "Yes I luf der sunsets. I get up here often."

"You do," Harry chuckled. "I get up here, too, but I must confess that I've never seen you here before. Apparently I stay on the port side and you're over here on the starboard side."

She laughed. It was a warm, friendly laugh, the infectious laugh he remembered before he made an ass of himself. Once again he began to feel comfortable in her presence.

"Der sunsets are beautiful out here on der ocean. Dey are truly vun of God's masterpieces. He paints der sunset vis der brilliant strokes of Matisse or Gauguin," she said pointing toward the distant clouds. She took a deep breath and exhaled. "Und der air, so clean und fresh." She breathed deeply again.

"I agree," Harry replied taking a deep breath, holding it momentarily and then slowly exhaling. He leaned against the railing close to her. In silence they stood looking out across the rolling seas watching the sun turn into a brilliant orange ball which slowly disappeared below the horizon.

The golden glow of the clouds turned into a dull, blue-gray, then to a somber, deeper hue. The ocean, too, changed, taking on a deeper, foreboding demeanor. Night had descended engulfing the two in darkness.

Harry finally broke the prolonged, almost embarrassing silence. "Uh, about the other night, as I said, uh, I am sorry. I guess I got a little bold and –"

"No. Please. I understand. It is done," she said. Turning toward him, she leaned forward, her lips lightly bussing his cheek. "It is hard sometimes to be a vidow such a short time, to review my life, to restructure my life knowing I must go forvard, dat I can't go back. Ven you touched me der odder night, it brought a new feeling; toughts entered my mind." Her voice became almost a whisper. "I tried to fight such toughts, der toughts I entertained after you kissed me, sinful toughts." She looked away into the darkness.

"How long have you been widowed?" Harry asked, knowing, but feeling he had to draw it out of her, to let her talk, to be a good listener. Maybe he could help her, could be a better friend to her. Something was troubling her, that he was sure of.

"Since last August," she said. "Rudy, my husband, vas killed in an auto crash." Her voice was halting, as though finding it hard to speak. Tears brimmed in her eyes, and then began streaming down her cheeks. Harry pressed his handkerchief into her hand. She took it, dabbing quickly at her eyes, but the tears wouldn't stop. She turned her back to him, her body shaking convulsively.

"I'm sorry, I —" Harry started to speak, feeling helpless, wanting to help her, but how? He wanted to hold her, to take her in his arms and console her, to let her know everything would be all right. Time heals. Yet, if he moved to hold her, she might get the wrong impression, shades of their first encounter, and then he was pulling her close, turning her around, resting her head lightly on his shoulder as he wrapped his strong arms about her. "There, there, it's hard to lose someone you love, someone you care for." As he spoke his hands gently massaged her shoulders in a soft, soothing manner.

"Don't be sorry," she sobbed, turning her tear-stained face to his. "He vas a terrible man. I vas married to him for tventy years und I tought I knew him, my own husband, but I didn't." She pulled away from him, dabbed at her tears and, in a choking, strained voice, continued. "He vas running around mit a young girl, a whore! A cheap little whore!" The word whore seemed to explode from her lips, and she twisted the handkerchief anxiously in her hands. "Oh, it hurt, it hurt ven I found out about dem. He cheapened our marriage." The tears continued, her body wracked with spasms as she gasped out her story.

"There, there," Harry whispered consolingly, not knowing what to say, finally deciding saying nothing was the best course of action.

"I'm sorry, Harry," she sobbed, "I vas a good vife. I did my vifely duties. I tought he vas happy. At least he appeared to be happy." Osa pressed the damp, wrinkled handkerchief to her eyes, then wiped at her cheeks and chin. "Dere ver no children. Ve agreed dat our careers ver der most important, dat sex und children ver not dat important in our marriage, dat our luf for each odder vould be all ve needed. I tought he lufed me, only –" She began crying softly again. Tearfully, she spoke. "I asked him how he could say to my face dat he lufed me und den go out und haf sex vis a –" She spat the word "whore!" Her face contorted in sudden anger. "He svore he lufed me, but dat she did tings for him, different tings to him, vulgar tings, tings dat no voman vould do for her husband. He actually told me, vulgar, vulgar, vulgar!" She buried her face in his shoulder, sobbing, shaking.

"There, there, let it all out," Harry whispered consolingly, as his hands moved tenderly over her shoulders and back. After a while she seemed calmer, nestling her face against his neck, her warm breath tingling his skin. The headiness of her perfume and erratic, panting gasps of her breath tantalized his thoughts.

Dammit! Here he was in the middle of the Pacific Ocean with a beautiful woman in his arms, only she had more problems on her mind than Carter had liver pills, and she sure as hell didn't need one more problem, namely horny Harry Martin.

A cool breeze swept across the deck. Osa shivered. Harry held her closer. "It's getting cooler," he whispered "Do you want to go?"

She didn't make any move to break free, offering only the faintest nod of her head and a whispered, "No."

Harry rubbed his hands vigorously up and down her back.

"This'll warm you," he whispered, continuing the vigorous motions. Her sleeveless cotton blouse and cut-off jeans didn't offer much protection from the cool breeze. She huddled closer to him, her breath warm and tingling against his throat, with tremulous little gasps.

The extent of his rubbing inched lower and lower until his hands slid down across her buttocks, momentarily kneading the firm mounds, then back up the length of her back. Osa made no attempt to stop him or break away as his hands moved down again, this time massaging the mounds. Her breathing came in shorter, faster gasps. Her head tilted upwards and their lips met in a warm, lingering kiss, her hands moving to the back of his head, fingers caressing his neck sending a shiver of excitement through him.

Harry dug his fingers into her buttocks pulling her tightly against his growing hardness, grinding against her, feeling her respond, the firmness of her pelvic bone. Their kiss became more impassioned. His tongue probed at her lips, sensed a momentary hesitation, and then they surrendered, parting, accepting as it drove deeply into her mouth. She moaned, sucking at the invader, then drove her tongue deeply within his mouth. As their tongues dueled in growing passion he ground his solid manhood harder against her, pleased at her response, the undulating thrust of her hips. His hands moved over her blouse encompassing her breasts, fondling, molding the soft resilient flesh. Desire she hadn't known in years swept through her body. A yearning sublimated for so long screamed for release, and yet, it was wrong; she had to stop him before it got out of hand.

She broke free of his kiss, gasping, covering his hands with hers. "No, ve must not," she cried, yet unable to force his hands away as they continued caressing her heaving breasts. "Oh, Harry," she mewled, her voice a hoarse whisper. "Ve must stop; dis is madness."

When his lips sought hers, she responded feverishly, parting to receive his probing tongue, answering in kind, passion raging uncontrollably throughout her responding, wanton body, knowing she didn't have the strength to resist, nor wanting to.

His hands moved under the back of her blouse. Osa, in a last futile attempt to stop him, reached behind her but his hands had moved quicker, the bra hooks parted easily and her breasts broke free to the coolness of the night. His hands caressed the soft, pliant flesh, fingers toying with turgid nipples. "Harry," she moaned as he pinched the hard tips. Her hips arched forward of their own volition grinding hungrily against his erection, a wetness in her aching loins.

She resigned herself, almost anticipating his urgent, forceful touch.

Her hand moved between them over the hard bulge in his pants, running the length of it, then jerked away as though she had touched fire.

Harry peeled her blouse back exposing the two ivory globes, nipples jutting starkly against the dark horizon and then he was sucking, moving from one to the other, her moans encouraging, thrusting her breasts upwards for his enjoyment, gasping as his teeth nipped gently on the sensitive buds.

Yet, her mind reeled in confusion. What was happening was lustful, sinful, her body being used for his sexual pleasure. Her mind may have sent frantic danger signals but her wanton flesh responded, enjoying. It had been such a long time since she had felt this way, so very long.

Rudy had paid the price for adultery; no sex for over a year. But it hadn't stopped him or his wayward ways. Who was the victim of frustration, not him, but her, alone, every night for over a year until that fateful day. Divorce had been out of the question. Her parents had been married fifty-five years. No one in her family had divorced; it was a subject not discussed. Rudy would have come around; it was just a matter of time.

Still, it was wrong what they were doing. It was sinful. They had to stop. Her argument was lost as her flesh succumbed to Harry's tender sucking. As his hand moved down over her stomach, she squeezed her legs together. "No, Harry," she whispered plaintively, and then his fingers popped the snap of the waistband of her jeans, the zipper sliding downwards. "No, Harry, please, no," she pleaded but his hands were already inside her panties easing behind, clutching at the pliant orbs, kneading the soft resilient flesh. In spite of her trepidations her body writhed to the tempo of his firm hands. "Harry," she groaned, suddenly arching upwards, grinding her pelvis against his hardness, her breath hot against his neck.

"Let's lay down," he gasped trying to ease her down to the deck.

"Noooo, Harry," she cried out, her pelvis grinding faster, harder against his erection, and then she emitted a long gratifying moan, shuddering as she collapsed against him.

She orgasmed! It struck him like a hammer blow. She'd orgasmed! In a complete state of frustration, he unzipped his pants and pulled out his swollen member wrapping her fingers around it. "Do me," he commanded. Osa, drained at her sudden emotional release, mechanically jerked at his rigid organ.

Just as quickly, Harry grabbed her wrist stopping her, the painful jerking motion so reminiscent of his wife. "Let's lay down, on the deck," he whispered kissing her fervently as he hurriedly shucked loose of his pants and shorts exposing himself to her. "C'mon," he pleaded. "Down on the deck."

The response was not there, not the passion they had shared only moments ago. She looked at him, hesitant, unsure, then at her hand, which she quickly jerked away. "No, please."

"C'mon," he said, and pulled her to him, kissing her, mashing his lips to her's, tongue darting feverishly inside. "I'm almost there, just a few seconds," he pleaded. His hands clutched the sides of her head, and then he was forcing her downwards. "On the deck," he hissed, "ohh, yeah, this will do the trick!"

Osa looked up into his lust-contorted face as he forced her downwards. Suddenly she realized what he wanted of her, what a whore would do. "No!" Her hands slapped upwards knocking his hands free from her head. "No!" she snapped, rising unsteadily to her feet, eyes blazing with anger as she faced him. "Dat is not nice vat you vant me to do. I don't do tings like dat."

Harry looked at her not believing what he heard. "Christ!" he roared. "One minute you're hot to trot and the next minute you're back to being an iceberg!" He shook his head in disbelief. "What the hell's with you, lady?"

"My husband vanted me to do tings like dat. I tell him no. I tell you der same ting. Whores may do dat. I don't! I don't need sex dat bad dat I got to do tings like dat."

She was shaking with anger, at the same time trying to dress herself. Bending forward, she dropped her breasts back into their respective cups, reached around and snapped her brassiere together. "All you men are alike, all sick, all animals! Sex, sex, sex, dat's all you vant from a voman!" She buttoned her blouse, zipped up and snapped her jeans. "Animals, sick animals!"

"Well, I'll be damned!" Harry snapped, finally finding his voice, feeling anger welling inside him. Talking to her through gritted, tightly drawn lips, a cynical tone to his voice, he said, "Well, I'll be damned. You sure as hell enjoyed sex a few minutes ago when you were being satisfied. But when it comes to satisfying your partner, to hell with him, and tings like dat ain't so sick and dirty!"

He was jamming his deflated penis back inside his shorts, pulling up his pants, zipping up. "How two people enjoy sex is their business. Sick and dirty are in your mind!"

He pointed at her head. "You remind me of my damned ex-wife. You probably never learned another damned thing about sex after your first week of marriage because you were taught sex was dirty and 'good girls' don't think about sex, nor encourage sex, and only have sex because its, as you said, 'their wifely duty'."

Glaring at him, Osa yanked down her blouse and tucked it in her waistband. "You are sick! All men are sick! You don't know how to treat a lady!"

"Show me a lady and I'll show you how to treat her," he quipped just as nastily as he faced her with equal anger seething inside. Yet, there was a feeling of pity for her, knowing now how she felt about men, how she must have felt about her husband. The poor bastard! No wonder he was looking elsewhere for action.

Still glaring at him, Osa straightened her clothes. She heard him. She ignored him. He was nothing but a filthy pervert. She turned away walking down the deck.

"When you get ready for sex, come see me," he called sarcastically after her.

She stopped, turned, face livid. "You vill be der last person on earth I vill ever turn to for sex. You are a pervert, a sick, sick person. You cannot haf sex visout luf. I don't ever vant to see you again. Ever!" With that she turned and stalked off down the deck.

"To hell with you, bitch!" he shouted after her but his words were lost to the rising winds.

In the solitude of his cabin after having stood under a cold shower and relived the nightmare, he now stood before his reflection in the mirror muttering to himself. "I swear the palm of my hand is going to be covered with hair by the time I get to China and get relief." His eyes narrowed as he faced his image, "but I'll tell you one thing, Martin, one thing is for sure. If I ever get a chance I'm gonna rub her snooty nose in mud. She'll never get me screwed up again, never!"

Chapter 41

PLASTIQUE EXPLOSIVES BELOW DECKS

Coming off watch the next morning, Harry headed straight for his quarters, stripped, showered and hit the sack. It had been a miserable watch. He was still fuming over Osa, his mind in an angry turmoil: Osa the iceberg! One day he'd settle the score with the bitch, her and her damned Victorian attitude.

Rolling on his side, he yanked the covers over his head forcing his mind to think of other things. Yet, sleep eluded him. He tossed and turned for the best part of two hours. Peter's snoring aggravated him. How the hell could he sleep so soundly. It wasn't human.

Finally, in disgust, he slipped from his bunk, dressed and headed for the galley. Hurrying through the line he decided a cup of black coffee and a sweet roll would do the trick. If the bitch sticks her neck out the kitchen door, so what? Who gives a rat's ass! Give her the finger!

He found solitude in a far corner of the galley, yet sitting where he could watch the kitchen door. One moment he was angry with himself for being stupid enough to even touch her; the next moment angry with her for even allowing him to touch her. She'd strung him along, a willing partner to the point of her release. The bitch! Even a cold shower hadn't cooled his anger.

You deviated from your game plan, Martin, he chastized himself. Your jacket's still in the corner of your locker where you threw it. Get back on track. Your time is limited. You've got a hell of a lot of work to do and damned little time, and you don't have time for any thoughts of her. Yes, his day would come; he knew it.

And there she was again in his mind's eye, her face, holding her in his arms. Maybe he had come on a little strong. It hadn't been his intention. He wanted to be friends, to listen, to console. He hadn't planned what happened; it just happened. She had allowed it to happen. She led him to believe she was ready and willing. Her response was encouraging, passionate as any female he'd ever had before, even Sandy.

Goddamn frigid prude! No wonder her husband was out with that young bimbo if that's what he had to come home to every night.

He took a sip of coffee, then a bite of roll. It was thick, doughy in his mouth. He washed it down with another sip of coffee. The way she treated sex; what'd she call it, a married woman's "responsibility." Bullshit! What damned Victorian thinking is that? She had to have been a classmate to his ex-wife. He shook his head. He figured they'd broken the mold when his ex-wife was created: cold, frigid, now here was another one.

Except for his honeymoon, he couldn't recall a time when they really enjoyed sex, talked about sex or experimented with sex. The constant arguments about sex had taken the edge off enjoyment, eventually killing any desire for her. The divorce had been a welcome relief, a door opening to a new life, to an attainment of sexuality he had sought, and found, with Sandy.

Sandy was the only one he'd met with a healthy, lusty attitude toward sex, a veritable free spirit. She was emphatic about sex; it made the world ago 'round. They sure had some great times he recalled, the best of times. Why was it so damned many broads over the age of 40 still lived the Victorian syndrome: sex is dirty.

He sipped at his coffee. It was still biting hot. The roll had disappeared. A number of early risers were starting to go through the breakfast line. He held off going through the line not wanting to see her.

For some unexplained reason, he felt edgy today, not just here in the galley and the chance that the bitch would show her face, but something he couldn't place his finger on. It was an inner feeling, a kind of sixth sense warning him. Was it Peter, the way he seemed so aloof last night, so damned testy in his commands, so seemingly wrapped in thought? Was it China? At the rate they were moving, they'd soon be there and he hadn't finished his jacket. Stan? Somehow he knew the bastard was out there somewhere just biding his time. Ernst? Yeah. He'd pulled off a con job on them, he was sure of that. Putty? Putty, my ass! Plastique explosives and putty don't look that much alike. The jerk had been too condescending in his efforts to clear up the misunderstanding.

Harry pulled the piece of putty from his pocket and unrolled it from the piece of paper toweling. The stuff was crumbly, a white residue flaking off on his fingers.

"Hello, Harry. Haf you been doing anymore exploring lately?"

Harry glanced up. Chief Engineer Svenson, a broad smile playing across his ruddy face, was making his way to his table.

"Naw, not lately," Harry shrugged knowing the word about his mistaking putty for plastique explosives was probably the butt of jokes around the ship.

"Vell, I've got some good news und some bad news dat vill probably be of interest to you."

"Oh. What's so important that I'd be interested?"

"You von't haf to be vorried about Ernst anymore. He fell down a ladder und broke his leg. He is in bad pain. I tink he has internal injuries, too."

"What?" Harry looked at the chief not believing what he had just heard. "Ernst, injured!"

"Yah. He is hurt bad. Peter said he has to be evacuated."

"When did this happen?"

"Just a little vhile ago. A helicopter is already headed dis vay. In der next hour Ernst vill be on his vay to Vake Island. Hopefully dey can fix him up and den he can be returned to der ship ven ve come back dis vay from China."

A cold chill ran down Harry's spine. The remark Karl, the oiler, had made regarding Ernst had stuck in his mind; Ernst had left the sister ship *Nuergren* because of a serious injury only hours before the ship suddenly and mysteriously sank that night in the deepest part of the Indian Ocean with the loss of all hands.

Nurad was approaching the deepest part of the Pacific Ocean, the Bonin Trench. Now, all of a sudden, Ernst is badly injured and is about to be transferred off the ship to Wake Island!

Excusing himself, Harry jumped to his feet brushing past the chief, bolting for the exit. Now he was certain Ernst had set plastique explosives. He stopped momentarily in his cabin to grab a flashlight, then hurriedly, two steps at a time, descended into the bowels of the ship.

He slipped past the engine room and continued quickly down along the lower passageway to the dimly lit walkway where he first noticed the putty. In moments he was at the spot. Flashing a light beam up the ribbing he saw a big gob of putty had been plastered tightly against the hull. Only now, there was something else, a fuse cap and a timing device implanted in the putty. Plastique explosives.

Carefully easing the timing device and fuse out of the plastique explosive, Harry saw the unit was ticking. It was set for 9 p.m. The ship would go down that night with all hands, just like its sister ship. No warning. Only one survivor.

Moving quickly along the passageway, he found a second gob of explosives and disarmed it. Then a third and fourth. How many had Ernst set? Sweat stood out on his forehead as he feverishly made his way back toward the engine room. All the explosives had to be found immediately or they didn't stand a snowball's chance in hell of living.

The helicopter! Had it arrived yet to pick up Ernst? He was the only man who knew the exact location of all the explosives. Quickly, Harry dashed up the ladder to the main deck. A crowd had gathered at one of the hatch covers where Ernst lay on a stretcher attended to by Captain Andress and Peter. Already Harry could hear the screeching thok, thok, thok of a jet engine as the helicopter approached the ship.

Harry raced down the deck barreling his way roughly through the crowd. "Don't release him!" he yelled at Captain Andress making his voice heard above the high-pitched whine of the approaching helicopter. He thrust the fuses and timing devices into Ernst's face. "You aren't pulling this shit a second time!" he screamed.

Strapped in a metal stretcher, Ernst paled at the sight of the fuses and timing devices. He looked at Harry fearfully.

"Yeah. You recognize this stuff don't you, you scheming bastard!" Harry screamed in Ernst's face. "You thought you could kill us with your damned explosives, but you're not. You're not getting off this ship! You'll die with the rest of us!"

"Vat is dis?" Captain Andress demanded, startled at the way Harry had shoved him aside, at his screaming at the poor injured sailor. He jerked Harry around. "Vot do you haf dere?"

"Timing devices to blow up the ship, sir," Harry replied holding the devices before him. "This son-of-a-bitch planted plastique explosives below deck. When I heard he'd fallen and was injured, and was to be taken off the ship, I remembered what was said about his leaving *Nuergren*, how he was the only survivor. I found these, but not all of them. We're the next victims for his ship sinking scheme."

Captain Andress took the devices from him, examining them.

"He told Peter and me it was just putty down there in the hold," Harry continued. "Putty, my ass! It's plastique explosives. There's enough down there to send this ship to the bottom in seconds with no survivors. Nine o'clock tonight and BOOM! No more *Nurad!*"

Captain Andress turned his attention to a cowering, cringing Ernst. His expression served as his confession. Looking up at his first officer, the captain asked, "Is vat he says true? Vy vasn't I informed of dis?"

Peter gave a half-hearted shrug. "Ernst said it vas putty. It's der kind ve use on board ship. He showed Harry und I. I believed him."

"You believed him? Vat Harry is showing us is serious. Look at dese devices."

"It seemed minor at der time," Peter replied defensively with a wave of his hand. "It vas brought to my attention. I took care of it."

"You may have bought his explanation but I didn't," Harry yelled, "especially after I learned he'd survived the sister ship sinking." He turned to Ernst. "You remember the *Nuergren*, don't you? You were the only survivor!"

Ernst looked away without answering.

"Keep him on board and he'll sink with the rest of us!" Harry screamed making his voice heard above the increasing noise of the fast approaching helicopter. The chopper swung in past the bow appearing suddenly over their heads, hovering back and forth, aligning itself over the hatch where Ernst lay.

A wave of fear crossed Ernst's face. He glanced quickly at Harry, then Peter, who turned away looking up at the chopper, and then over at the captain. There was no sympathy in the look from the captain.

"He is wrong!" Ernst cried out. "Captain Andress, please, I hurt bad, send me to Vake Island. I need help. Please! I got to go to Vake Island!"

Captain Andress knelt close to Ernst, his stern face only inches from the injured sailor. "Is vat Harry says true? Did you plant explosives on board dis ship?"

Ernst looked away. "No! Is not true! I know nossing of vat he says. Nossing!"

Captain Andress grabbed Ernst by his collar, jerking his head up till they were eyeball to eyeball. "Don't lie to me," he demanded. "Don't lie to me! Is vat he says true? Did you set explosives on dis ship?"

Ernst trembled, his eyes breaking contact, shifting away, and avoiding the intense look of his captain. Peter knelt close watching, waiting.

"Ahoy on board ship —" a voice boomed from the helicopter. "We are ready to hoist your injured man on board. Please hook the descending cables to either end of the stretcher and secure them tightly."

Ernst looked up at the helicopter, at the descending cables; his chance for freedom.

"He stays on board!" Captain Andress snapped, glancing up at Peter "Vave dem avay! He vill stay vis us. Ve get to der bottom of dis or so help me."

"No! NO! I must go to Vake Island! Please, Captain Andress," Ernst begged. "I am badly hurt, I am in pain. Please! I know nossing of dis, nossing. Please!" But his pleadings fell on deaf ears.

The cable from the helicopter dangled just above their heads now. A crewman reached up to grab the two end sections.

"Don't!" Captain Andress barked. "I said to vave dem off!" he snapped at Peter. "Did you hear me?"

Peter jumped at the sharpness of the command. "Aye, sir!" he replied backing away, frantically waving at the helicopter.

"No! I need help! I tell! I tell!" Ernst screamed. "I tell. Just get me to a doctor. Please."

"Der location of each and everyvun of dem," Captain Andress yelled. "Every single location on dis entire ship."

Harry yanked a pen and small lined pad from his shirt pocket and began writing down the locations as Ernst rattled them off.

"What's the deal?" boomed the helicopter speaker. "Why the wave off?"

Peter spoke into his walkie-talkie yelling that there would be a slight delay.

"Are dese all der locations?" Captain Andress demanded when Ernst stopped talking.

"Yah. All of dem."

"No lies?"

Ernst shook his head. "Dose are all der places I set explosives."

Harry reached down and grasped Ernst's broken leg squeezing it tightly, grinding the broken bone. Ernst screamed in pain trying to break the man's grasp on his leg. Harry tightened his grasp. Terror stricken, Ernst looked into his face. "The truth," Harry hissed. "Are these all the places?"

"Yes! I tell der truth!"

Harry relaxed his grip on the man's leg.

"If dis ship sinks, you vill be held accountable," Captain Andress said. "I vill radio dis information to der autorities at vunce." He stood, and then looked at those surrounding him. "Go. Search dis ship from top to bottom. Bring back all explosives, timers und fuses. Go now!"

There was no need to repeat the order. The men dashed below to search out the explosives knowing their lives depended on it.

"What's your decision on deck?" came the helicopter speaker. "We have a limited fuel supply. Hook him up or we'll have to leave him behind."

"Should ve keep him on board?" Peter asked.

"Hook him up. Get him out of my sight. He disgusts me!" said Captain Andress. "I vill notify der American autorities who vill hold him for shipment back to Stockholm und prison." He stepped back shaking his head sadly. A man he had known and trusted, trying to sink the ship, killing his own shipmates, men he had sailed with, drank with, broken bread with. It was insane. The man must be insane.

In the meantime, Peter had grabbed the two sets of cables and was kneeling down to connect the cables to the stretcher. Mr. Helmstrund knelt to assist him but Peter waved him away. "No. I vill do it by myself," he snapped brusquely. Mr. Helmstrund quickly backed off.

Peter waved, giving the thumb's up signal to the helicopter to haul away. The chopper rose slightly and the winch started reeling upwards, lifting the stretcher clear of the hatch. Out over the side of the ship, the stretcher started swaying dangerously in the downdraft of the huge blades.

"Oh!" someone screamed.

One of the hooks had broken loose and the stretcher was flipping back and forth in the downdraft. Ernst, strapped tightly onto the stretcher, was screaming in pain, in fear.

The downdraft intensified the jerking motion of the stretcher and it began twisting violently. Paralyzed, Harry watched helplessly with the others, horrified at the scene unfolding before them. Suddenly they gasped as the last cable snapped, and the stretcher and it's screaming patient plummeted into the ocean.

They all rushed to the railing. There was no sign of him, nothing but a turbulent ocean.

Peter gripped the railing, knuckles white. "I am sure I had it hooked properly, I am sure of it," he kept repeating, a tremor to his voice.

"We can't see any sign of him," the helicopter speaker boomed. "He's gone."

Captain Andress waved them off. The helicopter turned and headed back for Wake Island. Consolingly, Captain Andress laid his big, beefy hand on Peter's shoulder "Don't take it so bad. It vas an accident. It vas justice."

They stood at the railing for several minutes before Captain Andress started away. Finding a few crew still on deck, he angrily yelled, "Don't just stand dere. Turn dis ship inside out. Do not leave vun nich unsearched. Go! Go now! Your lives depend on it!"

Chapter 42

A VISIT WITH THE CAPTAIN

Second Officer Helmstrund caught Harry just as he entered the galley for a well-deserved break. "Der captain vants to see you right now. It is urgent."

"Can it wait a couple of minutes?" Harry asked. "I wanna get a cup of coffee. I'm bushed." All he wanted was a few minutes to sit back, relax, and collect his thoughts. It had been one hell of a grueling day.

"He said urgent!" Mr. Helmstrund retorted sharply.

"Yes, sir!" Harry retorted just as sharply, snapping off a salute. He turned, brushed past the officer and headed for the bridge on the double. Urgent must be important as hell, he decided taking the steps two at a time. And Helmstrund, what a dink! Not even time for a cup of java. What a dink!

Did it matter to him that the captain had ordered him to take charge of the search relieving him of the noon watch? Did it matter to him that for several hectic hours he and the crew searched every damned nook and cranny for the hidden explosives and, in fact, had brought a staggering amount of explosives, timers and fuses up and stacked them on deck? Not even time for a cup of coffee! What a dink!

And then a thought chilled him. Osa! He came to a screeching halt on the steps. The conniving bitch must have told her uncle that he tried to rape her out on the bow of the ship last night. Dammit! That must be it; he was headed for the brig!

All of a sudden his legs turned rubbery, and could not support him. His mind was frazzled. No. He wouldn't let the bitch get the best of him. The captain had to hear his side of the story.

"You wanted to see me, sir?" Harry gasped on entering the bridge, exhausted from struggling up the last set of steps.

"Yes. I sent a communiqué off to Stockholm detailing all dat has happened today. I requested a search of Ernst's files, bank account und an investigation of der people he has associated vis in der past two years. Dere may be a clue as to his actions in vanting to sink dis ship." He stopped, glancing past Harry at the radar scope. "Dammit! Get dat electrician up here to vork on der radar. It is malfunctioning again!"

Turning his attention back to Harry, Captain Andress continued, "I vas amazed at der amount of explosives he had stashed on board our ship. Ve haf pictures of everyting. I had der stuff trown overboard as a safeguard. Now, tell me about dis incident, every detail."

A feeling of relief came over Harry. It wasn't about the bitch at all. She hadn't told him – yet. The incident, yes. Starting slowly, for the next half hour, Harry recounted the details of the incident with the so-called putty, the trek below decks with a fawning Ernst, the comment that Ernst had sailed on *Nuergren*, had been injured and removed from the ship before it sank, and that when he heard Ernst had been injured and was being removed from this ship, it triggered a horrible thought – the deepest part of the Pacific Ocean was dead ahead, the Bonin Trench.

Captain Andress eyes widened at the news of Ernst's sudden departure from *Nuergren* due to a bad accident, so similar to what had happened today. As he listened, he asked an occasional question, took time to light his pipe, puffing clouds of blue-ish smoke into the air.

"Und Peter never suspected anyting?" he asked when Harry finished speaking.

"No, I don't think so. He was concerned when I told him of my finding what could be plastique explosives, but said he would get to the bottom of it before bringing it to your attention. He seemed satisfied at the explanation Ernst gave –"

"But you veren't?"

"No. I felt Ernst had pulled a con job."

"It appears somevun targeted dis ship for sabotage. I don't know vy but at least der home office is now alerted. Anyvays, tanks to you, ve got der culprit." Grinning, he gave a hearty slap to Harry's shoulders. "I vant you to repeat der entire incident into a tape recorder for der record."

Sitting alone at one side of the bridge, Harry repeated his story into the tape recorder. When he was done, he handed the recorder to the captain. Captain Andress thanked him, adding, "On behalf of all of us, tank you for being so alert. Trough your qvick action you saved der ship und all our lives."

Embarrassed, Harry mumbled that he was sure anyone else would have done the same thing. On that note he left. Once off the bridge, he felt a wave of stupidity for not being able to accept the captain's praise. But then, he was not one for being in the limelight.

Peter was waiting for him when he arrived back in their cabin. He appeared agitated. "Vot did der captain vant?" he demanded.

"More details. He wanted me to record the whole incident on tape," Harry replied. Knowing Peter was distraught about his role in the incident, his not suspecting Ernst of skullduggery, and his handling of the lines which caused the man's untimely death, Harry downplayed the report to the captain.

"I told him that Ernst had tried to con us into believing that cock and bull story about the stuff being putty. I had a hunch he was lying but I didn't let on that you weren't aware of the scam. I guess because you've worked with him over the years, you probably took him at face value."

"Yah. I trusted Ernst," Peter replied. "I haf known him for many years, even before he came back to dis ship. I guess you can't take anyvun for granted." He paused seemingly relieved at what Harry had told him. "Der captain vas satisfied vis your report?"

"Yes."

"Good." Peter strode to the door, stopped and said, "I must go und check out some details for tonight. I vill see you later."

Harry gave a wave of his hand, plopped down in the desk chair, stretched and propped his feet on the edge of the desk. Folding his hands behind his head, he stared reflectively at the overhead reviewing the events of the last several hours. It's mind-boggling, he thought, mind-boggling!

Glancing at his watch, he saw he still had time for a quick snooze before dinner. As his feet slipped off the desk, one foot caught the edge of the wastebasket spilling the contents across the deck. "Shit!" he swore, stooping down to pick up the bits and pieces of paper. Several scraps were from a ship's cable. Curious, he flattened the pieces out on the desk fitting them together as a jigsaw puzzle.

The message was from the ship's headquarters in Stockholm and addressed to Peter.

SORRY FOR LOSS. STOP. IMPERATIVE THAT VOYAGE PLAN BE SUCCESSFUL. STOP CONTINUE OPERATION AT ALL COST. STOP. LINDSTROM.

Harry read the message a couple of times. It had no meaning for him, just management sending a supportive message to continue the voyage. But why was it sent to Peter? Why not Captain Andress?

He re-read the message. On an impulse, he folded the pieces of the cable and stuffed them in his shirt pocket. The rest of the spilled papers were dumped back into the wastebasket. Climbing into his bunk, he pulled a blanket over him settling down for a couple of hours of well-earned sleep.

Chapter 43
COLLISION AT SEA AVOIDED

The ship was directly east of the Ryuku Islands when Harry reported to the bridge for the midnight watch. He noticed they had made a course change heading more northerly, a straight line to Shanghai. The weather report indicated a moderate tropical storm brewing dead ahead. Outside the bridge, a balmy breeze swept across the ship.

Peter seemed unusually quiet, pre-occupied, less than his normal communicative self. Harry shrugged it off. Yesterday had been one hell of a day. Today had to be better. Peering into the darkness he could see a scattered layer of low-lying clouds. Occasionally stars twinkled through the broken edges of the clouds as the layer moved on. Off the port bridge Harry saw the faint lights of small villages along a distant shoreline they'd be passing before long.

About an hour into the watch Harry reached over and tapped the radar screen. It hadn't made a good sweep in the past several minutes. Blips appearing on the screen would not show up the second and third time around. These were busy waters with many small coastal vessels on the move and the radar was very necessary. The last radar sweep showed the area devoid of shipping, yet, visually, he knew there was a small coastal off his starboard that would pass astern.

He tapped the screen again. Ships couldn't be appearing and disappearing that fast. The damned radar was definitely malfunctioning. One big blip suddenly appeared, but was gone the next sweep. Now there was nothing.

"Peter," Harry called. "This damned radar is screwing up again. What should I do, throw the damned thing overboard?"

Peter smiled at the comment. Stepping over, he examined the unit. He tapped it several times. "Hmmm, I am not an electrician. I vill call him."

Picking up a phone, he dialed. After several rings someone answered only to have his ears blistered by a not too pleasant First Officer ordering him to the bridge on the double.

"He vill fix it right dis time or he doesn't leave der damned bridge," Peter said, slamming the phone back in its cradle.

Within minutes a sleepy-eyed older man reported to the bridge carrying a large tool case. He offered an apologizing look in Peter's direction, shrinking back at the harsh look he received in return. Quickly he turned to the task of repairing the radar. Soon, parts of the radar were strewn about him as he worked feverishly under the scrutinizing observation of the First Officer.

Harry looked at the jumbled mess and shook his head. "Hell, if I did that I'd never get all the parts back together again."

Peter smiled at the remark, turned and walked away placing the binoculars to his eyes, scanning the horizon. "Sir," the electrician ventured. "I must go to der electrical shop for a part. Vun unit is broken. I know I fixed it before, but it is broken again."

"Go. Be qvick about it!" Peter retorted harshly. "Der damned ting should haf been fixed right days ago."

For a moment it appeared the man was about to argue the point but thought better of it and beat a hasty retreat from the bridge.

Harry watched amused. The poor guy had worked on the damned unit so many times he probably thought he'd fixed it. Turning back to steering the ship, he casually glanced out the port window as he did routinely during the watch, and then forward. All of a sudden his head snapped back to the left as he suddenly realized that the lights of the distant villages along the shoreline were being eclipsed by a large wall topped with moving lights.

Harry dashed to the port wing door and jerked it wide open. "Oh, my God!" he exclaimed, eyes wide with fright, the color draining from his face. "Oh, my god!" he repeated.

"Vas is?" Peter asked.

"A ship! A goddamned big sonofabitchin' ship is right on top of us!" Harry yelled dashing back inside, instinctively grabbing for the handles of the telegraph. "Peter, we've got to give the order to reverse engines immediately. We're on a collision course!"

"Stop! Don't!" Peter commanded.

"But we'll hit them broadside!" Harry yelled over his shoulder at Peter, and then froze. Peter was aiming a pistol at him.

"What th –" Harry started.

"Step back, Harry. Move away from der telegraph."

"For God's sake, Peter. Use your senses!" Harry screamed looking beyond the gun aimed at his head to the man. "We're on a collision course. We'll all be killed!"

"I know," Peter said calmly, advancing toward him holding the gun in his face. "Jus' step back a bit furder," he motioned with the gun forcing Harry to step away from the telegraph. "Dat's it, und don't try anyting stupid. You vill die vun vay or der odder."

"You?" The message in the cable suddenly made sense: "to the successful sinking of *Nurad*."

"They promised you a captaincy if you sank *Nurad*!" he gasped. "Ernst was your partner! You killed him!"

"Yes, it vas necessary. He vas no longer useful to us, more of a detriment dan anyting."

"But what about your shipmates? Your friends? If you crash the ship you'll kill all of them."

"No. You vill kill dem. Ernst said you brought a curse to der ship, dat dey vould all die. If anyvun should happen to survive, dat's vat dey vill tell der autorities."

"You'll die, too. When we collide, you'll be killed along with the rest of us."

A harsh laugh escaped Peter. "No. I von't die." He pointed to a large package in the corner of the wheelhouse. "My escape raft. You see, Harry, I haf planned dis out carefully. I had broken der radar earlier before you came on duty. By a stroke of luck, I happened to see dis big ship on der scope at dat time. Ven der ships collide und der *Nurad* sinks vis all hands, as I haf planned, I vill be der only survivor. Ven I am picked up from my raft I vill tell dem I realized you intended to sink der ship. Ve struggled und I had to kill you vhile you ver lashing der vheel for a collision course. Only trough der grace of God vas I able to survive und launch a life raft."

"You'll never get away with it!"

"But I vill." Peter reached into his pocket pulling out a thin nylon line and threw it at Harry. "Please lash der vheel."

Harry automatically reached out to catch the line and then let it fall to the deck. "No dice. I won't do it."

"Do it or I'll shoot you right vere you stand?"

"Screw you." Harry stood his ground, not moving. Not a muscle twitched as his eyes stared right into Peter's eyes.

"Do it!" Peter snapped, agitated at Harry's rebuff, a crack appearing in his composure. "Tie der damned vheel!" He stepped forward aiming the pistol at his head. "I am not fooling!"

"Shoot. Shoot me and you'll have a room full of company up here so fast it'll make your head spin," Harry shot back, bluffing, doubting that anyone would hear a single shot.

"Damn you!" Peter screamed charging at him, swinging the pistol down at his head. Harry ducked catching the blunt of the blow on his shoulder.

"My God!" a voice screamed. Peter glanced at the direction of the voice. The electrician had returned standing wide-eyed.

Taking advantage of the distraction, Harry spun about lashing out with his foot, kicking Peter's hand and sending the pistol clattering across the steel deck.

Peter flung himself after the gun. Harry was right on top of him in a split second, both of them struggling for possession of the weapon. Peter's finger curled in the trigger guard. Harry grasped his wrist in a vise-like grip, smashing his hand hard on the deck. The gun went off with an ear-shattering explosion punching a hole in the door to the starboard wing. A second shot screamed past Harry's head ricocheting off the overhead.

"Vat's going on here!" came the thundering voice of Captain Andress, bursting into the wheelhouse, jerking up his pants over his pajama bottoms with one hand while trying to snap a suspender over his shoulder onto his pants with the other. "Stop! Dat is an order!"

Peter automatically stopped at his captain's command before he realized his error. In that instant, Harry smashed a right cross to his chin knocking him backwards where he sprawled unconscious against the front of the wheelhouse.

"Vat der hell is happening?" Captain Andress demanded. "Vy are you fighting?"

"We're on a collision course with another ship!" Harry yelled. "The damned thing's right on top of us!"

Captain Andress glanced out the port window. "Shit!" he exclaimed seeing the gravity of the situation. In one quick move, he rushed to the telegraph, racking the handles around, throwing them into reverse engine position.

"Their damned lights blended with the shore lights," Harry cried out. "I caught sight of them visually at the last minute."

"The vheel," he called to Harry. "Ve must turn der ship avay!" Both men turned to the task, their powerful hands grasping the wheel, spinning it around, holding it far over, praying the huge ship would respond in time to avoid a collision.

"Hold it hard over," the captain gasped, releasing his grip, moving to the control panel where he slammed his hand hard against the ship's klaxon. In the same motion, he grabbed for the ship's whistle, frantically sending a series of sharp, spine-tingling blasts across the water.

"You vill all die!" Peter screamed, rising from the corner, pistol in hand. "You vill all die!" The pistol jerked. Harry felt a momentary sting at his shoulder.

A second shot rang out. It was a louder sound. Harry glanced to his left. Captain Andress was holding a smoking .45 caliber automatic. Turning back to Peter, he saw him leaning back against the bulkhead slowly slumping downwards, an incredulous look on his face as he clutched at his chest. Bright blood oozed out between his fingers.

"Are you okay, Harry?" Captain Andress asked, rushing to his side, his gun still aimed in Peter's direction.

"Yes. He nicked me," he replied with only a quick glance at his shoulder, seeing a small patch of blood. "But I'm okay."

"Good." Dropping the gun into his pocket, Captain Andress threw his considerable bulk to the task of helping Harry turn the ship. "Now ve vork!"

Grunting, straining, they held the wheel as far over as it would turn. Harry could sense a change in the ship; it was slowly starting to turn. His eyes were transfixed on the on-coming ship, unable to turn away. He could hear the terrible blaring of the klaxon and the screeching sound of their whistle. It was a terrifying sound clutching to the depths of his soul.

"We're doing it," he grunted to the captain. "We're turning!" It was met by an agreeing grunt.

Nurad was shuddering at the sudden reversal of its engines, begrudgingly responding to the dictates of its master. All motion at the moment seemed stilted, as if in slow motion. Yet, slowly, agonizingly slowly, *Nurad* was responding. The huge screws were grabbing up tons of water, churning it into seething, frothing pools as the ship began turning.

The vessel vibrated and groaned, straining with the demands placed upon it. But it was turning. There was no doubt of it as Harry could see, could sense it happening. Maybe there was a chance after all, just maybe.

With a sense of desperation, the two watched as the huge wall of steel moved closer out of the darkness of night, its deck suddenly ablaze with lights as it moved ever closer. Now they could see what it was, a large crude carrier supertanker. Harry recalled reading that even with all an LCC's engines dead, the behemoth would take fifteen to twenty minutes and at least three miles to come to a dead standstill. *Nurad* had only a matter of minutes to change course to parallel the LCC and avert a disastrous collision.

"The way she's riding, the damned ship must be carrying at least 200,000 plus tons of oil," Harry yelled at Captain Andress. "If we hit, we'll fry tonight!"

"Hold her hard over," the captain barked. He rushed to the PA system and announced, "Stand by for a collision! All hands report to your abandon ship positions!"

"Damn you, Peter!" Harry screamed at the fallen man slumped

against the bulkhead, his head angled over in a contorted position. "Damn you!" But there was no response. His profanity fell on deaf ears.

"Ahoy, carrier!" a sharp voice crackled over the radio. "Stand by for collision!" There was a momentary pause. "Can't you people see us? What the hell's going on in your wheelhouse?"

On *Nurad's* deck crewmembers rushed to their lifeboat stations. They stood frozen, mesmerized by the huge vessel bearing down on them. In fear of impending death, several had fallen to their knees praying to all-mighty God for forgiveness of their mortal sins.

Osa, her lifejacket thrown hastily over her nightgown, looked with drawn face toward the bridge. Like the others, she turned to face the fast-closing ship, standing helplessly, waiting, watching, paralyzed.

The sound of the ship's whistle only added to the drama of fear. Both ships whistles bleated into the chill night, a cacophony of high-pitched, sorrowful screams as the ships drew ever closer as magnets drawn to one another. There was no place to run, no place to hide, all spectators to the forthcoming disaster frozen in the glare of lights.

In the wheelhouse, Captain Andress re-joined Harry, perspiring freely, holding tightly to the wheel, and forcing it over as far as possible. The gap between the two ships was closing fast now; collision was eminent.

Sluggishly, *Nurad* continued it's sweeping turn, ever so slowly beginning to parallel the course of the huge crude carrier. In the corner of the wheelhouse, the electrical engineer stood frozen, not believing what he was seeing, sweat standing in beads on his forehead.

"Now!" yelled Captain Andress. "Now!" With that command, they spun the huge wheel hard over to port which would bring the ship more quickly into a parallel alignment with the crude carrier.

"Hold it tightly! Hold it tightly!" Captain Andress implored as he ran to the telegraph, grabbed the handles, and jammed them to full forward. Within moments, the ship again shuddered violently as the massive screws reversed, now propelling the ship forward.

"Ve must vatch out for der vacuum. Keep alert!" the captain called to Harry. Harry knew well that if the ships came too close together a natural affinity, a vacuum, would pull the two vessels crashing together.

In awed silence, they watched the crude carrier looming close at hand as it started to move along the port side of the ship. Less than one hundred feet now separated the two ships and they were still gravitating toward each other.

Captain Andress stepped out onto the port bridge wing to monitor the situation. Almost immediately he returned jamming the telegraph handles to slow speed forward. Again, there was an anxious pause before the ship responded. Harry felt the change at the wheel. He knew it would allow for better control of the ship and faster passage of the LCC along the port side.

Now the starboard side of the LCC was passing. Less than fifty feet separated them. Harry could almost sense the vacuum as the ships continued to pull closer together.

Captain Andress had once again stepped out onto the port bridge wing to monitor the situation. On the LCC anxious faces peered out the windows of their bridge. An eternity seemed to fly by instead of a scant few moments, as the LCC's stern finally cleared *Nurad* with less than twenty-five feet between the bow of *Nurad* and the stern of the LCC. And suddenly, *Nurad* was astern and clear of the other ship, wallowing in its wake. A loud cheer erupted from those on deck followed by clapping hands and joyous shouts of praise.

"Ahoy! Swedish ship *Nurad*!" came a rankled voice crackling over the radio. "That was too close for comfort. Can't you people see us? We're only three football fields long!" The sarcasm was harsh, crisp.

"Ve are sorry," replied Captain Andress speaking wearily into the microphone. "Our radar equipment failed us." As he spoke, his eyes zeroed in on the quivering electrical engineer. The message in the captain's eyes was evident. The engineer hastily squatted amidst the scattered parts of the radar unit and feverishly set to the task of repairing the equipment.

"Ve caught sight of you visually at der last minute, und ver able to take evasive action," Captain Andress continued. "Ve ver confused by your lights. Dey blended vis der lights on der distant shoreline."

"You better run your ship more efficiently than that, Mister, or you'll find yourself at the bottom of the Pacific Ocean one day!" the crisp voice retorted. "You can rest assured there will be a report made on this incident. What is the full name of your vessel, its registry and the name of the captain."

Harry, standing exhausted at the wheel, watched a tired Captain Andress suddenly come staunchly erect, eyes ablaze, his face redder, eyebrows deeply furled. He grasped the microphone tightly in his beefy fist, knuckles white. He was quiet, contemplating his reply. Of a sudden, he turned to Second Officer Helmstrund who had entered the wheelhouse only minutes before. "Ve are on der east-vest shipping lane, right?" Captain Andress snapped at the Second Officer.

"Ve vere on der east-vest shipping lane, dat is before ve changed course to avoid der supertanker, sir," he replied looking at the compass.

"I see," he said and turned to Harry. "Bring us back on our previous course, Harry."

"Aye, sir," Harry was quick to oblige, swinging the wheel around, bringing the ship back on previous course.

"Und vitch of us had priority, Mr. Helmstrund?" the captain questioned the Second Officer.

"From der position of der two ships, ve had priority, sir. Ve ver to his starboard. He should haf passed astern of us."

"Tank you."

Clutching the microphone to his lips, speaking in a firm, even tone of voice, Captain Andress replied, "Supertanker captain, dis is Captain Karl Andress of der Swedish ship *Otto J. Nurad*, out of Stockholm, destination, Shanghai. I, too, vill report dis incident. Ve ver der privileged vessel to your starboard. I vill report dat you ver in violation in not respecting der rights of dis ship according to der positions of der two ships. You should haf passed astern of us. Perhaps you should review der International Rules of Navigation on der high seas." He paused, an expression of satisfaction appearing on his face. Again, he put the microphone to his lips. "The qvestion comes to my mind; vy didn't you see dis ship earlier und take appropriate evasive action?"

There was a long pause before the speaker crackled again. "This is Captain Julio Antonelli of *VLCC Oricon*. Captain Andress, let me state that we, too, have the latest in sophisticated navigational aids on board. Unfortunately, according to my first officer, your vessel did not appear on our radar screen. I apologize for not having seen you, or for taking appropriate evasive actions immediately."

Captain Andress smiled, nodding attentively as he listened. There was an impish twinkle in his eye. Clearing his throat, he answered. "Perhaps, Captain Antonelli, ve should all go back to operating ships using human lookouts in addition to our modern 'sophisticated' equipment."

"Amen," came the reply.

Captain Andress blew the ship's whistle. *Oricon* returned the salute as it disappeared into the night.

"Take command of der ship und continue on course, Mr. Helmstrund," he ordered. "Bring us back to full speed."

"Aye, aye, Captain," Mr. Helmstrund replied. Turning, he ordered Harry to maintain the current course as he brought the telegraph to full forward. Sluggishly, the huge leviathan began to pick up speed, the decks shuddering once again under the demands placed on the giant screws.

Captain Andress stepped to the ship's PA system and ordered all hands to secure from abandon ship stations. With a look of despair, he observed his first officer slumped against the bulkhead laying in an ever-widening pool of blood.

Kneeling by the fallen man, Captain Andress checked for a pulse, yet knowing there was none. Tears brimmed in his eyes, and then trickled down his ruddy cheeks. He made no attempt to wipe them away. Peter had been his friend, his trusted assistant for many years. How had they gotten through to this loyal man?

With a deep sigh, he rose, wiping at his tears, and faced Mr. Helmstrund. "You are now next in command. Get two crewmen up here to take care of Peter's body. Ve vill haf burial at daylight."

Stepping beyond Mr. Helmstrund, the captain reached forward and shook Harry's hand. "Tank you, Harry. But for your qvick action —" He stopped abruptly as his eyes caught sight of Harry's bloody shoulder. "He did shoot you!"

"A grazing shot, sir," Harry replied glancing at his shoulder. "A little iodine and a bandage should take care of it." He tried to make light of it; it was just that, a simple grazing wound.

"Get der medic, Bjorg, up here on der double to take care of dis man, und get a replacement for him!" the captain snapped to Mr. Helmstrund. "He's done more than his share of vork tonight."

"Please, no, sir," Harry interrupted. "I'd rather stay on duty." He looked in the direction of Peter. "I'd feel bad going back to our cabin at the moment; he was a good friend. I'd rather work if you don't mind."

With a condescending sigh of understanding, Captain Andress agreed to his request "As you vish. But if it pains, tell Mr. Helmstrund und he vill haf somevun replace you." Waggling his finger under Mr. Helmstrund's nose, the captain said, "Make sure you keep an eye on dis man. He is valuable to us."

"Aye, sir," Mr. Helmstrund replied.

"Oh, und make sure all dis information is entered in der ship's log. Harry can report vat caused der incident, und I also vant to report der *Oricon*. Ve ver in der right." Again, he looked at Harry. "Ve talk later. Ve haf much to discuss."

Turning his attention back to the electrical engineer, who knew he was being watched as he worked feverishly, the captain fixed him with a blistering look, roaring, "You fix der damned radar right dis time or I vill personally trow you overboard to der sharks!"

Satisfied that everything was once again shipshape, Captain Andress departed the bridge. A loud cheer rang out from the thankful crew who still milled about on the deck. The captain stuck his head in the wheelhouse and called Harry to come outside with him. Under the glare of lights, Captain Andress raised Harry's arm high with his, a sign of victory. Again, the cheers and hand clapping rang out.

On deck, Osa clapped her hands together, looking up at her uncle and Harry with mixed emotions. How could she tell her uncle what a sadistic person Harry was when he was such a hero. Uncle Karl's eyes had lit up with admiration when he talked of Harry and how he had found the explosives, and now this!

She had relived the other night a thousand times, sickened at the vulgar thing he had wanted of her. Yet, up to that point she had enjoyed being held in his arms, the press of his body to hers, being kissed, even being caressed.

"Dat Harry Martin is vun good man," Gueder said as he passed by "Ve are lucky to haf him on board ship."

"Yes," Osa found herself agreeing, and she turned quickly heading for her cabin. What could she do to drive all thoughts of the man from her mind!

Chapter 44
COGNAC WITH THE CAPTAIN

Harry awoke with a start. Had he heard Peter snoring? He rolled over and glanced down at the bottom bunk. It was empty. Peter was dead. Last night had all the makings of a bad dream, but it was real. The man was gone.

Emitting a soft groan, he rolled over on his back. Every joint and muscle in his body ached, tested to the maximum during the frantic effort to avoid the collision.

An over-sized bandage was taped to his shoulder. Luck had been with him. It was only a flesh wound, the slug barely breaking the skin, nothing to get overly worked up about, but an hour further into his watch the captain had returned to the bridge and ordered him relieved of duty through the rest of the day. No argument; he was relieved.

Glancing at the clock, he let out another moan; he'd slept the day away. It was almost dusk. Soon it would be time for his watch again. "Shit," he muttered under his breath. Sliding off his bunk, he stood on the deck stretching, trying to loosen up aching muscles. A light tap at the door startled him.

"Yes. Who is it?" he called out.

"Hans. I haf a message for you."

"Come in," Harry called reaching for his pants, sliding into them, pulling them up just as the chubby-cheeked cabin boy who served in the galley entered, cap in hand.

"Well?" Harry asked eyeing the youth.

"Captain Andress asks dat you join him in his cabin," Hans replied, staring in awe of the man who had twice saved the ship. The stories about his heroic efforts had been flying rampant throughout the ship the entire day.

"Now?" Harry asked. "Like this?" he gestured at his unkempt appearance.

"Yah, if you vould, please," Hans said apologetically.

Harry studied the boy. Captain Andress had brought him aboard as cabin boy, a favor to his mother when he started running around with an older gang of kids, tough kids bent on getting into trouble. Now, he assisted Osa in the galley and as runner and cabin boy for the captain.

"Damn," Harry muttered under his breath. He glanced at the clock again. "Tell you what, Hans. You tell the captain that I'll be there in fifteen minutes, time to clean up a bit and look more presentable. Okay?"

"Yah. Okay." Hans beamed. "I vill tell him." He backed awkwardly toward the door.

"Did I miss any good meals today?" Harry asked.

"Yah. Good food," he grinned. As an afterthought, he said, "Mrs. Peterson vas not feeling too good today. She has spent most of der day in her cabin. Probably a headache."

Harry smiled. Probably wearing her halo too tight.

Fifteen minutes later, showered, shaved and looking somewhat presentable, Harry headed for the captain's quarters on the double. A myriad of thoughts raced through his mind. What does he want to talk about? The ship? The near collision? Peter? My wound? He recalled the captain saying early on in the voyage that one day they would get together and talk about the good old days in China.

Or was it Osa? Maybe he wanted to talk about Osa. Maybe she had gone blubbering to her uncle about his attempt to seduce her, had probably even exaggerated, telling him he tried to rape her. Shit! From hero to jerk, just like that, he thought with a snap of his fingers. The conniving bitch. Then he stopped: she wouldn't have, would she?

He hesitated outside the captain's cabin, and then taking a deep breath, he knocked on the door. "Come in," boomed the captain's voice. Harry steeled himself for the inevitable, then entered.

"Harry, good of you to come on such short notice," a smiling, cordial Captain Andress greeted him. "Come, sit down." He waved Harry toward a large overstuffed chair. "Vould you care for a glass of cognac?"

"Ahhh, yes, thank you," Harry replied somewhat hesitantly. "A glass of cognac sounds good."

Crossing the room, he settled in the plush chair. A sweeping glance of the small room showed it to be tastefully decorated but sparsely furnished. A couple of nice, comfortable chairs, coffee table, end tables with lamps. Two large framed black and white photographs of vintage World War II cargo ships hung on either wall. No frills, but cozy. A plus was the thick carpeting. The room definitely conveyed the bold, masculine personality of the captain. All it lacked was a fireplace and a crackling fire.

Harry could see into his bedroom. A double bed, dresser and mirror, and beyond that the bathroom with a tub. That's a plus for command, he thought. Except for Osa's cabin, all the other cabins he had seen were furnished with showers.

Harry rose and crossed to one of the large photographs. "Interesting ship," he commented. "One you sailed on before?"

Captain Andress, who was engrossed in pouring two snifters with cognac, replied without looking up, "Dat vun is my first command, der *Viking Prince*. Ve ver in Shanghai in 1937 ven der Japanese attacked. My captain vas killed by gunfire. I took command to get us der hell out of dere. Ve had hundreds of refugees on board. Sadly, ve ver torpedoed just north of der Philippine Islands. Tragic.

"Der odder photo is der *North Star*. I vas in Shanghai vis der ship ven der Marines left in 1949 und der communists took over der country. I barely got out dat time, too. Dey vas firing machine guns at us. Again, I had lots of refugees on board. Only dis time ve got avay safely."

"Shanghai wasn't exactly your cup of tea then," Harry observed, with a light chuckle.

"Shanghai is okay. It's you damned Marines alvays leaving ven I'm in port." He winked at Harry as he approached with two snifters of brandy.

"To der rest of der voyage und dat it be successful und less eventful," Captain Andress said, chuckling as he handed Harry a snifter of rich, amber cognac.

"Amen," Harry agreed touching his glass to the captain's. A warm burning all the way to his stomach greeted his first sip. "Good," he nodded. The captain beamed.

"Are you feeling better now?" the captain inquired.

"Yes, sir, but a little worn." He rotated his shoulder for effect. "I don't know about you, sir, but I ache all over. I mean, I really ache. I didn't realize I'd strained my poor old body so badly –"

"Me, too," Captain Andress roared. "I am pooped! Dat is der most vork I haf done in ages." He took a sip of cognac. "Harry, ve must admit it; ve are getting older, older but viser. Yah?"

He emptied his glass at that remark and raised it, a sign for a refill. "Sure thing," Harry responded downing the last of the liquid and handing the glass to his host. Why not, he thought. It tastes good and he's offering.

"Ve missed you at der funeral service," Captain Andress said while refilling their glasses. "It vas sad sending a shipmate to der bottom of der sea."

Harry jerked erect. "I'm sorry!" he blurted, shocked that they had held the service so soon. "I was asleep. Someone should have fetched me."

"Don't be upset. It is done." He handed Harry a fresh cognac, and then sank down in his chair. "We haf no means of keeping a body for any length of time. It vas necessary to bury as qvickly as possible."

He took a sip of cognac, and then set his brandy snifter on a coaster on the small end table next to his chair. Searching through a collection of pipes in his pipe stand, Captain Andress finally selected an ornately carved meerschaum pipe. Harry watched silently as he tamped fresh tobacco into the bowl. Then, using three matches to get it lit to his satisfaction, he blew clouds of bluish-white, aromatic smoke out across the room.

"I listened to your report of der incident," he said nodding toward a tape player on the coffee table. "Interesting. I am sad about Peter. He served vis me for over ten years. I had high hopes he vould become captain of vun of our ships, even as early as next year."

"Someone had promised him a promotion to captain," Harry interrupted.

"Yah. I haf been in contact vis der home office. All hell is breaking loose back dere. It is hard to believe dat such scurrilous people exist. Money and power. Dat's all dey vanted, no sense of guilt or responsibility about the loss of human lives, der ship or cargo. Vun man scheming to get more money und more power. Lindstrom. Der bastard! I am sorry Peter und Ernst got involved in dis scheme to sink ships for der insurance monies, und Peter, just for a command, a command he earned und vould haf gotten in anodder year or two."

He sat back puffing on his pipe, his mind slipping away deep in thought. Harry sipped at his cognac, watching, waiting. He'd let the man talk. Be a good listener. He recalled the phrase from his days working in public relations. You couldn't learn a damned thing while you were talking. Listen, be a good listener. The phrase had stuck with him, and he felt, had benefited him.

"Yah, I feel sorry for Peter, but more-so for his vife und children. It vill be devastating to her ven she learns of his disloyalty, und it may scar der children for life. Who knows?"

Harry nodded in agreement. "I thought Peter was a square shooter," he said, not wanting an answer. "There wasn't a sign, not the least indication that he was involved in anything underhanded. Someone had to promise him the moon to get him to go along with sinking this ship."

"Never can I recall any incident in vich I could fault der man. Not vunce in all dese years."

"I'll admit I became somewhat suspicious when he bought Ernst's story about the putty. Yet, I could see where he was coming from, believing in one of his shipmates, a man he trusted. But then, they were in it together. Even the cable from the home office advising him to continue the mission had me confused at first. I thought it odd that the cable went to him and not you."

"Ahh! Dat's ven I suspected him!" Captain Andress bellowed, jerking forward to sit on the edge of his chair. "Sparks brought me a copy of der cable. It made me vunder vy der vice-president of our company vould send a cable to Peter und not to me. I vas very upset. I vas going to demand an explanation from Peter, but I held off. After all, he vas upset over the unfortunate loss of Ernst. Yet, late last night chust before going to bed, I read it vun more time. Ven I read it, it suddenly came to me – der bastard vas a part of dem! Dat's ven I hurried up to der bridge."

"And just in the nick of time," Harry added.

"Yah. I jus' knew someting vas wrong. I had to get to der bridge in a hurry. I vasn't even avare of der odder ship."

He took another long draw on his pipe. It looked small in his big, beefy hand. Another cloud of smoke curled upwards toward the overhead. "Again," he said leaning forward patting Harry's knee, a sincere look on his face, "Ve are grateful to you for your qvick tinking. Both times der ship could haf been sunk."

Harry squirmed back in his chair, uncomfortable at having praise thrust upon him.

Captain Andress sensed his uneasiness and, with a wave of his hand, moved on to a new subject. "How does it feel being at sea again after all dese years?"

"Good, sir. Good to have the feel of a solid deck under my feet again, especially after I finally got my sea legs."

Laugher erupted from the captain. "Dey surely gave you a hard time about being seasick. Ahh, dat is part of life, being able to poke fun at ourselves. Ve must haf some fun, even at our own expense." Another cloud of smoke billowed upwards as he puffed contentedly on his pipe.

Harry watched, smiling, recalling several years before when his wife had practically begged him to smoke a pipe. It was the "manly" thing to do, she had stated quite emphatically, almost inferring that he was less than manly for not smoking. To keep peace in the household, he had struggled with the habit trying several pipes and various blends of tobacco, but never actually embraced the habit. Then, one day, his wife introduced him to her pipe-smoking boss, a "successful" businessman. Three pipes and five packs of rich, aromatic tobacco ended up in the wastebasket that very day.

"Are you getting along vell vis der operation of der ship? Any problems or suggestions on how ve might improve our operation and efficiency?" Captain Andress set his pipe down. "You know, sometimes an outsider can see tings dat are so obvious, but vich ve don't see. Vat's dat old saying, you can't see der forest because of der trees?"

"Yeah," Harry chuckled. "I know what you mean. Actually, you run a good ship, a tight ship, a ship with a dedicated crew who know what their jobs are and do them well. The only foul up I've seen was the radar."

"It had better be vorking right. Dat scoundrel knows he vill be trown overboard if he screwed up again." He laughed. "He is number vun on my shit list!"

Harry laughed. "I'd like to have been a mouse and seen him when he went back to his room. I bet he cleaned a pile of shit out of his pants after the way you read him out."

"Yah," the captain laughed. "He should haf shit his pants!"

Abruptly, he rose and fetched back the bottle of cognac, offering a refill to Harry, who raised his glass in acceptance.

"You keep your cabin, Harry," he said. "You earned it."

A feeling of relief warmed Harry. He had been concerned about where he might end up what with Peter gone. It would be more difficult to work on his special project surrounded by a dozen crewmen in their quarters. "Thank you," he replied. "Much appreciated."

"You vill be vorking vis Second Officer Sigmund Helmstrund now. He is a nice chap. Young, headstrong at times, but a very good officer. Strictly by der book. But I tink you vill like him. I haf already spoken to him about you. He seems to haf a favorable impression of you. Yah, der two of you should vork vell togedder."

Harry nodded, smiling for his benefit. What could he say? Helmstrund was a dink! He was young and overbearing, a damned know-it-all. Oh well, he reasoned, the voyage can't last forever. Maybe my first impression of him was wrong. I'll give him the benefit of the doubt, keep an open mind.

"How old did you say you are?" the captain asked.

"I'll be fifty-four in August, sir."

"Ahhh, a Leo. I am a Gemini. My birthday is May 29. Ven is yours?"

"August fifteenth."

"Good. Good. My cousin, Benji, vas born on August fifteen."

He paused, picked up his pipe and puffed at it for a couple of puffs, silently reflective for several moments. Harry sat quietly, sipping the amber liquor. "Yah, Benji vas lost off a fishing boat in der North Sea und drowned tree days before his tventieth birthday." His eyes misted. He blinked, then dabbed at the corners. "Damned smoke smarts ven it gets in my eyes," he said quietly. "He vas a great influence on my life, urged me to go to sea. He vas my idol."

Suddenly, with a slap of his hand on his knee, startling Harry, he said, "But enough of dat. Ve are getting older. I enjoy birthdays. Dey are fun times, especially vis my family und friends. Dat's vy I am happy ven I am home to celebrate. My vife spoils me rotten." He laughed heartily. "She is a great comfort to me. I look forvard to retirement, to staying home und being spoiled by her."

"Well, I've got several more birthdays to celebrate before I consider retiring," Harry replied. "I've got a hell of a lot of living to do between now and then."

"Osa has a birthday coming up soon. She vill be forty-five. Now don't you tell anyvun I told you dat!" he exclaimed shaking a finger at Harry.

Harry laughed. "No, sir. I won't tell a soul."

"She is a good voman, jus' reaching her prime. She is smart und is very attractive." He loosed a long sigh, and then took a sip of cognac. "It is too bad vat happened to her. Did I tell you?"

"No, sir," Harry replied. "I heard –" but he had no chance to mention having heard about Osa from Peter as the captain had already launched into a lengthy explanation of what had happened to her.

Harry saw just talking about Rudy upset the captain, the sudden rapid puffing on his pipe, the plumes of smoke shooting upwards like the puffing of an old coal fire driven steam engine, and the sudden refilling of their glasses.

"I had seen him vis dat young whore shortly before der accident dat killed dem. It made me sick. I tried to talk to him vunce before about his vomanizing, but to no avail. I should haf beat der crap out of him!

"Osa is a nice girl. He really hurt her. He vas a sick man. She don't deserve to be hurt. She deserves to haf a good life. She is my favorite niece, a nice, clean girl, high moraled, und very intelligent. Vun day she vill meet a good man, a man who appreciates der beauty und luf of a fine voman." He poured yet another cognac for himself, nodded to Harry, who held out his glass. "Just a touch, Captain."

Captain Andress filled both glasses to the brim, then set the bottle down close at hand, and settled back in his chair. He studied Harry for several seconds before speaking.

"I'm sorry about your lady friend back in Saginaw. It is terrible to lose somevun you luf. I hope dey catch der murderer."

"He'll pay," Harry said, grimly recalling the vision of the Chink hurtling over the railing, disappearing in the murky waters of the Saginaw River.

"Do you haf any odder lady friends back in Saginaw?"

"A few casual acquaintances. Nothing serious. Sandy was my steady. We felt comfortable with each other. I kind of figured one day we'd –"

"Yah. I understand," Captain Andress nodded as Harry's voice trailed off. "It must be interesting being single at your age."

Harry sensed what was coming. The old coot was trying to play matchmaker. Apparently Osa hadn't said anything about their last screaming encounter to her favorite uncle. Too bad "Uncle Karl" doesn't know his niece is as cold as an iceberg. That's probably why her husband was out chasing all that hot young stuff. He smiled. "Yup. I'm still hoping to meet the right girl, someday,"

He took a sip of cognac, watching the captain's eyes light up like the tilt lights on a pinball machine. Too bad the captain doesn't know what I'm smiling about, he thought. There's no way in hell that I'm chasing after the iceberg; she's his problem.

"After Sandy's death, I decided to go to sea," Harry continued. "I needed a chance to think, to clear my mind."

"Yah. I can understand dat," Captain Andress added, jumping on the remark. "Being at sea gives a man a lot of time to tink. Dat is precisely vy I brought Osa along on dis trip, to give her time to tink. She needs a lot of help. She is confused, trying to find her vay. She is hardheaded at times. I haf told her to relax, enjoy. I am sure, like you, she must haf many frustrations dat need to be taken care of." A sly, knowing smile crossed his face.

"Of course," Harry said, with no outward indication that he acknowledged the intended meaning of the remark, rather, letting it slide by. "You hate to see a beautiful woman such as Osa, so bereaved, so torn over the past, when she should be thinking ahead, of the future, the care of a loving man, a new home, a new life. Yessir, I can understand your concerns about her." He emptied his glass with one quick swallow. Looking the captain straight in his eyes, he said, "If there's anything I can do to be of help to you, to her, just let me know. I'll be happy to oblige."

"Dat's der ticket! Dat's der kind of response I vould expect from a gentleman like you!" Captain Andress bounded to his feet beaming, grabbing Harry's hand, pumping it enthusiastically. "Tank you for offering. It means much to me. After all, you are an older man, a wiser man, older dan der rest of der crew, und you could do much in der vay of comforting her. I know she has spoken highly of you in der past, so I know she vould appreciate a helping hand from you."

"Yes, sir," Harry replied with a somewhat uncomfortable feeling, having risen to his feet trying at the moment to extract his hand from the captain's tight grip. He glanced at a large wall clock. "Wow! I didn't realize it was this late. Mr. Helmstrund will read me the riot act. If you'll excuse me, sir. I have to get up to the bridge for duty. Thank you, again, for inviting me here. It was most enjoyable."

"Yes, of course, uh, tank you for coming, Harry. It vas most enjoyable," He backed away at the sudden nervous response of his guest.

Stopping at the door, Harry turned back to the captain. "Don't worry about Osa. I'll try to make her trip as interesting as possible." He winked.

Captain Andress cut loose with a huge roar of laughter. "Go," he shushed with a wave of his hand. "Und do come back again, soon. It has been a delightful evening."

Walking down the corridor, Harry started chuckling aloud. It's a good thing Osa hadn't told her uncle about the other night. The good captain would probably have him keel-hauled. "Hell," he muttered, "she's so damned far from my expectations of what a woman should be, it's pathetic!"

He headed up the steps two at a time. Inside, he felt warm from the cognac, maybe a little loose, but damn it had tasted good, too good. It allowed his mind to wander back to her again, the warmth of her nestled in his arms, and then the screaming match. No. She'd be just as frigid thirty years from now. It'd take a miracle to change her provincial attitude toward men and sex, especially sex. "And like they say, you can't teach an old dog, or an old broad, new tricks."

He laughed at the remark that had just escaped his lips. Yeah, he thought, better to continue our mutual dislike and shoot for something a little younger and sexier back in Saginaw. Still, the thought crossed his mind, how come she hadn't reported him to her uncle?

Stopping outside the entrance to the bridge, he reached in his pocket for a packet of gum, unwrapped a stick and stuffed it in his mouth. There, maybe old Helmstrund wouldn't notice his breath. Well, if I'm gonna work with the guy I might as well get to know him.

With his jaw set, he entered.

"Reporting for duty, Mr. Helmstrund, sir."

Chapter 45

SHANGHAI DEAD AHEAD

Early into the noon watch of the forty-fifth day, Harry stepped outside onto the port wing bridge. Moving to the railing he looked out across the seas. They were running fast with roiling brownish-green waves topped by frothy whitecaps. He inhaled, breathing deeply several times, and then smiled.

"I think we've entered the East China Sea, Mr. Helmstrund," he said enthusiastically as he re-entered the wheelhouse. He rubbed his arms briskly as a sudden shiver swept through him. "It's getting colder, too. Back to winter, or is it spring now?" He laughed. "I've lost all track of time. One day is the same as the previous."

"It is easy to lose track of time at sea, Mr. Martin. However, it is still winter." Mr. Helmstrund's reply was curt, to the point. He was always business.

"Yeah. Right, sir," Harry replied returning to the helm, the enthusiasm fading from his voice. Ever since the man took command of the watch he'd been aloof. Was it because he had to work with the American, or because the captain showed a bit of favoritism toward him for his efforts in saving the ship? Whatever it was, it bugged Harry no end. For several days he had tried to find a chink in Helmstrund's armor, the one thing that would say: "Hey! This guy is human after all." But he always maintained aloofness, arrogance, an anti-social air that was even evident in his demeanor and the crispness of commands.

Harry knew he had to do something about it, if for no other reason than clear the air and establish what kind of working relationship they were going to have.

It was do or die time, Harry thought, and taking a deep breath, he said, "Mr. Helmstrund, sir, do you mind if I ask a question, rather, a favor of you?"

Mr. Helmstrund, who had been looking out across the seas through his binoculars, lowered them and turned toward his helmsman with a somewhat disdainful look. "It depends. Vat do you vant, Mr. Martin?"

"Well, if we're gonna be working together, how about we call each other by our first names and not stick so much to formalities, 'cept when other officers or dignitaries are on board. It'd make for an easier working relationship. Call me Harry."

There, he's said it. Now the ball was in Helmstrund's court. He could run with it and be friendlier, or he could bobble it and, well, it could turn out to be a hell of a lot longer trip.

Second Officer Helmstrund had heard the request but there was no immediate response. Actually, he thought, as he mulled over Harry's request, the man made a good point. He was a good sailor and they worked well together. He raised his binoculars to his eyes peering at a speck in the distance, a plume of black smoke, probably a coastal freighter.

Harry stood at the helm, eyes forward scanning the horizon, waiting, a sinking feeling building in the pit of his stomach.

"Dat is a good suggestion, Harry," Mr. Helmstrund finally replied, turning back to him. "Please feel free to call me Sigmund." There was no smile, no nodding of his head, not even a friendly wink, nothing but his aloof approval.

"Right, Sigmund," Harry acknowledged. Whew, he breathed, a real breakthrough. He knew it was a really condescending gesture on the part of Sigmund, but it was the first step. Perhaps there was a streak of humanity behind that austere facade the Second Officer portrayed. Anyway, now they could begin anew, Harry thought. We might even find we enjoy working together.

"Incidentally, Harry, your remark about being in der East China Sea vas correct. Ve are in it now und getting closer to China."

"Really? I knew it. I just knew it."

"How?"

"I don't know, really. There's something about the seas off the coast of China. They seem different, more turbulent. I always recalled the seas being a shit-brindle brown. That's the way the seas looked this morning, a shit-brindle brown."

An amused smile broke across Sigmund's face.

"More dan likely an oil slick, but you are right. I checked der charts earlier und ve haf entered Chinese vaters."

"How about that," Harry grinned. "Fantastic recall, huh?"

Sigmund's smile broadened. He nodded, and then went back to the business of operating the ship.

Harry shrugged. He'd find the guy's funny bone yet. He can't be serious all the time.

As *Nurad* hove into view of the Chinese coastline a lone seaplane appeared, circled the ship, then headed back upstairs where it circled above them in a monitoring position. Within an hour they saw the smoke from a ship approaching toward them. Soon they were able to determine it was a warship.

"Probably a destroyer escort to bring us into Shanghai," Sigmund said. He picked up the phone and alerted the captain. Within minutes, he was on deck in full uniform.

Through binoculars, they watched as the ship drew closer. It made a wide sweeping turn and settled in on a parallel course about three thousand yards off the starboard side.

"It looks like an old Russian navy ship," Captain Andress said scanning the ship. "Destroyer class. Several guns und torpedo tubes." After a long pause, he said, "Vy haven't dey contacted us?"

Harry watched along with the others. It was apparent that the destroyer had no intention of contacting them, only to lay off the starboard side as an escort.

Glancing at the outside thermometer, Harry saw it registered 6° celsius degrees. The weather was steadily turning colder. He recalled March in Shanghai. It had been cold like this. It was the same kind of weather you'd find in Chicago or Saginaw, cool with occasional snow flurries and damp, chilling, cold nights.

Nurad moved closer toward land. Along the shoreline patches of snow dotted the landscape. The hills were terraced, much like the hills north of Tsingtao at the base of the Lao Shan Mountains.

The summer of '48 at the mountains, Harry recalled with a smile, the lush terraced hillsides rich with greenery and rice crops against the background of the taller mountains. The terraced hills carried right down to the sandy beaches where at the end of a small cove sat a small, quaint village nestled close by the ocean. It was a tranquil setting except for a thousand Marines playing war games, rushing ashore in waves from landing craft, setting up their command posts, charging up the beaches, digging countless foxholes and gagging down remains of World War II C-Rations. No one had foreseen Korea only a scant two years away.

Slowly *Nurad* moved into the Yangtze River, easing along the carefully manicured shoreline. A small, motor-driven launch chugged out from the near shore and drew alongside the ship. A ladder was dropped over the side and a Chinese pilot, resplendent in his high-collared uniform, climbed nimbly up the ladder to the main deck where he was quickly ushered to the bridge. Shanghai was close at hand. The destroyer made a wide turn and headed back out to sea.

Large high-sterned sea-going junks, their dull sails swollen with a favoring wind, glided silently by moving outbound for the open seas and distant ports of call. The Yangtze River proved long and twisting and *Nurad* passed a great number of foreign ships: freighters, some dull with rust from stem to stern, heavy-laden tankers, a couple of Russian ore boats, their flags flapping in a stiff breeze and at least three more gray destroyers, another grain carrier and several others. Smaller sampans darted about like small black water bugs, skittering dangerously close in front of the larger vessels, yet escaping from harm by the skillful oarsman sculling the single long graceful oar with a mastered touch. Although beautiful to watch, they were a menace to the command of a ship trying to avoid them.

Soon, they entered the Huangpo River. Coming around a bend in the river a panoramic view of Shanghai's skyline suddenly unfolded before them. At first glance, Harry thought the city seemed to have changed little since he had last seen it over thirty years before. It appeared to be the same bustling, mysterious international city. Many more ships of all sizes and shapes were tied up along the wharves and docks or anchored in clusters in mid-river. Approaching the heart of the city, Harry could see the Bund teeming with hordes of people. Quaint, colorful shops dotted the main thoroughfares and crowded side streets.

Nurad's main deck had become crowded with crewmembers standing along the railings, gawking, getting their first glimpse of the ancient, nefarious city. Harry enjoyed watching the crew's reactions, gesturing excitedly as new points of interest unfolded before them. He smiled as he recalled his first visit to Shanghai. Hopefully, they would have shore leave here.

Several small Chinese tugboats belching plumes of black smoke into the chill morning air, nestled against *Nurad*, easing the ship up to the Whang Poo dock. The docking crew quickly dropped hawsers to the dock where a rag-tag gang of longshoremen quickly secured the ship to huge steel bollards.

The troopship, *General J.C. Breckenridge* had been eased up to this very dock back in '47 and hundreds of Marines and military dependents had gotten their first close look at China and the Chinese that cold, gray morning. Dozens of sampans with hawkers selling their crafts, ornate wood carvings and other wares had already moved in next to the ship to make fast sales. Sailors quickly unlimbered fire hoses and showered them with cold water.

The *Breckenridge* had not even been docked, the screws still churning the dirty waters of the river, yet the sampans continued to crowd in. One sampan erred, caught in the flow of water along the side of the ship, and was sucked under the stern and into the churning screws, becoming splintered pieces of wood suitable for firewood. The owner and his wares disappeared beneath the brown water.

The *Nurad's* gangway was lowered over the side to the dock, and several waiting Chinese authorities quickly clambered onto the deck where they were met by Captain Andress and Second Officer, Helmstrund. Formalities were quickly dispensed with and Captain Andress led them to the bridge to check the ship's manifest, ships papers, bills of lading and other important papers, and to discuss the unloading of the grain.

Harry noticed that, unlike the ballyhoo and press coverage they had received in Saginaw at the loading of the grain, the Chinese authorities were low key, handling the event almost as an everyday occurrence.

The port authority personnel wore drab brown uniforms; the military personnel, by contrast, wore darker uniforms, crisply starched, with red epaulets on their shoulders. A red star was prominent on their service caps.

Nurad's crew stood on deck awaiting orders to start the unloading process. Already a long line of huge Russian-made trucks with large, high-walled trailers, were lined up along the dock, like piglets eager to receive nourishment.

Captain Andress and Mr. Helmstrund reviewed the ship's manifest carefully with the Chinese authorities. One military officer pointed out the procedure for unloading grain, the trucks first for shipment into the interior, then the rest being sucked up into large grain elevators located adjacent to the ship. Captain Andress agreed to the procedure. All parties satisfied, they followed the captain on a brief tour of the ship before the unloading process would begin. After about thirty minutes, Mr. Helmstrund gave the order over the PA system: "Prepare to unload cargo."

The crew quickly turned to, hatch covers were hurriedly removed and winched off to one side. Large suction pipes were burrowed deep into the grain-filled hold siphoning off the golden kernels into waiting trucks. Crewmen, with bags tied around their ankles, moved the huge siphon pipe nozzle, called a "camel," around, siphoning up the grain. It was hard work with only brief stops as one filled truck moved out and another empty one quickly replaced it. Precautions were taken not to spill any of the precious cargo.

Working in shifts allowed each man time to relax briefly, time to grab a sandwich, coffee, cigarette and head break before returning to work.

Harry welcomed the temporary relief when it was his turn. His muscles ached from the pushing and tugging of the huge siphon. The mood in the galley seemed quite relaxed compared to the hectic pace on deck. Conversation was at a minimum, most too tired for anything more than a quick comment, no lengthy conversation.

Osa was serving food. As Harry approached, she turned and moved into the kitchen. Screw you, he thought as he continued through the line then picked a quiet spot on the far side of the galley. Out of the corner of his eye he saw her return with a fresh tray of sandwiches. Was it coincidence, her going to the kitchen for another tray of sandwiches just as he started through the line? He shrugged. To hell with her; he had a lot more important things on his mind than playing games with a grown woman playing with a child's mentality. He washed his food down with a couple cups of coffee, made a pit stop, and then headed topside to work.

In spite of the temperature dropping to 8°celsius degrees, the men were sweating profusely. It was a relief when Mr. Helmstrund announced the trucks were loaded. Within minutes, large pneumatic siphon hoses were lowered from the huge grain elevator and the suctioning process continued. The grain shot up the intake pipes with a swishing, rattling noise. In the hold the trimming gang moved the nozzle sucking up grain and, in the process, made sure the remaining cargo was leveled.

Finally Mr. Helmstrund called a halt over the PA system. The allotment for Shanghai had been unloaded. The hatches could be replaced and secured.

The men cheered at the order. Quickly the huge, bulky hatch covers were replaced, secured and made watertight. It was 1600 when the last hatch was secured. On the dock, the last truckload of grain slowly disappeared through a gate as it headed into the city.

A hungry band of men descended upon the galley where, true to her word, Osa had prepared fresh sweet rolls and fresh coffee, a treat for them when the work was done.

"Attention," the loudspeaker blared across the galley and throughout the ship. "Ve haf been given special permission by der port autority for der personnel of der *Nurad* to go ashore in Shanghai. Dose members vishing to go ashore vill please report to der bridge immediately for passes."

A loud whoop rang out as a scramble of bodies rushed for the exit. Harry laughed at the mob scene so reminiscent of the Marines aboard *Breckinridge* when they heard they had shore leave in

Shanghai. Older now, and, hopefully, much wiser, he decided to take his time. He sat back and slowly devoured the last jellyroll, then washed it down with coffee. The room had quieted. Glancing about, he saw he was the only one there. "I guess now is the time to get your pass, Martin," he told himself. Wiping his lips, he dumped his dirty cup and headed for the main deck and then the bridge.

The corridor was jammed with chattering, laughing, happy crewmembers returning from the bridge flashing their passes. Osa passed him talking to a couple of men, telling them of the many purchases she wanted to make in Shanghai.

Harry felt he could have been invisible. She stared right past him as though he didn't exist. "Shit," he exclaimed as he stepped on deck. "I won't go into town. It'd be my dumb luck to run into her."

He walked along the deck finally coming to a stop, resting against the railing, admiring the commanding view he had of the city. The sun was setting lower. Evening clouds were moving in, bellies dark and heavy laden with moisture. It might snow tonight, he thought. Down along the dock, laborers were scurrying about. He smiled as he watched them. What was that old saying, they all look alike? From his vantage point, they did.

The lights of Shanghai were beginning to blink on. Harry breathed deeply, his nostrils assailed by a variety of odors. Shanghai's air was so different, a blending of various scents: oil, smoke from ships and chimneys, from small cook stoves on sampans, from a thousand different homes, shops and restaurants and the pungent fragrance of mysterious wares housed in the many warehouses along the teeming shoreline. The scents tantalized, enticed. It was the same Shanghai of thirty years ago. He recalled the excitement that flooded his very being at that time, the same excitement coursing through his body right now.

"Hell!" he exclaimed slapping the railing hard with his bare hands "You only go around once in this old world, Martin. You may never get the chance to walk the streets of this damned city again. By god, you're going ashore! Look out, Shanghai, Harry Martin's coming ashore!"

Mr. Helmstrund was just leaving the bridge as Harry arrived.

"Got any passes left?" Harry grinned.

Sigmund shook his head no but the grin starting to break across his face was a dead giveaway, much to Harrys' relief. "Yah. Just vun left. I vas going to bring it to you. I know you vanted to go ashore."

"Thanks, Sigmund. I appreciate it. I guess I've still got the spirit of adventure burning in me, got to see what the old city's like today, thirty years later."

"Haf a good time, Harry, but behafe yourself."

Harry grinned. "You bet." He took the pass and skipped down the steps heading for his cabin and a shower, shave and dressing for a night on the town. Thoughts of laying a beautiful, dark-eyed, black haired Chinese whore blocked out any thought of Osa the iceberg.

Chapter 46
LIBERTY IN SIN CITY

Harry inspected himself in the mirror. After all these weeks at sea it was hard to believe the clean-shaven, well-groomed man looking back at him was really him. It felt different being reasonably dressed after living in work clothes for so long. He checked out his black dress slacks and black flannel shirt again. Even his dress shoes felt light, awkward, after heavy workshoes. He looked down several times to assure himself he was wearing shoes.

Flaring the collar of his shirt, he held up the heavy gold pendent to his neck, then hesitated. Naw, he thought after a moment, with a subtle shake of his head, Sandy would have liked it. Maybe he was getting a little too old for pendants and bracelets. He'd let it pass for now. Dropping the pendent back in his dresser drawer, he reached beyond it to a pair of rolled up socks. Unrolling them, he took out a roll of bills. Peeling off four fifties, a couple of twenties a few ten spots and several singles, he balled the rest back into the socks and stuffed them to the back of the drawer. Good old American greenbacks ought to pay for a hot night in Shanghai.

Slipping on his old leather jacket, he grabbed a pair of warm leather gloves, stuffed them in his pocket, picked up his pass from the desktop and headed for the main deck humming to himself.

Evening was the nicest time of the day, he thought, as he watched the late slanting rays of sunlight breaking through the cloud cover, reflecting off the dull, dirty windows of several taller buildings. He shivered. It was chilly. Hurriedly, he made his way down the gangway and headed for the guardhouse by the main gate. He showed his pass to a Chinese soldier with a burp gun casually slung over his shoulder and was waved through.

Harry stood just outside the gate and looked about him. No rickshaws? Not even a pedicab. What gives, he wondered. The street was crowded with people, and as he looked at them closer, he saw they all seemed to be dressed alike in blue and black Mao jackets, even the women. No chatter, no hustle, no "Hey, sailor, no momma, no poppa, need money, can get you a deal, got my sister –" Nothing. And not one damned rickshaw in sight! He'd have to hoof it up to the Bund on foot. And any action, he thought, well, just looking at the female population wrapped up tight in high-collared Mao jackets was not really a turn on. Hell, there had to be a place for action, even in Communist China. Sin couldn't have been outlawed; where there was a will, there was a way. He was sure of that.

Thirty years, and a lifetime earlier, he'd taken a rickshaw to the Enlisted Men's Club in Shanghai. That turned into a hell of an experience when the screaming rickshaw boys suddenly surrounded him asking for more money. Thankfully, an MP Sergeant had come to his rescue, beating his way through the crowd with a billy club. This time he wasn't the "boot" Marine wet behind the ears. No. He was ready.

It didn't bother him that most of the crew had headed ashore an hour earlier. The last time he'd been in Shanghai, he'd felt really rushed tagging along with his buddies, having to see as much as possible, to get to the Enlisted Men's Club, the shops, everything before liberty ended. This time he planned to shop, to look around, to enjoy himself, not rushing helter-skelter through the city. If Shanghai hadn't changed too drastically under Communist rule, he might even find himself enjoying sexual gratification in the arms of a dark-eyed Chinese whore. The thought excited him. Shanghai; he mulled the name several times. It was exciting to be here.

He started off walking at a fairly brisk pace making his way through the teeming crowds, watchful for pickpockets, inhaling the smell of garlic and onions, dodging a sea of bikes, older model cars and the press of people as he made his way along the Bund. Before long, he headed in toward Nanking Road. Here, he took time to windowshop, to browse in several small, obscure shops, stopping to check the prices on embroidered jackets, carved ivory, jade and native made bric-a-brac. Pickings were slim. Although the gates to China had been open for a while, there was still a limited supply of "touristy-type" goods.

He wandered along listening to the sing-song sound of the Chinese thronging the streets, occasionally recognizing a familiar word, smiling back at the faces who smiled curiously at him. For the most part, the people were dressed in the traditional, distinctive, high-collared blue and black jackets and black trousers. He noticed that the younger men looked at his dress with a twinge of envy, wanting to get out of the traditional look and into something modern. American, English or even French or Italian.

Most women had the short-clipped haircuts, unattractive clothes, and unattractive shoes. They wore a bored, beaten down look, seldom glancing up, never smiling. Harry caught an occasional one who would look up at him. He'd smile, wink if she was attractive. She might offer an embarrassed smile in return but kept on going.

After several blocks he heard the distinct sound of English spoken, profane though it was, it was still English. The profanity came from inside a small building. He poked his head inside. A bar! Several people were seated at the bar, a few more scattered about the room at run-down tables. It was a mix of Asians, a couple of tough-looking sailors speaking in Russian, but no females. Harry settled in on the one empty stool at the bar. A bleary-eyed older man glanced up as Harry sat down. "What'll it be mate?" he asked. "Old Cheng Wang just got himself some good old American beer. Millers."

"Millers," said Harry. "Good beer." The old Chinaman behind the bar quickly popped the top on a bottle and set it on the bar.

It surprised Harry that they had Millers. Trade's improving, he commented to himself. The beer tasted good. The last time he could recall having a cold Millers in China was in Peiping at the Wagon Litz Hotel on a hot, sultry July day back in 1948. It was just as good now as it was then.

"You off that damned big Swedish grain ship?" the bleary-eyed one asked.

"Yes," Harry replied.

The man looked askance at him for several seconds. "You speak good English for a Swede," he grinned, taking a swig of beer.

"I'm American. Signed on for the trip."

Again, the man looked at him for several seconds, and then asked, "Ever been to Shanghai before?"

"Yeah. Thirty years ago. Marine Corps," Harry replied taking a deep swallow of beer.

"Marines? Hey, I was a Marine once, back in the thirties. Got busted from Staff Sergeant down to buck private. I had my time in so I got myself discharged here, worked for a big oil company. Pensioned out here." He waved his hand around indicating the room. "Names Johnson, Algernon P. Johnson. Call me Al." He reached out and shook Harry's hand. "Stupid place to retire. Sad. Japs. Nationalists. Communists. I been through all that crap. Even got re-programmed by the Commies. Hell, I should write a book about all the crap I've been through in the past thirty years. Pure crap!"

"Harry Martin," Harry offered. "What happened to all the rickshaws? I can't find one, not even one."

Al looked at him, and then smiled showing terribly stained teeth, a couple broken off. "An you ain't gonna find any in town either. The Commies eliminated them, said it was a rich man's burden on the proletariat. How about that?"

"Sounds like the town is buttoned down tight," Harry said. "What do you do for action?"

Al grinned. "Hell, I've got me a Chinese wife, five kids and twelve damned bratty grandkids running around. I got action, even at my age.

"The good old days are gone," he said with a deep sigh. "Back then we hung out at Jimmy's Place, swing band, lots of girls, good looking white Russians and slick Chinese, the old Imperial Club, the racetrack, all gone. Commies came down hard on sin. Now, if yer looking for action," and he leaned closer, breathing a whiskey breath in Harry's face, "ya gotta know yer way around this town. Underground, we call it."

Harry leaned back taking a deep breath. "What's the underground?"

"You got to know who's working the action. Now, I could get you a couple of whores if that's what you want," Al said kind of sizing Harry up, "but I think you want the good stuff. There's a hotel down the street, big old British run joint and I understand they've got some pretty good stuff, pretty pricey, though."

Harry listened, not saying a word. The guy was probably stringing him along, maybe going to put the touch on him.

"From one Marine to another," Al said. "You go to that hotel. Good food. Great girls. I know for a fact the local bigwigs are getting paid off under the table not to screw up the deal for the British. Those damned Englishmen have already made great inroads into trade with China. Locals don't want to upset the apple cart." He winked at Harry. "If you know what I mean."

"Thanks," Harry said, and slugged down the rest of his beer. He threw a tenspot on the counter. Al grabbed it, stuck it into his pocket and threw several wrinkled Communist notes on the counter. "Enjoy. Semper Fi!" Al called after him.

One thing became notably apparent as Harry continued his walk; no pimps hawking. By now he should have been accosted by no less than twenty pimps selling their sisters, wives, aunts, mothers, cousins, you name it, and all for a modest price. Tonight there hadn't been one pimp. The thought crept into his mind that the Communist government might have really cracked down hard on prostitution to the point of eliminating it. Damn!

His stomach growled. He had to find a place to eat. But this time, he wanted to find a restaurant that was different, ornate, old-fashioned, harking back to the pre-war period of the late thirties and early forties, the sophistication of the international settlement, and the rich foreigners with all their money. It had to be something that he could fondly recall in later life as one of the highlights of his last visit to Shanghai.

As he turned a corner heading down one of the narrow streets lined with quaint shops, he heard an argument taking place in one of the shops. He started to pass by, but there was no mistaking one of the voices: Osa. He stopped to listen, amused. She was pleading with someone about the price of an article of clothing. It was obvious by the tone of her voice that she was losing.

Harry poked his head in the shop door. "Need help?" he asked, not wanting to because of who it was, but compassionate to a fellow crewmember.

Osa whirled around, a look of exasperation on her face. At seeing it was Harry, she wailed, "Oh, Harry, vot should I do? I vant to buy dis silk blouse und nightie set but he vants too much money. I von't pay tirty dollars. No!" Her eyes wore a pleading look. "Vot should I do?"

Harry noted the silky garments she held before her, but his gaze was more directed to Osa. Under her open royal blue, fingertip coat she wore a smartly tailored powder blue suit accentuated by a white blouse with a flared collar, and offset by a strand of expensive pearls. High-heeled pumps accentuated her long, slim legs, but he knew they weren't worth a damn as walking shoes in this town.

"Vot should I do?" she implored.

"Haggle," he replied. "That's the way you buy in the Orient. "You haggle."

"Haggle?" she asked, confused. "Haggle?"

"Yeah. Haggle." He stepped inside the shop moving next to her. Taking the items from her he turned to the shopkeeper who had been standing, watching. "How much?"

"Thirty dollars American," the shopkeeper replied with a toothy grin. "Good deal."

"Too much!" Harry said with a shake of his head. "I'll give you five dollars and no more."

"No!" the merchant said with a sharp shake of his head, the smile suddenly gone. "Is worth much more."

"No they aren't," Harry countered holding up the material. "Pretty, yes, but skimpy, won't last long. Hell, it'll probably fall apart after the first wearing —"

"No! Is good material, finest silk. I buy myself. Is very good material."

Harry held the material up to the light. The silk was practically transparent, a white long sleeved blouse and wispy little white nightie and matching panties. "Seven-fifty for the whole lot — blouse and nightie," Harry said dropping the items in a heap on the counter. "Seven-fifty."

The merchant hesitated. Osa watched wide-eyed.

"Twenty dollars," the merchant countered, the inflection of his voice changing, aware that he was up against a seasoned haggler.

Harry sensed victory in his grasp. He turned to Osa and winked. "Open up your purse and show me your money," he said.

She hesitated, perplexed at his request.

"Do it if you want those items," he commanded in a whisper.

She opened her purse and dug out her wallet, opened it and showed the contents to him.

Harry shook his head turning back to the merchant. "You might as well forget the sale. All she's got is an American ten dollar bill and carfare back to the ship." He pushed the two items across the counter. "Sorry," he added, a regretful tone to his voice.

"Harry –" Osa started to protest, but he froze her with a sharp glance.

"No. American ten dollars is fine, ten is okay," the merchant beamed. "For our American friend and his lady, I cut my price. Ten dollars. Okay?"

Harry shrugged. "I'll ask the lady." He turned back to Osa winking at the flabbergasted woman. "Is ten dollars okay?" he asked.

"Y-yes," she stammered.

Harry reached into her billfold carefully slipping out a ten dollar bill from between two twenties, and handed it to the merchant.

"The lady is happy with her business transaction," he said. The merchant beamed his toothy smile as he took the money, examined it, and quickly stuffed it in his pocket. He placed the silky material in a rice paper bag that had the shop's name boldly emblazoned on the side, taking time, as he did, to slip one of his business cards in as well, an added gesture of friendship.

"Thank you. You have made the lady very happy," Harry commented, returning the smile. He picked up the package and handed it to Osa.

"Yes. Tank you," she said to the shopkeeper, "und you, too," she added turning to Harry, but he was already walking out of the shop.

Helping Osa was not on his itinerary of things to do in Shanghai. He was getting hungrier by the minute. He started down the street at a quickened pace. Somewhere in this town there had to be a place, a unique, different place where he could partake of a sumptuous meal and revel in its grandiose atmosphere.

"Harry! Vait! Please," Osa called after him, running to catch up. "Tank you so much for, how you say it, haggling for my clothes."

"That's okay. Have a good time. I'll see ya' later." He turned the corner continuing his fast-paced stride. He felt smug. He had helped the lady, much against his better judgment, and now had dumped her. Let her find her own way around Shanghai. I've got better things to do and they don't include the iceberg, he told himself.

Osa stopped, bewildered by his bluntness. She watched after him as he disappeared into the crowd. A chilling fear of being alone in Shanghai suddenly overwhelmed her. She looked around at the sea of Oriental faces. Not one Swedish shipmate, not even a white face. The staring faces, the sing-song language she couldn't understand, the darkness of night closing in all frightened her. Suddenly, she wanted desperately to be in the company of someone she could communicate with, anyone, even Harry. She ran after him.

"Harry, don't leave me," she wailed plaintively hurrying through the crowd after him. "Harry, it is getting dark. I don't vant to be by myself, please, may I valk vis you?"

Harry stopped, looking back at the pale faced female hurrying toward him. "Sure. Why not," he shrugged. Besides, they'd probably be bumping into some of the crew before too long and he'd dump her on them. He was sure they'd enjoy her company; she was a barrel of fun.

Osa struggled along beside him taking two steps to his one, gasping for breath, clutching her purchase tightly in her hand. After a bit, she slipped her arm through his, holding on firmly. Harry slowed his pace and they walked along in silence. In spite of his bitter feelings toward her, it did feel good having such a beautiful woman beside him.

"Is dere someplace special you are going to?" she asked, still trying to keep pace with him. The pumps were beginning to cut into her feet.

"Yeah. First a place to eat, then someplace to wind down, relax and have fun, a good time." It was a sarcastic reply.

"I am hungry, too," she gasped, the sarcasm having passed right over her head. "Maybe ve can find a spot to eat. I am famished."

"We'll see." He continued his pace, his eyes now desperately searching the streets and stores looking for other crewmembers. Dinner with her was out of the question; he had a different kind of meal, a different kind of companion in mind, not the bitch.

In spite of the increasing darkness and lateness of the hour, the streets were still solidly jammed with people. Vehicular traffic was held practically to a crawl. Horns blared, tempers rose, people walked in all directions oblivious of the screaming drivers.

The screeching of brakes startled Harry and Osa. A dark limousine had jerked to a halt at curbside just in front of them. An Oriental brandishing a machine pistol jumped out aiming a gun at Harry. He flung the door wide motioning for them to get in.

"Both of you," he commanded. "Inside. Hurry."

Osa started to protest but the Oriental cut her short with a sudden slap to the side of her face. Harry raised his fist to retaliate but the Oriental jammed the pistol in his face. "Get in!" he hissed.

They were shoved unceremoniously into the back seat and the door slammed shut. The Oriental jumped in the front seat, said something to his companion behind the wheel, and the car sped off.

"Are you okay?" Harry asked raising Osa's chin upwards, examining her face. A welt had already risen slightly on her cheek. "Yes," she replied. "Vat is happening?"

"I don't know —"

"Shut up! Sit still and be quiet!" the Oriental ordered. He had twisted around in his seat so that he could watch them . The machine pistol rested on the top of the seat, barrel aimed in their direction.

Harry glanced at the driver, also an Oriental. His eyes were glued to the road as he weaved in and out among the hordes of people, pounding on the horn, jerking forward, slamming on the brakes, and then forward again. Harry glanced at the speedometer. It registered twenty miles an hour. Great speed for a kidnapping, he thought. If it wasn't so serious, he would have laughed.

He turned his attention back to squint eyes. The kidnapper had a nervous habit of blinking his eyes. His face, however, had that stoic look Orientals are so noted for. The man's eyes never wavered as he watched the two of them, his finger curled around the trigger of the machine pistol. It wasn't the kind of weapon one challenged foolishly Harry knew from past experience.

"What's this all about?" Harry asked.

"Be quiet. You will see," the stoic-faced one replied, blinking.

"Stan send you?"

He didn't have to say anymore. Squint eyes looked like he'd been slapped, eyes momentarily widening, although the expression on his face never changed. "Shut up. You will learn soon enough!" squint eyes snapped. Just as quickly, his eyes continued their random blinking.

So Stan had sent a welcoming committee.

Harry caught a glimpse of a street sign: Zhongshan Road. Ahead was a large steel bridge over the Suzhou Creek. A bicycle suddenly swerved to its right in front of the car. Harry gasped. Osa screamed. The driver swerved. Pistol-packing squint eyes quickly glanced over his shoulder to see what was happening. That was all Harry needed.

As the man turned back, Harry's hand, steeled in a karate chop, was already in motion, catching squint eyes across the bridge of his nose. Even before the scream of pain escaped from his lips, Harry's hand had moved to its second position, smashing solidly up under the man's nose driving the cartilage sharply upwards into the man's brain.

The movement was quick, final, and accomplished just as his karate instructor had told him a hundred times. Smash the nose across the eyes, and then smash your opponent under the nose. The thrust will drive the cartilage into his brain killing the person. Remember, it's you or him!

As squint eyes slumped down in his seat, the pistol falling harmlessly from his hand, Harry's clenched fist smashed solidly against the right side of the driver's temple. The man's hands automatically jerked to his head. The car swerved off the road barely missing the errant bicyclist, but sending people flying out of the way as the car continued on mushing through several piles of snow before coming to rest, teetering precariously on the seawall.

Harry grabbed the startled, ashen-faced Osa's hand, jammed the car door handle down, threw the door wide and, in a fluid motion, jerked her out of the car just before it tottered over the edge into the oily, slick water.

"C'mon!" he snapped, steering her back up onto the sidewalk. He almost laughed when he looked at her, still clutching her purse and prized package.

"Vot about dem?" she asked.

"They're okay. Just gone for a swim."

Quickly he merged them in the crowd, walking at a brisk pace back toward the brighter lights of Shanghai.

"You okay" he asked not slowing.

"Yes. I tink so," She held tightly to him. "Vat vas dat all about?"

"I don't know," he lied. "I just knew we had to get out of there in a hurry. They were kidnappers. No telling what they might have done to us, especially you, a woman."

She clutched tighter to him, the thoughts of what they might have done chilling her. "But dose men ver still in der car. Von't dey drown," she protested.

"Yup. Better them than us. The guy with the machine pistol looked like he'd enjoy shooting us." He continued his fast pace. Stan had tipped his hand; he was here and Harry knew he had to be on guard every moment from now on.

Ahead they heard the chiming of the huge clock in the Custom Building. Six o'clock. The chimes struck loud and clear above the chaotic sounds of the street. The sound was pleasant.

Chapter 47

COOK'S NIGHT OUT

"Harry! Vait!" Osa called after him as he hurried along several steps ahead of her. "I must catch my breath."

He turned looking back at her. She had stopped in front of the Number One Department Store leaning back against the plate glass window. Her beauty was a sharp contrast to the several lifeless mannequins standing aloofly within the large windows.

Walking slowly back to her he kept an eye peeled for danger, catching reflections of people passing by, searching faces, alert to any sudden attack.

Her eyes wore a pleading look. "Must ve valk so fast?" she asked, still short of breath.

"Yes."

At his insistence, they continued. Turning the next corner Harry spotted an older, ornate hotel across the street at the end of the block. It was easily twenty stories high, overpowering, representative of the Victorian period of architecture still to be found in Shanghai. A large British flag waved in the breeze over the entrance.

Moving Osa along as quickly as possible, Harry angled across the street wending their way through the chattering throngs of people finally coming to a halt in front of the Monarch Hotel. A nattily dressed Chinese doorman opened one of the highly polished bronze doors for them. Inside, they found themselves standing in a cavernous lobby area, gawking at the ornate interior. It was as though they had stepped back in time to the turn of the century. The lobby was at least three stories high: the whole interior lavishly appointed in a rich Victorian style. Twelve huge crystal chandeliers hung down on large gold-plated chains. The floor was a highly polished Italian marble.

"Dis is beautiful," Osa said in awe, looking around the lobby. Harry grunted in agreement but was already moving them forward toward the registration counter, itself a deeply polished fruitwood. A directory stand caught Harry's attention. He read it. "There's a restaurant located on the eighth floor," he said steering her toward a battery of elevators.

"I must look a mess," Osa exclaimed, trying to catch sight of herself in the small mirror located next to the button rack in the elevator, starting to fuss with her hair.

"You look okay," Harry said pushing the eighth floor button. He gave a smile of approval.

The elevator stopped at the eighth floor and they stepped out into a large hallway leading directly into an elegant dining room.

Warm pecan paneling reached to the high ceiling on which was painted an ornate dragon resplendid in bright reds and golds. The colorful motif was overpowering, filling the entire ceiling, a masterful blending of Chinese art and Victorian architecture. Crystal chandeliers softly illuminated the room.

They crossed the hallway into the dining area where a hostess, a slender Oriental dressed in a beautiful, high-collared silk dress, greeted them. Harry asked for a table for two. They were ushered across the crowded room to a small table next to a large window that overlooked the city.

Using his best manners, Harry seated Osa, and then sat across from her. Through the window he found a commanding view of the Bund. Lights were on throughout the area.

"Isn't dat a magnificent view of der city," Osa said enthusiastically. "It reminds me of Stockholm on Friday night. Everybody is shopping." Harry nodded, but his focus narrowed on the far end of the Bund where he could see flashing red lights at about the spot where the car went into the river.

Yet, he had to agree. It was a beautiful sight, an ideal romantic setting if only you had the right girl. He glanced around the room. No crewmembers were visible. Probably too expensive for their wallets, he allowed, although he had an idea they were after something a little more exciting than food.

In looking around he saw an interesting mix of Caucasian and Oriental patrons. Many of the Caucasians appeared to be businessmen, perhaps opening new markets in China, or perhaps the first wave of monied world travelers. It was obvious from the way they continually glanced about that this was their first exposure to the orient. On closer scrutiny, he became aware that a number of the businessmen were accompanied by younger, very attractive Oriental women dressed provocatively in low-cut, form-fitting dresses. Obviously not their wives, he surmised.

"Dis is a beautiful place, Harry," Osa whispered across the table. "It must be very expensive. I don't tink I haf enough money vis me. Maybe I should go."

"Relax. My treat tonight, cook's night out on the town," he found himself saying. He chuckled. Did he hear himself right? He had actually offered to buy dinner for this female, the one who hated his guts, the female who said she'd never wanted to see or hear from him again – even if he was the last man on earth! He was going to spring for dinner for her! Goddam it, Martin, you're getting soft in the head in your old age!

"No. I vill pay my own way." She was upset with herself. Why him? Where were the rest of the crewmembers? He was the last person she wanted to be with. Anyone but him. What he had done, what he had tried to force her to do, still burned in her mind. Still, with no other crewmembers present, she would have to stay through dinner, and then she'd leave. Shanghai was not the place she wanted to share with him.

"No. I will pay," Harry insisted. "Call it a busman's holiday."

"Busman's holiday?"

Harry shrugged. "Trust me." It would take too long to explain. He waved it off. "Just consider yourself my guest for dinner." And he placed emphasis on the word dinner. "My pleasure. Okay?"

"Vell, okay," she responded hesitantly.

A waiter appeared with menus asking if they cared for a before dinner drink. Harry nodded yes and ordered a Miller's. He looked at Osa. She hesitated, then, smiling, ordered a scotch on the rocks.

The waiter thanked them and departed.

Both perused their menus "oohing" and "aahing" over the variety of appetizing dishes. Harry's eyes automatically went to the prices. He whistled softly. This definitely isn't your run-of-the-mill beanery, he thought. It was high class and it had the prices to prove it. Oh well, he admitted, Osa is a good cook and this is a chance to repay her culinary kindness. Besides, he rationalized, as soon as she's through eating she'll be heading back for the ship and then I'm off for a good time.

"Isn't dis a romantic setting?" she said, then cringed, shocked at herself for uttering such a statement in front of him.

"Yeah. It is." If you're with the right girl it would be the ideal romantic spot to start out an evening of fun, he thought. Dammit! Do a good deed and you get stuck, and her of all people.

As he glanced about he noted several shapely young Oriental females who, by their glances and movements, had fun time written all over them. There had to be sporting houses left; the town couldn't have gotten that clean in thirty years.

The waiter returned with their drinks and, in a polished manner, deftly placed a glass with ice in front of Osa. Would she like him to pour? She nodded, and he poured the large shotglass of scotch over the ice. Nice, Harry thought at the waiter's finesse. The waiter moved behind Harry, placed a tall, tapered glass before him and, with his nod of approval, poured his beer. I bet that movement will cost a small bundle, Harry smiled.

"Would you care to order now?" the waiter asked, extracting a pencil and pad from his inside pocket.

"Order for me, please," Osa asked, leaning forward toward Harry, her hand coming to rest on his.

Harry glanced down. Her touch had sent a tingle through him. "Two complete Peking Duck dinners with a red wine," Harry said, turning his attention back to the waiter.

"An excellent choice, sir," the waiter beamed. "We are known internationally for our exquisite Peking Duck dinners. I'm sure you will both enjoy your selection."

Harry was relieved; a good choice. Osa smiled approvingly. He felt like a hero. He took a sip of beer. Another good choice.

The sound of music suddenly filled the air as a small band started playing across the room. Within seconds the small dance floor was filled with twosomes moving to the beat of an old familiar tune, one that Harry recognized from the 'forties: "I'll be seeing you."

"Care to dance?" Harry found himself saying.

Osa looked at him. He pointed to the dance floor and smiled. Hesitantly, she nodded yes.

In moments she was in his arms moving lightly about the dance floor. To his surprise, she was an excellent dancer following his lead as though they had danced together all their lives.

When the music stopped, he started to escort her back to the table only to hear the strains of another old favorite: "If I loved you." He spun her around and she eased into his arms. As they moved, her body melted against his, moving to the slow, sensuous beat. Harry became aware of her hand warm against his neck, the aroma of her perfume tantalizing.

No! he found himself thinking. No! He wasn't going to fall into that trap again. He stopped, breaking free of her. Surprised, bewildered, Osa found herself being escorted back to the table and quickly seated.

"Uh, you'll have to excuse me, men's room," he whispered. She gave a somewhat embarrassed nod and turned away gazing out the window. She had to leave. The dance had made her aware that this was not right, his strong arms about her, the touch of his body against hers, that salacious feeling building inside. No, it would end up as before with them screaming at each other. She had to leave. She had to go someplace, anyplace but here. Poking through her purse she pulled out a guide to Shanghai. There had to be something.

While standing at the urinal, Harry couldn't help but overhear two men boisterously talking about their plans for the evening. They were laughing, chortling like a couple of schoolboys. The accents were distinctly British.

"Excuse me, gentlemen," Harry said, zipping up and stepping to the washbasin. "I couldn't help but overhear you. I'm new in town. Where's this action you're talking about?"

"You must be new," one chortled. "The hottest thing going right now, speaking in strict confidence you understand, is the new adult movie and lingerie show they have right here in the hotel. Very explicit films, beautiful models showing the latest hot lingerie –"

"The show starts in forty-five minutes," the second man said glancing at his watch. He giggled. "It's really great, old boy."

Harry grinned. "Is that why most of the businessmen I've seen with the sexy Oriental girls are here, for the show?"

"Right!" the first chimed in. "Business is business, whether it's yours or hers. Right, Alfie?" And not letting his friend answer, he continued, "Welcome to the underground. This hotel is off limits to the general public. It's maintained for those businessmen who are involved in opening trade with China. All hush hush. The powers that be turn their backs on the operation for a nice fee. I have no idea, but it must be good."

"Are you in Shanghai on business," Alfie asked.

"Yes," Harry lied. "I was told by a confidant about the underground, and, so, here I am." He grinned at them.

"For six dollars you can get into the show," the first one enthused. "If you have a date, the two of you get in for ten dollars, a chance to revel in sexuality. The films are first class, tastefully done, even got a plot to them. The lingerie is simply fantastic, old boy, clothing that will knock the socks off you. The Chinese girls are all gorgeous, simply gorgeous, and they don't hide anything from view, not one thing."

"Decadent. A real pick me up," the other added. He straightened his tie, ran his fingers through his hair and brushed one lightly across his thin mustache. "If you have a lady friend, take her along. Very educational. If not, they can supply a girl for a modest fee and you'll have a night you'll never forget. Do catch the show old boy. Simply delightful."

"Do," added the first and then they were gone.

Harry dried his hands. Already he could imagine himself in the arms of a beautiful Chinese girl. He shook his head. "Sounds good to me. Now all I have to do is get rid of the iceberg."

As he returned to his table, he caught sight of Alfie over at the side of the room talking to his waiter, pointing in his direction. The waiter nodded, then bowed to the man and headed across the room toward him. Alfie sat down next to a delicate, slender Chinese girl with long flowing black hair. She squeezed his arm at something he whispered in her ear, and then smiled.

Osa looked up, giving Harry a warm smile as he sat down. Almost simultaneously, the waiter arrived, announcing in a cheerful voice, "The show will start in forty minutes, sir. Will you and the lady be attending?"

Harry groaned, slapping his hand to his forehead. He'd thought the waiter had a better sense of discretion than to blurt out such information in front of the two of them, especially her. The least he could have done was whisper in his ear.

"We came to eat," he replied curtly, and then added, "Do they have a second show?"

"Yes, sir."

"Come back later. I'll let you know then." The waiter bowed in response to his request and hastily departed.

"Vat show is he talking about, Harry?" Osa inquired, the warm smile lingering.

"Oh," he replied, trying to appear nonchalant. "They're having a special movie and fashion show. It starts in forty minutes."

"A fashion show? Dat sounds vunderful!" she exclaimed. "Let's go! I vould luf it." Her face radiated anticipation.

"No." Harry raised his hand stopping her. How could he tell her the show was not for her, not an X-rated film? She was too prudish to get any enjoyment out of raw, basic sex. Better she should go back to the ship and continue her pure thoughts, or whatever it was she thought about.

"Vy not?" The smile had faded, her brow now wrinkled, eyes questioning.

Harry looked at her. He had to tell her. It would hurt her, but hell, hadn't she hurt him, literally emasculated him that night on the bow of the ship? Not tonight! There was no way he was going to get stuck with her tonight, not if there was a chance for action, a night spent in the sack sharing uninhibited sexual delights with a beautiful, desirable Chinese woman. Hell, it had been thirty years since he'd last screwed a Chinese whore. It was more appealing by the moment.

"Harry. Are you not listening to me? I said vy not?" Her voice had assumed that air of haughtiness, demanding.

He looked her straight in the eyes. If he was blunt, she'd grab her package and run right back to the ship.

"Adult entertainment," he said dryly. "Pornographic films, sex, and an adult style show showing the latest sexy clothing women can wear to turn their man on, to enhance love making. I'm sure you wouldn't be interested."

"Oh," she gasped. "Dat kind of show!" Color drained from her face. She looked like she'd just been slapped, lips suddenly pursed tightly together. Her fingers tightened around her glass, knuckles white. Sitting erect, she replied in an exasperated voice, "No. I vould not vant to go to anyting like dat!" Annoyance showed in her eyes, her voice. "I am a good Christian voman. Dat kind of prurient trash is below me. No vun in dere right mind vould vant to vaste time on such immoral filth like dat." Her voice suddenly choked with emotion.

Harry took a swallow of beer. That's for the night on the bow of the ship, he told himself smugly, and then replied. "I'm going in to see it. I enjoy seeing a good porno flick and getting some new ideas. I also enjoy a good fashion show."

At the moment, the waiter appeared with their dinners. Harry turned to him. "Waiter. Remind me about the show after I eat. Right now, I'm looking forward to enjoying your succulent Peking Duck"

"Of course, sir. I'll remind you," the waiter replied, setting his tray down on an adjacent stand. He glanced toward Osa. Harry shook his head no. The waiter nodded, and then began serving.

The die was cast. Harry felt smug. He wasn't going to strike out with the same girl three times in a row. Tonight was his night. With a faint smirk, he glanced across the table at Osa. She had turned away, gazing out the window, a tear glistening in the corner of her eye. If this was victory, why did he suddenly feel like an asshole?

The waiter had carefully removed the tops from each dish, held it momentarily under their nose, and then placed the dish before them. Uncorking the red wine, he passed the cork to Harry, who sniffed, then nodded approval. The waiter poured a sampling into his glass. Harry held the glass before him, swirled the ruby rich liquid around in the glass, sniffed the bouquet, and then tasted it.

"Excellent," he said. The waiter beamed. He filled both their glasses, lit the candle in the center of the table, and then stepped to the wall where he adjusted a rheostat softening the light over their table. The band had just started playing "Stardust." He smiled. It was a very romantic setting. They were a nicely matched couple. Bowing low, he turned leaving them alone.

"Osa," Harry ventured, attracting her attention. She turned back to him. He raised his glass of wine to her, and said, "To an excellent cook, and to smooth sailing." He smiled. It was a "trying to make amends" smile.

"To tonight," she responded, touching her glass to his, a Mona Lisa smile crossing her lips.

Now what the hell does she mean by that, he wondered, as he sipped. Why the cunning smile?

"Dis is really delicious, Harry," she said after several bites. She was suddenly her old self, exuberant, smiling as though nothing had ever happened between them, seemingly unperturbed at what had just transpired only minutes before.

Harry became wary. She had changed one hundred and eighty degrees from the iceberg to a warm, friendly dinner companion.

He found himself pecking at his food while noting her eating voraciously. The food was excellent, the best Peking duck he could recall since having it at the Hotel De Peking back in Peiping the summer of 1948. Although he felt uncomfortable at first, he soon warmed up as she chattered away on a variety of topics. It was the first time they had talked since traversing the Panama Canal.

Soon he found himself engaged in delightful conversation. They were surprised at the similarity in tastes in the love of the theater, gourmet cooking, enjoyment of classical music, visiting art museums, sailing, skiing, reading and on and on their conversation went. Before he realized it, the waiter was standing at his elbow. He coughed to gain Harry's attention, bent low and whispered in Harry's ear. The show would soon be starting.

Harry nodded somewhat upset at the interruption, surprised that they had such a welcome conversation for the best part of an hour. He asked for the check.

The waiter added up the bill and handed it to him. Harry glanced at it, then laid a fifty-dollar bill on the table and waved the waiter away when he started to make change. "Thank you, sir," the waiter said, bowing, picking up the bill and the fifty, then added, " the show begins in ten minutes –"

"Yes," Harry snapped cutting him short. He found himself in a quandary, wrestling with his conscience. He had enjoyed the evening with Osa thus far but he knew it would go nowhere, leading to nothing more than a luke-warm handshake, at the most. The films and fashion show offered much more of what he wanted for the night.

"Harry," Osa cooed from across the table in a soft, enticing voice. "Dis has been such a vunderful evening. I haf really enjoyed it. Vy don't ve do someting togedder, maybe shopping, take in der sights of der city, perhaps a play or someting like dat."

Harry looked across at his attractive dinner companion. In spite of the wonderful evening, he knew he wouldn't get anywhere with her, or would he?

At that particular moment there was a tantalizing, different look in her eyes. Was it a come hither look, an invitation? The thought of bedding her down flashed through his mind. It wasn't the first time he'd fantasized about making it with her. Then the thought struck him; she was probably the type who preferred sex in the dark, under the covers with her nightgown on, and she probably talked incessantly about the laundry, fixing meals, the price of groceries and other non-romantic gibberish.

The waiter coughed.

"Harry," she said, her voice beseeching, almost pleading. "You don't vant to go to dat kind of show. You are not dat kind of man, lowering yourself to such prurient tastes, lusting for such depraved sexual gratification, dat is not der vey I see you." Harry couldn't believe what he'd just heard; she'd reverted back one hundred and eighty degrees to the old, conniving, whining bitch. "You are an educated man," she continued, leaning forward, her blue eyes searching his face. "You are a man of stature, high morals, I - I can't see you lowering yourself to see dat kind of smut."

Harry listened. The lecture sounded all too familiar. If he closed his eyes and listened it would be reminiscent of the many times his wife had lectured him after one of their many famous, nearly nightly, battles about sex.

"Sex is not dat important dat it must be pursued like an animal," Osa said, coming on stronger with her redundant plea. "Man is a higher animal, able to control his lusting, not chasing after cheap, dirty whores und prostitutes. A normal man is able to pursue sex visin der normal bounds of love, not in dis kind of tawdry, sinful vay."

"Sisters under the flesh," Harry muttered aloud. She was building her case now, trying to persuade him that a night with her, sans sex, was better than a roll in the hay with a hot blooded Chinese woman. Bullshit!

"Harry, I tink you vould enjoy an evening vis me more dan dat trash." There was a conceited tone to her voice.

Thoughts of their last encounter flashed through his mind. All of a sudden she was beginning to irritate him. Alfie and his friend, and their two attractive Chinese dates, walked by. Alfie gave Harry a thumb's up. Harry nodded.

The time had come. An evening with her would be self-defeating. No damned woman would ever lead him around again; this he had determined a long time ago. This one was no different than his damned wife, Laurie. No, absolutely not. She wasn't dealing with just any man; she was dealing with Harry Martin – and he called the shots.

Maybe her husband hadn't had the balls to call the shots or he would have squared her away a long time ago. Well, I've got balls! No female is going to tell me how to run my life. There was only one woman: Sandy. She had changed his life. She was willing, in fact eager, to please him. They had found great satisfaction in pleasing each other. Osa was too much like his ex-wife, an iceberg. Thank god all women aren't like that. Piss on her. I'm going to the show!

His anger had peaked, and then waned. He raised his wine glass to her, and then drained it. "I'm going in to see the show. You're welcome to come along or, if you prefer, they can get you a taxi back to the ship."

Osa's mouth gaped open. She turned quickly away trying to mask her disgust. Why were men like that? They'd had a beautiful evening. Why couldn't he be content to be in the company of a lady, to share an evening of companionship? Why sex?

As much as she wanted to leave, in fact had planned to leave directly after dinner, she now found herself indecisive. She swirled the last of her wine about in her glass, and then sipped at it. Her mind was in a whirl; what should she do? Carefully, she placed her goblet back on the table on the wet ring where it had sat before.

"I've taken the liberty of ordering a booth for you," the waiter said, bending, whispering in Harry's ear. "If you wish, I can have a drink set up for you in the booth."

"Good idea. Make it a Millers."

"And the lady?"

Harry looked across at Osa, gleefully enjoying the moment, noting the dull bitterness in her eyes, tight jawline and tightly pursed lips. It'll take just a moment, he told himself, before her puritan ethic kicks in and she's out the door.

"Drink, Osa?" he grinned. "For the show."

He glanced at his watch. Almost show time. He could sense the excitement tingling through him, relishing watching a good porn flick. Sandy enjoyed them, too. They had gone to several together, even caught a lingerie show one time in Detroit. It had been a real turn on for both of them. They'd almost torn off each other's clothing before they got back to their hotel room. One hell of a night! He glanced back at Osa. Haughty bitch! He knew he had her. Exit Osa, enter love for the night!

Sensing the hesitancy of the man's date, the waiter politely added, loud enough for both to hear, "There are specially trained attendants inside the theater who can respond to your every need. They are especially responsive to the single man and welcome the opportunity of gratifying his every secret desire."

The grin on Harry's face widened. Osa's face, in contrast, turned cold, chiseled marble. Harry knew she had heard. Bye, bye Osa, he thought, rising.

"Order me a drink, Harry," she said softly, almost with a tone of dejection. She cleared her throat. "I go vis you." She gathered up her purse, package and coat as she rose.

No! I can't be hearing right! A look of incredibility crossed his paling face. She isn't going with me. I must have heard wrong. But she was standing beside him. He could swear there was the faintest edge of a smirk on her face.

She's playing some kind of game with me. The damned female is out to destroy my one night in Shanghai, the one night I had planned for, a night of lustful shacking up with some beautiful Chinese whore. No! Not her!

"Scotch on the rocks," she told the startled waiter. "Inside vis der gentleman."

"Very good," he gulped, clearing his throat. "Inside."

"Where do we go?" Harry snapped.

The waiter pointed toward the elevator. "Get off on the tenth floor and go to your left to a gold and red enameled door. Knock and give the hostess ten dollars. Tell her Wong has arranged for your booth. I, uh, I know you will enjoy the show."

Chapter 48
PAYBACKS ARE HELL

A small panel in the middle of the gold and red enameled door slid open and two coal-black eyes peered back at Harry. He held up a ten spot and mentioned Wong's name. The panel closed and the door swung open. A trim, graceful, Oriental woman with long coal-black hair greeted them, bowing low. As she did, Harry noted the dress she wore was breathtakingly sparse, two thin lacey panels of sheer material, a front and back, which were joined together at the shoulders, waist and hips with thin ties. The sides were completely open allowing an appetizing view of her lithe body. She wore nothing under the dress. The long open slits exposed creamy brown skin and a glimpse of small firm breasts and dark nipples.

"Thank you," she said softly taking the money. Harry felt a twinge in his groin. Nice, he thought, real nice, sexy nice. He feasted momentarily on the enticing view.

The woman led them through the dimly lit room to a luxurious booth which faced toward a large stage. A huge beaded screen dominated the wall behind the stage. Harry noticed there were a number of booths, each separate from the next allowing complete intimacy and, from the number of murmured conversations, sighs and occasional girlish squeals of delight, all were occupied.

He thanked the hostess, who again, bowed low exposing firm breasts which rolled freely forward. Damn, he said to himself, this is the place. He glanced around his booth. It was fairly large, with an overstuffed black leather couch that curved around the dark interior. In the center was a small table. Soft, lilting music filled the air.

Osa nudged him and he stepped aside allowing her to move past him, which she did, stiffly, and moved deliberately to the far end of the booth, as far from him as possible.

Harry said nothing, instead sitting down and staring forward. The bitch was out to ruin his night. He knew it. He had stalked out of the restaurant ahead of her, not bothering with manners, letting her walk behind. The ride up on the elevator had been in chilling silence. He crossed his fingers. He had one trump card left: Osa, herself. As soon as she got one good look at a couple screwing on the big screen ten times life-size, it'd blow her mind and she'd go running back to the ship. Then, WHAMMO!

Osa, too, sat in silence. She could hear the sounds of lovers all around them. She had steeled her mind, resigned herself to god knows what fate. Was he really worth it? She looked about the room with a hesitant glance, uncomfortable at being in such a place. She recalled the time when her girlfriends begged her to skip school with them and they had sneaked into an adult theater. It had been sinful and she had fled after several minutes. The vulgar images had stuck in her mind, had bothered her, upset her stomach to the point where she was sick for days afterward. Her friends had stayed through two movies and deliberately teased her for being such a prude.

Now, here she was with a man, Harry Martin. Was he worth the churning, nauseous feeling inside her, that feeling that she might at any moment throw up? Perhaps, she thought, he might still be persuaded to leave. She would strike at the right moment. Till then, she would endure the filth, the smut.

"Your drinks, sir," the waiter said appearing suddenly beside Harry at the opening of the booth. He set the glasses down sliding the scotch on the rocks toward Osa, the beer in front of Harry. "I told your attendant you might find need for her special attention. She'll be here soon." He leaned closer whispering in Harry's ear "Her name is Sunny, and she looks forward to brightening your evening."

Harry chuckled. Osa glanced at them, and then picked up her drink. Men, she muttered disgustedly. Glancing at the bill, Harry extracted his wallet, took out a ten spot and gave it to the waiter with a wave of his hand. "Thank you, sir," the waiter replied, bowing. "If you need help, Sunny can be very helpful. Otherwise, enjoy the show. I know you will have a good time."

No sooner had he left than Harry saw a tall, well-proportioned Chinese girl approaching with the warmest smile he'd seen in ages, and nothing much beyond that. She was dressed as a slave girl in a filmy costume right out of the Arabian Nights, replete with bracelets and chains. She was also breathtakingly beautiful and totally naked under the gossamer-thin material. Nothing was left to the imagination.

"Hello," she breathed in a warm, sultry voice as she stopped beside him. "I'm Sunny, and I'll be happy to do anything I can to make your visit here an exceptionally memorable occasion." She gave a knowing wink at Harry as she spoke.

Harry winked back, the smile on his face widening as his eyes traveled slowly down her delicious body. She moved slightly, modeling to accentuate her beauty points as his feasting eyes roved downward and then back up. Her smile continued, thrilled at the excitement in his eyes.

Osa coughed. It was an embarrassed cough.

Harry broke free of his beautiful vision to glance in her direction. She was glaring at him. Harry grinned impishly. Any minute now she's gonna flip out, scream some Swedish obscenities and go stomping out the door. The thought of her leaving made him feel good. He returned his gaze to Sunny's beautiful body already contemplating what he intended to do with her. Things were definitely looking "Sunny-er" by the minute.

"I'm sure you'll make my-our, stay a pleasant one." he said, clearing his throat, forcing his eyes beyond the fullness of her bosom, past the hard umber dark tips jutting against the diaphanous material, up to her delightful smiling face. He could feel a flush of lust coursing through his loins, blood pumping fiercely through his wanting body. The vibes between them were positive; he could sense it just looking at her. Tonight's the night! Just as quickly, his thoughts turned to Osa. Come on Osa, get pissed off and storm out of here!

Sunny smiled coyly, pleased with his approval, pleased that the American she'd been assigned was handsome, virile, a likely match for her sexual appetite. "We have any kind of drink or food you might desire," she purred. "We have seductively mature cherry wine that is very tasteful. It is rich, robust, a natural entree for lovers before the main course." There was a smoldering look in her eyes as she touched Harry's cheek with a soft brush of her fingertips. "I prefer several glasses before," she added in a soft whisper. "Wine puts me in a very receptive mood for anything my lover wishes to pursue."

Harry listened intently, enjoying the way she described the wine, the way her dark eyes intensified with desire, excited by the lightness of her touch. By the time she finished he had a burgeoning erection.

"We, uh, ate just before we came here," he said almost apologetically, looking into Sunny's dark inviting eyes that seemed to glow deeply with lust. "But, the wine –"

"Yes," she answered softly, ruby red lips slightly ovaled as she looked at him.

"Just bring us a bottle of vine!" Osa said sliding across the cool leather seat, leaning tightly against Harry. There was a syrupy softness to her voice, obviously mimicking Sunny. She slipped her arm through Harry's and smiled sweetly up at her. "Der vine vill be just fine," she cooed.

Harry's mouth dropped wide open, startled at Osa's sudden move. Sunny shrank back with a confused look, her eyes glancing from Osa to Harry. She abruptly pivoted and fled.

"What the hell was that all about?" he snapped, turning angrily toward Osa who deftly slipped her arm free of his. At that moment, the lights started to dim, the movie was about to begin. And just as casually as she had slid across to him, she was now sliding back across the padded leather seat, smug that she had nipped that little *tête-à-tête* in the bud.

"Bitch!" Harry muttered under his breath. He sat back hard against the leather backboard crossing his arms across his chest in disgust. Looking up at the screen, he saw the movie was starting. Although he was watching, his mind was already in motion thinking about his next move to get rid of the iceberg. The bitch was obviously out to ruin his one night in town. He had to get rid of her!

The title and credits rolled across the huge screen, vividly superimposed over an idyllic country scene of lush rolling hills, horses frolicking in a meadow and a meandering creek where, as the camera slowly zoomed in, could be seen a beautiful, blue-eyed, flaxen-haired young maiden taking a swim, hidden from view of the farmhouse and barn, but not from the consuming eyes of a naturally lecherous old hired man.

"Shit," exclaimed Harry as he realized he and Sandy had seen the same movie last summer in Saginaw. It was a good flick, but it was the unbridled passion they had shared afterward that he recalled best. He grinned. It had been one of their best times. Resignedly, he settled back to watch the film. He took a sip of beer. Was the beer flat, or was it just the way he felt?

Glancing over at Osa, he saw her hands covering her face, bulging eyes peering in disbelief between splayed fingers at what was unfolding before her. Her left hand stifled a gasp as the young maiden rose from the water facing the camera, beautiful in total nudity, coral tipped nipples centered on large breasts, a dark patch of pubic hair at the point her long slim legs joined her well-rounded body. Harry grinned; poor Osa hadn't seen anything yet. The good stuff was yet to come.

A monologue extolled the trials and tribulations of an innocent farm maiden who, although wanting to remain innocent and chaste, had become aware of her womanly charms which, in turn, had evoked a deep-seated yearning within her to be fulfilled as a woman, to know and enjoy the pleasurable aspects of sex. She had already observed the sexual matings of farm animals and, unbeknownst to her parents, had also watched their passionate couplings on a number of occasions.

Moving out of the stream, she stepped onto the grassy bank where she picked up her faded gingham dress. She hesitated at slipping into the dress, as though she preferred to remain naked, a free spirit. Behind a tree, the hired man stood watching, drool dripping down his chin. Finally, the maiden slipped the dress over her wet body covering her charms. Harry could see instant relief reflected on Osa's face.

Barefoot, the girl headed toward the farmhouse but she was

intercepted by the hired man, an obvious bulge in the front of his pants, who grabbed her wrist trying to drag her off toward the barn. She twisted away, stumbling, falling to the ground, her dress thrown up around her waist. The man's eyes were about to pop out of his head. He dived for her but she rolled away, scrambled to her feet and ran toward the farmhouse.

Osa sat nervously wringing her hands together. Harry snickered. She was obviously living the role of the young maiden vicariously, he thought, the way her eyes were riveted on the screen intently watching every movement. She breathed a sigh of relief when the girl reached the safety of the farmhouse. Weakly, Osa picked up her drink taking a deep sip.

The maiden's mother met her in the parlor, beaming, holding a letter before her. It was from her favorite aunt. The girl clutched the letter to her breast, then ripped it open and read aloud. It was an invitation to visit her aunt in the big city.

Looking apprehensively at her mother, the maiden pleaded with her for permission to go. After a moment the mother nodded yes. Excitedly, the maiden kissed her mother thank you, then hurried up the steps to her room, closed the door, threw herself on the bed and re-read the letter. She was going to the big city!

Bouncing off the bed, she took her suitcase out of the closet and threw it on the bed. Then, she began packing it with what sparse, dressy clothing she owned: dresses, skirts, blouses, underwear, shoes, cheap costume jewelry, hairbrush and makeup. She started to throw a couple of magazines in the suitcase, and then stopped. Glancing at the popular, naughtily illustrated romance magazines, the kind young girls love to read because they're full of exciting, passionate love stories, a yearning, hungry look came to her eyes.

Easing back on the bed, she began reading one of her favorite stories. As she read, her hand moved lightly over the bodice of her dress, fingers teasing, nipples rising hard against the soft material. Shortly, eager fingers undid the several buttons and pulled the material wide, exposing full, white, swollen breasts, gently massaged by the skillful demands of her hands, fingers pinching at hardened tips.

Osa, who had taken a sip of her scotch, nearly choked on her drink as she recoiled back in the seat, eyes flying wide open as the girl eased the hem of her dress up, bunching it across her hips to expose her nakedness, her most private parts.

Osa drew back, clutching at her chest at what she was viewing; wincing at the girl's lewd, degrading action, a scene filling the giant screen. Osa shook her head in disbelief. Yet, without a conscious thought to what she was doing, she brought the scotch to her lips and drained the glass.

Harry found it more interesting, actually amusing, watching Osa's reactions to the film. Quietly shifting about in his seat, he continued to observe her. This was worth the price of admission, the bitch viewing raw sex on a large screen totally unaware of his observing her.

The action on the screen shifted to the big city where the maiden had just arrived at her favorite aunt's home modestly tucked away in one of the finer neighborhoods. Her aunt was a tall, attractive, dark-haired woman with an alluring figure. She appeared not much older than her niece. Shortly, they were in a bedroom with the niece trying on several captivating gowns as her aunt informed her she had already arranged a date for her with one of her handsome young gentlemen acquaintances. The niece threw her arms about her aunt, hugging her, kissing her, thanking her for inviting her to the city.

The scene shifted again showing the home filled with the sound of music, gaiety, laughter, flowing wine and handsome men eager to dance with the aunt and beautiful niece. The two women were dressed in beautiful ball gowns, low-cut bustlines showing ample cleavage.

Osa relaxed for the moment enjoying the lightness of the scene. The handsome men looked equally elegant in business suits. Osa glanced at Harry, gave a nervous half-smile, then turned her attention back to the screen. It wasn't as sinful as she had first thought.

As the evening progressed, the young man's intentions toward the niece became a little bolder, more amorous. Their lips touched, lightly at first, then turned into a prolonged, passionate kiss. More kisses followed, each more passionate than before. The niece seemed receptive to his kisses, his whispered suggestions so exciting that she soon melted in his arms. Alone in the living room with the lights low and a glowing fire in the huge fireplace, they shared fresh wine as their kisses grew more intense. They had eased to the floor sitting before the fire watching the flames licking at the burning logs. The maiden had reclined back in his arms shyly allowing the man freedom to slip the straps of her dress, caressing her. As passion consumed them, he slowly undressed her. Soon they were naked, silhouetted before the dancing flames of the fireplace.

Harry watched the tension mounting in Osa, the sudden tautness of her chin line, hand clutching at her stomach, gasping as the maiden responded, aroused, wanton, to her lover. As the man seduced the innocent maiden, Osa flinched, glancing away, yet drawn back to the screen wide-eyed, watching in awe at the deflowering of the innocent maiden. The girl's face was contorted with passion, an eagerness in her body's response to their wanton sexual enjoyment.

Beads of perspiration stood out on Osa's face. Her eyes bulged following every move of the lovers on the gigantic screen. She tried to stifle a gasp at the close-ups of their copulation, hearing the moans and sighs of sexual rapture. In a state of heightened anxiety, Osa pushed back against the leather seat shaking her head in disbelief, not wanting to believe this was happening, that two people would partake of sex as the two were now doing on the screen and allowing it to be recorded on film.

The poor girl. How could she let this happen to her? This was terrible. Sinful. She knew she had to leave, to flee from this den of sin. It was not right. She would never have allowed Rudy the freedom to do that to her. No man would ever take her like that. And yet, the girl was smiling, happy eyes following everything the man did to her, and what she did for the man. No, she had to go. This was filth. She had to leave.

Observing Osa, Harry suddenly felt sorry for her. Maybe this was too much for her to handle. Maybe she wanted to leave. He'd ask her. If she wanted to leave, it was understandable.

"Hi," Sunny said easing in beside him, her bosom pressed tightly against his arm. "How's it going?" She had deposited a bottle of red wine on the table. Harry looked at the bottle. He almost choked; it had to be a magnum. How the hell would he ever get through that much wine? Before he could answer, Sunny was pouring two glasses with chilled cherry wine.

"So-so," he said, glancing at Osa. "The lady might be leaving shortly." Osa's head was shaking aimlessly back and forth, eyes welling with tears, softly bewailing what she was seeing, still pressed back against the seat.

Sunny kissed him lightly on his ear, swirled her tongue around, and then murmured softly, "Let me know." He slipped her a twenty. "Bring me a couple of scotches, doubles might be best." He nodded toward Osa. Sunny smiled. As she rose, he patted her buttocks. Solid. Sunny glanced back at him smiled, winked, and then was gone.

All feelings of remorse for Osa suddenly vanished. Instead, Harry found himself wishing she would leave now. "C'mon, Osa. Get really upset and leave. This isn't your kind of game," he heard himself whispering. Already, he could envision himself naked between Sunny's long legs, sweating, enjoying each other. He wanted to shout out loud, Osa! Go back to the ship!

He was so aroused thinking about Sunny he found his hand was shaking, spilling several drops of wine as he slid a glass across in front of Osa.

She hadn't missed seeing that brazen Chinese slut slip in beside him, seen her kiss him, whispering in his ear. It had happened just at the moment she was about to leave, insist they both leave, but now the little slut had ruined the moment.

Upset, she turned back to the screen. She could always cover her eyes. Degrading filth. Maybe just a little longer, even Harry had to be upset at such degradation. But she was definitely going to leave, and if he cared for her at all, he'd leave with her.

On the screen the beautiful aunt, now naked except for a black garter belt and black stockings, was happily satisfying two suitors at the same time. "Oh, my god," Osa exclaimed aloud, mouth agape at the horrid scene. She jumped turning quickly at Harry's touch. He'd pay hell getting her! He was pointing toward the table, the glass of wine.

"Oh," she choked. Grasping the glass, she raised it to her lips downing the chilled fluid in one long swallow. Just as quickly, her eyes moved back on the screen having wavered for that moment when Harry had touched her. She couldn't believe what she was seeing, what she was hearing, the gasping, the groans and sighs, the thrusting bodies. Disgusting! Yet, as she continued to watch, a warmth was spreading throughout her body, a tingling itch she couldn't understand, nor ignore. She felt flushed as prickling sensations began to stir within her, lascivious feelings of desire, prurient thoughts she had always masterfully held in check. No, she ordered her mind. No! Quickly, she held the empty glass in Harry's direction. He filled it.

The scene had shifted back to the niece and her lover. In stunning nudity, silhouetted in the soft glow of burning embers in the fireplace, she was kneeling over her lover, her kisses trailing softly down his firm body.

Osa unconsciously ran the tip of her tongue around one clenched knuckle, driving it deep into her mouth stifling a gasp of disbelief at how the maiden pleased her lover. Harry almost choked on his wine as he glanced from the maiden back to Osa, who anxiously chewed on her knuckle.

Harry turned away, his whole body convulsing with laughter, yet not daring to laugh out loud. Osa's vicarious reaction was the funniest thing he'd seen in ages.

Around him the muffled sounds of lovers, soft titters of laughter, gasps and occasional moans of pleasure were beginning to have an affect on him. He looked at Osa. Her eyes stayed glued to the screen where the young niece was now wrapped in the arms of her lover, gaspingly meeting his every thrust. Osa, too, was gasping, her breasts rising and falling in tempo with her labored breathing. Harry shrugged. What the hell. If I do, I'll catch hell; if I don't, I'll never know.

He eased over next to her slipping an arm around her shoulder. Osa glanced at him, glaring. "Harry, ve must leave now. Dis is not right," she implored as her head turned back to the screen. Yet, she hadn't pulled away from his arm. Taking it as a good sign, Harry leaned over kissing her lightly on her neck. She flinched but did not move away. He softly nibbled on her ear. She winced momentarily then seemed to relax, resting back against him. Emboldened, he rested his hand in her lap, then moved upwards under one heaving breast, cupping it. Osa's hand came quickly to her defense, stopping him, yet not pushing him away. After several seconds, his hand continued caressing moving freely between the heaving orbs. There was no rejection, only a prolonged sigh. Turning her face to his, he kissed her fully on her mouth, surprised as she responded warmly with a long passionate kiss. With shaking hand, he unbuttoned her blouse and reached inside feeling heated flesh. Easing one bra strap over her shoulder, he exposed one full, firm, hard-tipped breast. Osa moaned softly as he massaged the pliant flesh, squirming responsively as his tongue swirled about the hard tip.

Just then, the house lights suddenly came on, slowly increasing in intensity, the movie was over. Just as suddenly, Osa broke free from Harry, an embarrassed look on her face as she glanced about. Quickly she stuffed her breast back inside the bra, pulled up the strap and buttoned her blouse. She was upset with herself, face crimson. She glared at Harry, who returned to his end of the couch.

"Ve must go before somevun sees us here," she whispered hoarsely, gathering her coat and package. "Dis is all wrong."

"There's nothing wrong from my point of view," he replied not making any motion to move. "Hell, Osa, you're two times twenty-one. You can make your own decisions. You have a perfect right to be here, if you want. Besides, no one can see in the booth. We can have a great time together."

"Togedder, here, never!" she snapped. "Dis is all wrong, all wrong." A sigh of indignation escaped her. She had hoped they could become friends again. Dinner had been delightful up to the point where the waiter had interrupted, had told of this sinful place. This would lead nowhere. It was the path to ruination, tawdry, gutter sex. If he had only listened to her, had gone away with her. They could have strolled through the streets of Shanghai, shopping, talking, building their friendship.

True, her thoughts had strayed thinking of him in a sexual context but not in a setting like this, not now. Their feelings toward one another had to grow over a period of time. Sex would come gradually. If he cared at all, he would go with her. He had to go with her.

"Harry, please, let us go now," she implored.

"No." His answer was sharp, exasperated "If you want to leave, fine. Go. It's okay with me. I'm sure you can catch a cab back to the ship. Me. I'm staying. I kind of like what I've seen so far."

"But vat dey do is disgusting. Decent people don't do dat!"

"Says who? I don't practice everything that I see, but at least I keep an open mind. Not everyone looks at sex the way you do. Sex is whatever the two consenting parties agree to. I'm staying. This is my night in town, and I'm sure as hell going to enjoy myself."

Osa rose, confused, clutching at her coat and package, upset at his bluntness. Harry rose moving to one side to let her exit from the booth only to bump into the waiter, Wong.

"You're drinks, sir," he grinned, placing the two double scotches on the table.

Harry was surprised at seeing him. Where the hell was Sunny? The iceberg was leaving and it was time for the good times.

"Sunny is in the fashion show," Wong said answering the unasked question. "She'll be out shortly with our bevy of beautiful models."

"Thanks," Harry replied peeling off a ten spot and handing it to Wong with a wave of his hand, no change necessary. He shoved a double scotch over in front of Osa.

Her eyes glistening with tears, she continued to stand, still blocked by Harry from leaving the booth. "Harry," she whispered, "don't treat me like dis, please. I am not dat kind of voman, please, go vis me."

"No. I vant to stay. I vant to enjoy myself." He mimicked her pleading whine. "Have a good trip back to the ship."

Of a sudden, a loud, solid, sensuous disco beat filled the theater and a dazzling display of flashing, pulsating lights splashed a montage of wild colors around the room. The colors changed constantly to the throbbing beat of the disco brightly lighting the curtain that had closed in front of the movie screen.

Osa backed away from Harry collapsing on the seat burying her face in her hands, sobbing bitterly, unable to stop herself. She wanted to run but she couldn't; she felt paralyzed, confused that she was not in control of her feelings, confounded at the aching in her heart, the longing she felt for this man. She turned away from him facing the stage, tears streaming down her cheeks, yet knowing he had sat back down oblivious of her, not caring one bit about her feelings. Her hand wrapped around the double scotch and she downed it.

Chapter 49

LUST TAKES A POWDER

"Good evening lovers," a sultry female voice announced. "Now that you've had a chance to get to know one another better, to get in the mood, in the groove, and your motor's purring nice and easy, we proudly present our special fashion show, our *piece de resistance*, Fashions *ala* Freddie!"

The volume and beat of the music intensified as the large curtain parted. The sexy, sultry voice continued. "Our first model is Sunny, a native of Shanghai, and one of our favorite models. Sunny runs her own chic boutique in the lobby of the hotel during the day and models our special fashions in the evening. She's one of our most popular models."

Sunny had stepped through the curtain moving toward the audience. "Sunny is wearing a beautiful flaming red peignoir with low-cut bodice and, of course, her ever present smile." Osa's eyes followed the beautiful Chinese woman, the swing of her hips and the flagrant way she displayed her body. Disgusting. The wispy material barely hid her body from view of the audience.

Harry, too, was looking at Sunny, his eyes bulging. She was breathtaking. She had walked across the stage to a small ramp leading out into the audience. As she reached a point close to him, she stopped, winked, and slowly pirouetted before him ending in a bump for his benefit. Harry grinned, applauding. Tonight, he thought, tonight. She's gonna be the best damned thing to come into your life in ages, Martin, he told himself. Hot damn!

A tap on his shoulder brought his attention to his left. Wong held a small card before him. Harry held it up to the light and read it. He laughed, turned and thanked the waiter, cocked his head toward Osa shaking it no, and stuffed the card in his shirt pocket. "Not with this one. Maybe later, but thanks," he chuckled.

The announcer introduced the next model, Mei Ling, who came through the curtain alluring in a thin, silky transparent blouse and matching tap pants.

Harry took the card from his pocket, re-read it, and chuckled Osa looked over at him. She had seen the waiter stop and hand him something. They were making jokes about her.

"Vot is so funny?" she demanded "Are you making jokes of me now vis der vaiter?"

"No. Nothing's funny, and we weren't making jokes about you," he replied. "He gave me this card and I thought it was funny. It didn't concern you at all."

"Let me see der card."

"You won't enjoy it."

"I vill be der judge of dat." She grabbed the card from him and read it.

PRIVATE ROOMS AVAILABLE IN HOTEL. SOFT LIGHTING. SOFT MUSIC. WATER BEDS. LARGE MIRRORS ON CEILING AND WALLS. ADULT FILMS ON CLOSED-CIRCUIT TV. YOU WILL LIKE. LET YOUR WAITER OR HOSTESS KNOW OF YOUR DESIRES. THEY WILL MAKE ALL NECESSARY ARRANGEMENTS. THE MANAGEMENT.

"Disgusting!" she said thrusting the card back.

Harry took the card and tucked it in his shirt pocket. "Yup," he agreed ruefully, "especially if you've only got one night in town." He shoved the second double scotch over in front of Osa. Again, her hand wrapped around the glass.

The show continued. Osa watched in amazement at the gaudy fashions being shown by the models, clothing she would never buy in a lifetime, the kind of clothing she associated with cheap girls, harlots, whores, the kind of clothing only worn by women who gave freely of their bodies to satisfy the carnal desires of despicable men; women who subjugated themselves to the lustful, erotic perversity that men were known to crave, the kinds of things portrayed in the movie, things she never dared do.

Yet, in the darkness of the night lying restlessly in her bed, she had entertained such prurient thoughts, wondering what it would be like to recklessly abandon her body, to be totally submissive to a man, to Harry.

Since the moment they had first met she knew he would be special in her life. Glancing in his direction, she recognized the look of lust in his eyes as he intently watched every model parading across the stage, their bodies enticing under such thin lacey material. Her thoughts strayed back to those restless nights of late, lying in bed thinking of him, the way he had held her, his demanding kisses and the sexual longing that stirred within her as his hands encompassed her body. And then her hand would move stealthily down along her thigh slipping under the hem of her nightgown and, much like the maiden in the film, would bring wanton release.

No! She knew she had to leave even though it meant losing him. Good girls shouldn't be here, not in this place, not watching such prurient, suggestive films, explicit scenes that filled a woman's mind with lascivious thoughts, the thoughts she was now thinking. Her heart was heavy, mind confused, and that inner aching, that yearning to have Harry touch her, caress her, consume her blocked out everything else. No! She must push all prurient thoughts from her mind. She would leave right after the fashion show.

But another part of her told her to stay and enjoy, taste the forbidden fruit, enjoy the fulfillment of her innermost secret fantasies, the kinds of passionate moments she had seen so vividly portrayed on the large movie screen, fantasies she thought only she had ever dreamed. She carefully set the empty glass down on the table. A heady feeling seemed to encompass her as the alcohol flowed freely throughout her body, a relaxed feeling, somewhat akin to euphoria, a sense of bliss. She stole a glance at Harry. He was totally absorbed in the show.

The fashion show continued. Each model was as beautiful as the one before. All were tall, leggy, full bosomed, curvy-hipped and proud of their winning figures. The erotic display of lingerie drew applause and gasps from the attentive audience. The clothing included thin, almost transparent nighties, gowns, skirts with long thigh-high slits, sensuous French bikini panties, garter belts, thin bras, open-tipped bras, thigh-high stockings in a wide array of colors, Teddies, colorful thin silk blouses, even attractive dresses and suits for the after five cocktail hour.

The announcer ended the fashion show by calling all the models forward to the applause of a very enthusiastic audience. The announcer also added that all of the clothing was available at a modest price and to let their hostess know of their desire. "After all, men, these clothes were designed to show off and compliment the female form, and to stimulate you, her lover. Be nice. Buy your companion a gift. Let her know you care."

To continuing applause, the models left the stage as the curtain parted. Almost instantly, the lights dimmed and the next film began: *School for Marriage*.

Chapter 50
PEOPLE DO CHANGE

"I thought you were leaving," Harry said turning to Osa, somewhat irritated that she was still here. There was a sharp edge to his voice. His night of unbridled lust was about to begin in the arms of beautiful Sunny and he sure as hell didn't want any interference from the iceberg.

"Vell, I –" Osa started to speak but stopped short as Sunny swept into the booth. She was still wearing thigh-high black nylon stockings, satin French panties and an open-tipped bra, her nipples standing forth teasingly hard. She slid in next to Harry resting her hand on his leg, pressing tightly against him. Osa's mouth gaped wide not believing a woman would so shamelessly approach a man so scantily dressed.

"I had plans for us this evening," Sunny whispered softly in Harry's ear, emphasizing her intentions by swirling her tongue quickly around the inside of his ear. Harry sat electrified at her touch, an erection straining to burst out of his pants. Turning, he looked into dark eyes sultry with desire, red lips full of promise and then she was kissing him passionately, driving her long, slender tongue deep within his mouth snake like it its exploration, then withdrawing it leaving him breathless.

"I've got to go now," she murmured, her voice faltering. "I waited as long as possible for you, but –" and she gave a quick glance toward a still gaping Osa – "I have another 'friend' waiting. Sorry. I'll look for you tomorrow night, alone, and I promise it'll be special, just for you." She gave him another deep wrenching kiss and then fled.

Harry sat trying to catch his breath, trying to sort out what had just happened. "What a woman," he gasped. He found himself trembling at the thought of what it might have been tonight, just the two of them. "Dammit!" he swore softly to himself. The full impact of what had transpired hit him solidly like a punch to his gut; he was alone. He had struck out because of, because of the iceberg.

Jamming himself back in his seat, he folded his arms across his chest in disgust and stared up at the large screen. There it is shithead, he told himself. The only sex you'll get close to is right there on that big screen! That's your action for the night. He didn't bother to look at Osa. It made him sick to think she was still there, that her being there had cost him his one night in Shanghai.

Osa had watched the incident with Sunny in embarrassed silence, experiencing a pang of jealousy at the brazen way Sunny had touched, kissed and spoken to Harry. Never could she recall having felt this way about a man, not even Rudy, and they had courted through high school and college. It was as if she were once again a young schoolgirl competing for the attention of a boy, that first special boyfriend.

She had fought Helga Sorenson, wrestling her to the ground, pulling her hair, biting, punching, their pubescent bodies writhing on the fresh spring grass at the back of the schoolyard. She had won, had received a bloody nose, but to this day she couldn't remember the name of the boy.

In spite of her disgust at Harry's actions, he had sparked the embers of desire; she was about to burst into flame. Never had she wanted to possess a man, or be possessed by a man as she did at that moment. She blushed at the thoughts coursing through her mind as she slid across the cool leather seat and put her arm around his shoulder, her other hand resting lightly on his leg.

"But for tonight you're mine," she whispered huskily, softly running her tongue around the inside of his ear.

Harry jumped at her touch, startled, turning to see if it was really her. He found himself staring into sultry, inviting blue eyes. Damn, he thought, it must be the booze getting to me. This is the iceberg!

Before he could react, she pulled his head forward planting a kiss fully on his lips, driving her tongue deep within, searching, withdrawing, forcing it deeply within again several more times, then withdrawing leaving him gasping.

"I'm a fast learner," she whispered, her hand inching upwards along his leg. His manhood swelled, suddenly becoming uncomfortably hard. Her hand moved lightly across the bulge and she smiled. Moving her hand to his cheek, holding his face to hers, she kissed him again, whispering softly, "Der films are interesting, but I need a good instructor, you." She shifted around snuggling under his arm, pulling it around her shoulders. His hand coming lightly to rest on her right breast.

Harry was stunned at her change; she had just done another one hundred and eighty on him. What the hell was coming off? She snuggled closer emitting a sigh of contentment. A grin broke across his face. What the hell, when in Rome. He pulled her closer, his hand cupping her breast bringing a sigh of pleasure.

The film credits had rolled past already. As they looked up at the screen they saw it was a period film, one set in France at the time of Louis the Fourteenth. A young woman of virtue, wanting to learn all the intimate joys of sex so she could apply them aptly in her forthcoming marriage to a wealthy, elderly Count, had agreed to attend a marriage school, mostly at the insistence of her mother and her lady friends. It was for her benefit, they had chided. After all, the Count had been married twice before and, upon his divorces, had set his ex-wives up in a fine manner. Rumors circulated that he was most appreciative of a giving woman, happily sharing his extensive wealth in return for inventive sexual favors.

The plot was thin and Harry and Osa found themselves watching the young woman as she entered the marriage school learning from virile young men and women such techniques as would make her marriage more satisfying, more secure. The young woman went from one explicit scene to another, learning technique after technique and practice, practice, practice.

Harry shook his head at some of the erotic practices, even beyond the scope of his fertile mind. But he was impressed by the beautiful French maiden who was truly a fast learner and most active participant.

Soon the dark booth became equally exciting as Osa willingly shared intimate kisses, even an approving sigh as her blouse parted and moments later her bra slipped from her shoulders. His hands caressed and kneaded the naked mounds of soft resilient flesh. Osa mewled as Harry's fingers pinched her taut nipples and then one breast was drawn into his eager mouth. Her body and mind responded willingly to his every whispered suggestion with gasping sighs of approval.

By the time the French maiden was excitedly thrusting her way through graduation exercises under her pummeling instructor, the Swedish widow, naked to her waist, her skirt bunched up around her hips, was enjoying the personal instruction she was receiving and was just as excitedly looking forward to her graduation exercises. Harry tingled as Osa became the aggressive one, fumbling with the zipper of his pants, digging inside, and then boldly extracting his rigid manhood. She glanced up at him seeking approval. Smiling, she seemed to relish her task of giving him pleasure.

Yet, if it felt good, why, all of a sudden, did he have such a guilty feeling? Why did he feel like he was taking advantage of a highly emotionally charged situation? She wasn't that kind of woman. She wasn't like Sunny. If anything, she was really, basically naive.

He remembered that night on the ship, vowing to bring her down off that damned pedestal, debase her, rub her nose in it. That had been his goal, to shame her. And he had shamed her, shamed her into coming to the damned porno show. It was true; she had been shamed into it, put on the defensive. Yet, it seemed she was showing him she was capable of making her own decisions.

But it wasn't right because he was taking advantage of her. She wasn't that kind of girl. Sandy enjoyed porno flicks. They were a real turn on. But that was Sandy; she enjoyed sex. Osa didn't. It was that simple; they were that different.

Why the hell are these kinds of thought screwing up my mind, he thought as her lithe fingers worked magically. Even his ex-wife, the queen of prude, couldn't compare to Osa's gentle ministrations. She was indeed a fast learner, and damn, but it felt good.

But the guilt persisted. Why couldn't she have left earlier, told him to go to hell and continued her "saintly" ways. Hell, he could have lived with it. If it were Sunny he would have expected this from her, and more.

The fantasies he had daydreamed so often of subjugating Osa to his will, of breaking her shell of purity, were coming true here and now. He had wanted her to suffer, to wallow in lust, to get so damned turned on she'd be humping everyone in sight, and then he'd cut her off! But it wasn't turning out that way at all. Deep inside, he realized she meant more to him than just a one-night stand. She was human, understanding, loving, caring. She had feelings. If the truth was known, she probably wished she was somewhere else.

"I'm sorry, Osa," he whispered. "I know you don't like this place, the show, so if you want to leave, I'll understand."

Osa sensed something was bothering him. Still clutching him, she pulled his head close, kissing him passionately. "No," she replied in a gasping breath, "I vant to be here vis you. I am learning, you vill see. Just like in der movie" – she whispered in his ear – "I vill make you happy, you vill see." Her tongue circled within his ear, teeth nipping lightly at his lobe. Then, gently, she trailed hot, wet kisses down his neck and chest toward his groin.

"Hold it!" Harry gasped in a hoarse whisper, pulling her face back to his. "The lights are coming on; the movie's over."

Hastily, as the closing credits rolled across the screen, the two lovers scrambled into their clothing. Osa buttoned her blouse, tucked it into her skirt, then pulled the skirt down and smoothed out the material. She snatched her bra and panties from the floor and quickly shoved the items into her purse. Next to her, Harry managed to get his pants pulled up, shirt tucked in, zipped up, and his belt buckled as the house lights came up to full intensity.

Flushed, thoroughly aroused, the two sat back, glancing around, pretending nothing had happened in their booth just in case anyone might glance within, and hoped desperately for at least one more film and darkness.

Osa squeezed Harry's hand. "I haf never felt dis vay before." she whispered, not releasing his hand. "I vant you so badly I ache."

Harry kissed her. "I know what you mean I feel the same way. We gotta find a place, and quick!"

"Another drink, sir?"

It was their waiter staring down at them. Harry glanced at the table, at the empty glasses, the empty wine bottle, and the empty double scotches. The drinks must have evaporated somewhere along the way.

"No," Harry said. "Is there another movie?"

"Except for the fashion show, as the models are now busy with their guests, the two films will be repeated. There will be an additional charge. Do you wish to stay for a second showing?"

"No!" Osa blurted, suddenly reaching over and jabbing her fingers into Harry's shirt pocket, extracting the card. "Ve take vun of dese rooms instead!" She thrust the card up at the waiter. "I tink my teacher has some tings he vants to teach me, some tings I vant to learn better."

Harry extracted a fifty dollar bill from his wallet, thrusting it at the waiter. "And make sure there's plenty of booze in the room. I've got an anxious, eager student willing to learn."

It was a night neither of them would ever forget, exploring, experimenting, enjoying each other totally uninhibited, no hang-ups, no remorse. From the moment they entered the room, kissing passionately, touching, caressing, tearing at each other's clothing, the action never ceased. Harry couldn't believe this wanton, man-hungry female was the same iceberg he'd tried to ditch. She was beautiful in her total nakedness, aggressive in her desire to please and be pleased and bringing him back to life time after time to continue her lessons.

It was a happy, exhausted couple who finally emerged from the exotic, erotic Victorian hotel three hours later, not because they wanted to, but because they had to return to the ship by eleven p.m. curfew and he had the midnight watch.

Hand in hand they walked through the streets of Shanghai, stopping occasionally for a tender kiss, a soft caress, two lovers who had suddenly found themselves and happiness. And a satisfied Harry Martin was certain his lover had definitely left her Victorian scruples behind.

It was nearly eleven when they passed through the gate by the guard shack, waved through by the somber-faced, machinegun-toting guard. In the darkness behind the shack, Harry pulled Osa to him and kissed her, holding her tightly to him. She melted in his arms savoring the warmth and tenderness of his kiss.

"Thank you, Harry," she whispered, not breaking free of his hold.

"For what?" he whispered back, lightly kissing her neck. "Ummm, you smell good." He kissed her again.

"For helping me realize dat I can enjoy sex. Dis is der first time I haf truly enjoyed sex. Even on my honeymoon I vas scared und it hurt. Now I feel alive. I know dat it sounds crazy, but I feel better about sex now, und I know I can truly satisfy a man." She kissed him, hugging him tightly. "Especially you. You haf fulfilled me. Tank you so much."

Harry broke free adjusting the growing bulge in the front of his pants. "I think we better get on board ship. The guard will be over here in a minute wondering what's going on and I don't want to have to explain this bulge."

She laughed, lightly patting his erection.

Arm in arm they headed for the ship. On board, the watch commander checked them in. Then, boldly disregarding Captain Andress' off limits order, Harry escorted Osa back to her cabin.

"Thank you for a vunderful night," she whispered as she stepped into her cabin. "Later I vill model my new clothes for you, just for you,"

He laughed. Leaning forward, he kissed her. Her tongue brushed his lips, then thrust deeply into his mouth, a promise of things to come.

Chapter 51

CUTTHROATS ABOARD

"How vas shore leave?" Mr. Helmstrund asked in a mildly inquisitive voice as Harry reported for duty on the bridge. "Vas it as good as ven you ver here before?"

"Better," Harry replied, grinning as he poured a cup of coffee. "The best shore leave I've ever had in my life. Saw the sights of the city and tasted the passion of a beautiful woman. Great! Actually, nothing's really changed that much except the times and people, and the right people are changing."

Sigmund laughed. "Next time I vill go ashore, on our next trip. Den I vill haf some extra money to shop around und, as you say, taste der city."

"Let me know when you do. I'll supply the name of the place and the lady." Thoughts of Sunny and her promise of love came to his mind. She'd be a tiger in bed, probably more than Sigmund could handle. Who was the lucky guy that ended up with her, he wondered. He took a sip of coffee. Sunny, it would have been great.

"Harry, you amaze me. You are vat I vould call der constant stud. Do you tink you vill ever get it out of your system?"

"God, I hope not," Harry retorted. "Remember, older is better, and I'm getting a hell of a lot better."

Sigmund roared at the response.

"Did you happen to see Osa in town?" he asked wiping at his eyes, still chuckling. "She vent shopping by herself, vitch I tink vas dangerous, especially in Shanghai. Too many funny tings happen to foreigners in dis town."

"I, uh, saw her in town, bought her a drink and dinner. Then she took off shopping and, uh, I caught up with her again just outside the gate, walked her back to the ship."

"Dat voman. I vas just curious about vat she vould do in der city for so many hours by herself. None of der crew recall seeing her. It vas eleven ven you two came on board. I'm glad she valked back vis you."

"I'm sure the guys had other ideas in mind than shopping," Harry chuckled. "I did." He looked beyond Sigmund toward the bow. "Has anybody made the rounds of the deck tonight?" he asked changing the subject. He didn't want Sigmund, or anyone, to even remotely consider a tie between him and Osa.

"No. As long as ve are in port, Captain Andress vants periodic checks of der deck. He says dere are too many cuttroats roaming about. I suggest you should do it now before it gets too cold. It vas checked an hour ago on der last vatch, but ve should check it to be on der safe side."

"Consider it done, sir," Harry retorted with false bravado, snapping off a smart salute. Humming to himself, he headed out and down to the main deck. He halted at the railing for a moment listening to the cacophony of sounds on the river, the bleating of horns as ships arrived or departed, their forms dark against the blazing lights of the city. He felt good. It had been one hell of a good night, finally. By walking the deck he'd be able to reminisce about the night with Osa. She had turned into a wanton tigress in bed, wanting to do everything, taking the initiative, wallowing in erotic sexual perversions he never thought her capable of. It was what he had hoped to find in Shanghai. That he found it in the arms of Osa instead of Sunny was the most satisfying part of the night. Thoughts of her filled his mind as he savored every exciting aspect of their time together.

He started walking, taking his time as he rounded the stern of the ship, his heels clicking hard on the steel deck. The frigid widow had really thawed out. He found himself grinning time and again at some of the things she did, things she said she'd never done before, but now enjoyed with him. She had surprised him; she was a passionate, sensitive lover.

He stopped at the rail momentarily, the spot where he'd sent the

Chink to eternity. The bastard. He felt no remorse for him, nor for the two thugs who had kidnapped them. The river had swallowed them just like the Chink. No, he wasn't a cold-blooded killer, he told himself, just a survivor.

Stan had tipped his hand. He was in China, he was sure of that. There was no doubt that he had figured out how old Harry Martin had escaped from Saginaw, no doubt that he was following the progress of *Nurad* very carefully. Martin, he told himself, you'll have to be on guard every minute from now on.

Heading toward the bow of the ship, his hand went to his duty belt but it wasn't there. He stopped. "Dammit! You ass!" he chastised himself. Captain Andress had been explicit about the duty officer and bridge watch personnel carrying arms at all times while in port. The Colt .45 automatic and belt were in the wheelhouse. Oh well, he'd be back in the warmth and safety of the wheelhouse shortly. It was cold on deck. The temperature was supposed to drop to -2°celsius. He had no intention of staying on deck any longer than necessary.

At amidships, he stopped again looking across the sprawling city. Traffic was still moving along the Bund. A number of shops were still open, no doubt to serve the last of the sailors straggling back to their various home ships. Glancing over the side, he noted there were no sampan villages built around the ship.

Moving on, he saw a large cargo ship had moved in ahead of them. A British flag waved from it's stern. Several sailors were looking back toward *Nurad* pointing at something. Harry hurried forward toward the bow. What could it be? Nothing seemed amiss. At the port bow, he glanced over the side. Still nothing. Leaning far out, he strained his eyes searching the darkness. His gaze followed the length of the huge hawser that tied *Nurad* to the dock bollard. His gaze was momentarily obstructed by a large rat guard disc that encompassed the hawser about mid-way between the ship and dock. He concentrated his attention on the rat guard. There appeared to be a figure huddled just in front of the rat guard. The figure didn't move.

Harry moved several paces along the railing and looked again.

There was definitely somebody holding onto the rat guard.

"He's seen the little bastard," came a British voice. "He'll give 'em what for now!"

A sudden movement to his left startled Harry. Turning, he instinctively ducked, receiving a glancing blow to the side of his head that bounced off his shoulder. Dropping, he rolled over on his back as a dark-clad figure charged at him. Harry quickly drew his legs back tightly and then thrust violently outwards catching the assailant in the stomach, throwing him backwards.

Before the assailant could regain his feet, Harry was up and moving in for the attack. The figure lashed out with a Karate kick, but Harry countered, thrusting his arm upwards and outwards, knocking his assailant off balance. Savagely, Harry followed through with a crushing kick to the groin. The assailant screamed, falling to the deck, clutching at his crotch. Harry ignored the man's agony and pressed his attack, jerking the man to his feet and lifting him in one fluid motion over his head, then throwing him over the side of the ship bouncing him off the hawser. There were two distinct splashes as two bodies hit the cold, murky waters of the Huangpo River.

Harry squatted low, listening, his heart pounding, adrenalin coursing through his veins. Gasping, he tried to control his breathing in order to hear. Were there other intruders on board? There was only continuing silence, his pounding heart and his heavy, labored breathing.

After a couple of minutes, he glanced over the railing. Whoever they were, they were long gone. He raced the length of the deck and up the ladder two at a time to the bridge. At his report, Sigmund immediately stepped to the control panel and punched two switches. The ship was suddenly bathed in light from stem to stern, coming alive like a small city. Picking up the phone, Sigmund reported the incident to Captain Andress. Hanging up, he ordered Harry below to roust two crewmen to duty on deck watch.

"Und make sure dey are armed!" Sigmund added as he saw Harry strapping on his .45, making sure there was a full clip in the butt. Harry acknowledged with a wave of his hand and headed below passing Captain Andress on his way, taking a moment to relate the order to get men for a deck watch. He grinned after bidding adieu; if the skipper only knew, but then, what he doesn't know about his niece, the better.

After rousting two crewmen, both slightly hung over from shore leave, and both unhappy at being ordered on deck in the middle of the night, Harry returned to the bridge. Captain Andress curtly reminded him of his standing order to wear a sidearm while on duty in port. Harry apologized only to be met with a hearty slap on his shoulder for rebuffing the boarders.

"It reminds me of der old days, Harry," the captain said somewhat gleefully. "Many der times I haf trown der heathen scum overboard or hosed dem down mit a firehose." He laughed heartily. "I tought Chairman Mao had changed dis nation about. I guess times change but not der people. Yah, dere's no telling vat dose cuttroats might haf done. It is a good ting you ver alert, Harry." He turned to Mr. Helmstrund. "Carry on. If you need me, give me a call." With that, he left the bridge.

The rest of the watch proved uneventful. Harry found consolation in recalling intimate moments shared with Osa. It surprised him that Sigmund didn't ask any further questions about his night in town. Just as well, he thought; he'd just end up feeding the Second a bunch of bullshit.

Captain Andress arrived back in the wheelhouse before the end of their watch surprising them. Both were enjoying a cup of coffee. "I couldn't sleep," the captain said in response to their unasked question. "Anyting new to report?"

"No sir," Sigmund replied. "Der rest of der vatch has been visout incident."

"Good." Captain Andress glanced out the windows along the lighted deck. "I vant you two to stay here. I feel uneasy for some reason." Harry glanced at Sigmund, who shrugged as if to say, he's the captain; he gives the orders.

Before long daybreak slowly crept across the mottled skyline followed shortly after by a fiery, red-orange sun that rose almost imperceptibly through the morning haze. It's slanting rays reflected off the dirty, grimy windows of hundreds of buildings as it climbed higher over the city, washing across frosted ships, dock buildings and early morning traffic.

Shanghai slowly came to life. Birds flitted across the docks while seagulls dove near the ships seeking tasty morsels adrift on the surface of the muddy waters. The pungent aroma of burning wood and cooking wafted through the chill morning air.

Sampan traffic picked up along the river. Harry marveled at the ease with which the pilots gracefully sculled the fragile craft along. Most had the traditional eyes carved in the bow of the craft helping the sailor to find his way. A black military police boat chugged along belching black diesel fumes from its stack leaving a foul-smelling trail of smoke behind. The police sat boldly erect, sharply attired in brown uniforms with bold red epaulets, fur caps squared, red star emblazoned on the fronts.

Captain Andress poured a cup of coffee as he joined them. Although jovial, he was short on conversation tending to move about, peering out the windows, first forward, then aft. The river was bustling with activity with ships unloading and loading, two ships were being warped around ready to head out to sea while other ships were readied for their newly vacated berths.

"Are ve ready to sail?" Captain Andress asked.

"Aye, sir," Sigmund replied smartly. "All cargo hatches are secured und der ship ready to sail."

"Good. Ve depart at 0900 hours. Haf all vork details ready by 08:30 hours"

"Aye, aye, Captain," Sigmund replied, grabbing the P.A. mike, curtly announcing the departure time throughout the ship.

"Harry, it's a good ting you caught dose two heathen last night," Captain Andress said, pouring another cup of coffee. "Der captain of der British ship ahead of us reported dey ver docked here a couple of months ago und ver boarded by thieving cuttroats der first night. A crewman vas stabbed. Dey had to leave him behind to recuperate. He just re-joined der ship yesterday. You're qvick action last night probably saved us a lot of grief."

Picking up his coffee cup, the captain moved around the

wheelhouse busying himself with checking dials, the radar, stopping at the chart table to check the current chart in use, and moving on to other minute details that only he could check to his satisfaction. He was humming as he moved about.

The next watch entered the wheelhouse. Harry passed along his .45 to the next helmsman. Sigmund passed along standing orders and then he and Harry stood back waiting for the captain to decide what to do with them.

"Oh," Captain Andress said at seeing the two waiting. "Breakfast is ready. Osa seems particularly cheerful today. Radiant. You are both relieved from duty."

Harry couldn't help but think the last remark was for his benefit. He let it slide as they stepped out into the chill morning air. A light layer of frost had enveloped the ship. Carefully, the two made their way down the ladder from the bridge to the main deck. Stopping at the railing, they looked forward along the dock. Already a gang of rag-tag stevedores was busily engaged in unloading the British ship. Below the dockworkers were already standing by ready to assist in the departure of *Nurad*.

"Look at dat crazy vun down dere pointing up at us," Sigmund called, gesturing toward one of the laborers standing to one side excitedly pointing up at them. "He is pointing right at us. Vat do ve do, trow money or vave at him?"

Harry leaned forward to see who Sigmund was indicating. As he did, he felt a momentary tug at the neck of his jacket. Almost immediately after, he heard the crack of a rifle. Both dropped to the deck instantly crouching behind the railing. Harry looked at Sigmund. "You okay?" he asked. Sigmund nodded yes, but his eyes were as big as saucers as he stared at Harry's collar. Instinctively, Harry grabbed for his neck. No blood. As he ran his fingers around his neck again, his little finger caught in a hole in his jacket collar. Whipping off the jacket, Harry whistled; a hole the size of his little finger was punched neatly through it.

"If you had been standing erect instead of leaning over, you vould haf been shot right trough der neck," Sigmund gulped. He put his finger in the hole. "Right trough der neck!"

"That was close," Harry said with a sigh of relief. "Probably one of the guys from last night still holding a grudge."

"Lucky," Sigmund retorted with a shake of his head.

Harry burst into laughter. "On the other hand, it might be one of my bastard children from my last visit to Shanghai saying 'Hi' to their old man!" His laughter broke the tension and they sat on the deck laughing like a couple of kids.

More crewmembers appeared responding to the shot, wondering why the Second Officer and Harry were sitting on the deck laughing so insanely.

"Vot happened?" Captain Andress called from the bridge. "Is somesing wrong?"

"Everyting is okay," Sigmund answered. "Just a vild shot dat missed Harry. Everyting is okay."

Turning to the crewmembers, Sigmund said, " Please go about your business und prepare for our departure. Ve vill be sailing soon." As he spoke, both he and Harry got to their feet then started walking along the deck.

"You are lucky. If you had been hit und not killed, ve vould haf to leave you behind in a hospital to recover. Ve don't haf der facilities on board to care for any badly vounded person."

Harry nodded. There was no doubt that the bullet had been intended for him. In a hospital, Stan could get at him much as he got to Joe. Martin, he told himself, you're one damned lucky fella.

Osa's eyes sparkled with a new warmth when she saw Harry enter the galley. Quickly she straightened her outfit, smoothed down her apron, even patted several seemingly displaced hairs back in place.

"Good morning, Harry, Sigmund, how are you today?" she asked, but her question and attention was directed more toward Harry. "Did you haf a good vatch last night?"

"Good. No problems," Harry replied nonchalantly, watching as she took it upon herself to personally serve them, noting, too, the extra helping she gave him.

"He is modest," Sigmund said, holding up his plate for a dab more, figuring his plate should be as filled as Harry's. "You should haf seen him in action –"

"I vould like dat —" she interjected, winking at Harry. He felt himself flush.

"He beat off some boarders single-handed last night und den dis morning dey shot at him, right trough der collar!" He shoved a finger through the hole in Harry's collar. "See. Harry is lucky to be alive."

Osa gasped, dropped her serving spoon, and rushed around the counter to examine the bullet hole. "Oh, Harry, you should be more careful. I, uh, ve don't vant anyting to happen to you." She looked at the bullet hole, and then pulled his collar down to examine his neck. "You are okay, yah?"

"Yeah. Okay." He hated anyone fussing over him. "I'm okay, really." He picked up his tray and hurried away toward one of the far tables.

"Jus der same, you be careful," Osa called after him as she returned behind the counter.

"Women," Harry scoffed with a shake of his head as Sigmund joined him. "Fuss, fuss, fuss."

"Yah, but she is concerned about you," Sigmund retorted as he sat down. "I noticed her reaction ven she heard about you. She is concerned. You know vat, Harry? I tink she likes you."

Harry gave him a dour look. Sigmund smiled. They ate in silence. Several times Harry caught Osa looking in his direction out of the corner of his eye. When their eyes met he felt his heart skip a beat.

Returning to the main deck the two found the ship bustling with activity in preparation for departure. Small, ancient tugboats belching puffs of black smoke into the air had already moved into position to warp the huge ship around in the river to head downstream, outbound.

Sigmund took command of the forward deck crew, following the captain's orders to cast off and retrieve their bowline hawsers. At the stern, the process was repeated. A Chinese pilot stood next to Captain Andress on the bridge wing calling out commands to the dockhands and to the crews of the chugging, puffing tugboats.

Slowly *Nurad* was turned about in the river, its whistle blowing huge plumes of white smoke into the chill morning air. The ka-thunk, ka-thunk of the engine turning the huge screws and the noisy screeching of the tugboats all but drowned out verbal commands. Harry could sense *Nurad* beginning to move of its own accord, the powerful screws cutting deeply into the brackish water, churning up an oily brown slick that trailed after them.

The sun climbed ever higher in the sky. Harry could feel its warmth as he stood on deck looking back at Shanghai. He pulled his collar high and jammed his gloveless hands into his jacket pockets. He was startled when he felt an arm slip through his. Turning, he saw it was Osa. He smiled at her. Casually he glanced about to see if anyone was looking at them. They were alone. Osa slid her hand inside his pocket entwining her fingers with his.

"I vill alvays remember Shanghai, und cherish der moments ve spent togedder," she whispered, squeezing his fingers.

Harry squeezed back. "Me too."

Slowly Shanghai fell astern, loosing itself in the twisting curves of the Yangtze River as *Nurad* moved downstream toward a stormy East China Sea.

Chapter 52

ROMANCE HEATS UP

P hysically exhausted from the night's tour of duty and his near encounter with destiny, Harry sought the solitude of his cabin, the comfort of his bunk, and the peace that sleep would bring. Thoughts of Osa brought a smile to his face; one terrific lady.

He slept undisturbed, a child again, rocking in the arms of his mother in the old black walnut rocking chair in their parlor. He always felt secure when she held him in her arms and rocked him to sleep. The gentle rocking motion began to intensify. He looked wonderingly up into his mother's eyes as to why she was rocking him so hard, holding him so tightly that he struggled to breath. Stan was grinning back at him, a vicious grin. His arms tightened around Harry as though he were trying to squeeze the very life out of him. Harry started struggling, twisting, pushing, trying to get away, trying to stop the rocking. He had to escape.

Suddenly, sitting up, perspiration running down his face, gasping, he looked about, now groggily aware of his surroundings, safe in his own bunk. It had been a bad dream. He peered out the porthole. Wind-whipped whitecaps swept across dark greenish seas. Huge swells rolled the ship. Rain lashed across the porthole. Yet, in the distance he could see a faint glimmer of sunlight. They'd be out of the storm soon. But, and he gave a sudden shudder, Stan was still somewhere ahead.

Glancing at his clock he saw it was 15:30 hours. He'd slept the day away. His duty watch having been re-established beginning at 0400 hours the next morning, the rest had been welcome – except for the nightmarish dream. He shook his head to clear the cobwebs, still chilled by the thought of being at the mercy of Stan. Where and when would he strike next?

Dropping lightly to the deck, he stretched, rotated his shoulders and winced at the pain in his right shoulder where the boarder had struck him. He swung his right arm around several times. He'd work it out. Over the next fifteen minutes he moved through a series of exercises, leg stretches, arm rotations, sit-ups, push-ups, and capping off skipping rope in place 400 times, working up a good sweat. "There –" he gasped when he stopped. "Now for a hot shower and shave, then topside to see what's happening."

He reached into the shower and turned on the faucets, adjusting the settings to his satisfaction: hot and steamy. Then, kicking off his shorts, he stepped inside. Jumbled thoughts raced through his mind, that bastard, Stan, was aware of where he was, and most likely that they were headed for Tsingtao.

A grin broke across his face. Last night in Shanghai was indescribable, just the happenstance of bumping into Osa – as though it was meant to be – then being kidnapped, breaking free, dinner and dancing at the hotel, the movies and wine, and ending up in the arms of a definitely wanton blonde.

His body lathered in soap, Harry began singing loudly at the top of his lungs – "Eh, Figaro! Figaro! Figaro!" A draft of cool air swept through the stall, an almost imperceptible draft that Harry failed to notice.

Suddenly, the plastic curtain was yanked back. Harry jerked around, glowering, only to gasp with delight as Osa stepped into the shower wearing only a big grin. Letting loose with a roar of laughter, he pulled her close to him under the steamy spray planting a warm, wet kiss on her soft, yielding lips. Between fervent kisses they explored one another ending with her legs wrapped around his waist as he pummeled her against the shower wall. The stinging spray cleansed them as they continued sharing soft caresses and lingering kisses of the afterglow.

Begrudgingly, Harry finally turned off the faucets. She stood before him beaming, a look of satisfaction on her face. Water traced down her smooth body in twisting rivulets. "Vas dat good?" she asked happily, the eager, apt student.

"Terrific. You get an 'A' for that one," he replied. "Just magnificent! Where did you learn the legs around the waist bit?"

"From der second movie," she replied softly, wearing a devilish grin. "It vas ven der young bride-to-be made love under der vaterfall. Remember?"

Roaring with laughter, Harry threw his arms around his eager lover hugging her tightly, kissing her. "You really got a lot out of that film. You're the greatest. You really are."

Grabbing a couple of towels, they began drying each other off, laughing, kissing, fondling.

"Now if you'll excuse me," he said. "I have to shave to please a certain lady in my life." She stepped aside, taking a moment to wrap the towel around herself. Standing to one side, she watched as he applied lather, and then drew the sharp razor across his face and neck in long upward and downward strokes.

"Feel," he said sliding her fingertips across his smooth-shaven face.

"Ummm, dat is nice," she replied kissing him lightly on his cheek. He grabbed up a bottle of aftershave and splashed it on his face, hairy chest and around his groin. "Now how do I look?" he asked facing her.

"Very handsome," she replied allowing her towel to slide down her body as she moved to him, pressing her nakedness tightly to him, breasts mashed against his hairy chest. Her arms encircled his waist. "Uhmmm, I tink I am ready again," she whispered. "I luf der smell of you, so nice und clean. I vish ve could stay here all night und make luf."

Harry kissed her. "Me, too. But it's getting late. You're due up in the galley soon so we better get dressed. It'd be a little hard to explain your being here like this if they sent a search party looking for you. This time you're uncle would probably have us both thrown overboard." Just the thought of Captain Andress barging in the door sent a chill through him.

"You don't vant me?" she teased, her lower lip jutting out poutingly. "You say go but someting else says different," she said letting her hand encompass his growing erection.

"You know I want you," Harry replied, yet wondering if there was time to enjoy one more moment with her, his thinking dictated more by the growing hardness of his penis under her gentle touch, than any rational thinking. Yet, he knew she was due in the galley and her uncle would be looking to see her there.

"Vell, if you don't vant me, I vill leave!" she said as he pried her fingers away. "Poop on you!" With mock indignation, she wheeled about starting to leave the bathroom. Harry caught her with a sharp whack on her buttocks with his bare hand. "Oh!" she yelped jumping forward.

"Shhh –" he cautioned putting his finger to his lips. "That's for being a smart ass, and be quiet. People do walk by this cabin. We don't want any uninvited guests."

Rubbing her fanny, she snubbed her nose at him and proceeded to dress. Knowing he was watching, she deliberately took her time, stepping into her panties and drawing them sensuously up her slender legs until they encompassed her full, firm buttocks. Then, in the same manner, she donned her brassiere, bent forward and let each tantalizing globe settle into it's respective cup before straightening up, pulling the straps over her shoulders. Lastly, she stepped into a bold yellow jumpsuit and zipped up.

Turning to him with a seductive smile, she asked, "Did you enjoy der show? Vas it as good as der girls on stage last night?"

"Better. You're much better."

"I vish ve could re-live last night," she sighed as she slipped into her shoes. "I vould do tings even better for you. Really! I haf given a lot of tought to it. You vould be surprised." She beamed. "You vill be surprised next time."

"I'm already surprised. That was a unique shower."

She burst into laughter. Inside she felt good; she had pleased him. At the moment her whole being seemed to center around pleasing this man, the man who had forced his will on her, had dominated her, had made her face up to the stark reality of her life, and that love, no, sex. could be enjoyable.

"By the way, how the hell did you get into my cabin?"

"You didn't lock der door."

"Yes I did. I know I did. I'm sure of it."

She let out a girlish giggle, and then extracted a key from her pocket. "I got Peter's key from my uncle's key locker. See." She held it out before him, and then saucily dropped it back in her pocket. "For next time –"

Suddenly she cut loose with a screech. "My hair!" She had caught a glimpse of herself in the wall mirror. "Oh, no," she moaned. "I look awful. I vil haf to dryblow it. It is still vet. I must go now und take care of my hair." She gave him a quick peck on his cheek. "I see you at dinner, yah?"

"Yah." he answered as she let herself out. "Damn!" he grinned happily. "She is really one hell of a woman, one hell of a woman!"

Chapter 53
A NEW PARTNERSHIP

Osa was behind the serving line dishing out food to noisy, hungry crewmembers when Harry entered the galley. Picking up a tray and utensils, he moved through the line. He noticed her lush blonde hair was pulled back and tied with a white bow. Most likely, she didn't have time to fuss with it as she had wanted. Her warm blue eyes were enhanced with a touch of eye shadow, her lips a soft shade of red. An apron hid the freshly pressed outfit she was wearing.

Her eyes took on a special sparkle as she looked up to see Harry before her. She winked as he stopped momentarily before her, dishing up a healthy serving of food. He winked back, and then blew her a kiss. Surprised, flustered, she quickly looked about to see if anyone had noticed, then gave him a dirty look.

Grinning, Harry moved along filling his tray. He selected a table in the far corner of the galley where he could think, not of Osa, but of Tsingtao. The port was only two days away. As he pecked at his food, he strived to recall every minute detail about Tsingtao that he could dredge up from the recesses of his memory. Thirty years was a long time between visits; there were probably a million changes in the old town.

Closing his eyes, he forced himself to recall old familiar ground: the dock area, the old Japanese Compound with it's high wall around it, the rough stone road that went under the railroad bridge then curved around to the right leading into the main part of town. The main drag. Yeah, the Enlisted Men's Club with its famous mural on the back wall, Gizmo's Nightclub on Chu Fu Road, Wang's Cafe and the Tivoli Restaurant, even the old Welcome U.S. Allies Whorehouse. A smile crossed his face. No wonder his battalion had the highest VD rate.

Concentrating harder, he recalled the road past the Corporal's Club, then how it wound on up to the Marine Corps Compound, now the University. With eyes still closed, he retraced the routes several times trying to recall every minute detail, irritated that he couldn't remember everything. There was the park where the Chinese practiced their intriguing Tai Chai routine every day, and there was the YMCA and, beyond it, another road that led up to the compound. Yet, he had forgotten the simple route across town, a route he had traveled every workday for over two years. What was missing?

"Is der food not good tonight?"

"Huh? What?" Harry's eyes blinked open, startled from his deep concentration. Looking up he saw Osa's concerned face. "No. No. I was just thinking about some things I have to tend to. Personal. That's all."

"But you've hardly touched your food," she scolded. "I had prepared it especially for you."

"It's great." He looked at his hardly touched plate and took a big fork full of mashed potatoes, chewing hurriedly under her scrutiny, then wolfed down a second fork full. "Great. It's really great." And a bite of meatloaf disappeared into his mouth. "I'd personally like to thank the cook. Do you think that might be arranged?" He deliberately leered at her.

Osa giggled. Why did she feel so feminine around him, like a silly schoolgirl? She'd never felt this way around Rudy, not in all the years they shared the same bed, not even during their courtship. What was so different about this man? Whatever it was, she knew he was on her mind constantly. Again and again she had recalled the pleasures shared in Shanghai, even this afternoon. It was sinful, such thoughts, but so enjoyable, especially knowing it would happen again.

"Vill you be in your cabin later?" she whispered.

"Yeah. For a couple of hours. I've got some work to do but you'd be a very pleasant interruption."

"Shhh," she hissed, looking about. Satisfied that no one heard them, she added, "After I clean up der kitchen, I vill be down to collect my tip." With that, and a saucy flip of her head, she turned and walked away.

Harry watched after her, at the swing of her hips under the uniform as she moved through the galley. Nice. Now, where was I? he asked himself. Oh yes, Tsingtao.

It was only a short time later that he had his jacket and seabag spread out on Peter's old bunk and was painstakingly examining each item for the umpteenth time to make sure each pocket was sewn properly, each Velcro seal would seal properly to ensure the packets of money stayed tightly inside.

Peter's death had become a blessing in disguise. The entire cabin was now his thanks to Captain Andress, who said he deserved it to himself. There was little chance of interruption at work, or play.

He checked the seabag next, testing the false bottom inner lining of sailcloth he had added. Underneath the flap were several pockets to stash money. Closed, the false bottom kept any money safe from prying eyes.

Satisfied that he was ready, Harry moved to the desk, reached into the top drawer and extracted his small penlight, then three different sized screwdrivers, including a Phillip's head, and a metal pry-bar, all of which the engine room had unknowingly donated. Picking up the jacket, he opened it exposing the armpits which he had fitted with pockets. He slipped the tools into their respective pockets, then stood up and pulled on the jacket. It felt comfortable. Good.

Knowing Joe, Harry figured he'd be true to his word about having his loot in large denomination bills, perhaps hundred or thousand dollar or more. By putting the bills in packets of approximately one inch thick, or slightly thicker, Harry surmised he could easily stash away well over a million dollars in the jacket pockets. If necessary, he could make the packets even two inches thick. The jacket pockets would be filled first, then the seabag. The jacket would take on its former full, bulky look and no one would be the wiser.

Once on the fourth floor of the old barracks building it wouldn't take long to locate the money; just follow Joe's instructions, pull out the packets, and in a matter of minutes he'd be back out on the street headed for the ship heavier, but richer.

He smiled. It all sounded so simple. If it could only come off that simple. But there was Stan. What kind of surprise did he have in mind, Harry wondered. Or, had he already beat him to the cache?

Mentally and physically, Harry knew he was ready. He had been lifting weights with other crewmembers down in the lounge area for the past several weeks. By the time they had reached Shanghai, he had tested himself countless times: hoisting the seabag with about 100 pounds inside, plus carrying another hundred pounds strapped around his waist. He had circled the deck dozens of times at odd hours, undetected, carrying his load the equivalent of five miles. At first he had felt the strain, but after repeated episodes, he found he could carry the extra load with little effort.

Opening the bottom drawer of the desk, he extracted three big stacks of writing paper all cut to the size of standard United States currency, all tied in neat packets about an inch thick. The packets were already dog-eared from the many times he had practiced filling the pockets over the past two weeks. He knew he could accomplish the whole task in a matter of minutes. All he had to do was concentrate, not be distracted by the darkness or the fear of being caught. Concentrate and work methodically, he told himself again and again as he practiced for his big moment.

Now it was practice time again. He shrugged his shoulders. The jacket fit well, loose, comfortable. The tools fit snuggly under the armpits, their presence not detectable to an outside observer. Glancing at his watch, he called out, "Time!" and quickly dropped to his knees, slipped off the jacket and lay it before him. Coolly, efficiently, he extracted the tools pretending to unscrew several screws, all the while holding the penlight in his mouth, the beam trained on his hands and tools. Then he ripped open the jacket pockets. Methodically, he grabbed each packet and firmly stuffed it into a pocket and slapped the Velcro tab shut. "26...27...28..." he silently counted.

The door suddenly opened.

Startled, Harry looked up from his kneeling position, the penlight falling from his gasping mouth. Osa stood in the doorway, a perplexed look on her face.

"Vot are you doing?" she asked looking from him to his jacket, then back.

"Come in and close the door," he snapped. "Quickly!"

She stepped inside, closed the door behind her and leaned back against it. She was stunning in a knee-length blue leather coat.

"Vat is dis?" she questioned.

Harry didn't reply for a moment, instead, continuing to look at the packet of paper still clutched in his hand.

"Harry!"

"Uh, I'm working on a special project," he said trying to be casual, yet cursing himself for not locking the door as he usually did. He hadn't expected her for at least another half hour, time enough to rehearse his routine and put everything away.

"Vat kind of project? It looks like you haf made pockets in your jacket. Vat are you stuffing in dem? money?" She stepped forward taking the packet from him. "It looks like a packet of money but it is just paper. Vhy?"

"That's all it is...just paper."

She shook her head. "I don't understand."

"You will," he replied. Picking up the jacket, he said, "One day these pockets will hold real money, lots of money." As he spoke, he stripped the dog-eared packets from their respective pockets. Whether he had intended to have an accomplice, or not, he suddenly realized he was about to have one.

Since beginning his odyssey, he had wanted to confide in someone. Perhaps Peter, Sigmund, even Captain Andress, but certainly not her. He had wanted someone in a position of power, someone who could ensure his getting ashore in Tsingtao, could help him return, could even help in the event of trouble with the authorities. He recalled the night he almost confided in Peter, but held off, finally deciding it was best to pull off the caper himself. Yet, a back-up person could be a big help. Maybe, just maybe, fate had brought them together; Osa might be the most logical one after all.

"Osa, can you keep a secret?" he asked, now standing erect before her, his eyes sincere, staring directly into hers. "I mean a really big secret, one that might mean the difference between life and death?"

She caught her breath. "I-I don't know. I-I tink so. Yes, for you, I tink so. Vat is vrong?"

"Nothing's wrong. To make a long story short, a friend of mine stashed a lot of money away in a special spot in Tsingtao many years ago. He's been unable to retrieve it himself and, so, he asked me to get if for him. I said I would, and here I am. It's that simple."

"Vat is so dangerous about dat?" she asked, puzzled. "It sounds simple, as you said." She watched him extract the last packet of paper from the jacket.

"The whole thing sounds simple on the surface, except the guy who asked me to get the money was murdered."

A momentary gasp escaped her lips.

"The murderer is still at large and he knows I'm headed for Tsingtao to get the money." As he spoke, Harry folded the jacket, grabbed up the seabag, and placed them both back in the locker.

He sat down at the desk, reached out and picked up the several packets of fake money and dropped them back into the bottom drawer. "I know who the murderer is, but I don't know where he is. I do know he will kill for the money."

Osa stood silently as the impact of what he was saying sunk in. Her eyes never wavered as she watched Harry's every move, hung on his every word as he continued speaking.

"The two guys who kidnapped us in Shanghai, even the guy who shot at me, are probably members of the gang this guy commands," he said, with one more check to make sure everything was safely stored away. "If so, it might be more difficult to get the money. The advantage I have is that I know exactly where the money is. Hopefully, he doesn't know."

"Oh, Harry," Osa wailed, suddenly rushing into his arms. "I don't vant anyting to happen to you!" She buried her head against his chest clutching tightly to him.

"Hey, hey, nothing's going to happen to me." He wrapped his arms around her, tilted her head back and tenderly kissed her.

"Nothing's going to happen to old Harry Martin if he has anything to say about it." Grabbing a tissue from a box on his desk, he dabbed at a tear starting to trickle down her cheek.

"I vant to help you," she sniffled, looking straight into his eyes. "Please tell me vat I can do to help. I even go vis you into Tsingtao. Anyting, please –"

"Just knowing you know and care is all the help I need," he replied softly, assuringly.

"No. I am serious. I vill go into Tsingtao vis you. I can be of great help –"

"No! Out of the question." He held her face in his hands. "It might be dangerous." His lips brushed softly against hers. "All I ask is that if I don't come back, you'll contact my kids and tell them I was killed in an accident at sea."

"No. Dat is ridiculous. I don't do dat for you!" She pushed herself away, standing, glaring at him. "I vill go vis you und make sure you don't get killed." Her jawline was firmly set, eyes defiant. "I vill help you!"

"I won't let you. I mean it," he snapped rising, advancing toward her. "Harry!" she exclaimed starting to back away, coming to an abrupt halt when she bumped against his bunk.

"I mean it, Osa. You're not going!"

A curious look came over her face at that moment. She sniffed, then sniffed again, deeply this time. "Vat do I smell?" she asked. She sniffed again. "It smells like perfume." She moved closer to the head of his bunk. "It comes from dere," she said, pointing toward his pillow. Reaching up, she slipped her hand under his pillow.

"Vat is dis?" she demanded pulling the thin, pink satin bikini panties out and holding them before him. "You haf anudder voman?"

"Gimmee those," Harry said, flushed at what she had found, grabbing for the panties. Osa deftly jerked them away from his grasping hand. "So, Harry has anudder voman, huh," she teased, flaunting the panties before him. "Und she has expensive taste in perfume, too," she added sniffing as she passed the wispy garment under her nose. "My, my." She enjoyed seeing him squirm, beet red now, trying to grab the panties away. "Und who do dese panties belong to?"

With a sigh of exasperation, he backed away, surrendering the panties to her clutch. "Uh...well...they belong to a girl back in Saginaw. Somehow they got mixed in with my laundry, honest...."

"Oh?" Her eyebrows shot up and she gave him an impish grin. "You do your laundry togedder?"

"No, not really, well on occasion, it depended –" Geez, no matter what he said it sounded stupid. They had met at the laundromat by accident that one day, only a day or so before Joe Gionetti's call. They had laughed about their chance meeting, did their laundry together, threw it all in one large dryer, separated their clothing, or at least he thought they had, and then gone out for dinner. So, he ended up with her panties.

"So you brought her panties along to remind you of her?"

"No. Not exactly –"

"Most men prefer a picture of der voman to look at," she added with a slight touch of sarcasm, "not her undervare."

"Well...uh...I didn't do it deliberately, and I didn't know where to put them, so I just shoved them under my pillow for the time being –"

"Hah!"

He felt suddenly very uncomfortable at having to explain himself while she stood there with that supercilious grin, holding the wispy garment before him. "Besides, she never gave me a picture of herself...one that was halfway decent."

"Vell, I don't like it, not at all."

Osa moved past him to the desk where she dropped the panties in the wastebasket. Returning to the side of the bunk, she repeated her statement, "Not at all," as she started untying the belt to her leather coat.

"Harry," she said softly, facing him squarely, setting her legs slightly apart. With a devilish smile, she whipped the coat open, threw it back, and then let it slide down her arms to the deck.

Harry's eyes flew wide. If ever a man's fantasy of having a centerfold appear before him could come true, it had just happened.

There she stood all curvy, saucy, delectable, wearing the new silk nightie she had bought in Shanghai. It was a soft white and so shear it was almost transparent. Wispy little French-cut panties did little more than cover the darkness of her pubic mound, although it was quite visible to the eye of the beholder, who let out a long, low whistle. Her deeply tanned body contrasted sharply against the milky whiteness of her full breasts and white band around her hips.

"I give you someting better to keep," she said reaching under the hem of her nightie. Her thumbs caught inside the elastic band of her panties and she whisked them down over her hips, down her long slim legs and deftly stepped out of them. Raising them to her face, she pressed her lips tightly against the material leaving a full, red lip print on the material. She held them up before him. "Dere! Now you vill sleep better knowing I am close at hand." With that, she thrust the panties under his pillow. Turning back to him, she gave him a seductive smile, pursed her lips and blew him a kiss.

His gaze swept her full, lush body, breasts straining against the thin, diaphanous material, nipples taut. The slight ruffle of the hem of her nightie barely covered her hips, just enough to entice.

"C'mere," he commanded and she came to him, melting in his powerful arms.

"Take me, Harry," she whispered.

He locked the door and carried her to the bunk.

Chapter 54
TRUE CONFESSIONS

"What's the matter? Cat got your tongue?" Harry called out from where he was standing in front of the bathroom mirror. For some odd reason, she had become somewhat uncommunicative after they made love, had stayed back on Peter's old bunk avoiding any eye contact with him, or talking. It was obvious that something was bothering her, but what? "Hey! I'm talking at you!"

She averted her eyes, seemingly more intent on picking a piece of lint off the hem of her nightie. With a shrug, she leaned back against a pillow, crossed her legs and looked up at him.

"C'mon. Something's bothering you. Did I say something wrong...do something wrong?" He looked at her, his comb poised to run through his hair. "What is it?"

It was unusual for her to lay there so long in the near buff, the nightie hardly hiding her womanly charms. Whatever it was, he knew she'd let him know soon. One thing he had learned about Osa; she spoke her mind, at times being brutally frank.

With a listless sigh, she eased to the edge of the bunk, leaned forward and stood up. There was a forlorn look on her face. Another long sigh followed. "Harry, I am vorried, really vorried."

"About what?

"Vell, I haf dis vunderful feeling ven I am vis you...can't seem to keep my hands off you. I vant you all der time. I –" She hesitated groping for the right words to say, the right phrase. "I –"

"C'mon. What is it?" he demanded. "You can speak frankly to me. I feel we know each other well enough now that we can speak openly, even about sex."

"Vell, ven I vas married, I never tought of sex, Rudy und I had dis understanding, sex vas not dat important, at least dat's vat I tought. But since Shanghai, you and I, all I do is tink about sex und vays to enjoy it. I vant to be vis you all der time, to possess you, to have you possess me, all kinds of crazy tings, like in der movies ve saw –" Then, in an almost inaudible whisper, she added, "I tink I am turning into a, how do you say it? A nim-pho – nim-pho-may-nee-ack?"

Harry almost burst out laughing, but the serious look on her face stopped him. It was obvious that she was concerned. "The term is nymphomaniac, honey," he said spelling it out. "But I don't think you're one."

"I'm serious," she said, the forlorn look still haunting her beautiful face. "I tink I am vun of dose vomen. Ever since Shanghai, I tink I am over-sexed –"

"Aw, honey." He moved quickly to her side taking her gently into his arms. "You're not a nymphomaniac. You're a beautiful woman who has come alive. You've found out there's really more to life...how good sex can be when shared by two people who really care for each other." He kissed her lightly on her forehead, each cheek, then her soft lips. "And I'm the lucky guy," he whispered. "If you really want to know the truth of the matter, I'm always thinking of you, too. You're on my mind more than I care to admit. I don't think I've ever met anyone quite like you. You're really special to me –"

"Oh, Harry!" she squealed, hugging him tightly to her. "Do you really like me dat much? I-I tink, maybe you don't like me anymore because I am so forvard, like a –" Her eyes averted his, her voice a husky whisper. " – like a whore."

Harry squeezed her to his chest. His hands roamed up and down the smoothness of her back coming to rest on her resilient buttocks. "Every beautiful woman should have just a touch of whore in her," he whispered. "It's what makes a guy keep coming back."

"You don't tink I am a bad voman?"

"Hell no. I think you're a very nice girl, my girl," he whispered, continuing to massage her backside. "Sometimes I feel like a schoolboy chasing after his first girl. I want you to be my girl. I want to be with you, to do things for you, to do things with you, to share with you. I enjoy being with you."

Eyes brimming with tears, Osa pulled Harry's head close, kissing him longingly, deeply. "You make me happy," she sighed. "I never tought I could be so happy like I am now. I feel loved, fulfilled. Sometimes ven I tink of vat I haf done, vat ve haf done, I say to myself dat I should be ashamed, and yet, I don't. It is hard to explain. I really enjoy it, making love vis you –"

"Don't try to explain it. I know what you mean." He kissed her mashing her lips with his, exploring her mouth with his scalding tongue, feeling her eager response. Never had he thought he could feel this way about a woman again, not after Sandy. Yet, just holding Osa in his arms, knowing deep inside what he had just told her about wanting to be with her, to share with her, was from his heart.

"Harry," she whispered breaking free of his kiss, "I been tinking of us –"

"Uh huh –"

"I tink I vill go vis you into Tsingtao."

There! Dammit! She had done it to him again: another 180 from nymphomaniac to going ashore in Tsingtao. "No," he replied sternly. "Absolutely out of the question. I told you it might be dangerous. I don't want anything to happen to you."

"Hah!" She pushed free of him. "Ve vill see about dat!" She picked up her coat from where it lay piled on the floor, slipped it on, then stepped into her shoes, all the while ignoring his stern tirade as to why she should not go into town. With flashing hands, she tied the knot about her coat, then raised her right hand before him, stopping him in mid-sentence, her eyes glowing with deadly determination. "I haf made up my mind. I vill go vis you. I can help!"

Harry threw up his hands in total despair. "My god, woman, I appreciate your interest, but it's dangerous. Listen to me: DANGEROUS! I happen to care too much about you to put your life in danger."

"You really care dat much?" she squealed, delighted at his remark.

"You nut. You know I do!" He grabbed her, pulling her off

balance into his arms, smothering her with kisses. "Now get out of here before someone comes in and puts two and two together, like your uncle!" He whirled her around heading her for the door, giving her a healthy whack across her backside.

Osa jumped, turning, rubbing her rump, giving him a dirty look. "I get even vis you. You vill see." She stopped at the door and gave a coy look over her shoulder. "I love you. I am going vis you!" With that, she flitted out the door.

"Damned female!" Harry called aloud, grinning. "Nymphomaniac!" He broke into uproarious laughter, doubling over, tears streaming from his eyes. Nymphomaniac. She had been so serious, so damned serious. At least now, he thought, she does enjoy sex, and that's a healthy sign.

He crawled into his bunk for a catnap before duty called. Closing his eyes, he rolled onto his side sliding his hand under his pillow. At contact with the silkiness of her panties, he drew them out, then grinned at seeing the bold red lip imprint. He inhaled the heady fragrance of her perfume then switched off the light. Damn but the thought of her made him tingle.

Chapter 55
TSINGTAO; END OF THE LINE

"I just received vord from der harbormaster of Tsingtao," Captain Andress was saying to Sigmund when Harry stepped into the wheelhouse for the second watch. "A pilot boat vill meet us outside der harbor to put vun of dere pilots on board. He vill bring us into port. Ve vill be met by der harbormaster, a Mr. Ma, und der military commander, Colonel Pui. Dey vill be our official greeters so ve must be on our best behavior. I vant to make a good impression on dem for ve vill be coming back on future trips."

"Aye, sir," Sigmund replied. "I vill inform you der moment ve make contact vis der pilot boat. Der crew vill be alerted to be clean-shaven, clean clothes und most courteous at all times."

"Good. Dat is der ticket."

Harry caught bits of the conversation and already his mind was mulling over the name, Mr. Ma. The name triggered a thought from his past. Mr. Ma. He wracked his brain trying to recall the name and the face and locale that went with it. Yeah! There had been a Mr. Ma who worked with his battalion back in 1947 at the Old Japanese Compound. Could it be the same Mr. Ma?

He could picture the man. Stocky build, short, thick black hair, slightly balding in the back, ramrod straight, a former soldier who had fought the Japanese. Always wore black. Harry recalled that Mr. Ma had been a responsible person to work with, courteous but disciplined. There was no shirking by the coolies when he was around. He had said one day that "ma" had meant horse in Chinese, that he worked like a horse. They had laughed at his comment but he was a hard worker.

The bothersome thing he recalled about Mr. Ma was his quiet

reserve, a subtle arrogance. Harry had a feeling Mr. Ma felt he was superior to the Americans. In whatever they did, he seemed always to be challenging them, playing mental games, always trying to get the upper hand. Another bothersome thing was a chance comment made by one of the coolies to the "batu," who passed it along to him. They disliked the man saying he walked with the gait of a Japanese soldier. Harry had caught the inference; Mr. Ma was a survivor.

And what has happened to all the many fine Chinese people he had worked with, he wondered, recalling the office girl, Margaret, the Batu, the red-headed coolie he had befriended, the two orphan waifs the one battalion had "adopted" as mascots, even making them small Marine Corps uniforms. Had any survived the great Communist purge when the Reds overran China?

"Ve are getting close to your old home, Harry," Captain Andress said stepping behind him. "Are you getting excited?"

"What? Oh, yessir," Harry replied snapping out of his daydreaming. "Yes. I look forward to seeing the old place again."

Captain Andress slapped him lightly on his shoulder. "Later today, yah..." He turned to Mr. Helmstrund. "Vell, carry on. I vill be in my cabin. Call me as soon as ve make contact vis der pilot boat."

The night droned on. Sigmund came by to check the dials several times, halting as if he wanted to talk, then moved on to the front of the wheelhouse. Harry glanced at the radar; it was working fine. No more problems. He doubted they'd have any more trouble with it since the Captain chewed out the engineer.

While he mechanically fulfilled the duties of helmsman, Harry's thoughts strayed to Tsingtao. He could feel the excitement rising within himself: the journey's end. He had to control his feelings. Yet, the thought of being in Tsingtao yet today filled him with an exhilarating feeling. Mentally, he reviewed the old barracks building, the front entrance, the two end doors, and the steps leading to the fourth floor. Was the storeroom still intact after thirty years? Had the building been remodeled, the rooms remodeled? Was all this effort a wild goose chase? And what surprise had Stan prepared for him?

He shook his head. Think pleasant thoughts. He smiled as his mind switched to the incident of the panties, trying to catch a few winks but too excited to sleep, tossing and turning, wadding his pillow about, feeling the silkiness of Osa's panties. He almost laughed aloud as he recalled the way she whipped them off, planted the red lip print on them and stuffed them under his pillow. There was definitely a jealous streak in the woman. Dammit, there he was thinking of her, wanting her. No. He had to think of Tsingtao. Concentrate, he told himself. You've got a job to do that demands every damned minute of your time!

"Are you seeing Osa?"

"Huh?" The question startled Harry. He looked to his right to find Sigmund had moved in close to him, a serious look on his face. The question was curt, demanding an answer.

"Why?" Harry responded feeling his hackles rise.

"I saw her come from your cabin last night. You know she shouldn't be dere. Dat is off limits to her, you know."

"Oh, yeah, last night." He was suddenly more irritated with himself than at Sigmund. What he had feared most was that someone would see her leave his cabin. Damn!

"Vell?"

"She stopped by for a moment, dropped off my banjo albums. She had accidentally broken my Flint Banjo Club album. I guess I got a little nasty with her and —"

"Yes. And vat?"

"Well," Harry whispered, crooked his finger, drawing Sigmund closer, and continued, "keep this between you and me, okay?"

"Vat?" Sigmund asked with a questioning look.

Harry forced himself to keep a straight face as he started fabricating a fantastic cock and bull story for Sigmund's benefit. With a tone of intimacy in his voice, he continued, "She asked me if she could pay for the album but I told her no, that I'd take it out in trade."

Sigmund's eyebrows shot up. "You didn't!" he gasped. He slapped his hands together in shock. "Harry. You shouldn't haf said dat. She is a lady. Dat vas not a nice ting to say to her, to even suggest —"

"Yeah. You're right about that," Harry replied. "I got the distinct impression she didn't care for my suggestion. I thought she was going to slap me but you know what, she kept her cool. Instead, ya know what she says?"

"No. Not after a callous remark like dat. She should haf slapped you." He was all ears waiting for Harry's next comment.

"She asks me if I'm going ashore in Tsingtao? I says maybe, why? You know what she says then?" He watched the look on Sigmund's face, his eyes never wavering, attention riveted on Harry. "She says she wants to go into Tsingtao with me, says she'll buy me a drink to pay for the album. Now ain't that gutsy?"

"No. I tink dat is nice. It is fair of her to offer to pay for der album, even to buy you a drink. I haf heard from Captain Andress dat she said you showed her a nice time in Shanghai. You should be honored dat she vould vant to go ashore vis you in Tsingtao."

So she told her uncle she had a good time, Harry mused. Just how much did she tell him? And now Sigmund is drawing conclusions about the two of them. Better to shatter any such thoughts right now.

"Wait a minute," he snapped back at Sigmund. "Sure I enjoyed her company, but I had to work hard to ditch her for an hour so I could get a little action, if you know what I mean. After all, a guy's got to get rid of his sex drive somewhere!"

"Dammit, Harry! You haf a vun-track mind: sex, sex, sex! You should not tink of dose tings ven you are out vis Osa. She is a lady. Treat her vis respect. You are older now. Slow down. Dere are odder tings beyond sex. Try to raise your morals and toughts to a higher level."

Harry backed off seeing that Sigmund was really getting hot under the collar. "Yeah, well," he said, "maybe your right." He was getting the distinct idea they were all carrying Osa around on a silver platter, all protecting her because of the rotten incident involving her husband with the young hooker. Yet, he had to add one more touch of agitation. "I, uh, I gotta tell you this, then, but don't get upset. It just happened! Honest! When she says she wants to go ashore with me, I, uh, I asked her what was in it for me besides a drink."

"You didn't!" exclaimed Sigmund with a horrified look on his face, a look that quickly changed to anger, redness creeping up from his collar to his hairline.

"Afraid I did," Harry nodded glancing away momentarily, pretending to check several dials, but more-so to keep a straight face knowing Sigmund was seething inside.

"And?" came his voice through gritted teeth.

"She got the message. She hauled off and really slapped my face screaming that she wasn't that kind of woman. Boy was she pissed off. She stormed out of my cabin. That's probably when you saw her, and, well, anyways, that's what happened. I'm sorry." He wore the most sorrowful hound dog look he could muster for Sigmund's benefit. "Please don't breathe a word about what I told you. I realize I made a mistake so I'll square it away with the lady."

There, Harry thought, now you can chew on that line of bullshit, my friend. At least, hopefully, it got Osa off the hook for being in his cabin.

Sigmund loosed an exasperated sigh and walked to the front of the wheelhouse. Harry could sense the agitation Sigmund was feeling by the way he rubbed his hands together, then tightened them into fists. Finally, having calmed down considerably, he again approached Harry.

"If you don't mind my saying so, Harry," he said crisply. "I tink she vas right in slapping you. From vat you haf told me about your past sexual conquests, I tink you haf found out you finally came up against der vrong voman dis time. Osa is a fine voman, a high moraled voman. You deserved to be slapped. Dat vas terrible vat you suggested. I tell you for der last time, you vill treat her like a lady!"

Harry nodded, keeping his eyes forward, hoping his face wouldn't crack into a grin. He stared into the darkness of night feeling the contempt the Second Officer held for him at that moment, not believing this man could so demean such a fine woman.

"Osa is like a delicate piece of porcelain, very fragile," Sigmund continued. "She must be handled gently."

The thought of Osa in his shower stall with her legs wrapped tightly around him, thrusting madly against his manhood, came to Harry: delicate, yes, indeed.

"Dat is der only vay you vill ever become her friend." Sigmund said, pausing as a new train of thought came to him. "You know, Harry, I do tink she likes you. She speaks very highly of you. You must make it a point to be nicer to her." An idea suddenly struck him, his face lighting up into a smile. "Ahh, I haf it. Ven you get off vatch you must go immediately to her und apologize. Dat vill let her know you are a gentleman. Yah. You vill apologize."

Harry gulped to control a grin. "Yeah. You're right, Sigmund. That's exactly what I'll do. First thing when I get off watch!"

"Of course. I know I am right. You vill apologize und den you vill ask her to go ashore this evening, der autorities villing, und take her to dinner somevhere, show her a good time. Lofty toughts. No mention of sex. Let her know you are a vell-intentioned person, not a sex maniac."

"Well, I don't know about taking her ashore," Harry replied with a grimace. "I've got other plans for any possible shore leave —"

"No!" Sigmund bristled. "You must not try to chase down every whore in town to satisfy your lusting! I tell you dis, take Osa ashore instead. Show her a good time. It is to your advantage." He cleared his throat taking on a deeper tone of authority. "I don't vant to pressure you, but I am der deck officer who happens to give out der passes for shore leave. I could, shall ve say, run out of passes ven you ask for vun. Do you understand?"

Harry's jawline tightened. The bastard. He could do it, too. No shore leave; no money. Taking Osa ashore was the last thing on his mind. Getting ashore and getting the money would consume every moment of his time. Having her tag along would only slow him down. Then, too, there was the danger of the unknown — Stan Drezewski. There was no doubt in his mind that Stan would play his hand in Tsingtao. He had to be on guard every moment ashore and having Osa tag along would only complicate matters.

"Vell?"

"You made your point loud and clear."

"Good."

371

"So, I'll apologize and ask Osa to go ashore with me. It'll be my pleasure," he lied.

"Dat is der ticket, Harry. You vill feel better about it. Show her a good time like in Shanghai. She vill appreciate it. You vill see. I am right, and no mention of sex! Understood?"

"Understood," Harry retorted with a condescending nod of his head. Shanghai. He almost broke into a grin. What he doesn't know won't hurt him. At least she'd be happy he rationalized after a moment. Sigmund would be happy, the captain would be happy, and good old Harry, if he could ditch her for an hour and recover the loot, would be happy, and richer, he hoped.

And so the night continued: Harry staring into the darkness, brooding, trying to figure out another way to ditch Osa; Sigmund feeling better that he now knew the full story about her momentary visit to Harry's cabin. Osa was a nice lady. It's just too bad that Harry couldn't be as high-moraled; they would make a nice couple.

Chapter 56

A TASTE OF LOCAL HOSPITALITY

A myriad of long, thin, finger-like streaks of pink and purple began breaking across the horizon, stealing through the darkness. The distant clouds slowly turned a fiery red as the sun peeked over the horizon and day broke quietly astern of *Nurad* in the East China Sea. In the distance the rugged coastline of the Shantung peninsula could faintly be discerned.

Harry felt a tightness in his stomach. Tsingtao lay dead ahead. He was anxious to get into town, get the money and get out. Everything was ready for his mission ashore. Once back aboard ship it would be clear sailing back to Saginaw.

"Bring her two points to port," Sigmund called from the chart table. "Ve should be entering der harbor at about seven hundred hours. Der pilot boat vill meet us just outside der harbor entrance."

"Two points to port," Harry repeated. He wondered if he would be able to recognize the harbor, remembering how his ship, *General J.C. Breckenridge,* had moved slowly into port that rainy morning so long ago, how it had moved past the ornate pavilion at the end of the long pier, then circled around to the dock area adjacent to the Old Japanese Compound. Would the sounds and smells be the same? He smiled. Did they still use the old wooden "honey" carts? He'd never forget the time one of their military trucks hit a cart. Liquid shit flew in all directions drenching the dozen or so Marines standing in the bed of the truck with a smelly, clinging coat of brown. It had taken several washings to get the stench out of their clothing.

And fish! The way the Orientals carried them tied to the back of their bicycles through the dirty, dusty streets drawing flies, hundreds and hundreds of dirty black flies. How could they eat the damnable fish after it had been wheeled through the streets exposed to flies, dirt, dust and the hot beating sun?

"Don't forget, Harry," Sigmund cautioned. "You vill see Osa und seek her forgiveness, und ask her to go ashore tonight."

"Right. I haven't forgotten. Right after I get off duty."

"Good."

"I heard you mention a Mr. Ma when you were talking to the captain last night," Harry said, changing the subject. "Will he be the one bringing us into port?"

"I don't know. Vy do you ask?"

"Curious. I used to know a Mr. Ma many years ago when I was stationed in Tsingtao, back in 1947 through 1949, just before we pulled out of China. He was a likeable guy. We always got along well together. I thought it might be him meeting us on the pilot boat."

"Vell, it could be him. Stranger tings haf happened. Dis Mr. Ma might even be a relative of der man you know, perhaps a son, children do grow up in tirty years, you know." There was a wry smile on his face. "Some of us even get a little older, yah?"

Harry caught the inference. Thirty years. He was older; he'd gone through several career changes in the past thirty years; most likely this Mr. Ma was an entirely different person than the one he recalled.

A high-pitched whining sound that turned into a screaming, shattering roar suddenly enveloped them, a sound that jarred their minds, hands quickly slamming to cover their ears. Three Chinese MIG jet fighter planes flashed past the port side of the ship barely above the waves, red stars emblazoned on their fuselages. The planes roared skyward, did a barrel roll, and then headed inland toward the craggy hills of the Shantung peninsula. Probably headed for the old MAG airfield where the First Marine Air Wing was located, Harry thought as the MIG's disappeared from view.

"Vot der hell vas dat!" exclaimed Captain Andress bounding into the wheelhouse, pulling up his suspenders, gasping for breath.

"Tree Chinese jet planes, sir," Sigmund replied.

"I tought ve ver being attacked!"

"MIG fighters," Harry said. "A good morning wake up call."

"Vell dey succeeded," he fumed. "Every person on board must be up. Scared der shit out of me." And then he laughed. "Reminds me of ven ve pulled out of Shanghai back ven der Japs ver taking der city. Der damned Jap Zeroes vould zoom down shooting at us mit dose damned machine guns. Time and again. Killed a lot of people –" He stopped, the thoughts of that long ago time momentarily flitting through his mind.

"Lucky the Japs didn't have twenty-millimeter cannons and missiles like the modern jets carry," Harry said.

"Damned Japs," Captain Andress cursed.

A trail of smoke off the port bow caught Harry's eye. He squinted. Was it the pilot boat? "Boat off the port beam!" he called out. "Heading our way."

Both Captain Andress and Sigmund grabbed up binoculars and focused in the direction of the smoke. "It is der pilot boat," Captain Andress said. "Back off der telegraph to slow ahead."

Harry grabbed the handles and racked them around to slow ahead.

"You two stay on duty until ve reach port," Captain Andress said. "Harry, you know der port. Keep us informed."

Harry gave a wondering glance at the captain. Hell, he hadn't been in the port in thirty years. What the hell did he know about the damned entrance? He'd only sailed in that one day on the troopship *Breckenridge*, and besides, it was raining and he was just one of many Marines forlornly standing on deck in the rain looking at the dismal gray town and blurred hills.

Within minutes, Harry could feel a change in the operation of the ship. It was slowing perceptibly. The pilot boat was closing rapidly, black smoke belching out of it's stack, trailing far behind it. It was a squatty craft, similar in style to those he had seen in the Caribbean and other world ports. The boat came in at an angle and swung about easing up almost touching *Nurad*. A ladder had been dropped over the side of the ship. Riding close to the hull, the small craft seemed to ride the crest of the bow wake steering as close as possible without touching. Two Orientals, one in a tan army uniform;

the other in a black uniform, stood on the deck of the boat waiting to jump to the ladder. First one, then the other, successfully made the leap and clambered up the ladder to the deck of *Nurad*. They were greeted by Captain Andress, resplendent in his tailored uniform. There were cursory handshakes and then the Captain was ushering them toward the bridge. The small pilot boat, under a full head of power, headed back toward homeport.

"Dis is Mr. Lee Fong, our pilot, who is vis der harbormaster's office; and dis is Major Wan Sang, our military escort for Tsingtao," Captain Andress said introducing them to Sigmund and Harry. Again, there were handshakes all around. Mr. Fong spoke nearly flawless English. He quickly established that he was the pilot and in command of the ship as he gave Harry instructions for the course to steer into the harbor. Major Sang was more low key, moving to the back of the wheelhouse out of the way, content to observe the operation, quick, however, with a big toothy grin.

In about thirty minutes Harry could see the harbor entrance. Goosebumps swept over his body as he saw the temple at the end of the Tsingtao pier. Soon, he told himself, soon.

Major Sang said something to Mr. Fong, who turned to Captain Andress asking to see the ship's manifest. The three moved to the chart table where Captain Andress opened the document for their perusal. Major Sang reviewed the document, the smile on his face all the time.

Seemingly satisfied, Major Sang had another sing-song exchange with Mr. Fong, who next asked to see the ship's crew listing. Captain Andress seemed somewhat surprised at the request, but, in the spirit of cooperation, he pulled the listing off the shelf and brought it back to the chart table for them to look at. He commented briefly about his crewmembers, and the loss of one officer and one oiler, as they leafed through the document.

"Ah yah," Major Sang uttered, the smile widening.

"Somesing der matter?" asked Captain Andress.

Harry recalled the Chinese were always saying "Ah yah." Sometimes it meant nothing, or it could mean everything, depending on the inflection given.

"No," Mr. Fong replied. "We wanted to get a count of the number of crew members you have on board."

"Oh."

Interesting, Harry thought. Funny they didn't ask for that kind of information when they docked in Shanghai.

Mr. Fong stepped in closer to Harry standing just behind him. "You are an American?"

"Yeah. Why?"

"Nothing. It seems unusual to have an American on board an all-Swedish manned vessel." He raised his glasses and scanned the harbor entrance.

Harry shrugged. Big deal. He glanced over in Major Sang's direction. The man was looking at him, his eyes squinting, the big smile still present. Interesting, Harry thought, interesting.

The long pier and pavilion passed by as they moved into the port of Tsingtao. The city lay sprawled before them much as it had thirty years before. It was nestled along the waterfront and sprawled back inland around and through many hills. Still standing starkly above the town, high astride one of the hills, was the Mayor's house looking almost the same as it did so many years before. It held a commanding view of the harbor. Beyond it, on the next hill, Harry could faintly discern the buildings that once comprised the old United States Marines Compound. What was it now? Oh, yes, the Shantung University.

Nurad moved slowly around the harbor joined by two ancient, black smoke belching tugboats. Then Harry saw the dock area. A lump formed in his throat as he saw the dirty red brick fence around the old Japanese Compound, the tiled roofs of the many godown storage buildings clustered within. Many of the old landmarks were still evident including the dirty, grimy railroad bridge where the dead coolie had lain for two weeks that winter of 1947 because no one would claim the body and be responsible for the burial of the remains.

To the right a new building had been constructed on the site of the old Nationalist Army supply depot that had exploded into smithereens one sunny summer morning killing at least 500

Nationalist soldiers and civilians. The Marine brass had warned the Nationalist command countless times about the potential danger of storing gasoline and ammunition adjacent to each other. A spark was all it took to kick off the holocaust. And, apparently, that was what happened. The sight of the dead, of headless corpses, legs, arms, and live, unexploded shells laying about the ground still haunted him.

"Come to full stop," Mr. Fong ordered, to which Harry quickly responded almost automatically. Shortly, the tugboats had warped the huge ship in closer to the dock where anxious docking crews stood waiting. Reminiscent of Shanghai, a long queue of large Russian built trucks lined up along the length of the dock ready to receive the golden grain from America. Harry felt a gentle bump as the ship nestled to the dock. The *Nurad* had arrived; the telegraph was secured.

The dock crews and deck crews labored feverishly in the cool morning air to tie off the ship as huge hawsers were lowered, then winched tight against the large steel bollards. It was 0800 hours when *Nurad* was officially secured and ready to discharge it's cargo.

Relieved by the next watch, Harry stepped out onto the starboard bridgewing. It was cold, much like the morning he'd first stepped ashore in Tsingtao so long ago. At least it wasn't raining. Not surprisingly, the same feeling of excitement he had felt then as a young Marine Private still tugged within his chest.

As several trucks had deposited them in front of the 12th Service Battalion that rainy morning a Captain had met them. Tall, ramrod straight, his chest bedecked with medals, he bluntly warned them they were guests in this country and they would be held personally responsible for any unsavory action. He also warned that they would be held responsible for the reduction of venereal disease in the battalion which, Harry soon found out, had the highest incidence of infection on the whole compound.

The second piece of "good news" came from their Master Sergeant. All Marines had to serve a minimum of two years before being eligible for rotation back to the states, unless in the case of an emergency. Harry recalled glancing around at the bleakness of the compound and shaking his head; two damned years in this god-forsaken place. It had been a depressing thought.

A smile broke across his face, at least this time he'd be out of the place in twenty-four hours, time enough to unload the grain, time enough to get his loot and git!

His thoughts were interrupted by the arrival of a large, old black 1949 Buick limousine. He watched as it moved slowly down the dock past the long line of empty trucks, watched as the dock personnel fell back clearing a path for it, watched as it came to a halt in the shadow of the ship close by the gangway. The driver hopped out and dashed around to open the door on the far side for his passengers. Two Chinese officials stepped out. Each was resplendent in crisply tailored uniforms, one military brown, the other in black. The latter wore a captain's cap replete with scrambled eggs.

They stood momentarily looking up at the ship. Mr. Fong stepped up beside Harry, looking far over the railing, waving and shouting to get their attention. The two officers nodded, and then proceeded up the gangway.

Unable to find Captain Andress, who had disappeared moments before the car arrived, Sigmund scurried down the ladder to the main deck racing to greet the two officials, arriving just as the two stepped on board. He snapped off a smart salute, which was promptly returned. There were brief exchanges of pleasantries and handshakes, and then Sigmund was escorting them to the bridge.

Harry noted all the activity along the dock had ceased. Apparently any action was dependent on the approval or disapproval of these two men. He was about to leave the bridgewing for the galley and a welcome breakfast when Sigmund entered the wheelhouse with the two officials.

Almost immediately, Harry recognized one of the men, the man in black: it was Mr. Ma. There was no doubt in his mind. This was the same Mr. Ma he had known so long ago. Time had been kind to him. His hair was silver-gray at the temples. Yet, under the brim of his cap could be discerned the countless wrinkles of aging etched across his forehead and in the fine lines of his face. He still stood erect with a military bearing which Harry recalled so vividly. Black piercing eyes took in the wheelhouse in a glance. His eyes stopped momentarily as they came across Harry, then moved on, with no sign of recognition on his part.

The other officer, too, took in the wheelhouse in a continuing gaze not uttering a word, just looking.

At that moment, Captain Andress arrived, slightly out of breath, buttoning his coat, a wide grin on his face, and apologizing for his tardiness in greeting the two Chinese officials.

Harry smiled. What a hell of a time for the call of nature. He hoped it wasn't an omen for the next twenty-four hours.

Chapter 57
PLEASED TO MEET YOU

"Captain Andress," Sigmund said as he approached, "I haf der pleasure of presenting Mr. Ma, director of der Port Autority, und Colonel Wen Pui, Military Attaché to Mr. Ma."

Thrusting his beefy hand forward, Captain Andress encompassed the smaller hand extended by Mr. Ma, shaking it vigorously. He repeated the procedure with Colonel Pui.

"Ve are most pleased to meet you," Captain Andress said. "It is an honor for us to be here today for dis truly historic occasion, to haf der S.S. *Otto J. Nurad* delivering dis important cargo to der people of China."

Mr. Ma nodded politely. "We awaited the day your ship would arrive. On behalf of the Chinese government we sincerely want you to know how greatly your effort is appreciated."

"Tank you," Captain Andress beamed. "Of course," he said, continuing, "you have met my First Officer, Mr. Helmstrund, and dis is our helmsman, Harry Martin." Both Mr. Ma and Colonel Pui nodded in recognition. "Harry vunce served here in Tsingtao mit der United States Marines, ven vas it, Harry? 1948?"

Harry nodded. "1947 through 1949."

Mr. Ma's eyes focused sharply on Harry. He smiled. "Yes, of course, I thought your face looked familiar. I think I recall you in an office setting...here on the dock area, am I right?"

"Yes, sir," Harry smiled. "Right over there, the old Japanese Compound. I used to be Corporal Harry Martin then. Twelfth Service Battalion. I had the pleasure of working with you in the compound in several of the old godowns."

"Of course, of course," Mr. Ma replied and then turned to

Colonel Pui and explained to him in Chinese of having worked with Harry so many years before. Colonel Pui listened attentively, looked at Harry, and then smiled broadly, nodding.

"I had wondered at times what ever happened to you and all the other fine Marines after you left China," said Mr. Ma turning back to Harry. "Did you fight in Korea?"

"No. Went home. Went to college. Got married and raised a family." Harry sensed he was blurting out his life story in a matter of seconds, almost choking at the thought his life hadn't been that exciting. He stopped to take a breath, adding, "And that's about it in a nutshell." His eyes met a smiling Mr. Ma and he wondered what was behind the smile. "I, too, wondered often about those I left behind, all my friends here in Tsingtao –"

"Correction, Harry," Mr. Ma interjected sharply. "It is now Qingdao. Our names are no longer Anglicized. Beijing instead of Peiping or Peking. Qingdao instead of Tsingtao."

"I see," Harry replied, bothered at the blunt correction. "Anyways, I enjoyed serving here in Qingdao – I hope I said it right – with you, Margaret Chang and all the other nice people. In the back of my mind I kind of hoped the day would come that I could return, and now," he shrugged, "and now I'm here."

"I'm sorry to report that many of those you worked with did not make it through the great purge that swept our country. Margaret, I'm not sure of, but the people's courts were swift in dispensing justice."

A feeling of disgust shocked Harry at the thought that Margaret might have faced the swiftness of Chinese justice. He had seen it with his own eyes back then as the Nationalist Chinese defenses were crumbling and the Americans were preparing to vacate. He had watched, sick at heart as hundreds of alleged communists prisoners, boards strapped to their backs, the tops sticking up above their heads bearing their printed criminal charges, were marched past the Marine headquarters building to a site where they would be executed by machine gun or beheaded by the swiftness of a sword. Most mornings Harry could recall seeing at least two or three hundred prisoners march past. The communists, too, were equally swift in meting out justice in the same manner when they came into power. Could that have been Margaret's fate?

"But, as you can see, Harry, I survived to become an important member of the People's Party, a leader in my community and director of the Port Authority," Mr. Ma added, breaking into Harry's thoughts.

Survived. Harry caught the subtle notation that he was a survivor. The comment the Chinese coolies had made so many years before came to his mind: Mr. Ma was one of the few who had survived through the Japanese occupation, now the Communist occupation. He worked opportunities to his advantage; he was indeed a survivor.

"Well, that's some consolation," Harry said forcing a smile. From office flunky to head of the Port Authority; that's a big jump, Harry mused. Now he's letting me know he's a big shot. His smile suddenly broadened. Maybe the big shot might be the ticket for his getting ashore later on. It was worth a try.

"What brings you back to Qingdao, Harry," Mr. Ma asked. "I would think being married with a family would keep you at home working to support them."

"Long story. Suffice it to say I got divorced, chucked my old job and decided to become a free spirit, dedicated to spending the rest of my life pursuing the things I want to enjoy."

"Ahh, a free spirit, something we all want to be at some time in our lives. Good. And your freedom brings you back to Qingdao. How interesting. Is it the adventure of sailing the many oceans of the world or is there something else that brings Harry Martin back to our ancient shores? We must find time to talk, to fill in the years." He smiled giving a slight nod, then turned his attention back to Captain Andress. "Are you prepared to unload the grain, Captain?"

Harry stood with his mouth agape. He had hoped to pursue their conversation a bit longer, had hoped to get around to going ashore to see the city. Mr. Ma had cut him off abruptly, had turned back to the business at hand.

"Ve are ready to unload with your approval, Mr. Ma," replied Captain Andress.

"Good. But first, I would like to inspect your holds."

"Of course." Captain Andress replied, and led the small delegation from the bridge to the main deck.

"Dat vas interesting, Harry," Sigmund said watching after the departing trio. "Vy does he vunder dat you should vant to return to China? It seems he is playing some kind of mouse und cat game vis you." He shook his head. "I don't trust him. I don't know vy. I just don't."

"Aw, he's okay," Harry retorted, sloughing it off. "He was the same way when I was here before. Just natural curiosity, I suppose. I guess I'd probably wonder the same thing. Probably not that many ex-Marines beating a path back to Tsingtao, oops! I meant Qingdao." He loosed a light chuckle.

But, now that Sigmund had brought it to his attention, Mr. Ma's question had bothered him. It seemed like an innocent question, wondering why he would want to return half way around the world back to Qingdao. Hell, maybe Mr. Ma could read his mind. The damned cache of money was uppermost on his mind of late, except for stolen thoughts of Osa. Naw, let it ride, he decided. No sense in reading anything into an innocent remark.

As he headed below to get a now belated breakfast, Harry passed close behind Captain Andress and the two officials who were watching as the large cargo covers were being removed. Captain Andress reached back grabbing his sleeve. "I vant you to stay on deck und talk to dose officials. Ve could use some good public relations vis dem. You know Mr. Ma. He seems pleased dat you vould return to your old Marine base. Talk. Talk. Besides, I haf some paper vork to get done. Okay?"

"Sure," Harry agreed, "be happy to." He ignored his grumbling stomach and joined Mr. Ma and Colonel Pui at the ship's railing. They exchanged small talk watching as the unloading operation got into full swing.

"It sure takes quite a number of trucks to unload all this grain," Harry commented as the large siphons were driven deeply into the grain, the rattling sound of grain noisy as it moved through the system and then spilled into waiting trucks.

"There are many, many hungry mouths to be fed," Mr. Ma replied.

"Yeah. As I recall, there were a lot of hungry people way back then. I guess Tsingtao, excuse me, Qingdao, hasn't changed that much in the past thirty years, hunger, poverty –"

"Oh but it has, Harry," snapped Mr. Ma reacting to what he felt was an inferred slur. "You should see the way the city has grown and expanded since you Americans left us. It is vastly improved. There is much progress...much progress indeed. It's just that we had a bad grain harvest, and had to ask for foreign assistance. Isn't that right Colonel Pui?"

"Yes," replied Colonel Pui with his always ready nod. "Mr. Ma is right. We have made great progress."

Harry was surprised to hear the Colonel speak. His English was fluent. Apparently Mr. Ma was the head honcho. He did all the talking so the Colonel kind of blended into the background, a yes-man.

Harry well knew the Chinese were having a rough time; millions of people and too little food. It wasn't just a grain shortage this year but for many years, and it wasn't worth getting into a negative discussion about. Instead, he decided on a different approach, one more favorable to one, Harry Martin.

"I'd like to see the old town again," he said with a note of enthusiasm, "a chance to walk where I once walked as a youth so many years ago, a nostalgia trip, so to speak, but –" and Harry sighed deeply, " – I guess after we've unloaded the grain our ship will be leaving port and returning to the United States for the next shipment of grain. Besides, I haven't heard that we received authorization to go ashore as we did in Shanghai, so we must be sailing."

"That can be changed, Harry, that can be changed," Mr. Ma said. He wore that famous, inscrutable Oriental smile. Turning to Colonel Pui, he spoke brusquely in Chinese. The Colonel whipped open his attaché case and pulled out several official looking documents which he quickly handed to Mr. Ma.

Skimming through the documents, Mr. Ma pulled one out, then read it. Taking a pen proffered by Colonel Pui, he signed his name to the document with a flourish, and then held it up before Harry.

"Believe me, Harry, when I say I am an important man in this community –"

"Vell, how is everyting?" came the jovial voice of Captain Andress approaching the group.

"Very good, Captain," Mr. Ma answered. "I was just telling Harry that I am an important man in this community. To show you what I mean, and to thank you and your crew for what you have done for us, I present you with this document authorizing your crew to have shore leave in Qingdao until midnight tonight. It will give your men an opportunity to become better acquainted with our people and our new China."

"Vunderful! Tank you very much, Mr. Ma," Captain Andress beamed accepting the document. "My men vill certainly velcome dis varm gesture of friendship." He glanced at the document. "Dis is vunderful, just vunderful."

Mr. Ma smiled, too, pleased with the response, but did admonish, "I will ask that you remind your men to remember that they are visitors in our fair land and not to get into trouble or to cause trouble. Colonel Pui's military personnel and our civilian police are harsh on those who break our laws."

"Yes, of course. I shall pass along your offer of shore leave und a varning to der crew before dey go ashore."

Mr. Ma bowed stiffly. Almost as an afterthought, he added, "It would be my pleasure to have you, Mr. Helmstrund and, of course, Harry, as my luncheon guests today. It that possible?"

Captain Andress glanced at Harry, saw the way his eyes lit up, and replied, "Of course. Ve vould enjoy dat very much."

"Good. I will pick you up at noon."

With that, and apparently satisfied with the way the unloading process was proceeding, Mr. Ma and Colonel Pui excused themselves and departed. At the bottom of the gangway, Mr. Ma stopped, talking earnestly to Colonel Pui. Suddenly Colonel Pui snapped to attention, snapped off a salute, and turned heading back up the gangway. Mr. Ma entered the black Buick limousine which quickly sped away.

A somber Colonel Pui stood off to one side observing the unloading process. He made no effort to rejoin either the captain or

Harry, seeming to prefer being by himself.

Harry drifted down to the galley, which was deserted for the moment due to the unloading process, found a couple of jellyrolls, grabbed a cup of coffee and sat off to one side munching on a roll, sipping coffee.

Qingdao, the end of the trail. Maybe he could con Mr. Ma into showing him the city, could figure out the old route up to the compound. Hopefully, things hadn't changed that much that he couldn't figure out how to get to the cache.

"Penny for your toughts," came the pleasant, lilting voice of Osa as she settled into the chair next to him. She looked radiant in a white short-sleeved blouse and white skirt.

"Hi," he grinned, looking her over. "Man you look great!" He glanced around; the galley was totally deserted except for the two of them. Before she could react, he reached over, grabbed her by the back of her head and pulled her close mashing his lips to hers in a warm, heady kiss.

"Harry!" she exclaimed, breaking free, quickly looking about. "Not here. Vat is der matter vis you?"

He laughed. "Where's your kitchen helper?"

"He's vorking on der unloading. Vhy?"

"Oh, nothing." He gave a casual glance about again. "I can't recall you're kitchen area. Do you give tours?"

"Tours?" A perplexed look crossed her face.

"How's about a tour, say now?"

A sudden sparkle of recognition of his intent came to her eyes, and her face shown with a new radiance.

"Yah, a tour," she giggled pulling him after her. Osa moved hurriedly through the swinging doors into the kitchen area, back to the far recesses of the kitchen where he had first touched her, had first stolen a kiss. Passionately they kissed as their hands frantically explored, buttons popping loose, buckles coming unbuckled, zippers sliding down as hands touched and teased, and their clothes fell aside. And then they were as one.

I'm apologizing Mr. Helmstrund, Harry grunted, sweating.

Chapter 58

SHANTUNG UNIVERSITY: THE OLD MARINE BASE

Promptly at noon the black Buick rounded the end warehouse and came to a stop beside the *Nurad* where Captain Andress, Sigmund and Harry waited. The two officers looked distinguished in dress black uniforms and braid. Harry looked equally impressive in casual slacks, opened neck shirt, sweater and his leather jacket.

The doors of the limousine were swung wide by the attentive driver and the trio was warmly greeted by Mr. Ma. Opting to rank, as the two officers climbed into the back, Harry eased into the front seat next to the driver who immediately shifted the car into gear and headed inland away from the dock area.

"Der men haf been informed about shore leave," Captain Andress said, addressing his remarks to Mr. Ma. "I suspect dey vill haf der ship unloaded by 1500 hours at der rate dey are vorking now." He laughed. "Dey are anxious to get into town. Vat's dat saying about a fool and dere money."

"There is much to see in Qingdao," an amused Mr. Ma said. "We have culture, theater, movies, dance troupes, acrobats, a museum and much more."

"Good. It vill be good for der men to go ashore. Dey vill haf a better understanding of der Chinese people und der culture," the Captain continued. "Und dey vill get all der shenanigans out of der vay before dey come back on board ship for der long trip back to Saginaw."

"I know what you mean," Harry agreed. "I think this town has much to offer."

"It's not vat you're tinking, Harry," chuckled Sigmund with good-natured sarcasm. "He means der men can move about, see some of der sights mentioned by Mr. Ma, get a few beers, valk around und haf a chance to relax."

"No offense, Harry, but dose houses you vunce frequented probably no longer exist," grinned Captain Andress. He gave a good-natured wink toward Mr. Ma. "In fact, I doubt dey haf any of dose kind of vomen in Qingdao, right, Mr. Ma?"

"Not that the authorities know of," replied Mr. Ma.

Harry turned away from them facing front, grinning. "Where there's a will, there's a way," he whispered to himself. "Ever since Adam and Eve..."

The limousine sped past the entrance to the Old Japanese Compound and on under the railroad bridge then turned sharply to the right toward the main part of town. Harry found his head swiveling from side to side recalling locations and places. Qingdao was still a bustling seaport. The streets teemed with hordes of people milling about, walking somewhat aimlessly, gawking, talking, standing in groups about the small open air markets, deftly dodging the ever present bicycles and motorized traffic in an unperturbed manner.

The driver braked constantly, impatiently banging on the horn. His efforts were, at the least, futile. The incident reminded Harry of his recent kidnapping in Shanghai and the speed with which the driver attempted to race away. It brought a grin to his face. They were going at almost the same speed.

As they topped a rise, Harry recognized where they were almost immediately, the main street. The car moved slowly down the street and Harry glanced around vaguely recalling old haunts.

The car rolled to a stop at curbside, stopping before a large restaurant. Harry's mouth dropped open; it was the old Tivoli Restaurant.

Alighting from the car, he took in the immediate area with a sweeping look. No U.S. Allies Whorehouse, no Sparky's bar, no Enlisted Men's Club. But the Tivoli, damn but it was the same as he recalled it some thirty years ago. He shook his head. Remarkable.

"You find it interesting?" asked Mr. Ma stepping in next to Harry.

"My God, yes! I spent a lot of time walking around this area, these streets, a lot of time. I got goose bumps just standing here, here in Qingdao, here in front of the Tivoli."

"You may wish to return later today and once again recall pleasant memories of the past," said Mr. Ma. "For your pleasure, we are eating in the Tivoli today. They are awaiting us," he added. Leading the delegation, Mr. Ma strode briskly toward the entrance where a doorman quickly swung the door wide. A grinning, bowing maitre'd in starched uniform, greeted them. Turning, he led them through the restaurant to a private room at the back. A bevy of equally starched waiters stood against the far wall awaiting them, dark eyes watching intently as they approached one of the larger tables which was appropriately adorned with fresh-cut flowers.

Crisp, starched white linen napkins, arranged in the shape of a fan, sat on an equally crisp, starched white tablecloth. Amy Vanderbilt would have been pleased at the sight, Harry thought, as he surveyed the table: everything was precisely arranged.

"Please be seated," Mr. Ma said. At his nod, the maitre'd clapped his hands and the army of waiters descended upon them. Water glasses were filled, wine glasses filled.

Rising, Mr. Ma held up his glass of wine. "This is a vintage white wine, a blend of grapes from our new winery located on the Shantung peninsula, a first for the area." Then, he led off with a toast to China, relating how China has taken the initiative to improve international relations. This was followed by a toast to the Swedish sailors for their adroit seamanship in transporting the precious cargo of grain to Qingdao. A true diplomat, Mr. Ma offered a special toast on behalf of Harry's return to the orient, that he was the first American Marine to return to this fair city, and to their renewed friendship and his quest of adventure, whatever it may be, and that it be successful.

Harry thanked him, getting into the spirit of the occasion, calling for a toast to the many happy times he had spent in Qingdao, the pleasure of having worked with such great men as Mr. Ma, and assuring him that although his stay in port would be short, they would meet again one day. Mr. Ma touched his glass to Harry's assuring him they would.

A toast was offered by Captain Andress on behalf of the citizens of Sweden, and the American government for making this journey a reality.

A gourmet meal followed served in eight courses, beginning with sliced eggs, pineapple and rice cakes, fried minced shrimp patties, soup cooked in melons with meats, nuts and chick peas, chicken breasts with vegetable inserts, green vegetable stalks with cream sauce, fried rice with pork and eggs, and a small sweet cake along with sweet rolls and oranges to top off the meal.

Attentive waiters hovered over each guest ensuring they had plenty to eat and drink. Beyond the sing-song chattering and the table discussions could be heard the melodic strains of Chinese music.

"Whew. I haven't eaten such a delicious meal since, I guess since the last time I ate here in the spring of 1949," Harry said pushing away from the table, patting his bulging stomach. "Excellent. Simply excellent. The Tivoli was noted for it's fine food way back then and I'm pleased to see it has retained its high standards for culinary excellence."

"You have a good sense of recall," Mr. Ma beamed. "Did China make that deep an impression on you?"

"Yes, it did," Harry replied after a moment. "I guess it did impress me. This was my home for almost three years. I spent a lot of time exploring this town and the outlying area, the smaller villages and rugged terrain. I especially enjoyed the Lao Shan Mountains to the north of us, the beautiful terraced hills and colorful little coves, the small fishing villages nestled along the shoreline, the people, their quaint dress, your melodic language and your warmth. Yes, I guess you can say I have fond memories of my time in Tsingtao."

"Qingdao," Mr. Ma hastened to correct.

Then, quick to follow on Harry's positive response, Mr. Ma added, "I hope, like you, that many other former service men will one day return to pay us a visit, perhaps bringing their families with them so all might experience our land and our peoples."

After a momentary hesitation, he looked directly at Harry, asking, as though another thought had crossed his mind, "Is there something else that brings you back, Harry? A long lost love, a quest to recapture your youth, something else of equal value? After all, you are the first ex-Marine to return."

Harry gave a light shake of his head, a whimsical smile coming to his face. "Correction," he said. "There are no ex-Marines, only former Marines. Naw, just dumb luck brought me back, being in the right place at the right time, getting on board *Nurad* which was headed for China." His smile grew more rueful. "Nothing of value here to return for, maybe a couple of blue-eyed Chinese bastards running around that'd love to see their old man, but nothing I'd deliberately come half way around the world for. At least not for a couple of bastard kids." He laughed.

Mr. Ma was not amused, his smile having turned coldly stoic.

Captain Andress and Sigmund offered embarrassed laughs.

Harry sensed a pregnant pause and knew his flippant remark had caused it. How could he change the subject gracefully and get back into Mr. Ma's good graces. To his surprise it was Mr. Ma who changed the subject.

"Are you in a hurry to get back to your ship, Captain Andress?" he asked.

"Vell," he glanced at Sigmund, who shrugged, "not really. Everyting is under control, but I am sure you haf many demands on your time, und ve don't vant to delay you."

"Nonsense. You are my guests today," hastened Mr. Ma. "If your appetites have been satiated, it would be my pleasure to escort you on a brief tour of our fair city."

"As long as ve are not imposing," replied Captain Andress.

"No. Not imposing. I look forward to it, a chance to share my city with you." He waved the maitre'd over to the table complimenting him on the meal and the attentiveness of his staff. "My guests are most impressed," he said as Captain Andress, Sigmund and Harry added their thanks. "Come, now, gentlemen," he said to his guests, rising, "a tour of the city awaits you."

Outside the restaurant, Harry noted a change in the weather. The bright, warm sunlight was being overshadowed by a thin layer of clouds. This time of the year the weather could bounce from twenty below to fifty or sixty above, as it was now, only to plunge to the twenties again at night. And snow was forecast for tonight.

The limousine moved along the harbor drive at a leisurely pace. Harry recognized the old YMCA building where he had spent so many pleasant hours. At the corner, the driver turned left heading inland up a winding road that twisted ever upwards, then straightened. Harry's heart skipped a beat: they were headed right for the old Marine Corps compound.

"You might find this spot of interest to you, Harry," called Mr. Ma tapping him on his shoulder. "You may recall some of those impetuous youthful days spent here." He laughed. Harry glanced back over his shoulder, grinning. "How true! How true!"

A long chain-link fence paralleled the road for several hundred yards before terminating at the main gate. Harry was surprised to see it was still standing after all these years. He was more pleased when he saw the dip where the small stream still meandered under the fence and across the edge of their old playing field. The gap in the fence above the stream was still there. It would be like the old days coming in late from liberty, he thought, making a mental note that tonight he would use the same old routine again.

Beyond the fence Harry could see the old field, a combination parade ground and exercise field. Today, several youths were standing about in the center of the field flying ornate kites. But, just seeing the field brought back a flood of memories, the baseball games between rival battalions and other bases; the last baseball game he played in was against the team from Guam and he played opposite his old high school buddy, Sergeant Quick. Too, the field had been the locale for any number of rough and tumble football games, all with the same intense rivalry between battalions. He could visualize muscular Corporal Black the day he stopped the Third Marine Battalion receiver with a heart-stopping tackle as he slammed into him, knocking him cold. And the old slopshoot was no more, just a grassy knoll.

Mr. Ma ordered the driver to enter the campus through the main gate. The car swung right driving under a handsome sign heralding: Shantung University.

"The Marine Compound has been converted back to a

university," said Mr. Ma. "The Central Party determined it should be named the Shantung University. There are about five hundred students presently enrolled, with plans to double in size in the next few years. As soon as we acquire additional funding, we will provide space for more young men and women who are eligible for higher education, giving them the opportunity to advance and help China move forward as a world leader.

"Although the university has existed for a number of years, the emphasis on education has only come about under our new chairman of the Communist Party. Emphasis is being placed on a broader understanding of world cultures, economics and languages. Agriculture is also one of our major programs. With almost a billion Chinese mouths to feed daily, it is important to manage our soils properly." He paused for a moment to let his words sink in, to impress his guests that China, although struggling at the moment, was indeed moving forward.

"We are also stressing birth control and family planning. Many of these students will return to their own villages and will be responsible for reducing the number of unnecessary births through educating the masses. We love our children, but we must be a responsible nation. Getting back to our other classes, you will be pleased to learn that all of our government officials, police officers and other government employees are now required to learn English. As a matter of fact, most of our Qingdao police officers now speak English fluently."

"Interesting," Harry offered.

The limousine continued along the narrow drive adjacent to the large field. "As you can see some of the students are flying kites, an old Chinese tradition," said Mr. Ma. "Soon, as in the United States, we will be playing baseball again. It is becoming very popular here. The field is also used for soccer and other activities."

As the car turned left at the first corner, Mr. Ma said, "This is the engineering trades school." Harry knew it as the old Third Marine barracks. "And ahead of us you will see our literature and fine arts school—"

Harry felt a tightness in his chest. It was the old 12th Service

Battalion barracks. Without trying to be obvious, he studied the building. It stood as they had left it, except it was cleaner now under a new coating of paint and landscaping. Along the far side wall leading to the fourth floor he could see the steps the Marines had built, shelves for potted plants to add a dash of color to the drabness of the barracks they had told the administrative brass. In actuality, the steps had been built as an accommodation to sneak Chinese whores up to the fourth floor storage room where they held frequent "parties."

Glancing up along the line of steps, Harry could faintly discern the outer hinges of the secret door, almost invisible to the naked eye because of the way they had constructed it. Now, several additional coats of paint all but obliterated the location of the door. A slight grin broke across his lips as he savored the memory of those crazy nights; horny Marines and wanton whores; what a crazy combination.

"You probably recall this building, Harry," beamed Mr. Ma. "I believe it was your old barracks building. Would you like to see how we have remodeled it into functional classrooms?"

"Wha-what?" Harry replied, startled from his reverie, realizing Mr. Ma was speaking to him. "What did you say?"

"Would you like to get out and take a tour of your old barracks in order to see what we have done in converting the space into functional classrooms?"

"Yes. Of course I would," Harry answered quickly.

The limousine came to a stop in front of the gleaming white building. The group got out and stood before the building. To Harry it was like stepping back in time. Staring at the entrance, it seemed as though 1949 was only seconds ago.

The basic structure of the entrance was the same, only now it was adorned with a bold sign proclaiming it to be the School of Literature and Fine Arts. The grounds surrounding the building were landscaped with an abundance of ferns, cedar, and other shrubbery. Early crocus were already breaking through the cold mantle of black soil and dirty snow.

Students were all around, talking, sitting on benches, soaking up the warmth of a spring day, or moving on to their next classes.

The delegation followed Mr. Ma as he led them into the building. On entering, their attention was immediately drawn to a giant picture of Chairman Mao. A scholarly looking older man approached them from the administrative office. Mr. Ma bowed slightly, and then introduced them to Dr. Wei, school administrator.

Harry nodded and shook hands. His attention was drawn to the office, the old guard shack. Inside sat a pretty young secretary pecking away at a typewriter. She must have sensed she was being stared at for she turned, her dark almond eyes meeting his. She smiled. It was a warm, inviting smile. Harry smiled and waved. She laughed.

Dr. Wei had taken command of the tour. Waving once again, as the blushing secretary returned to her typewriter, Harry joined the group as it moved along the corridor. Dr. Wei stopped at the juncture where the corridor met the stairwell. He explained the alignment of the rooms and the arrangement of the classes on this floor and the upper floors.

While Harry listened, an eerie feeling came over him. The resonant sound of voices along the corridor was so reminiscent of the past. He half expected to see Novak coming back from working out, a towel wrapped around his neck, or the Indian arguing with the Sergeant for a pass, the always smiling Mexican kid from El Paso. A flood of names and faces suddenly overwhelmed him: Netzinger and Ertel from Wisconsin, Bailey and Johnson, Olson, Griffith, Sapp, Winterhalter, Pope, Byrd, Kellerman, even Johnnie Baker and Parks from California and Virgil Leeson from West Virginia. Faces from a hundred different towns and states.

A bell rang startling the group, and suddenly the corridor was flooded with students moving to their next classes. Their sing-song voices sounded strangely pleasant to Harry's ears. They smiled and nodded in passing.

Dr. Wei continued the tour leading the contingent down the length of the corridor, stopping periodically to show them a classroom, a moment to observe. It was obvious he was very proud of his building and his students and instructors.

As he peered into the old central lecture hall, Harry could almost feel the presence of his old comrades, could almost smell the pungent tobacco smoke wafting from Shorty Donelson's old corncob pipe, could recall the look of rage that crossed the faces of Joe and Stan when they were dragged away that day.

On climbing to the second floor, Harry popped his head inside the first doorway, his old barracks room, and his bunk being just inside on the left. A desk now occupied the space. A slightly built, but very attractive girl, was seated at the desk. She looked up at him, smiling. He smiled back. Everyone was friendly. She was not only friendly, but also damned cute. He always wondered what mysterious thoughts lurked behind those dark eyes, whether deep in conversation or making love.

He saw the others were ahead of him, waved, and hurried to catch up. The room-by-room tour continued up to the third floor. At one point, Harry glanced inside one of the classrooms noting the students were intently looking at something behind a screen as they sketched, making quick strokes in charcoal. His curiosity aroused, he stepped forward and peeked around the screen. A naked girl striking a pose glanced up at him. Harry flushed. Just as quickly he stepped away, but not before he noted the girl's body had taken on a distinct pinkish hue.

At midpoint of the third floor, Harry stopped at the base of the steps leading to the fourth floor. He looked up the steps. At the top was a thick metal door.

"As I recall, these steps led up to the fourth floor supply room where we kept all our clothing supplies, winter parkas, boots, carbines and MI rifles and other items," he said not directing the statement to anyone in particular.

"Yes, storage. It is still used for storage," said Dr. Wei picking up on his comment. "It is too small for a classroom so we keep old records up there. It is too cold for any practical purpose. I don't think the room has been touched in many years."

"Probably not since you were here thirty years ago," said Mr. Ma. "Would you like to see it?"

"No," Harry said with a shake of his head. "Just old memories."

"Ahh, memories. Yes, memories are like beautiful pieces of

treasure, to be recalled and enjoyed again and again," Mr. Ma said with a warm smile.

"I'm sure Mr. Martin has many fond memories of this structure," said Dr. Wei. "Fine memories."

"Yes, and I do treasure them, each and everyone," Harry said. And, he thought, by a stroke of luck, the money might still be in the storage areas right where Joe hid it if the place hasn't been used over the years.

The tour ended back at the main entrance with a brief exchange of cordialities. Dr. Wei wished them a pleasant day and safe voyage back to America. The secretary had stood up beyond him, stretching, long black hair trailing to the middle of her back. She was thin, yet nicely proportioned, small breasts pushing against her cotton blouse. Her eyes met Harry's and he saw a mischievous, subtle smile. Harry grinned letting the subtle invitation pass.

Sigmund, too, had caught her stretching, had stared at her. He was surprised when her eyes shifted to him, the invitation still in her eyes; was he interested? His face reddened as he caught the meaning of her look. Turning, he beat a hasty retreat out the door.

Having seen the interplay, Harry chuckled. All Sigmund had to do was nod yes and love was his for the taking. He'd have to talk to the boy. He was definitely missing out on life. Still grinning, he sauntered out of the building. Where there was a will there was a way. The old town hadn't changed that much. Sex was still available.

"She probably gets off at five," he whispered to Sigmund. "You ought to come back this afternoon and check it out. I think she likes you. Maybe it's the uniform."

Sigmund gave him a dour look, then turned away.

By then, the others had joined them and all settled back in the limousine with the tour of the university continuing. "I'm just amazed at what they did with our old barracks," Harry said. "They took those old beat up rooms and remodeled them into such attractive classrooms. Just amazing."

"You must remember, Harry, that before the Japanese and Americans came, this was a university. Now, it is one again."

The car moved on past the Administration building and up past the Agricultural Science School, which Harry recognized as the old First Marine Battalion barracks. Students milled about outside the front of the building. Love was in the air, boys and girls walking hand in hand. The world never changes that much, Harry thought. He was surprised to see a new, modern field house on the spot where the old Tarver gymnasium had collapsed back in 1948.

Captain Andress and Sigmund were exchanging small talk with Mr. Ma about the landscaping, the attractive look of buildings and the neatness of the campus. "Do you haf evening classes?" the Captain asked.

"No. We have not advanced that far yet. The university actually stops operation at 6 p.m. and the gates are locked for the night," replied Mr. Ma.

Thank you Captain Andress, Harry thought. You couldn't have asked your question at a more appropriate time. No night classes. Things were falling into place better than he had hoped for. With luck he could get on campus after dark, get into the building and get the money, and be back to the ship with no problems. With the warm weather today, he had noted many of the building windows were open. There'd probably be a window or door unlocked in the building, or he could jimmy a window to get inside. At this point, all systems were go!

Mr. Ma ordered the driver to leave the campus by the back gate. Circling around the hill, Harry recalled the road came out by the old racetrack. He was surprised to see the track and grounds had been converted into a huge People's Park. At the far end of the grounds were a series of apartment houses. Do the white Russians still live in the area, he wondered, recalling the slim blonde with the blue eyes the officers all dated.

Before long, the limousine was moving along the dock toward the *S.S. Otto J. Nurad*, slowing to a stop in the shadow of the giant ship.

"Tank you for a most enjoyable luncheon und tour of your beautiful city," Captain Andress said alighting from the car. "It is very kind of you, Mr. Ma. Ve sincerely appreciate it."

"Yes. Very enlightening," added Sigmund. "Tank you."

"I agree, and thank you, too, for stopping by the University of Shantung. Meeting you again, being here in this beautiful city, seeing the old Marine compound and the way you have so successfully changed it into a university. Well, all I can say is you've done a marvelous job, and I thank you again for rekindling some very fond memories," Harry said. "It was very thoughtful of you."

An enigmatic smile crossed Mr. Ma's face. "It was my pleasure, gentlemen." He slid across the seat close to the door. "On behalf of the people of China, I want to thank you, Captain Andress, and your noble crew, for bringing this cargo of badly needed grain to our people. In case I don't see you before you depart tomorrow, have a safe journey and we look forward to your return trip."

He reached forward, shaking each one's hand, holding onto Harry's a moment longer. "Till we meet again, Harry. It's been too long since we last met; I trust it won't be as long next time."

With that, he closed the door and the black limousine sped off.

"An interesting man," said the Captain as he turned heading for the gangway. "A likeable fellow, yet –"

"I feel dat vay, too," Sigmund chimed in. "Dere is someting about him dat bodders me."

Harry shrugged it off. Mr. Ma was always subject to discussion, even in the old days. He slapped Sigmund on his shoulders. "You going back into town to check out that cute secretary?"

"No," came his curt reply.

"She was cute, built nice. She gave you an invitation –"

"She vas nice," Sigmund interrupted. "Maybe der next trip. I haf been assigned deck officer tonight."

"Bummer."

Harry followed him up the gangway. "You got to strike while the iron's hot," he said to Sigmund's back. "Prime stuff there. Someone else could serve your watch. She might not be around when you get back."

Sigmund chose to ignore the remark, instead walking quickly away as they stepped onto the deck of the *Nurad*. At the hatchway, he turned, "Don't forget, you are taking Osa into town, und behafe yourself. Also, be back early. You haf der midnight vatch," and then he disappeared into the bowels of the ship.

Harry stopped short. It was obvious Sigmund didn't like to be teased, especially about female relationships. And, yes, he was well aware of the need to take Osa into town. But, at the moment, he had more important things to think about, last minute preparations to be made, and, yes, he'd be back in time for the midnight watch.

Chapter 59

LOVE: THE TRUTH WILL OUT

The galley was deserted when Harry entered a couple of hours later. Satisfied, from his point of view that he was ready to go ashore tonight to retrieve the cache, he had to have a serious talk with Osa. It was imperative that she not go ashore tonight.

Stopping by the huge coffee urns, he poured a cup of coffee then pushed through the galley doors into the kitchen area. Osa was at the stove checking several simmering pots. As she opened the oven door to check on a roast, Harry slipped in close to her lifting a lid off one of the pots.

"Ummm, smells good," he said sniffing loudly.

"Oh!" Osa gasped, turning quickly, surprised at seeing Harry. "You startled me."

"Sorry," he grinned. "Just came down to see what's cooking."

"You tease me." She slapped his hand causing him to drop the lid. "I am not in der mood for teasing."

Jerking his hand back, Harry asked, "What's the matter?"

"Sigmund. He came down here a vhile ago telling me most of der men ver going ashore tonight, even my kitchen help! I planned for a special meal for our last night in China und now it vill all be vasted."

"If it helps any, I'll try to eat as much as I can to make you happy," he said trying to appease her.

"No," she laughed, then her face changed to a frown. "Besides, I'm upset vis you, too."

"Me? Why me?"

"Vat you told me about all dat money und dat odders ver looking for it. I don't like dat. I tink ve should stay aboard ship tonight."

"Whoa! Hold on!" Harry snapped. "I came half way around the world to find that money and I intend to leave with it. I was up at Shantung University this afternoon and, after having seen the place, I'm sure the money's still there. All I have to do is get in, get it and get out. Simple as A.B.C."

"But if dose odder men know about it, know you are here, dey might kill you for der money." She turned away, afraid she was going to cry. "I couldn't stand losing you," she whispered in a choking voice.

"Hey, no one's going to hurt me," he said moving to her, placing his hands on her shoulders, his face close by her ear.

"I've lived all these years and I plan to live many more years. Don't go writing off Harry Martin, yet. Besides, he's got plans and those plans include you."

Osa whirled about, beaming through her tears. "Me?"

"Yes. You."

"How?" Her eyes glistened through the wetness and a warmth replaced the melancholy look of only moments before. "How?" she asked again.

"You'll find out when I get back to the ship and not a moment sooner," he replied with a wink.

"Harry!" She gave an exasperated sigh. "You get me so angry, so confused." She turned back to the stove. "I don't haf time for your babbling nonsense. I must finish my dinner und put it out for dose men who vant to eat." She yanked the oven door open, took a towel for the hot pan and eased the steaming pot roast out placing it on the counter. "It must cool," she said as she wadded the juice-stained towel and threw it across the kitchen where it landed in the sink.

"Hey, take it easy. Don't get so uptight," he said moving to her, rubbing her shoulders, his strong fingers gently massaging tense muscles. His rubbing motions traced downward to the small of her back, then up, then back until he was gently massaging her buttocks. Osa leaned against the counter not offering any argument. That tingling feeling was moving through her and she knew where it would lead. She had to stop him, but for the moment – and she loosed a long sigh, closing her eyes, enjoying his touch.

"I've been thinking about tonight," he said in a soothing voice. "You seem to be too keyed up. Why don't you stay on board ship? I'll make a dash for the cash and be back –"

"No you don't!" Osa snapped breaking free of his hands, whirling about. "You don't try to sweet talk me out of it. I go vis you. Back rub, hah! I got your number. I know vat you had in mind und it von't vork. Ve go togedder!"

"Dammit! No! I'm serious. I don't want you to go. I don't want anything happening to you."

"No! No! No!" She pushed him aside, storming past him to lift a lid on a pot. "I vill put der food out for der men, den I get dressed und ve go ashore."

"Osa!" Harry implored, grabbing her, jerking her around. "Listen to me. I don't want your life endangered. You're not going ashore and that's final!"

"Oh?" Just as quickly, her eyes softened and a kind of smirk crossed her face. With one eyebrow raised, she replied prissily, "Sigmund said ve vould go ashore togedder –"

"Screw Sigmund! I don't want anything to happen to you!"

"Vy don't you vant anyting to happen to me?" she asked, baiting him. "Am I dat important to you?"

"Yes. You mean an awful lot to me."

"Really!" she squealed. "You really mean dat?"

"Yes, dammit. Yes."

She threw herself into his arms smothering him with kisses, her arms about his waist. Laughing, Harry tried valiantly to extricate himself from her grasp, but it was to no avail. She wrapped her arms around his waist holding tight, nestling her head to his chest.

"Ever since Shanghai, all I do is tink of you," she whispered. "You are on my mind all der time. I haf all kinds of toughts about you about us. I find myself vanting you at der craziest times, find myself tinking of vays in vich to make love like in der movies. I blush ven I tink of how often I haf such pleasurable toughts about you. Ven you ver just rubbing my back I vanted you to continue, to make love to me."

He wrapped his arms around her holding her close. "My little nymphomaniac," he whispered, chuckling.

"It's true. I tink I am a nymphomaniac. I tink of you all der time."

"You're just a beautiful woman whose found out sex is a beautiful thing when shared by two people in love."

"You do love me den?" she shrieked, pulling back from him. "Oh, Harry, I luf you, too. I really do."

There was a warmth and tenderness he'd not seen on her face before. He had to admit it, he was in love. In spite of their early tiffs, anger and skulking, their being thrown together time and again had turned into a deeper appreciation of one another. It made him realize he had deeper feelings for her, feelings he knew all too well as love.

"I really do love you," he said. "I don't know why. You give me a hard time all the time, but yes, I do love you."

And then they were kissing. The irritating buzzing of a timer interrupted them, a sound that registered in Osa's mind and, with a gasp, she broke free exclaiming, "Oh! Der food! I must get der food ready for dinner." Hastily, she dashed to the stove, shutting it off, and then scurried around getting the food set out for dinner. Harry watched after her, shook his head and poured another cup of coffee to replace the one now gone cold.

In minutes, Osa was back standing before him. She took his hand in hers, squeezing it. "Vy do you love me?"

Harry grinned. "Let me count the ways, eh?"

"Be serious. I vant to know."

He scratched his head for a moment before answering. "I guess it's because you're beautiful, 'cause you're warm and sexy, 'cause you're a darned good cook, 'cause you look good in a bikini bathing suit, 'cause even without anything on, as a matter of fact," he said, which caused her to blush, but her eyes remained transfixed on his. "I love you because you're intelligent, witty and charming, 'cause you like the kinds of things I like, 'cause you like to make love in bed, showers and other places, but mostly because you're you. And that's why I love you."

Tears streamed down her cheeks as she continued looking up at him. "I luf you, Harry Martin. I could shout it from der highest most point of dis ship: Harry Martin. I luf you!"

Then, in an almost inaudible whisper, she continued. "You haf made me proud to be a voman. You haf helped me learn dat a voman can do much to please a man, and a man to please a voman. I luf you for all der same reasons you luf me, und ven ve get back to der ship tonight, I vill show you. I got a lot of ideas from dose movies dat I vant to try yet. You vill see." She grabbed a large knife and started carving the roast as she spoke.

Harry laughed. He shook his head. His argument for her staying aboard was losing strength. He had to say something, do something drastic to keep her on board.

"Hello," came Sigmund's voice as he poked his head into the kitchen. "Oh, Osa, Harry –"

"It's okay, Sigmund," she replied sweetly. Ve ver just discussing vere ve vould eat dinner in town. Vot do you suggest?"

"Only vun place. Der Tivoli," he retorted. "Right, Harry?"

"Right."

Of all the dumb times for him to enter the kitchen, Harry thought, and he sure as hell didn't need his suggestions for where to eat dinner.

"You vill enjoy der Tivoli, Osa," Sigmund said. "Harry vill show you a good time in town. I hope it is as good as ven you ver in Shanghai."

"Yes!" Osa beamed. "I certainly hope so."

Harry caught the impish look on her face. He couldn't help but grin. Just how much did Osa tell the captain about their fun in Shanghai? Well, Qingdao would be different; this wasn't for fun and games. He had a job to do and he was determined to get it done.

"Here's your passes," Sigmund said handing across two liberty passes which Osa quickly snatched. "Enjoy," Sigmund said retreating back behind the doors. "Is der food ready, yet?"

"Yes. Please help yourself," Osa called. "Self-serve tonight." Turning to Harry, she grinned as she slipped the passes inside her blouse pocket. "Now ve go to town?"

"Yes," he mimicked with an exasperated sigh. "Now ve go to town, my little nymphomaniac. Wear black and be ready by six o'clock, eighteen hundred hours. Got it?"

"Yes, Harry," she grinned back. "Black und eighteen hundred hours." With that saucy response, she whipped off her apron, threw it on the counter and, happily humming to herself, slapped him hard across his buttocks as she left the galley. Harry jumped at the smack, and then laughed. Crazy female, he chuckled, and then dumped his cup of cold coffee for a fresh one.

Unconsciously, he began nibbling on bits and pieces of food still sitting on the counter. "Shit," he muttered under his breath. Things weren't going exactly as he had planned, not one damned bit.

Chapter 60

LIBERTY AND THE SEARCH FOR HIDDEN TREASURE

Harry waited impatiently on the cold deck for Osa. He stomped his feet several times to keep the circulation going. Where the hell was she? He shivered. Without the alpaca lining, his jacket was thin, too thin to stop the chill air cutting through him. Even having the folded seabag tucked under his jacket did little to ward off the cold. Most of the crew had long departed for the city and its many attractions. A cloud layer had moved in blanketing the city. Flurries of large snowflakes whirled about him. And still he waited.

Osa stepped on deck striding leisurely toward him as though she had just stepped out of an exclusive women's apparel shop. Wearing tailored slacks, black boots, and a hooded ski jacket with a fur collar over a black turtleneck sweater, she was breathtakingly beautiful, and he had to admit, well worth the wait.

"I am excited to go," she said joining him.

"Yeah. Just follow my directions and everything will come off okay," he said sternly, which erased her warm smile.

"Yah. You are der boss." She was miffed that he hadn't commented on her appearance. The fact that she had spent the past hour or so selecting just the right clothing, makeup and perfume upset her.

"And you look absolutely gorgeous," he smiled grabbing her by the arm and steering her toward the gangway where Sigmund was standing.

"Enjoy der Tivoli," Sigmund said waving them through. "Make sure he shows you a good time, Osa," he added for Harry's benefit. Harry gave him a dirty look as he passed. Osa flashed a quick smile. "He vill."

As they started down the gangway a break in the low-lying clouds revealed higher, blood-red tentacles of thinner clouds that to Harry, looked like long bloodied fingers. Was it an omen, he wondered?

Just past the main gate guard shack, Harry saw what looked like a long line of pedicabs. A boy immediately dashed forward calling out, "Trishaw! Trishaw! his three-wheeled unit bouncing along beside him. Carefully, the twosome climbed into the tight confines of the back seat, cuddling close together. "Cozy," Harry said slipping an arm around Osa's shoulder. "I never rode in vun before," she giggled, as Harry called to the boy to take them to the Tivoli restaurant.

The boy started peddling, the trishaw swaying and bumping along the rough stone road. Harry held Osa close, enjoying the warmth of her body next to his, the fragrance of her perfume. It may have been cold but the lovers were unaware of it, only the jiggling, yawing sensation of the trishaw moving along. The labored breathing of the boy could be heard as he paced himself through the crowded streets, up several small hills and around toward the central part of town.

Harry kept a jaundiced eye on the boy for any sudden, uncalled for movement. It took only a second to leap off the seat, dumping passengers out on to the street. Just as quickly, there'd be a dozen cutthroats falling on the helpless victims, beating them unconscious, robbing them, taking anything of value, even slashing or killing them. Allen, from Philadelphia, had his tongue slit, and "Ski", from Chicago, had an ear cut off when the rickshaws they were riding were dumped, and they were attacked. Harry was always alert. At least he left China back then with all parts intact.

Within minutes the driver had topped the last hill and there, below, only a couple of blocks away was the brightly lit Tivoli restaurant. It was a fast, jolting ride down the hill. With trepidation, Harry wondered whether the boy could stop in time. But, with a sudden jerk, he stopped his rig exactly in front of the restaurant, then politely helped his passengers out. He wore a big grin as he extended his hand to Harry.

"How much?" Harry asked, reaching into his pocket for change.

"Two dollars, American," the grinning boy replied, his hand extending further.

"Two dollars? Boy inflation has hit China, too," Harry said opening up his wallet. He extracted three singles and slapped them in the boy's hand. "Sesh-in-ee," he added, smiling, hoping he hadn't forgotten all his Chinese.

"Ding hao," the boy replied, laughing, tucking the bills away.

"Well, at least I remembered some of it," Harry chuckled.

"Look!" gasped Osa pointing just beyond the Tivoli.

Turning, Harry saw his engine room friend, Karl, walking along with the young cabin boy, Hans, both with their arms around the waists of slim Oriental girls.

"Dat is disgusting," Osa snapped. "He is too young for –"

"He'll be a man before the night is over," Harry countered steering her toward the entrance to the Tivoli. "Everyone has to learn about it, some sooner than others –"

She started to reply, then stopped.

They continued on into the restaurant and turned right into the bar. "We'll have a drink first," he said, helping her onto a barstool. "Tsingtao piju, that's a beer for me, and a scotch and water for the lady," he said to the bartender. "See Osa, I remembered; scotch and water." She smiled, but he wondered what kind of scotch it would be.

Harry slapped a ten spot on the bar. While they waited for their drinks to arrive, he looked around the bar, and then into the dining room. No familiar faces of the crew, or others he knew. Only one white haired old man who was sitting far back in the corner.

"Pay the man for the drinks out of this," Harry said to Osa, pushing the ten spot in front of her. "I'll be back before the beer gets warm. Order yourself another drink, if you want, but stay here. That's an order!"

"But Harry," she started to object, but he grabbed her head between his hands and kissed her fiercely, crushing her warm lips to his. "You stay here," he said, parting. "Right here."

"But you said I could go vis you."

"Sorry. Change of plans."

"Harry!" Her eyes snapped in sudden anger. "Dat is not nice."

"Sorry, babe. I've got a feeling about tonight. I can't explain it. I just know you'll be safer right here. I'll be back in less than an hour, then it's dinner on me."

"Yes. Dat I am sure of."

"If I don't get back in an hour and a half, go back to the ship immediately –"

"Harry! No I don't even vant to tink such toughts."

Her attention was distracted at that moment by the bartender setting their drinks on the bar. Turning, she shoved the ten spot across to him, and then turned back only to find Harry was gone. She swore softly in Swedish, taking the scotch in her hands, resigning herself to the fact she would have to wait. One hour, and then what?

On the street, Harry looked around searching passing faces, looking for one in particular, the bearded face of Stan Drezewski. But there were no bearded Caucasians or clean-shaven Caucasians, just slant-eyed Orientals, hundreds of them. Maybe luck was with him, he thought as he started off, quickening his pace as he moved through the dark streets ever angling upwards toward the university.

He pulled his knit cap low across his forehead hoping it would be harder for anyone to recognize him. The streetlights were sparsely located and offered little in the way of bright lighting. People passing paid scant attention to him, just another face in the crowd, exactly what he wanted.

The walk became more demanding, more grueling as he moved up the winding street. Automobile traffic was at a minimum, perhaps four or five cars passing by in either direction during the twenty minutes it took to reach the point just shy of the main gate where the fence paralleled the athletic field. Stopping for a moment, he checked the area. No one at hand. Slipping and sliding on the wet grass, he hurried down the embankment toward the fence then moved along the fence until he found the opening where the drainage ditch passed under the fence. The ditch smelled foul. Kneeling down, he crawled under the fence staying clear of the narrow stream.

Once inside the fence, he ran along the edge of the stream in a crouched position, leaped the stream and found himself at the bottom of the embankment behind the old Third Marine barracks.

Stopping, listening, assured no one was close at hand, he made his way up the embankment and moved to the shadow of a large tree. Again, he stood motionless for several minutes, cautiously observing the buildings and grounds, wondering what kind of security was employed, if any. Seeing no unusual movement except for the sound of branches clacking together, moved by a cold breeze, he quietly moved to the corner of the building where he could peek around the corner and observe the old 12th Service Battalion building.

Straining his eyes in the darkness, alert to any unusual sounds, he stood silent, yet felt his ragged breathing, the trip hammer pounding of his heart, the adrenalin rushing through his tense body. His nerves were on edge, alert, honed for this moment. He half grunted, almost chuckled aloud; Novak would have laughed his ass off if he could see him now. How many times had the two sneaked back on base this way, snockered to the gills, and damned lucky they weren't caught or blown away by trigger-happy guards?

Using the shadows to his advantage, he moved stealthy across the street to the end door of the old barracks. Grabbing the door handle, he twisted. Locked. Damn! Staying in the shadows, he moved along the building toward the front entrance, methodically checking each window along the way. All locked. Damn! Even the front entrance was locked. He didn't want to chance breaking a window and attracting attention, so he kept on moving, continuing along the front of the building, checking each window. Someone had to have goofed. It had been a warm day and there were several windows open. It was a natural thing for a student to leave at least one window unlocked.

At the far end of the building, adjacent to the old administration building, he came to another door. He grabbed the doorknob and twisted. The door was unlocked; someone had goofed! He knew students, he smiled smugly. It was exactly what he was looking for, hoping for.

Easing the door open, he slipped inside, quickly closing the door behind him. Standing motionless, he peered into the darkness of the hallway, waiting, allowing his eyes time to adjust to the dark before moving on.

"One false move and I'll blow your damned head off!" came a guttural voice hissing from the darkness. At the same moment, Harry felt the coldness of steel pressed to his temple. He froze. Strong hands grasped his and a rope was quickly knotted about his wrists. Then, a gag was thrust into his mouth. "Now move," the voice commanded and, prodded by the gun, Harry moved forward into the darkness.

Chapter 61
STAN'S SURPRISE

"Stop here," the voice commanded after awhile. Harry stopped, listening to the man's breathing, caught the foul smell of cigarettes on the man's breath and clothing as he reached past him. Too, he knew there was another person, the one who had tied his wrists, but the person was quiet save for his footsteps.

A creaking door was swung wide, and then he was shoved forward, tripping, trying to regain his footing, running abruptly into a rough-textured wall before regaining his balance. The door creaked shut finalized by the clicking of the lock. Pretty rough handling for security, Harry thought. Too rough, in fact. Was it Stan?

There was another click and the room was suddenly bathed in light from one bare bulb hanging from the center of the ceiling. Harry blinked several times to adjust his eyes, then focused on two figures facing him. Stan and Mr. Ma, both armed.

"Hello, Harry," Stan said. "Long time no see."

"I told you we would meet again, Harry," grinned Mr. Ma.

A movement to his left caught Harry's attention. Turning, he felt his heart leap into this throat. Osa was sitting back against the far wall, hands and ankles tied and a gag stuffed in her mouth. Her blue eyes were filled with terror. Harry winked at her trying to bolster her spirits, and then turned back to Stan and Mr. Ma. He wanted to swear, to tell them she had nothing to do with it, to let her go. But the gag stifled any comments.

After what seemed an eternity, Stan stepped forward close to Harry. His beard was scraggly and unkempt. A smell of whiskey and tobacco fouled the air with his every breath. His deep-set, piercing black eyes never left Harry's as he pulled up his pistol, a long barreled .38 with a silencer attached. He jammed it hard under Harry's chin forcing his head sharply back against the wall.

"I've spent a lifetime trying to find that damned money," he hissed. "I know Joe told you where it's hidden 'cause yer here for it. Right?" He jammed the gun harder into the soft flesh. Harry felt pain, blinked back tears that welled in his eyes. "Now yer gonna tell me where Joe stashed the dough, and I mean right now!" He yanked the gag from Harry's mouth. "Now, dammit. Now!"

Harry ran his tongue around the dryness of his mouth several times before answering. "I don't know where the money is. Joe never told me any –"

"Bullshit!" Stan exploded, slamming the barrel of the gun sharply across the side of Harry's head. "I know damned well he told you!"

Harry staggered, seeing stars, falling to his knees. Another sharp blow landed on his shoulder sending him crumpling to the floor. A terrified Osa screamed out in horror, the sound muffled in the dirty rag stuffed in her mouth.

"Harry," said Mr. Ma in a pleasant voice as he knelt beside him. "Why do you think I went to all the trouble of showing you how to get up to the University today if it wasn't to help you find your way back to get the money? I saw the way your eyes lit up when we toured the building. You know where the money is. We know you know. You can save yourself a lot of grief. Just tell us where the money is. It's just that simple."

He reached over grasping Harry's wrist, twisting it backwards until Harry gasped in pain. "As I said earlier, there must be a reason you came back, and I know it wasn't to renew our old friendship. Tell us, Harry."

"I don't know," Harry gasped through clenched teeth. He tasted blood, feeling a rawness where his face had smacked against the floor. "Joe was gonna tell me when I came back to the hospital to let him know I was gonna go back to China." He grimaced as more pressure was applied to his wrist. "Stan and the Chink had already killed him. He never told me anything, just that the money was in the building."

Mr. Ma applied more pressure. Harry gasped, the pain shooting up his arm, sure his wrist would break off. He knew he had to resist or he was dead. "All I know is it's in this building," he gasped, struggling for release from the pain.

Stan, who had been standing off to one side admiring the simple tactic applied by the black-belted Judo master, Mr. Ma, suddenly lashed out kicking Harry in the stomach with a sharp, snapping kick. Harry grunted and fell forward, coughing, spitting, curling up on the dusty cement floor.

"Hold my gun," Stan ordered, handing his piece to the surprised Mr. Ma. "I'll show you how to get information from the bastard!" He grabbed Harry, jerking him to his feet, and then slammed him back hard against the wall. "Joe didn't tell me a damned thing. Nothing!" Stan hissed through gritted teeth. "That little sonofabitch knew I was coming after him so he told you. I know he told you! That's our money, not Joe's! That little shit hid it on me. He was supposed to share it with us, not you. It's not your money. It's our money!"

He slammed Harry hard against the wall again. "I saw yer name on the hospital registry. You got there before me so I know he told you. I know he did!" In a rage, he bounced Harry off the wall several times. "Tell me where the money is! Tell me!"

"I don't know!" screamed Harry.

Gasping for breath from the physical exertion, Stan pinned Harry against the wall with his arm thrust under his throat. Looking into his bloodied face, he gasped, "Remember how we used to shake down the gooks, Harry. Remember how we shook 'em down and what we did to 'em when we caught them stealing? Ya' remember?"

His fist caught Harry hard in his stomach. Harry choked, gasping for air. Stan followed with a flurry of punches to his ribs and, suddenly, cracked Harry across his face with an open-handed, tooth-jarring slap that sent him staggering headlong into the corner. As his legs turned to jelly and he started to fall, Stan lashed out kicking him hard in his stomach once more.

Harry crumpled in the corner writhing in agony, afraid to

scream out, his body shocked with pain. If his hands were free he'd kill the bastard!

Just as quickly, Mr. Ma was on him, grabbing his wrist, bending it backwards, sending a searing lightning bolt of pain the length of his arm. If he screamed, he knew they'd be on him like a couple of jackals, ripping him apart. He had to endure, had to wait them out. It wasn't just for him, but Osa: both of their lives were at stake.

Mr. Ma placed his knee into Harry's neck cutting off his breath. Harry struggled, feeling his Adam's apple slowly turning to applesauce. He couldn't breath, could feel himself falling away, unable to struggle, to fight for his life. Even kicking out with his legs trying to break free was to no avail. This is a hell of a way to have your life end, he thought, as he slipped into unconsciousness.

The splash of cold water brought him around. He hurt like hell. He shook his head. His eyes opened slowly: same room, same cast of characters. In the corner Osa stared at him through tear stained, fearful eyes.

Harry wiggled his hand; it pained terribly at the wrist from the damned twisting, but it still worked. He had thought the damned fool was going to twist it off. Sucking in a deep breath, he felt sharp pains shoot through his stomach. His ribs ached. At least I'm alive, he ventured.

Stan squatted down grabbing Harry's head and twisting it so their eyes met. "You've caused me a lot of headaches, Harry, a lot of headaches."

"Bullshit!" Harry spat.

Stan shook his head. "Joe didn't want to tell us where the money is. Now he's dead. That little trick of yours back in Saginaw, she didn't want to tell us either." He grinned ruefully. "The Chink had a good time playing with her. Now she's dead!"

"So's the Chink!"

"Oh!" Stan replied, eyebrows raised. "I wondered about him. Thanks. He was getting greedy."

"I supposed those were your people down in Shanghai, too?"

Stan grinned. "I was gonna save you all the trouble of coming clear up here to Tsingtao, Harry. You cost me two good men."

"One of them was my son," Mr. Ma added. "My eldest son."

Harry thought better than to make a sarcastic comment about those playing with fire getting burned.

"And the rifleman on the dock?" he asked.

"He was supposed to nick you, put you in the hospital for a few days, long enough for us to get to you and get the information. Sloppy shooting." He paused, and then added nonchalantly, "He's not around anymore, either."

Jerking Harry's head up, Stan looked at him. Shaking his head slowly, he said, "I keep asking myself why old Harry Martin comes back to China? Why he comes back to the old barracks after dark? He says he don't know where the money is. Just a nostalgic trip, Harry?" Leaning forward, his face only inches from Harry's face, speaking in an ominous tone of voice, he continued, "I say bullshit. I say Harry Martin's here looking for my hidden money."

He thrust him away and stood up. His eyes traversed the length of his adversary. "Interesting jacket, Harry," he said suddenly squatting and grabbing at the material, jerking the jacket wide open. His eyes suddenly widened at seeing the seabag tied around his waist. He jerked at it, yanking it loose, and held it up before Mr. Ma.

"Lookee here, ain't this something! Old Harry says he don't know where the goddam money is, but he just happens to be carrying a seabag with him. What'cha gonna carry in the seabag, Harry? Our goddamned money, that's what! He threw the bag in Harry's face. "You lying son-of-a-bitch! You know damned well where the money's hid!"

In a rage, Stan lashed out, punching Harry solidly on his jaw, bouncing his head against the floor.

"Untie me, you bastard, and it'll be a different story," Harry hissed, shaking off the punch.

"Screw you!" Stan retorted, grabbing him, jerking him to his feet and throwing him bodily against the far wall. Harry hit solidly, his head bouncing, and he collapsed heavily to the floor. More cold water brought him around. Stan splashed another cup for good measure. Slowly regaining consciousness, Harry once, again, looked into the sneering face of Stan Drezewski.

"Well, Harry, what'll it be? More fun and games, or the location of the money?"

Harry shook his head trying to get rid of the cobwebs. Feebly, he responded. "I told you, I don't know."

"We'll see," Stan grinned, rising. "We'll just see." He raised his foot aiming it at Harry's stomach, and then drew back. Harry closed his eyes anticipating a hard driving kick. "How many kicks do you think you can take before you bleed to death internally?" asked Stan as he prodded the point of his boot into Harry's stomach.

"Stan! Wait! The woman, maybe she knows," exclaimed Mr. Ma, grabbing Stan's arm. "Harry brought her ashore with him for some reason. Maybe he told her where the money is hidden."

"Good thinking."

Stan and Mr. Ma both turned their attention to Osa, now trembling with fear, looking from one to the other. Her face blanched white with terror. She had heard, they had killed another woman, that friend of Harry's. Now would it be her?

Chapter 62

TROUBLE IN THE OLD STORAGE ROOM

Peiping was hot and muggy in July, Harry recalled as he and several other Marines began their five-day leaves in the ancient city. The fifth floor of the Hotel De Peking was reserved primarily for visiting American servicemen. Pimps were quick to meet you when you arrived, knocking on the door of your room, a bevy of girls in tow ready to service you. For twenty bucks you could rent a whore for a week. There was a ledge, approximately three feet wide that ran along the length of the fifth floor. The whores were a happy lot, always eager to please, running around in the scantiest of attire, and they delighted in flitting from room to room along the ledge, popping in to see who the newcomers were, and what women they had selected.

Stan had barged into his room with a couple of other Marines, all soused, feeling no pain. He had spotted the girl as she entered the room from the window ledge. She was young, spirited and lithe, chattering away in her sing-song language. No free samples without payment first, she had laughingly told Stan as he had drunkenly grabbed for her breasts, lightly stepping away from him as she spoke. In a sudden rage, he smashed her fully in her mouth, his fist breaking teeth, and before she could utter a cry of pain, he hit her again, then grabbed her arm and spun her across the room where she toppled out the window and across the ledge. She fell five stories to her death.

Stan had shown no remorse. He said the girl had slipped. The authorities shrugged; others had slipped and fallen off the ledge. What was the loss of one more whore?

Watching Osa at that moment, Harry's heart went out to her.

Life meant little to Stan. He would kill her if he wanted, much as he had killed the young whore in Peiping. He could still see the crumpled, lifeless body of the young whore lying on the pavement outside his hotel.

An evil grin appeared on Stan's face as he dragged the helpless Osa to her feet. The grin turned to laughter at the look of fear in her eyes. Turning to Harry, he said, "Ya know what, Harry. We tailed you since you left the ship. Could have picked you up anytime. Anytime. But we had to see what your game plan was, to see if you really were going for the money. We knew you were making your bid for it when you left the restaurant and started up the hill toward the old compound." He laughed derisively. "This dumb broad was easy to sucker away from the Tivoli. All Mr. Ma had to do was tell her you'd been injured and she came right along." He laughed again. "As a matter of fact, you are injured, and soon you'll be dead!" He roared with laughter at his comment, which elicited a chuckled from Mr. Ma.

Then, as though turning off a water spigot, the laughter stopped as he faced Osa. Grabbing her face in his hand, dirty fingers digging into her cheeks, he growled, "Do you want this woman dead, too, Harry?"

"No! She doesn't know anything about this!" Harry cried out. "Let her go!"

Stan removed the gag from Osa's mouth. "Let's see what she has to say."

"Harry," she pleaded in a trembling voice, "who are dese men?"

Before Harry could answer, Mr. Ma had moved behind her grasping her wrist, twisting. A scream of pain burst from Osa's mouth, a scream that chilled to the depths of Harry's soul.

"Don't hurt her!" he screamed. "She doesn't know!" In a futile gesture, he tried to rise, to move to her defense, but Stan caught him sharply with a backhanded blow knocking him back down. Almost immediately his pistol was aimed at Harry's head.

Osa screamed at seeing Harry fall, and then screamed in pain as Mr. Ma applied more pressure to her wrist.

"Stop!" Harry yelled. "The money's up on the fourth floor, in the old supply room."

"Where in the room?"

Harry hesitated. Osa's gasping scream brought an answer.

"Turn her loose and I'll take you to it." He knew if they found the money he and Osa would be killed. He had to fight for time, time to keep them alive, time to figure another way out.

"Now we're getting somewhere," Stan grinned.

Mr. Ma slipped his gun inside his belt, pulled a knife from his pocked and flicked it open. The polished metal gleamed as he knelt before Osa. With a quick motion of the knife, the rope around her ankles fell to the floor. "We go upstairs," he hissed, stopping momentarily to pick up the seabag and a satchel by the door.

Jerking Harry to his feet, Stan snapped off the light and the foursome moved slowly out into the darkness of the corridor. Gingerly, they made their way along, and up the steps to the fourth floor. The building was silent except for their labored breathing and intermittent sobs escaping from Osa.

With a heavy-duty bolt cutter, Stan made short work of the lock on the storage room door. The door opened wide and Osa and Harry were roughly shoved into the room. Closing the door securely, Stan turned on a flashlight and shined it around the room. It was small, cramped, and dirty with a thick layer of dust covering the floor and several boxes stacked just inside the door. It was obvious from the cobwebs hanging in the corners and strung out across the room that no one had been in the room in ages. Just about the way they had left it so many years ago, Harry observed. Even the old chimney in the center of the room was strung with cobwebs and covered with a layer of dust.

Stan moved close to Harry, shining the light full in his face. "Where?" he hissed.

Harry nodded toward the far wall. "There, in the wall, behind the plaster."

Stan played the light on the broad plaster wall. Some of the graffiti written by Marines was still faintly visible under a thin covering of whitewash, now a soiled gray. Except for a heat register, the wall was barren.

"Where in the wall?" Stan demanded.

"In the wall, that's all I know, that's all he told me."

Mr. Ma flicked on his flashlight and stepped over to examine the wall. He started tapping the plaster. "It could be plastered behind the wall, Stan. It's hollow."

"You son-of-a-bitch!" Stan snarled, giving Harry a sudden shove. Harry reeled backwards until he abruptly bumped into the chimney. "You said you knew where the money was. Now we'll have to punch out the whole damned wall!"

Harry slid down the rough-chinked brick of the chimney to a sitting position. If they found the money, he and Osa were dead. At least, for the moment, they were alive and as long as they were alive, there was hope.

Stan was tapping the wall now, moving along, thumping at it feverishly, as though the money would suddenly jump out at him if he struck the wall just right. Mr. Ma returned to the prisoners shining his light first on Harry, then up at Osa. Tears streamed down her cheeks in endless ribbons, punctuated by periodic, gasping sobs.

Harry's heart went out to her. He wished he'd never told her about his quest for the money. She would never have ended up in this damned mess.

"Sit down, please," Mr. Ma said, pushing Osa toward Harry. She knelt, and then rolled backwards leaning up against the chimney next to him.

"I'm sorry, Osa," he whispered. "I had no idea it would come to this." It was little comfort as he listened to her soft, gasping sobs. Maybe, he thought, if he could just get around to her, to touch her, to comfort her, maybe even get our hands together, perhaps they could untie the knots binding their wrists. It was a long shot, but then, anything was worth a try.

At the far wall Stan and Mr. Ma had begun pounding on the plaster, cursing with every thumping of the wall. From the sounds of their voices, their tempers were getting shorter by the minute. Harry struggled, twisting his wrists, trying to loosen the knots, forsaking the idea of getting Osa to help. She was so terror-stricken, she was almost a basket case. "I wish I'd taken that damned magic course," he swore to himself.

Now the two were punching holes in the plaster. They're making enough noise to raise the dead, Harry thought, even to bring the security police to the rescue.

Frustrated at his inability to undo the knots, Harry leaned back against the dusty, grimy chimney. His body was dulled with pain, his mind muddled. Glancing to his left, he could faintly see the old secret entrance they had built in the other outside wall. He could faintly detect the outline of the hinges glinting in the dim light from the distant flashlights.

Neither Stan nor Joe was aware of the door. It had been built after the two were sent back to the States to a federal prison. Even the commanding officers were unaware of the door. It had been pre-fabricated and put up in less than an hour, the time the officers were at mess.

Maybe if he could get to the door, just maybe he could get out. He looked at Osa. No. Any attempt to get out the door would be futile. They'd be dead before he got to the door.

"God damn it, Harry!" Stan swore, his breathing raspy as he came back to the chimney, brushing cobwebs out of his way. "You know more than you're telling us!" He squatted in front of Harry grabbing his chin so that he looked right into his eyes. "Where's the damned money?"

"I don't know. Joe said it was in the far wall. It's supposed to be hollow."

"It's hollow all right, in places! If we don't find that damned money soon, you're a dead man!" He glanced over at Osa. "You'll both be dead!"

"It's there," Harry replied. "Joe said it was there. It's there, somewhere..."

Stan glared at him, stood, and moved back to the wall. "Keep going," he called to Mr. Ma. "It's gotta be here." With renewed effort, they continued punching large holes in the plaster, cursing each empty hole.

Harry edged forward and started rubbing the rope binding his wrists up and down against the rough bricks at the corner of the chimney hoping to fray the rope enough so he could break free. Maybe, he thought, I can catch Stan with a lucky punch when he comes back and get his gun.

The rope caught against a piece of the mortar and a brick pulled loose. "Dammit," Harry muttered. This was the only spot he could rub against without drawing attention to his actions. He sat silently, dejected. The damned brick couldn't have come loose at a worse time. Osa's soft sobbing only added to his plight.

From his right came the loud thumping, crunching sound of holes being punched in the wall by Stan and Mr. Ma, each empty hole followed by their curses. Soon they would run out of wall. Time was growing short. Harry realized he had to make an effort to escape, and quick.

He tried to raise up above the loose brick but couldn't without drawing attention. He sat back. Maybe, he thought, if I can get the brick loose and wedge it, I can then saw the rope along the rough edge of the brick 'till it's frayed enough to break.

Slowly, his fingers grasped at the brick, wiggling it back and forth, easing it ever outward until it came free in his hands. He breathed a sigh of relief. Then, all of a sudden, he stopped, almost breaking into a chuckle. There was a chance, just the slightest of chances after all. He was suddenly alive with new hope.

Chapter 63
A TWIST OF FATE

Easing his fingers back into the opening where the brick had been, Harry touched cloth. My old K-bar, he breathed. He could visualize the knife, long and with a razor sharp edge he had personally honed. The moment he had hidden it back in '48 came flooding back, the investigation surrounding Joe and Stan and the theft of cigarettes, the investigation moving into the barracks. The whole building had been thrown into bedlam. The MP's were scouring the building confiscating illegal weapons, pistols, swords, rifles, non-issue knives, anything that wasn't government issue. Rather than part with the knife, it'd make a good hunting knife after my tour of duty, Harry thought. He remembered wrapping it in an oily cloth and hiding it in the chimney behind a loose brick.

In the rush to get out of China before the advancing onslaught of Communists Chinese soldiers, he'd forgotten the knife, leaving it behind. Now, it was in his hands again.

Quickly, he eased the cloth out of the opening and carefully, awkwardly, unrolled the material until he felt the coldness of tempered steel, the cutting edge and point still sharp. He held the knife between his fingers and sawed back and forth on the rope. Within seconds, the rope loosened, then fell away and he felt the prickly sensation of blood rushing through his hands again. He was free.

"Harry! You lying bastard! You just bought it!" came Stan's raging voice as he stormed across the small room. "You lied to me for the last time. It ain't in the wall!" He was gasping heavily from exertion, sweating profusely, beads of sweat standing across his forehead. "I know it's in this room somewhere, but I don't know where –" He raised his silencer-equipped pistol up leaning the barrel against Harry's temple, the flashlight full in his face. Harry blinked, trying to move out of the glaring light, and at the same time his fingers were wrapped tightly around the handle of his knife.

"You know where the money is! We can't find it, so if we can't have it, neither can you!" He pressed the barrel tighter to Harry's temple. "Say yer prayers, Harry. Yer a dead man!"

Almost at the same moment he finished uttering the words, an incredulous look crossed Stan's face as the K-bar swiftly penetrated into his body, the sharp point continuing to drive deeply into him, thrusting far up under his rib cage, as far as Harry could force it with his remaining strength.

The flashlight dropped from Stan's grasp, it's beam dancing crazily about the room as it came to rest on the dusty floor. With his dying breath, Stan squeezed the trigger. The "thok" of the silencer was heard, but the bullet caromed harmlessly off the bricks of the chimney and burrowed into the ceiling.

Osa screamed, "Harry! Harry! No!" Her scream trailed off into a frightful wail.

"Is he dead?" called Mr. Ma, almost in a knowing manner. When there was no immediate response to his question, he asked, "What's the matter, Stan?"

Harry grabbed the gun from Stan's lifeless hand. Quickly, he picked up the light and aimed it at Mr. Ma. "He's dead," Harry replied, his voice husky.

Startled at hearing Harry's voice, Mr. Ma grabbed his pistol from his belt swinging it around in the direction of the light, getting off a snap shot that splattered off the chimney. In the same movement, he rushed toward Harry.

Harry squeezed the trigger. The gun kicked hard in his hand. The bullet entered just below Mr. Ma's right eye, knocking him off his feet as it continued smashing through his brain, blowing off the back of his skull, splattering bone, brain, flesh and blood against the pock-holed wall. Mr. Ma fell dead at Harry's feet next to his partner, Stan.

Holding the smoking .38 still kicked high in the air from firing,

Harry looked down at the carnage before him, thankful that he was still alive.

"Control!" he breathed aloud, still visibly shaken. "Got to control myself. Got to get us the hell out of here!"

Yet, already, his mind was working at break-neck speed, reviewing his options: Grab Osa and run, get out of the building and get back to the ship as fast as possible. No. Get the money, and then run! The two had made one hell of a racket pounding holes in the wall. If anything, it should have attracted the police bringing them on the run up to the room.

Hold your breath and listen, he commanded himself. He strained to hear the sounds of footsteps, voices, sirens, anything, but there was nothing, nothing save the sobbing, distraught Osa.

"It's okay, honey, it's okay," he whispered, moving to her, kissing her, wiping at the tears. "We're alive, everything will be okay now."

He yanked the knife from Stan's lifeless body and cut the ropes binding her wrists. "Oh, Harry," she sobbed rubbing her wrists vigorously trying to restore circulation, "ve must get out of here. I'm so afraid." She looked apprehensively down at the two dead men. "Ve must leave now."

"We will, but first the money. We'll leave with the money."

"But –" she started to protest, only to have him raise his finger to his lips.

"Listen," he uttered.

They listened in silence. There was no sound except for their labored breathing. "I don't hear anyting," she said with a questioning look. "Not a ting."

"That's just it," he said. "You'd think there'd be a thousand police swarming over the place by now what with all the noise those two made. Nothing. We've got to take advantage of the time now to get the money. It's now or never!"

He turned shining the light across the two bodies lying grotesquely, blood oozing from their lifeless forms. Harry stepped over and took the gun out of Mr. Ma's hand. He replaced it with his knife, squeezing his fingers tightly around the handle. Next, he wiped any fingerprints off Stan's gun, and then put the gun back in Stan's hand molding his hand to the weapon, his finger clutching the trigger. Standing back, he flashed a light over his handiwork. It gave the appearance of a falling out between two thieves.

"Dis is terrible –"

"Hey. Don't say that. Terrible? In another minute it would have been us lying there. It was them or us. Don't worry about them; they're both killers. The world is better off without 'em."

Picking up Mr. Ma's pistol, he looked about. "Now what'll I do with this damned thing?" he said. He had no intention of walking down the street with it in the event they were stopped. How do you explain to the police why you're carrying a gun with a silencer on it? "I gotta get rid of this thing," he said, "but where?"

On the edge of the light beam he saw the strands of rope that had bound them. "Christ! These too!" Reaching down, he snatched up the pieces of rope. As he did, the light fell across the brick. "Why not," he grinned as the answer came to him. "Why not."

Quickly, he wiped off any fingerprints on the pistol with the oiled cloth, then wrapped the pistol in the cloth and slipped it into the opening in the chimney. It slipped in easily and was quickly followed by the strands of rope. Harry replaced the brick fitting it snuggly back into place, flush as it was before. Shining his light on the spot, he defied anyone to find which brick had been replaced. "Maybe when they tear this building down they'll discover the gun," he mused.

"Okay. Come and help me now," he said grabbing Osa's wrist. "Don't ask questions; just do as I tell you."

Osa, who had been watching his busy activity, seemed somewhat puzzled but was snapped out of her thoughts as he literally yanked her across the room.

"Oh, God, Harry!" she screeched as the beam of light shone fully on the blood splattered wall, at the bits and pieces of Mr. Ma scattered across it's length. She turned away sick to her stomach.

"Don't look at it," he said releasing her. He looked at the wall, at the many holes punched in it. They hadn 't come close to the money, but it was there before them all the time.

"Der money isn't here or dey vould haf found it," came Osa's anxious whisper. "I tink ve should leave right now, don't you?"

"They didn't know where to look," Harry replied. "Just hold on for a few more minutes."

As he had rehearsed so many times before in the solitude of his cabin, Harry quickly stripped off his jacket, reached up under the armpits and extracted three screwdrivers, a pry-bar, steel saw blade and penlight. "Now hold the light on the heat vent cover," he commanded, kneeling before the vent. Selecting a Phillips's head screwdriver, he unscrewed the two large screws holding the faceplate. Dropping the screws on the floor, he pried the plate loose and set it to one side. Next, he picked up the flathead screwdriver and, reaching several inches back into the opening, unscrewed a set of four slotted, round-head screws. A thin metal frame fell forward and he extracted it, setting it next to the faceplate.

Then, facing the unit, he reached inside, grabbing a tab on either side of the ductwork and slid a long section of the heat duct out into the room. Back about two inches from the face of the ductwork were four more screws, two on either side. Using the Phillip's head screwdriver again, he unscrewed the four screws, and then popped off the front section of the duct. He felt inside, his fingers touching plastic.

"Bingo!" he chirped, winking at Osa.

He grabbed the plastic tightly and pulled. A large section of black plastic conforming to the shape of the duct, slid out. Quickly, Harry unwrapped the plastic covering spewing packets of money on the floor. He fanned through the packets, large denomination American bills. His eyes lit up. Osa gasped.

Harry quickly pulled the entire duct unit out from the wall, tilted it on end and shook it, watching as several oblong plastic packages slid out, piling on the dirty floor. When it was empty, he shined the light inside the empty duct just to make sure, then knelt at the opening and shined the light back into the ductwork. There was nothing but wood framing. He slid the empty container back into the opening, and then reversed the entire procedure until the faceplate was finally back in place. No one would ever be the wiser. Ingenious, he thought. Even now, heat was pouring out of the duct.

Except for Stan and Mr. Ma, finding the money had been relatively easy, just as old Joe said it would be.

"You knew all der time," Osa whispered, wide-eyed.

"Of course. Telling them or not telling them made no difference. They were determined to kill us anyways. I had to use the information and give it out sparingly in order to give us additional time, time to do some fast planning, to keep us alive."

"I-I guess you're right," she nodded with a sudden shudder of revulsion. "I just don't like to see people get hurt, to get killed."

"I know. I feel the same way. Taking a life isn't right. But when it comes down to his life or mine; better his."

He glanced at his watch. "We have to hurry. It's 10:00. It's getting late and we have much to do."

He began ripping open all the pockets of the jacket, then systematically stuffed packets of money inside each pocket, sealing each in turn as Osa stripped open the rest of the plastic packages and handed the money to him. "The seabag," he said continuing to stuff money into the pockets as he had so methodically rehearsed a hundred times. "They were kind enough to bring it with them."

Osa opened the seabag wide and started stuffing packets of money in the hidden inner lining. Soon, all the money had been tucked safely away. As an afterthought, Harry stuffed the plastic covering into the bottom of the seabag. The tools were replaced in the jacket armpits and it was done; he had the money. They could leave now.

Shining the light carefully about the room, he was satisfied. There was no indication that anyone except Stan and Mr. Ma had been in the room. Good. He glanced at his watch. It was 10:30.

"C'mon. We've got to get out of here," he whispered as he hoisted the seabag up and flattened it against his stomach. Pulling a piece of twine from the jacket pocket, he tied the seabag off around his waist. Excruciating pain cut through him from battered ribs and tender stomach as he snugged the seabag tight, suffering with every breath.

Stan had hurt him but as far as he could determine, nothing was broken. He'd have to endure the pain in order to get back to the ship. Too, it was best Osa didn't know. As distraught as she was, he felt she really couldn't handle much more.

Then, slipping on the jacket, he buttoned up. It felt snug. With the addition of the money, the bulky appearance was once again restored to the jacket, which pleased him. At this late hour no one on board ship would notice the change in his appearance, at least that was his hope.

Moving to the door, Harry eased it open, and listened. It was quiet in the darkness of the stairwell, too quiet. A sixth sense warned him that someone might be waiting there, part of Stan's gang of cutthroats. One? More than one? He couldn't risk it. He closed the door and locked it.

"Vas is der matter?" came Osa's hoarse whisper, surprised that he locked the door.

"Shhh," Harry cautioned. He flicked on his penlight. "There might be someone down there waiting for us. Can't chance it."

"How do ve get out den?" she asked clutching his arm, a tightness in her voice, terrified at the thought they might be captured again.

"Come with me," he whispered. Taking her hand, he led her back across the room, stepping over the two bodies now laying in ever-widening pools of dark blood, to the far outside wall. "Perfect," he breathed as the penlight shone on the painted hinges. They were still intact. Reaching up, he grabbed at one of the open studs and jerked sideways. Nothing happened. He jerked again, then again. Still nothing.

"Vot are you doing, Harry?" she asked, an urgency in her voice, puzzled at his action. "Ve must get out of here. I am frightened."

Harry glowered at her. Didn't she think he knew that. With a growing apprehension, he jerked at the stud again, even harder this time. Suddenly the wood moved ever so slightly. He squatted down and jerked at the stud about a foot off the floor. It was stuck, not budging. In desperation, he gave it a sharp karate chop. The wood popped to one side and then he could see the two screw heads, one at the top of the stud, one about two feet off the floor.

Relieved, he took a flathead screwdriver and eased each screw a begrudging half turn, wincing as the screws squeaked, spitting on the metal to silence the noise. The slotted heads were now in a horizontal position. Dousing the light, he pushed against the wall.

It swung outward, squeaking as it moved, opening ever wider. Stepping out onto a narrow ledge, Harry surveyed the area. Nothing. Not a damned soul in sight.

Reaching back inside, he took Osa's hand and guided her out onto the ledge and motioned for her to stand still and not move. Stepping back inside, he jerked the studding back in place covering the two screw heads.

Once again out on the ledge, he swung the door closed. Fumbling in the dark, he felt for the outside screwheads. Finding them, he stuck the screwdriver into the slot and twisted each a half turn clockwise and, once again, the door was secured.

"See," he whispered. "If anyone's waiting inside the building they'll go nuts trying to figure out how we got out of the place without being seen." He gave a muffled laugh. "Now let's get the hell out of here."

Chapter 64

TSINGTAO FOREVER

Standing in the shadows next to the old Third Marine barracks, Harry took a moment to look back at the old 12th Service Battalion building. He had led Osa down the side of the building walking on the cement planter steps they had built so many years ago. He had to admit it; the planter steps did enhance the architectural beauty of the building, just as his commanding officer had said.

Crouching low, using the shadows to their advantage, he guided her down along the athletic field to the small stream and gap in the fence. He rolled under the fence, and then pulled up on it to allow her to roll under. Brushing themselves off, they moved up the grassy embankment and quickly hurried down the street.

"We can't risk going through town," he whispered. "If the cops ever stopped us they'd want to know what happened to me."

Osa gasped as she caught a glimpse of his face in the dim light of a streetlamp as they passed under it.

"We'll have to take the side streets to get back to the ship," he continued. "We'll have to hurry. C'mon!" Even as he spoke, he started jogging and she quickly fell in step beside him praying he knew the way.

Straining under the added weight of the money, he continued on, cursing himself to keep on going. Waves of nausea swept over him forcing him to stop several times to catch his breath, to let the feeling pass. "The police, the police, got to stay away from them," he kept telling himself.

It was colder. A gentle snow was falling, large flakes drifting down about them, on them. Yet, Harry was sweating profusely. Wracked with pain, hurting with every breath, he had to stop frequently, feeling the extra weight starting to drag him down. This wasn't the way he had planned it, not the beating, not the painfully sore ribs, and certainly not her. He could tell by the way she looked at him, at the way she glanced about that she knew they were lost.

Stopping under a streetlamp to catch his breath, he glanced at his watch. It was 11:15, forty-five minutes to curfew. Time was running out. They had to get back to the ship, but where the hell was it? He'd become confused running aimlessly, first down one street, then another, down to his left, down to his right, stopping momentarily to catch their breathes, then running again.

Ahead of them loomed a central fountain surrounded by several tall lampposts. Stopping at the fountain, gasping for breath, Harry dropped heavily onto one of the cold stone benches encircling the fountain. God, the fountain looked so familiar to him, so damned familiar. Why should it? Why should it stick in his mind? It meant something to him, but what?

Osa had reached into her pocket pulling out a handkerchief which she dipped into the fountain. Wringing it out, she gently dabbed at the blood caked on Harry's face. He winced but endured the washing without uttering a sound.

"I know it hurts but dis vay you don't look so hurt," she said apologetically, trying to comfort him, continuing to wet the handkerchief and wiping his face clean.

"Just so I look good for you," he managed with a painful grin.

"Dere," she said after a moment, taking one last swipe at his face. She stood back looking at him. "You look much better, like the man I luf."

He laughed.

She bent forward, kissing him.

"What's that for?"

"Because I love you."

He shook his head. Women! Here they were, lost, in danger and she tells him she loves him. He gave a nervous laugh.

It was time to move again. Standing, he glanced around the area. Damn but it looked familiar. Old memories locked in the recesses of his mind began opening as he forced himself to remember, to recall the Tsingtao of his youth. He knew he'd been past this very fountain a hundred times; he was sure of it.

Sammy's joint down by the dock, the accordian player, Tsingtao beer, the white Russian bar girl who could suck a cigarette to ashes with one long suck. Yeah! He had it!

Clutching Osa to him, he kissed her enthusiastically. "We've got it made," he gasped, pointing past her. "That's the way to the dock area. I remember, I remember, c'mon, let's go!"

He pulled her after him, starting down one of the side streets. They were close now and a feeling of elation swept through him.

"Shemma," a voice rang out. "Shemma, shemma!"

The two froze. He remembers those words. Chinese police used to call out – What, what! Turning, He looked back, and then felt a sinking feeling in the pit of his stomach. A police officer was advancing toward them, his gun drawn. Looking up, he saw a stonewall, a possible chance to escape, but it was topped with shards of broken glass.

"Damn," he breathed, "so close, so close." He couldn't lose now, not now.

As the police officer approached, Harry suddenly swept Osa in his arms, kissing her. "Speak Swedish to him," he whispered in her ear. "We're lovers looking for our ship." He kissed her again.

"Why were you running?" the officer demanded, speaking in broken English, his gun still drawn as he approached closer, wary at their sudden embrace, wondering what they were up to.

Osa turned to him speaking in Swedish. Harry could tell by the blank expression on the officer's face that he was totally confused. Smiling, Harry spoke brokenly in English. "I am sorry, officer," he said haltingly as though searching for the right words, gasping as he deliberated, wiping the sweat from his brow, trying to keep his face partially covered. "Ve are from der Svedish ship in der harbor, der grain ship, und ve vant to get back to it before der midnight bell, but ve are lost. Perhaps you could tell us vitch vay to go?"

"Ahh yes," the officer sighed, holstering his pistol. "The dock, ahead over next hill," he said pointing down the street. He looked at his watch. "You have minutes. Fifteen. You quick, quick." He pointed in the direction once again. "Go that way."

"Tank you, tank you very much," Harry said, grinning, nodding. "Ve appreciate your help." He took Osa's hand in his and they started off running down the street in the direction the officer had indicated.

"If the guy's going to shoot us he better do it now," Harry wheezed, but nothing happened.

Topping the hill, they could see the dock area and *Nurad* nestled against the dock. They stopped to gaze down at the scene. *Nurad* had never looked more beautiful nor more inviting as it did right at that moment.

Osa, still gasping for breath, suddenly started laughing uncontrollably.

"What's so funny?" Harry gasped.

"You, speaking like a Svede trying to speak English. It vas funny, simply funny."

He laughed. They stood looking at each other laughing like a couple of kids. With bolstered spirits, they walked hand in hand down the hill and passed through the guard shack, submitting their passes. Harry glanced at his watch. It was 11:50 p.m.

Just inside the gate he noticed a restroom. Excusing himself, he stepped inside where he examined himself in the mirror. His face was bruised and puffy, but not notably distorted out of shape. He took his handkerchief and wiped off additional bloodstains and grime, then combed his hair, pulled his cap back on and hurried out to a shivering Osa.

"How do I look?" he asked stopping before her.

She looked him over, and then grinned. "You look like you had a nice time in town," she replied. "I especially enjoyed der Peking duck und der Tsingtao beer, but der floor show vas a bit rough." She laughed.

"I owe you one special dinner just for two with candlelight and soft music at our next port of call," Harry said apologetically. "And we'll skip the floor show."

"I vill hold you to your promise," she retorted. "Remember, I don't forget dat easily."

"Promise."

Taking her hand in his, they walked down to the ship kicking through the light layering of snow. *Nurad* was lit up like a small village, beautiful under big fleecy flakes of snow that continued falling all about them. As they moved up the gangway, Harry reached over and kissed her lightly.

"Vell, you two just made it," Sigmund said as they stepped on deck. "Did you forget you haf duty in five minutes, Harry?"

"Oh, shit!" Harry exclaimed, slapping his forehead. "I forgot all about it! I'm sorry, Sigmund. We were having such a good time, got tied up and forgot all about the time. You know how it is when you're having fun! Jeez, I'm sorry." He felt Osa squeeze his hand at his comment. "Do I have time for a quick shower before I report for duty?"

Sigmund broke into a big grin. "Don't vorry. Captain Andress tought you might be tired from taking Osa into town und suggested dat I haf anudder sailor serve your vatch tonight. So go to bed. You look beat."

"Truer words were never spoken," Harry responded with a glance toward Osa. "I really feel beat. It's amazing what a woman can get you into."

Osa bit her lip trying to keep a straight face, trying not to burst into laughter. Poor Sigmund, she thought, if he only knew.

"You men are all alike," she chided after a moment, showing mock indignation. "Vy is it alvays der voman's fault? I am tired, too, trying to keep up vis dis man. He is not der only vun tied up." With a twit of her nose, she turned and started away. "I tink I go to bed now. I am tired."

"G'night, Sigmund," Harry called over his shoulder as he hurried after her. "Wait up, Osa. I'll walk you to your cabin."

He put out his arm in a gallant gesture so obvious that even Sigmund might notice, and she slipped her hand through it with an equally noticeable response. "Tank you," she smiled.

As they turned a corner out of sight of Sigmund, Harry made an abrupt change in plans steering her to his cabin. There was no protest from Osa. Once inside, behind a closed, locked door, he grabbed her tightly to him.

"God, it's good to be alive," he breathed, pressing her tightly to him, enjoying the feeling of his arms around her, realizing how much she meant to him. Her head was buried against his shoulder, arms around his neck. They were silent for several long moments just holding onto each other.

After a while, Harry tilted her head up and lightly kissed her. "Are you all right?" he whispered.

"Yes." Tears streamed down her cheeks.

"Why the tears?"

"Happy tears," she said. "I tought dey ver going to kill you. I vas so scared." She raised, kissing him. "I luf you, Harry. I really do..."

"I love you, too," he replied huskily. "I really mean it.

He winced as her hand touched softly to his face. "I'm sorry," she gasped. "Does it hurt much?"

"Honey, I ache all over," he said. "They did one hell of a number on me." He eased away from her starting to take off his jacket. "I better get out of these clothes and see how much damage they did to this old bod, 'cause I sure as hell hurt."

He motioned toward the desk. "There's a bottle of cognac in the lower right hand drawer. Get it. We need a celebration drink."

He shrugged off the heavy jacket and untied the seabag letting both fall to the deck. Continuing to disrobe, he yanked off his black turtleneck and then his T-shirt. Naked from the waist up, he began examining his body, especially his ribs. Large red welts appeared on his chest and stomach where Stan had beat and kicked him.

Osa glanced over at him from where she was pouring two full glasses of cognac. "Oh, Harry, you got red splotches all over you. You are badly hurt?"

"I'm tender, but nothing's broken," he answered with a sigh of relief. "Just badly bruised."

"I vill take care of you," she said setting the two glasses over to the edge of the desk and moving to him. She ran her hands lightly over his hairy chest and across his broad shoulders. "I vill make you vell, and den some," she said smiling mischievously.

Harry wrapped his strong arms around her and squeezed her buttocks, kneading the firm flesh. "I bet you will. I just bet you will."

He released her and picked up the two glasses of cognac. "To our successful treasure hunt, " he said, handing her one of the glasses. "To our Tsingtao treasure." He touched his glass to hers, then brought it to his lips and drained it in one long continuous swallow. It burned all the way to his stomach. Osa stood flabbergasted, amazed he could down the scorching liquid so quickly. "More," he grinned holding out his empty glass. "More, it burns so good, and I hurt so bad."

She laughed. "You are crazy." She filled his glass again.

"Very observant," he nodded accepting the glass and tipping it, emptying it.

"Harry!" she exclaimed.

He set his glass down, grinning at her. "Now, my love," he said pulling her down on the carpet, "Let's see what we got for all our effort."

"Oh, Harry," she giggled. In the spirit of the moment, she took a deep swallow of the amber fluid, enduring the burn, then tipped the glass, emptying it, wiping away sudden tears.

She filled the glasses again. Then, cross-legged like a couple of kids, they pulled the money from the jacket and seabag and began counting. There were large denomination bills: thousand dollar, five hundred dollar, hundred dollar and even fifties. Excitedly, they leafed through the bills, counting, stacking.

An hour later, an empty bottle between them, the money all neatly stacked, they sat grinning and giggling at each other.

"How does it feel to be engaged to a multi-millionaire?" Harry asked, his words slurred. "That is, if you'll become engaged to me." He giggled at his *faux pas*.

Osa laughed uproariously, her head thrown back.

She crawled over to him on her hands and knees pushing him over on his back, laying across him. Through slitted eyes, she looked at him, a silly grin on her face. "I accept your proposal," she said smothering him with kisses. "Und how does a man who has over two million dollars und his new fiancé make love?" she giggled.

"Like dis," he said, laughing, wrapping her within his strong arms.

THE END

WHO NEEDS A ROAD?
The Story of the Longest and the
Last Motor Journey Around the World
by Harold Stephens & Albert Podell
ISBN: 09642521-5-5
487 pages, with photographs, $14.95

**THE STRANGE DISAPPEARANCE
OF JIM THOMPSON**
And Stories of Other Expatriates in Southeast Asia
by Harold Stephens
ISBN: 09642521-7-1
260 pages, with photographs, $14.95

**TAKE CHINA
THE LAST OF THE CHINA MARINES**
A Novel dedicated to
The Men of the 29th Marines Sixth Marine Division
by Harold Stephens
ISBN: 09642521-8-X
366 pages, $14.95

Leslie F. Harcus
Newly Made Corporal
1947

Leslie F. Harcus
Today